Some of WBAI's Charter Members

Photographs from *The Golden Anniversary History of Kappa Beta Pi, 1908-1958*
Biographies from *The History of Kappa Beta Pi*, June 1937 by Alice C. Edgerton, Grand Historian

ALICE MARIE CRAIG (MRS. CHARLES H. EDGERTON)

And now comes your historian, with a great deal of trepidation and self-consciousness, and sets forth her own biography.

Alice Marie Craig was born on a farm in southeastern Wisconsin—the only child of Mr. and Mrs. Asa H. Craig. There she attended district school and made playmates of birds and animals in the neighborhood, including canaries, dogs, cats, lambs, pigs, and on one occasion, a woodchuck. She attended Carroll College in Waukesha, Wisconsin, where she was an honor student. After her graduation, she taught in the county grade schools for two years. During most of this time she studied music—piano and vocal; also painting.

She was then married to Mr. Charles H. Edgerton, of Florida, who passed away a few years later. Mrs. Edgerton was at that time living in Chicago and, with a great deal of nerve and absolutely no business training, she secured a job as stenographer in a law office. As her stenographic knowledge was entirely self-taught, she says that she had literally to remember the first few letters which were dictated to her. After three years of this work, she became a private secretary to the Judge and Clerk of the Probate Court of Cook County, which position she held for four years. It was during this period that she attended Chicago-Kent College of Law.

Both she and her father are listed in *Who's Who in America*. Her name also appears in *American Women, Who's Who in Law* and *North American Authors*.

Alice is of medium height, slender, with grey hair and brown eyes, and possesses a keen sense of humor. She lives alone, with a small white dog, in a big white house, to which come the other founders (and Cora Green and Ella Sullivan) on the first Saturday in June of each year for a week-end houseparty. A special feature of this occasion is always an old-fashioned New England boiled dinner.

She loves books and movies, but her particular hobby is raising melons. During the season she takes a vacation from her desk and ships to customers as far east as Boston and Washington quantities of fine cantaloups, which were originated and raised for thirty years by her father. They are grown on the old Craig homestead which has been in the family for 100 years.

ALICE CRAIG EDGERTON

Admitted to Illinois Bar in 1910; to Wisconsin Bar, March, 1926.
Chicago-Kent College of Law, L.I.B.
Practice—General, specializing in Probate
Member: Women's Bar Association of Illinois

During her first year at Kent, she won a $100 prize for highest grade in a class of 150, and received a scholarship the following year. This, she hastens to add, was again due to her memory and not to a particularly logical mind. She was admitted to the Illinois bar in 1910 and received her master's degree from Chicago-Kent the following year.

After the death of her mother in 1923, Mrs. Edgerton moved to her father's home in Mukwonago, Wisconsin, where she was admitted to the Wisconsin bar and has since been engaged in general practice. She is also the local Justice of the Peace, having served in that capacity since 1927.

Mrs. Edgerton has filled the following offices in the sorority: first President and Dean (re-elected in 1914), member of the first Board of Directors, Grand Marshal, Editor of *The Quarterly*, and is now Honorary Grand Dean. She is one of the founders of the Women's Bar Association of Illinois, and a member of the Waukesha County Bar and Wisconsin State Bar Associations. She is also a member of the Order of Bookfellows, the Order of the Eastern star, of which she is Past Matron, the Waukesha Women's Club, and several local societies.

Mrs. Edgerton devotes a portion of her time to literary work, having published two books for children, one book of debates (as co-authored with her father), and two books of original speeches. She has also written poems, articles and feature stories for books, papers and magazines. Thanks to a syndicated article regarding her work, she has acquired something of a reputation as a ghostwriter, and prepares speeches for people in different parts of the country. This makes her daily mail rather exciting. She frequently talks on legal or quasi-legal subjects before clubs in nearby towns. Although living ninety miles from Chicago, she never misses a Kappa Beta Pi celebration or a Founder's Day dinner in that city. She occasionally attends chapter meetings in Milwaukee and Madison.

Alice inherits her literary inclinations from her father, who was an educator as well as farmer, and the author of several books.

CHARLOTTE DOOLITTLE (MRS. HARRY A. WHITE)

Charlotte Doolittle was born in Charles City, Iowa, spending her early childhood on a large farm owned by her parents. Fortunately, it was just outside the city limits, which enabled her to attend school in town. She graduated from high school shortly after her sixteenth birthday. For a year she attended college in Wisconsin, and the following year took a business course in Minneapolis, Minnesota.

The founder of her family in America was Abraham Doolittle who settled in New Haven, Connecticut in 1640. Her paternal grandfather was the late United States Senator James R. Doolittle, from Wisconsin. Her father was a graduate of Annapolis, and at the beginning of the Civil War he organized his own regiment at Racine Wisconsin, serving practically the entire four years of the conflict and attaining the rank of Colonel of the Cavalry under General Rosencranz. AT the close of the war he finished his law course at Ann Arbor, Michigan. He was later appointed Collector of the port of New York, leaving there to make his home in Iowa where he practiced law and operated a farm. Lieutenant James Doolittle, the well known aviator is a distant relative.

Miss Doolittle came to Chicago in 1906 to accept a position on the Record-Herald. However, the urge to study law was so strong within her that she resigned from the paper and secured a position in a law office the year she began her course at Chicago-Kent College. Charlotte passed the Illinois bar examination during her senior year.

On November 29, 1911, Miss Doolittle was married to Harry A. White—the culmination of a law school romance, Mr. White also being a member of the Chicago-Kent class of 1910. The other founders were guests on this occasion.

In 1923, Mrs. White became a member of a prominent law firm in Chicago, where she specializes in corporation law, income and inheritance taxes, wills and trusts. For several years she handled this type of law work for the Fort Dearborn Trust and Savings Bank, for which her firm were attorneys.

Mr. White is also a member of Chicago's most prominent law firms—attorneys for a large public utility in that city.

Mr. and Mrs. White have a large, beautifully furnished apartment on the near north side, which is a favorite gathering place for Kappas and other women lawyers. Early in 1936, when Epsilon Alumnae chapter entertained undergraduate members and pledges, Mrs. White opened her home for the occasion and served tea to over 65 girls. She has the happy faculty of making her guests fell perfectly at home, which has won her the reputation of being a wonderful hostess.

Charlotte was a member of the first Board of Directors of Kappa Beta Pi and served as dean in 1910-1911. She has also held offices as Secretary and Treasurer, and has always been active in sorority affairs, both local and national. She is a charter member of the Women's Bar Association, of which she is a past president.

Mrs. White studied music for years—both piano and voice. Even after coming to Chicago she took vocal training at the Chicago Conservatory of Music. She posseses a sweet voice and is always ready and willing to sing for the Kappas.

She is a lover of all animals and from childhood road horses, broken and unbroken, and some os the accounts she gives of the unbroken ones are rather hair-raising.

Charlotte is tall, with a graceful, dignified carriage. She has beautiful dark auburn hair, the natural wave in which is the envy and despair of all her friends. She posses a sunny disposition, a vast amount of common sense, and is unselfish in her devotion to her family and friends. She has several hobbies. One is Buddy, a parrot, whose "Come on up" is a welcome to whoever rings the bell. Another hobby is the collection of beautiful bric-a-brac and furniture from places which she and her husband visit during their long vacation trips together. And at Christmas time her family and friends remember that she is inordinately fond of beads.

MARTHA ELVERT

Miss Elvert enjoyed the distinction of being the first Dean to be elected by the delegates from two chapters, and doubtless she was therefore the first to rightfully bear the title of Grand Dean.

Martha was Kappa Beta Pi's first candidate, and from the date of her initiation in the fall of 1909 at the home of Katharine Clark, she was one of the sorority's most ardent supporters. She was outstanding in her loyalty, her tireless energy and her exceptional executive ability. So closely was she associated with the founders as almost to be considered one of them. IT was on her motion, made January 13, 1917, that the founders of the sorority were made life members of Alpha chapter, with all rights and privileges of active members.

For many years Miss Elvert was a successful court reporter, maintaining her own office. After her admission to the bar she combined this work with her general practice. She was a deep student, delving into psychology, astrology and kindred subjects. She loved to travel and to visit out of the way places. Having a fine imagination and being a good reconteur, she was able to share these pleasures with her friends.

Martha was above average height and well proportioned. She had brown hair and gray eyes. Although living alone, she always maintained an apartment, in which Kappas frequently gathered. She possessed a highly cultured taste for the finer things of life, and many of her gowns were rich and beautiful.

Miss Elvert was the first of that early band of associates—the first of the Grand Deans—to go. She passed away suddenly at her home in Chicago on September 16, 1935. She had no near relatives and those of the founders who were in the city went to the home immediately and took charge of all arrangements for the funeral. The services were largely attended by members of the Women's Bar Association and by sorority members, who came to express their love and respect for the devoted, loyal member of Kappa Beta Pi.

THE FIRST 75 YEARS

TURNER PUBLISHING COMPANY
Paducah, Kentucky

Photograph of bust of Myra Bradwell, courtesy Northwestern University School of Law.

Turner Publishing Company

Created and designed by
David A. Hurst, Publishing Consultant

Written and coordinated by
Charlotte Adelman, WBAI Archivist

Copyright © 1992
Womens Bar Association of Illinois
and Turner Publishing Company

This book or any part thereof may not be reproduced without the written consent of the Author and Publisher.

The materials were compiled using available and submitted materials; the publisher regrets they cannot assume liability for errors or omissions.

Library of Congress Catalog No. 91-75256

ISBN: 978-1-68162-560-7

LIMITED EDITION

Additional copies may be available directly from the publisher.

CONTENTS

FOREWORD

FOR USA/ILLINOIS WOMEN LAWYERS THE PAST IS ENTWINED

by Charlotte Adelman

The history of women lawyers in Illinois is, in fact, the history of women lawyers in the United States.

Until 1869 there were no women lawyers in the nation.

In 1869, two women applied for admission to the bars of their respective states, Illinois and Iowa. Had the Illinois Supreme Court granted Myra Bradwell's application, she would have been one of the first two women admitted to the bar in the United States. But the Illinois Supreme Court refused her application, and Illinois lost that distinction.

In rejecting Bradwell's request, the court ruled that she could not be a lawyer because of her disability of being a married woman and, upon appeal, because of her sex. Until such disability shall be removed by legislation, the court said, it was powerless to grant her application.

In 1869 Iowa became the first state in the country to admit a woman to the bar. She was Belle Mansfield, who, ironically, never practiced law.

However, Illinois was the first state where a woman graduated from law school: Ada Miser Kepley of Effingham in 1870 became the first woman in the United States to graduate from law school. She attended Chicago University Law School, predecessor to Union College of Law, later known as Northwestern University School of Law.

But Illinois refused to admit her to the bar.

Nevertheless, Kepley was the first woman in the United States to practice in a court of law. In 1870, while Myra Bradwell's case was pending before the Supreme Court, Effingham County Judge Decius permitted Kepley to practice in his court.

In 1871 Alta Hulett of Rockford petitioned the Illinois Supreme Court for admission to the bar. She was rejected. She reacted by drafting legislation that would prohibit sex discrimination in employment and this gave women access to the legal profession. Hulett, Bradwell and Kepley all worked on the bill, which was enacted in 1872.

A year later, Illinois admitted its first woman to the bar. Alta M. Hulett. In 1881 it admitted Ada Kepley. In 1882 Bessie Bradwell, Myra's daughter, graduated from Northwestern Law School. In 1890, the Illinois Supreme Court granted Myra Bradwell a law license on her original application filed in 1869. (It was too late for her, however; she was dying of cancer.)

In 1899 the American Bar Association still refused to admit women membership. (In response, New York women lawyers founded the Women Lawyers Club.) In 1901 *The Chicago Legal News*, founded by Myra Bradwell, noted, "It is with pride and pleasure we mention the fact that Illinois has more women lawyers than any state in the world and Chicago has more than any other city in the world." (Sept. 14, 1901, page 29.)

In 1908, the first legal sorority in the United States was established in Chicago by female students at Chicago-Kent College of Law. It flourished throughout the United States especially in Washington, D. C., and had chapters abroad.

Illinois, in 1913, passed a law giving women partial suffrage, only in presidential and municipal elections making Illinois the first state east of the Mississippi to grant women suffrage in a presidential election. In 1914 WBAI was formed.

When the 19th Amendment was passed, giving the women the right to vote, Illinois was the first state to ratify it on June 10th, 1919.

For most states, this was followed by giving women the right to sit on juries. Unfortunately, Illinois lagged behind. It was only

Ada Kepley

Class of 1870, law department of Chicago University. SHE WAS THE FIRST WOMAN IN ILLINOIS AND THE UNITED STATES TO RECEIVE A LAW DEGREE. However, because Illinois did not allow women to enter learned professions, she was refused a license to practice. Her husband, Henry B. Kepley, wrote the bill granting women the right to enter professions. It was passed in the Illinois legislature in 1872. Ada Kepley received her law license in 1881, but was not active in the field. (Courtesy Mabel Brown Collection, Northwestern University School of Law)

Alta Hulett

First woman lawyer in Illinois. (Courtesy Chicago Historical Society)

Judge Mary Bartelme

Class of 1894, Northwestern Law School, first Illinois woman attorney elected to judgeship. Judge Bartelme retired in 1933 after more than 35 years of service on behalf of the delinquent and misunderstood youngsters of Cook County. She served as Circuit Court Judge in charge of the juvenile system for more than nine years. She was president of WBAI in 1927. (Courtesy Northwestern University School of Law)

Sophonisha Breckinridge

First woman to graduate from University of Chicago Law School, 1904 (Courtesy University of Chicago Law School)

after 20 years of lobbying by the Women's Bar Association of Illinois and other groups that legislation giving women this right passed in 1939.

In 1919 Matilda Fenberg was the first woman admitted to Yale Law School. She later became a prominent Chicago attorney. (Harvard Law School didn't admit women until 1950; Notre Dame Law School in 1969; and Washington and Lee Law School in 1972)

Different and worse treatment for women law students and lawyers was the norm until passage of the 1964 Civil Rights Bill.

After that, it was illegal to discriminate against women in employment. Women started asserting their rights and could help guarantee them by filing lawsuits and making other demands. Law schools and employers slowly tried to comply with the law.

In 1990, women law students nationally numbered 54,100, up from 6,700 in 1970, according to ABA statistics. Women lawyers are regularly hired by public agencies and private law firms. Television depicts them as an accepted component of the litigious world of trail lawyers.

But what does the future hold? In 1991, "There are a few litigators among attorneys but even fewer female litigators, and it starts at the law school level with the presumption and assumption that this is not something women should do or are capable of doing." said Roxanne Barton Conlin, president-elect of the Association of Trial Lawyers of America, a former U. S. attorney for the Southern District of Iowa.

Discrimination that starts in law school presents an alarming situation, in view of the steadily rising number of women in law school.

How can employment discrimination be challenged?

University of Chicago law professor Mary Becker notes that sex discrimination law suits are an effective way. But, she says, "Such suits are good for women in general, but to the individual who does it, the personal costs are exceedingly high."

Personal costs include being ostracized for being openly critical of the powers that be. After toiling through law school and passing the bar exam, exclusion from law practice is devastating. Thus, few women lawyers file such suits. This explains why discrimination lingers. When harm is not exposed, there is no reason for those doing the harm to stop.

In her book, *The Invisible Bar*, Karen Berger Morello, a New York attorney, speculated about what might happen as a substantial number of women enter the legal profession.

She concludes it will not necessarily mean women will rise to higher levels of the profession. Rather, she predicts, they will be relegated to a second tier, much like teachers in primary schools are mostly women while teachers in higher grades are men.

She believes the forces that once kept women out of the law have shifted to keep them out of powerful positions in the law.

For women attorneys to achieve parity with their male counterparts, one thing is clear: Women cannot afford to be complacent. Women lawyers still present a challenge to the male establishment. To overcome continuing resistance, women must be prepared to dig in

for the long haul.

The Chicago Tribune's Nina Burleigh commenting on Anita Hill's testimony during the Thomas hearings said, "Successful women must emerge from their positions of relative security and strength and tell their stories."

Perhaps inspired by Hill, many women lawyers and women judges have increasingly done just that. For change to occur, women together with fair-minded men, must strongly support those courageous enough to speak out.

References

Cynthia Fuchs Epstein, "Women in Law."

Meg Gorecki, "Legal Pioneers: Four of Illinois' First Women Lawyers," Illinois Bar Journal, Oct. 1990, Vol. 78, No. 10.

Karen Berger Morello, "The Invisible Bar."

"How We Started - 75th History of NAWL," National Association of Women Lawyers.

Chicago Sun-Times, Aug. 21, 1991.

Chicago Tribune, Oct. 8, 1991.

Willard & Livermore, "Women of the Century" (1893)

Reprinted from the *Chicago Daily Law Bulletin*.

Dear WBAI Members:

For more than three quarters of a century, The WBAI has been witness to remarkable breakthroughs for women in the legal profession and the work place in general. With all due humility, we would like to think that our efforts have in no little way influenced this trend. The history of the WBAI in front of you—which in itself is a unique celebration of our origins—is both a commemoration of our past successes and a reminder of the many hurdles we have yet to overcome. It is peopled with a number of members we can only hope to emulate, but never duplicate, as we move toward our centenary. When our charter members paid $10.00 to incorporate on June 23, 1914, their object "to promulgate, promote, advance and protect the interests of the women lawyers in the State of Illinois" was a reasonable goal. Today, it is our mandate.

Carole Siegel
WBAI President

Past Presidents

1914-1915 Nettie Rothblum Loew
1915-1916 Nellie Carlin
1916-1920 Catharine Waugh McCulloch
1920-1921 Esther A. Dunshee
1921-1922 Charlotte D. White
1923-1924 Ada M. Cartwright
1924-1925 Pearl M. Hart
1925-1926 Edna E. Barnett
1926-1927 Mary D. Bailey
1927-1928 Hon. Mary M. Bartelme
1928-1929 Rebecca Willner Liss
1929-1930 Irene V. McCormick
1930-1931 Helen M. Cirese
1931-1932 Mary G. Kelly
1932-1933 Bertha L. MacGregor
1933-1934 Anna Florence Nelson
1934-1935 Edna Devlin Bowens
1935-1936 Elizabeth H. Buchhalter
1936-1937 Elsa C. Beck
1927-1938 Kathryn Barasa Rinella
1938-1939 Marion Marshall Mulligan
1939-1940 Jean Smith Evans
1940-1941 Ellen Nylund Whitsett
1941-1942 Hon. B. Fain Tucker
1942-1943 Charlotte E. Gauer
1943-1944 Eva Pollack Glaser
1944-1945 Helen W. Munsert
1945-1946 Katherine Nohelty
1946-1947 Dorothea Blender
1947-1948 Katharine D. Agar
1948-1949 Coula P. Butler
1949-1950 Jeanne Brown Gordon
1950-1951 Elanor Y. Guthrie
1951-1952 Bess Sullivan Heptig
1952-1953 Edna G. Perraton
1953-1954 Mary Anastasia Johnson
1954-1955 Alice M. Chelberg
1955-1956 Alice M. Bright
1956-1957 Thelma Brook Simon
1957-1958 C. Lois Samuelson
1958-1959 Charlotte Hornstein
1959-1960 Jeanne Hurley Simon

1960-1961 Hon. Helen F. McGillicuddy
1961-1962 Esther R. Rothstein
1962-1963 Dolores K. Hanna
1963-1964 Sylvia M. Cervenka
1964-1965 Theodora Gordon
1965-1966 Mary Avgerin Pappas
1966-1967 Hon. Rosemary LaPorta
1967-1968 Helen Hart Jones
1968-1969 Elaine Strauschild Blatt
1969-1970 M. Lois Dierstein
1970-1971 Patricia E. Mullin
1971-1972 Georgia Lee Lipke
1972-1973 Helen Viney Poter
1973-1974 Hon. Odas Nicholson
1974-1975 Hon. Mary Ann McMorrow
1975-1976 Dr. Rowine Hayes Brown
1976-1977 Hon. Mary Hooton
1977-1978 Katherine Abraham
1978-1979 Hon. Margaret G. O'Malley
1979-1980 Dawn B. Schulz
1980-1981 Teresa M. Conway
1981-1982 Hon. Loretta Douglas
1982-1983 Hon. Marilyn Rozmarek Komosa
1983-1984 Mary Frances Hegarty
1984-1985 Charlotte Adelman
1985-1986 Hon. Barbara Disko
1986-1987 Susan C. Haddad
1987-1988 Jacqueline S. Lustig
1988-1989 Ina S. Winston
1989-1990 Jewel Klein
1990-1991 H. Candace Gorman

Charter Members

Elizabeth Hoffman Buchhalter
Alice C. Edgerton
Mary M. Epperson
Eunice D. Martin
Mae L. Minock
Nettie Rothblum
Charlotte D. White
Ella Zoelzer
Martha Elvert

MARY E. MILLER.

Miss Miller, the secretary of the Alumni Association, first beheld the light of day in Calhoun county, Michigan; graduated in the French and Latin courses from the Marshall High School and the Ypsilanti State Normal School, taught in the High School of Portland, Michigan, the year following her graduation from the Normal School; came to Chicago in 1888, where after pursuing a course of study of stenography and typewriting, she entered a commercial house as stenographer. After a little more than a year in commercial houses she entered the office of Charles H. Aldrich, ex-Solicitor General of the United States, and from that time until July, 1895, was employed in law offices, her duties ranging from stenography pure and simple to general office manager.

In the fall of 1893, with the view of making the active practice of the law her life work, she entered the Chicago College of Law, graduating therefrom with honor in May, 1895. In July of that year she opened her law office in the Monadnock Building. During the summer and fall of 1895, she practiced in the Criminal Court with a considerable degree of success. Her first jury trial was under the following circumstances: One day while by chance she was in the court room a man was brought in for trial whose attorney did not appear. The judge (being the Hon. Frank Baker, who always believes in giving a woman a fair chance to earn an honest living) appointed Miss Miller to defend him. The charge was burglary. There were no witnesses for the defense save the prisoner. He was tried, the proof was overwhelming that he had committed some kind of a crime, was found guilty on the indictment

MISS MARY E. MILLER,
Secretary of the Alumni Association.

and sentenced to the penitentiary; Miss Miller discovered a flaw in the indictment, made a motion to set aside the judgment, and the prisoner was taken to the penitentiary.

The motion was called up for argument, but the judge refused to grant a writ of habeas corpus for the return of the prisoner, until he should hear Miss Miller's argument, saying, that if it should then ap-

(Continued on page 339.)

CHICAGO LEGAL NEWS

Lex vincit.

MYRA BRADWELL, Founder and Editor for 25 years.

JAMES B. BRADWELL,
B. BRADWELL HELMER, } Editors.

Published EVERY SATURDAY by the
CHICAGO LEGAL NEWS COMPANY
NO. 87 CLARK STREET.

TERMS:

TWO DOLLARS AND TWENTY CENTS per annum, in advance. Single Copies, TEN CENTS.

☞ The Chicago Legal News Office is at No. 87 CLARK St., directly opposite the court house. Telephone No. 7.

THE CHICAGO COLLEGE OF LAW.
(Continued from page 338.)

pear that there were good grounds he would grant the writ. She presented her authorities and after hearing her argument the judge granted the writ; the prisoner was returned; the judgment and verdict set aside; a new trial granted and the prisoner was allowed to plead guilty to petit larceny and taken Bridewell sentence of a few months. Had it not been for the services of Miss Miller this man would not have escaped from a five years' sentence in the penitentiary. The indictment was for burglary in the night.

These services were rendered without compensation, as the friends of the prisoner who are well to do eastern people (as is often the case), utterly refused to assist him in any way.

Miss Miller says that his term is now ended and he is at work in the city trying to redeem his past and to pay her fees, and she has every hope that he will lead a different and better life. She was informed by the representatives of the state's attorney's office that it is the first time in the history of the Criminal Court that a writ of habeas corpus has been granted for the return of a prisoner from Joliet under similar circumstances.

Miss Miller has not practiced in the Criminal Court since last fall and we are pleased to be able to state that her civil business is steadily increasing and the outlook for her is very encouraging, considering the length of time she has been practicing.

She went as speaker to the National Council of Women held in Washington, D. C., 1895, was a speaker at the Art Institute for one of the Congresses in 1893, and has often appeared as a public speaker on different occasions.

In addition to the regular course of two years, she took the post graduate course and received the degree of Bachelor of Laws in 1896. We predict for her a successful professional career.

The program was carried out to the letter. We regret that space prevents us from giving a more extended notice of the exercises. There seemed to be an energy and enthusiasm about the members of these two graduating classes which astonished us. The boys and girls who graduated seemed to feel the importance of the occasion to them, and gave evidence that they mean to do all in their power to achieve success in their chosen profession. Elmer E. Barrett, Secretary, announces that the prize of $100 offered by Messrs. Callaghan & Co., Law Booksellers of Chicago, to the member of the Senior Class who passed two full years at this institution, and who, during the Senior year, at-

tained the highest general proficiency in his studies, was awarded to Richard Boddinghouse.

Those worthy of honorable mention are Robert K. Reilly, Eva M. Reynolds and Quin O'Brien.

EVA MAY REYNOLDS.

Miss Reynolds is a hoosier girl, having first opened her eyes to the beauties of this blessed world of ours, in Parke County, Indiana, several years "after the war." Her parents moved to Indianapolis twenty

MISS EVA MAY REYNOLDS.
Received honorable mention.

years ago, and she received her education in that city, noted for its admirable common school system. After graduating from the high school she was engaged as stenographer and private correspondent with the D. H. Ranck Publishing Company, and came to Chicago, when the office of that company was moved here in the spring of 1893. She is at present the secretary and subscription manager of that company. Of keen, analytical mind, and a persistent student, she has a natural fondness for the study of the law. This led her to take a course in the Chicago Law School, from which she recently graduated third in a class of 178 students, and received honorable mention. This speaks well for the ability of women to compete with men in the study of the law. Miss Reynolds, by being placed third in the class stands ahead of the three other women in the class, and of 172 men.

NELLIE CARLIN.

Miss Carlin is a Chicagoan, twenty-seven years of age. She attended the public

MISS NELLIE CARLIN.

schools of this city and about seven years ago took a course of instruction in the Chicago Athenæum Business College in stenography and bookkeeping. She held a position as stenographer and bookkeeper

for five years with the Grant Baking Powder Company, and a like position with Graham & Sons Bank, and is now employed in the law office of the well known lawyer and Democratic orator, C. S. Darrow, of this city.

Miss Carlin is deeply interested in social problems and has made a study of sociology; is a believer in equal rights for all, irrespective of race, color, creed or sex, but she says "I am not a woman suffragist, not, however, because I think women should not have the right of suffrage, but my study of philosophy, especially the writings of Herbert Spencer, has led me to question the right of the majority to rule. This opinion has not been changed since my study of the law, which latter science, according to my opinion, is sadly in need of reform and is a Herculean task should any one have courage to undertake it."

Miss Carlin is an independent, original thinker and is not of views upon any subject banquet attracted considerable She will be heard from in the profession to which she has just been admitted.

MILDRED ELWELL TREMAINE.

Miss Tremaine was recently congratulated on being the youngest lady lawyer in Chicago. She is a lawyer, in the sense of having a right to practice, but has no intention of exercising that right at present. Miss Tremaine was born and has always lived in Chicago. Since leaving Oberlin

MISS MILDRED ELWELL TREMAINE.

College, where she spent some time, she has undertaken several branches of usefulness. Her purpose in studying law was simply to "grow," as she says, and to better fit herself for any line of work she may hereafter adopt. That work will probably be one into which she can pour all the accumulations she has made in her various lines of thought and study, including, as they do, music, art, ethics, politics and improved dress for women—a subject which she holds most dear. Her pen will therefore probably occupy her attention in the future, as she has already found time to contribute to some of the current magazines, and surely her earnestness and ability can find no better outlet.

ANNA MULLIN.

Mrs. Mullin, just graduated from the Chicago College of Law, is a Chicago business woman, who studied law, not with a view of practicing at the bar, but to educate herself generally. She believes that a knowledge of the principles and rules of law is essential to a broad understanding of business relations, and that business women, no less than men, should make an effort to acquire that knowledge, even at the cost of considerable time and money

that it might seem easier to spend otherwise.

Mrs. Mullin conducts a large commission business and is always to be found at her post, having had but one day of vacation in nearly six years.

She has recently accepted the position of treasurer in "The Forward Movement," a new college settlement on the West Side, and expects to devote much time and energy to the work. She is well adapted to assist in many capacities, having taught

MRS. ANNA M MULLIN.

in the Chicago schools, being a fine Latin scholar as well as a thorough student of English literature. Mrs. Mullin's time is largely absorbed in business, but her heart is singularly free from it, as many friends and beneficiaries testify. In fact, this quiet, unassuming woman is a living denial of the old fallacy that a woman loses her womanliness by entering men's sphere (so called), and proves conclusively in her life that experience and responsibility enrich us all, and that the more one has in himself or herself, the more he or she can give the world.

Myra Bradwell, founder of the Chicago Legal News.

5

HISTORY OF THE WOMEN'S BAR ASSOCIATION OF ILLINOIS

In 1869, Chicago's courthouse was in a sorry state. Cows, goats and the good citizens of Chicago had trampled the grass in the courthouse square. The windows were filthy and the walls worn and defaced. The squalid condition of the courthouse did not seem to bother anyone - with the exception of Myra Bradwell. This remarkable woman had just established the *Chicago Legal News*, a weekly publication designed to provide up-to-date case law and legal information to lawyers and also to improve everything connected with the practice of law. Restoring the courthouse was part of her ambitious campaign. (See: *The First Century* by Herman Kogan) At a time when, in the whole of the United States there were no women lawyers, and women did not yet have the vote, what was her motivation?

Myra Bradwell was a schoolteacher from Vermont who married James B. Bradwell, a lawyer. She had begun to study law in her husband's Chicago office, intending merely to assist him in his law practice. As her studies progressed, she decided that she would also become a licensed attorney. This quest was interrupted temporarily by the Civil War, during which Bradwell worked for passage of laws granting women fair property rights, the right to serve on juries and urging the admission of women to university law departments.

Bradwell also served as Secretary of the Illinois Women's Suffrage Association, whose goal it was to ensure that Illinois become the first state to permit women to vote. Through all the turmoil, she steadfastly worked toward her goal of becoming an attorney.

In 1869, Bradwell passed the bar examination and was certified to the state supreme court for admission to the bar. Had this been permitted, she should have been one of the first two women lawyers in the United States. However, the Illinois State Supreme Court denied her application. Its reason was that her "married condition" constituted a "disability" which impaired her ability to keep a client's confidence. That year, Iowa admitted Belle A. Mansfield, who became the first woman in America admitted to the bar.

Bradwell immediately requested the Illinois Supreme Court to reconsider. The chief justice, in an opinion indicating general approval for women's rights, harshly affirmed the original denial (55 Ill. 535). Not only would Bradwell's admission to the bar be denied because she was a married woman, ruled the court, it would be denied because she was a woman. The court reasoned that women had not been known as attorneys at common law. Women might have a detrimental effect upon the administration of justice.

When the legislature gave the court the power of granting licenses to practice law, it was with not the slightest expectation that this privilege would be extended equally to men and women. Since God had designed the sexes to occupy different spheres of action, and it belonged to men to make, plan and execute the laws, the court chose to not exercise its discretion to admit women.

Bradwell promptly filed a writ of error to the United States Supreme Court. It affirmed, ruling that admission to the bar was not a privilege belonging to citizens of the United States which individual states were prohibited from abridging. The Court noted that "the laws of the Creator" had placed limits on the functions of womanhood. There was one dissent.

Bradwell made no subsequent attempts to attain admission to the bar. She devoted her time to legal reform, her newspaper, women's rights, working for the formation of what would eventually be The Chicago Bar Association and encouraging other aspiring female attorneys. However, on its own motion and four years before her death, in 1890, the Illinois Supreme Court granted her a law license, based on the application which she had made on August 2, 1969, 21 years before. Two years later, the United States Supreme Court admitted her. Although she never practiced law, Myra Bradwell was perhaps Illinois' most outstanding attorney.

In June, 1870, the first woman in the U.S.A. graduated from law school. She was Ada Kepley from Effingham, Illinois. She attended the law department at Chicago University. In 1873 after her graduation, Chicago University and Northwestern University entered into an agreement to jointly manage the department and it became known as the Union College of Law. In 1891 it was formally integrated into Northwestern University. However, Illinois refused to permit women to enter the so called "learned professions". Ada Kepley was not then allowed to practice law.

In 1870, while Bradwell's request for admission to the Illinois bar was pending, a courageous judge in Effingham permitted Adah H. Kepley to practice in that court. He stated that although the Illinois Supreme Court had refused to license a woman, it was in another case, and he believed Kepley's motion was proper and in accord with the spirit of the age.

In 1871, Alta Hulett, who had passed the bar examination at age 18 and studied law in a Rockford law office, applied for admission to the Illinois bar; she was refused. Hulett, assisted by Bradwell, Kepley and others who had also been refused admission to the bar, drafted a bill which provided that no person could be discriminated against in any employment, except the military, on account of sex. With the help and encouragement of Myra Bradwell and the *Chicago Legal News*, the bill passed in March of 1872. It was the first law in the United States prohibiting sex discrimination in employment.

On Hulett's 19th birthday, June 4, 1873, Illinois admitted her as its first woman lawyer. (Tragically she died in 1877.) From 1875 through 1879, one woman was admitted to the bar each year. In 1880 and 1881, two women were admitted one of them, Adah Kepley. In 1882, one woman was admitted; in 1884 through 1887, two were admitted, each year. In 1888, one was admitted; and in 1889-90-91, three were admitted each year. In 1892, the number increased to five. From that time on, the number varied. One of those early admittees was Bessie (Helmer) Bradwell, Myra Bradwell's daughter, an 1882 Northwestern University Law School (Union College) graduate.

In 1880 Helen Schuhard was appointed Master or Chancery in Union County, Illinois, despite a challenge that women could not legally hold the office. J. Ellen Foster was a defense attorney in the 1880's who gained a new trial for her client, a woman facing execution. This enhanced her reputation as an attorney; she was also a temperance leader.

An early leader in the suffrage movement was Catherine Waugh McCulloch, an 1886 Northwestern School of Law graduate (then Union College of Law) who was admitted to the Illinois bar in November, 1866. She was also a noted club woman. The Equal Suffrage Association, under her leadership, held conventions throughout Illinois.

By 1890, boasted Kate Kane Rosse, a Chicago attorney, she had "either prosecuted or defended every crime known to modern times except treason and piracy". In 1890 the Illinois Supreme Court granted Myra Bradwell a license, on its own motion, on her original application filed in 1869.

In 1891, Ellen Martin, a Chicago lawyer noted the Town Charter of Lombard had omitted the word "male" in its voting ordinance. She demanded the right to vote. Shocked, the judges permitted it, and she produced 14 other women, who also voted.

In 1894 Florence Kelly graduated from Northwestern Law School. She went on to work in a child labor reform, through Hull House and as Chief Factory Inspector in Illinois. She left Illinois for New York in 1900.

In 1894, the first black woman was admitted to practice law in Illinois; her name was Ida Platt. When she was admitted, one of the Illinois Supreme Court justices commented, "We have done today what we never did before - admitted a colored woman to the bar. Now it may truly be said that persons are admitted to the Illinois bar without regard to race, sex or color."

The first legal sorority in the United States was established in 1908 in Chicago by some of the Chicago-Kent College of Law's female students. It flourished throughout the United States, especially in Washington, D.C., and had chapters abroad.

In 1913, the Illinois law was passed giving women partial suffrage: they gained the right to vote, but only in presidential and municipal elections. Illinois became the first state east of

6

CHICAGO LEGAL NEWS.

VOL. XXXII. JUNE 2, 1900. No. 41.

The Courts.

WOMEN LAWYERS OF ILLINOIS.

By James B. Bradwell.

1.—MYRA BRADWELL.

MYRA BRADWELL was the first woman in Illinois to apply for admission to the bar.

August 2, 1869, she applied to the then official examiners and passed the examination for admission to the bar. The following is the certificate of examination.

CERTIFICATE OF EXAMINATION.

The undersigned have examined Mrs. Myra Bradwell as to her qualifications to enter upon the practice of law, and finding her qualified therefor, recommend that a license be issued to her.

CHICAGO, ILL., August 2, 1869.

E. S. WILLIAMS,
Judge 7th Judicial Circuit.
CHARLES H. REED,
State's Attorney.

MOTION TO BE ADMITTED.

Robert Hervey, of the Chicago bar, at the September term, 1869, of the Supreme Court of Illinois, filed the certificate of examination and of character from Judge Jamieson of the Superior Court of Cook County, and the application of Mrs. Bradwell, giving the reasons why she should be admitted. For all of which see 2 CHICAGO LEGAL NEWS, p. 145.

On the 6th of October, 1869, she was refused admission by reason of the disability incurred by her married condition. November 18th Mrs. Bradwell filed an additional brief combating the position taken by the Supreme Court. The Supreme Court, after considering the additional brief, in January, 1870, filed a written opinion refusing the application upon the sole ground that the applicant was a woman. For the additional brief and opinion of the court see 2 CHICAGO LEGAL NEWS, pp. 165-167, also reported in 55 Ill. 535.

Myra Bradwell sued out a writ of error from the Supreme Court of the United States to the Supreme Court of Illinois and removed the cause to that tribunal. For the argument of Hon. Matt H. Carpenter, counsel for Mrs. Bradwell in the Supreme Court of the United States, see 4 CHICAGO LEGAL NEWS, p. 108.

The opinion of the United States, Supreme Court, from which Chase, C. J., dissents, affirming the judgment of the Supreme Court of Illinois refusing to grant to Myra Bradwell a license to practice law upon the sole ground that she was a woman, will be found in 16 Wallace 130, and in 5 CHICAGO LEGAL NEWS, p. 885. Also for full report of this case see 2 History of Woman Suffrage, pp. 601 to 626.

LICENSE GRANTED ON COURT'S OWN MOTION ON ORIGINAL APPLICATION.

When Mrs. Bradwell was in Mexico, in March, 1890, without her knowledge, the court granted her a license on her original application filed in 1869. Hon. S. P. Shope, the then Chief Justice of the Supreme Court, wrote to James B. Bradwell, saying: "It gave me great pleasure to, at least, do justice to Mrs. Bradwell, and also to be able to say to you that after the matter was canvassed and understood, every member of the court cordially acquiesced in granting on its own motion, license as attorney and counselor at law to her. I am pleased, both because I recognize her great service to the profession, and uniform kindliness and courtesy toward the court."

Myra Bradwell was, on motion of Hon. W. H. H. Miller, Attorney General of the United States, on March 28, 1892, admitted to the bar of the Supreme Court of the United States.

Myra Bradwell was the founder of the CHICAGO LEGAL NEWS, and its editor for more than a quarter of a century. This publication is an enduring monument of her great ability as a legal writer and her sound judgment as a woman.

MYRA BRADWELL.

Mrs. Bradwell passed over the silent river February 14, 1894. For a sketch of her life, so full of service to humanity, see 26 CHICAGO LEGAL NEWS, p. 200.

Mrs. Bradwell was the first woman to become a member of the Illinois Press Association, also the first woman to become a member of the Illinois State Bar Association, and the only married woman in the world whose earnings were given her by a special act of the Legislature. The Legislature gave her a special charter for her paper and passed several acts making it evidence in the courts and a valid medium for the publication of legal notices. She was a member of the Soldiers' Home Board in Chicago for nearly thirty years, and for several years its treasurer.

She was one of the Board of Lady Managers of the World's Columbian Exposition and chairman of the Woman's Committee on Jurisprudence of the World's Congress Auxiliary of 1893.

The present law of this State giving a married woman her own earnings was drawn by Myra Bradwell.

Mrs. Bradwell was a delegate at the organization of the American Woman's Suffrage Association at Cleveland. 1 CHICAGO LEGAL NEWS, p. 76. For law allowing women to be admitted to the bar in Illinois, see 4 CHICAGO LEGAL NEWS, p. 186.

In 1870 sixty of the leading lawyers of Chicago petitioned Governor Palmer to appoint Myra Bradwell notary public, but the Governor refused upon the sole ground that she was a woman.

Governor Beveridge appointed Mrs. Bradwell a delegate to the Prison Reform Congress at St. Louis. The Governor of Illinois appointed Mrs. Bradwell as one of the Illinois Centennial Association to represent Illinois in the Centennial Exposition at Philadelphia, in 1876, and she was made treasurer of the woman's branch of the association. During the war Mrs. Bradwell was active in receiving and caring for the sick and wounded soldiers. She was a member and secretary of the Committee on Arms, Trophies and Curiosities of the Great Northwestern Sanitary Fair, and was the leading spirit in producing that artistic and beautiful exhibition in Bryan Hall in 1865.

She was a charter member and matron of Marion Family of the Eastern Star, organized October 6, 1866, being the first body of that order in Illinois; was a member of the Woman's Club; Daughters of the American Revolution; The Woman's Press Association, and the National Press League.

2.—MISS ALTA M. HULETT.

Miss Alta M. Hulett began the study of law in Rockford under the direction of Hon. Wm. Lathrop. She mastered the elementary text books with marvelous rapidity. After passing a very creditable examination under the statute passed in 1872, to secure to all persons freedom in the selection of any profession or employment without regard to sex, she was admitted to the Illinois bar at Mt. Vernon on June 6, 1873.

Miss Hulett at once engaged in the active practice of the law in Chicago. She had a fine legal mind and was a most successful practitioner until her brilliant career was cut short by her untimely death.

3.—MISS MARY FREDRIKA PERRY.

Miss Mary Fredrika Perry (Michigan University, LL.B., 1875,) commenced the study of law in 1870, in the office of Shipman & Loveridge, with whom she remained until the fall of 1873, when she entered the law department of Michigan University and graduated in the class of 1875, and in the fall of that year came to Chicago and was examined with the regular class at Ottawa for admission to the bar. One of the examiners who was opposed to the admission of women in the profession, informed Mrs. Bradwell, the editor of the LEGAL NEWS, that Miss Perry took the court, the examiners and the bar by surprise, and passed by far the best examination of any member of the class. Her license bears date September 17, 1875.

Miss Perry was a thorough student and entered into the practice of law with a good knowledge of the principles upon which it is founded. Practicing in the days when there was so much prejudice against women in the legal field, Miss Perry was one to allay hostile criticism and to win the respect of all who made her acquaintance. She was connected in the practice of law with Miss Ellen A. Martin until the time of her death, which occurred June 3, 1883. So devoted to the memory of Miss Perry is Miss Martin that she still uses the firm name of Perry & Martin. See 8 CHICAGO LEGAL NEWS, p. 8, and 15 CHICAGO LEGAL NEWS, p. 331.

For resolutions on the death of Miss Perry see *Ib.*, p. 339; for proceedings of the meeting of the Chicago bar on the death of Miss Perry presided over by Judge Tuley, and the remarks of Judge Tuley, Ellen A. Martin, her law partner, James P. Root, John W. Ela, A. J. Grover, C. B. Waite, Alexander McCoy and Hon. John H. Batten, see 2 Obituary Memoranda of the Illinois State Bar Association, p. 13 to 19.

4.—MISS ELLEN A. MARTIN.

Miss Ellen A. Martin, (Michigan University, LL.B.,) after passing a successful examination before the Supreme Court, was admitted to the Illinois bar January 8, 1876. See 8 CHICAGO LEGAL NEWS, p. 128.

Miss Martin, after her admission, entered into a law partnership with Miss Mary Fredrika Perry, under the firm name of Perry & Martin, and continued to practice in Chicago with Miss Perry until Miss Perry's death in 1883. Miss Martin is so devoted to the memory of Miss Perry that the sign Perry & Martin may be seen to-day on her office door at 84 LaSalle street. Miss Martin has been in active and successful practice since her admission. She is a woman of ability, a good lawyer, and has done excellent service in the ranks of those who believe in the equality of men and women before the law.

Miss Martin is the secretary of the National League of Women Lawyers.

Miss Martin, and Miss Perry's mother, now over seventy years of age, were two of the fifteen women who voted at the charter election at Lombard, a suburb of Chicago, April 6, 1891. See 23 CHICAGO LEGAL NEWS, p. 278, and for article of Miss Martin on "Women Voters of Lombard," see *Ib.*, page 270. For remarks of Miss Martin on the death of Miss Perry at the meeting of the Chicago bar, see 2 Obituary Memoranda, Illinois State Bar Association, p. 13 and p. 1[illegible].

It was through the efforts of Miss Martin as chairman of the law department of the Queen Isabella Association, that a meeting of women lawyers was held during the World's Fair, August 3, 4 and 5, 1893, at which thirty women lawyers attended, and she delivered an address upon "The Myra Bradwell Case in Illinois."

ELLEN A. MARTIN.

5.—ABBEY S. COLTON.

Abbey S. Colton was admitted to the Illinois bar January 15, 1877.

6.—MISS ALICE D. MERRILL.

Miss Alice D. Merrill (Union College of Law, LL.B., 1878,) was admitted to the Illinois bar June 13th of the same year.

Miss Merrill was a printer by trade and for a time worked in the office of the CHICAGO LEGAL NEWS. She still resides in Chicago.

7.—MRS. MERIETTE B. R. SHAY.

Mrs. Meriette B. R. Shay was admitted to the Illinois bar June 17, 1879; was a graduate of the Bloomington Law School, and wrote a book entitled, Students' Guide to Common Law Pleading," which was published by Callaghan & Company, and printed by the CHICAGO LEGAL NEWS Company.

8.—MISS CORA A. BENNESON.

Miss Cora A. Benneson, (Michigan University, A. B. '78, LL.B. '80, A. M. '83,) formerly of Quincy, Ill., was admitted to the Illinois bar June 5, 1880. Miss Benneson is a woman of scholarly attainments. In 1887, she held the fellowship in history in Bryn Mawr College. She is engaged in literary pursuits, and has lived for many years in Cambridge, Massachusetts.

9.—MRS. PHEBE M. BARTLETT.

Mrs. Phebe M. Bartlett (Union College of Law, LL.B., 1880,) was admitted to the Illinois bar September 18, 1880.

Mrs. Bartlett was for a time in the office of Judge Van H. Higgins in this city.

10.—MRS. ADA H. KEPLEY.

Mrs. Ada H. Kepley, (University of Chicago, LL.B.,) the wife of H. B. Kepley, a practicing lawyer of Effingham, was admitted to the Illinois bar January 13, 1881. For her admission as a law student to the law department of the Chicago University, see 2 CHICAGO LEGAL NEWS, p. 44.

She graduated from the law department of this university in the class of '70.

Judge Decius, of the Circuit Court of Effingham County, in defiance of the opinion of the Supreme Court of Illinois, on motion, entered an order allowing Mrs. Kepley to practice in his court, November 16, 1870. 3 CHICAGO LEGAL NEWS, p. 60.

Mrs. Kepley has been in active practice with her husband in Effingham since her admission, to the present time. She is a woman of ability, and has a large circle of friends, and is respected by all who know her. She celebrated the 32nd anniversary of her wedding, November 4, 1899. See 32 CHICAGO LEGAL NEWS, November 18, 1899.

Mrs. Kepley is an honorary member of the Illinois State Bar Association.

11.—LOUISA LUSK.

Louisa Lusk was admitted to the Illinois bar, June 11, 1881.

12.—MRS. BESSIE BRADWELL HELMER.

Mrs. Bessie Bradwell Helmer (Northwestern University A. B. 1880, A. M. 1884, Union College of Law LL.B., 1882,) received her early education in the public schools of Chicago, graduating from the Chicago High School in 1876 as valedictorian of her class. After the completion of her college course at Northwestern University she entered the Union College of Law and was chosen by her classmates at the law school to deliver the valedictory at the commencement exercises. She was admitted to the Illinois bar June 15, 1882.

Mrs. Helmer edited twelve volumes of the Illinois Appellate Court Reports and has been associate editor of the CHICAGO LEGAL NEWS since 1894. Mrs. Helmer has taken a deep interest in securing money for fellowships for gifted women of scholarly attainments, and for many years has served as chairman of the fellowship committee of the Association of Collegiate Alumnae, of which organization she was at one time president. She was vice-chairman of the woman's committee of the Law Reform Congress of the World's Congress Auxiliary, is secretary of the Soldiers' Home Board in Chicago, and an honorary member of the Illinois State Bar Association.

13.—MRS. KATE KANE ROSSI.

Kate Kane (now Mrs. Rossi), formerly of Milwaukee, now of Chicago, spent one year in Michigan University law school, and one in the law office of A. A. Jackson, at Janesville, Wis.; was admitted to the Wisconsin bar, July, 1878, practiced five years in Milwaukee, and was admitted to the Illinois bar March 24, 1884. She is a woman of ability, a good speaker, and is ever ready to defend her rights in or out of court. Mrs. Rossi has been practicing law at the Chicago bar for the past sixteen years. She is equally at home in prosecuting a civil suit or defending a criminal. Mrs. Rossi took an early interest in having matrons appointed for the police stations in this city.

CHICAGO LEGAL NEWS.

14.—LAURA B. SHEPARD.

Laura B. Shepard was admitted to the Illinois bar May 14, 1884.

13.—KATE KANE ROSSI.

15.—ALICE C. NUTE.

Alice C. Nute, after passing a successful examination before the Appellate Court of this district, was admitted to the Illinois bar March 20, 1885. She was for years one of the ablest shorthand

ALICE C. NUTE.

writers in Chicago. See 17 CHICAGO LEGAL NEWS, p. 225.

Miss Nute died March 18, 1898, in Chicago. For sketch of her life see 30 CHICAGO LEGAL NEWS, p. 273.

16.—EMMA STRAWN.

Emma Strawn was admitted to the Illinois bar at Springfield, June 9, 1885. She practiced law for several years at Lacon.

17.—MRS. CATHERINE V. WAITE.

Mrs. Catherine V. Waite, (Union College of Law LL.B., 1886,) wife of ex-Judge C. B. Waite, of Hyde Park, was admitted to the Illinois bar June 15, 1886. Many years ago Mrs. Waite was principal of a private school for girls in Chicago. She is a woman of broad education and business ability; was prominent among woman suffragists; was president of the Illinois Woman's Suffrage Association.

Thirty-four years ago Mrs. Waite applied to one of the medical colleges of this city for admission as a student to study medicine, but was refused on the sole ground that she was a woman. She has now a daughter who is a skillful physician—Dr. Lucy Waite. See 18 CHICAGO LEGAL NEWS, p. 331.

Mrs. Waite has recently removed to Colorado.

18.—MRS. CATHERINE WAUGH MC-CULLOCH.

Mrs. Catherine Waugh McCulloch (Rockford College A.B., Union College of Law LL.B., 1886,) was admitted to the Illinois bar November 9, 1886, and practiced law for four years at the Rockford, Illinois, bar.

Miss Waugh was married by Rev. Anna H. Shaw to Mr. Frank H. McCulloch, May 30, 1890. See 22 CHICAGO LEGAL NEWS, p.326. Mrs. McCulloch has been in active practice for years in Chicago, in connection with the law firm of Prussing & McCulloch. This firm has recently been dissolved, and she is now a member of the firm of McCulloch & McCulloch, husband and wife, with offices at 1113 The Rookery.

Mrs. McCulloch is a woman of talent; an eloquent and ready speaker; an able lawyer; one of the leaders and officers of the American Woman's Suffrage Association, president of the Illinois Equal Suffrage Association, and has taken an active part in the legislative work to place women upon an equality with men.

Mrs. McCulloch has been a member of the Illinois State Bar Association since 1891, and is now treasurer of the National League of Women Lawyers.

She was a member of the committee of the Woman's Branch of the World's Congress Auxiliary on Jurisprudence and Law Reform.

19.—MISS LETITIA L. BURLINGAME.

Miss Letitia L. Burlingame, formerly of Joliet, was admitted to the Illinois bar May 9, 1887.

Miss Burlingame has been dead for some years.

20.—MARY MERRILL.

Mary Merrill was admitted to the Illinois bar June 14, 1887.

21.—ANNA MCCOY.

Anna McCoy (Union College of Law, LL.B., 1888,) was admitted to the Illinois bar June 16, 1888. See 20 CHICAGO LEGAL NEWS, p. 842.

22.—MINERVA A. DOYLE.

Minerva A. Doyle (Union College of Law, LL.B., 1889,) was admitted to the Illinois bar June 12, 1889.

23.—BERTHA E. CURTIS.

Bertha E. Curtis (Union College of Law, LL.B., 1889,) was admitted to the Illinois bar June 12, 1889. See 21 CHICAGO LEGAL NEWS, p. 357.

18.—CATHERINE WAUGH MCCULLOCH.

24.—MRS. MARY A. AHRENS.

Mrs. Mary A. Ahrens (Union College of Law, LL.B., 1889,) was admitted to the Illinois bar June 12, 1889.

Mrs. Ahrens is a woman of very decided ability; a fluent speaker; has been

in active practice at the Chicago bar for eleven years and in addition to her professional duties has devoted much time to philanthropic work. See 21 CHICAGO LEGAL NEWS, p. 357; 25, p. 431.

Mrs. Ahrens occupied one law office for more than ten years and always has taken a pleasure in her law practice. During her recent serious illness she

MARY A. AHRENS.

said feelingly to a friend, "Please do not let it be forgotten that Mary A. Ahrens was a lawyer, is a lawyer and always will continue to be one."

Mrs. Ahrens was a member of the committee of the Woman's Branch of the World's Congress Auxiliary on Jurisprudence and Law Reform.

25.—MISS L. BLANCH FEARING.

Miss L. Blanch Fearing, of Chicago, (Northwestern University, LL.B., 1890,) was admitted to the Illinois bar June 10, 1890. See 22 CHICAGO LEGAL NEWS, p. 345.

Miss Fearing is in many respects one of the most remarkable women practicing law in the United States.

She has literary ability of a high order. Her published articles and poems have received very favorable mention from literary critics and the opinion has been expressed by some of her friends that it is a pity one who is so gifted should not devote her entire time to literature. Notwithstanding the fact that she is blind, Miss Fearing has since her admission practiced actively at the Chicago bar. Possessed of a keen, analytical mind, she is an able lawyer.

26.—MRS. FLORA V. WOODWARD TIBBITTS.

Mrs. Flora V. Woodward Tibbitts, after graduating at the Union College of Law, was admitted to the Illinois bar June 10, 1890. See 22 CHICAGO LEGAL NEWS, p. 345.

She received the degree of LL.B. from the Chicago College of Law in 1891; did brief work, and practiced for several years in Chicago; is a woman of decided ability.

27.—MISS EMMA J. H. BAUMANN.

Miss Emma J. H. Baumann, of Chicago, (Chicago College of Law, LL.B., 1891,) graduated from the Chicago College of Law in the class of 1890; received the degree of LL.B. from that institution in 1891 and was admitted to the Illinois bar October 21, 1890.

Miss Baumann is now in the employ of the well-known law firm of Hatch & Ritsher.

28.—MISS CORA B. HIRTZEL.

Miss Cora B. Hirtzel graduated from the Chicago College of Law in 1890, and was admitted to the Illinois bar October 31, 1890. Miss Hirtzel was for some time

in the law office of Hon. W. C. Goudy. In 1897, when Charles S. Thornton was Corporation Counsel, Miss Hirtzel was appointed Assistant Corporation Counsel of the city of Chicago, and is the only woman who ever held that position in the great Metropolis of the Northwest. She performed the duties of that office with credit to herself and to the entire satisfaction of the profession and others transacting business with her.

A large portion of her practice has been preparing briefs for the profession. She is an able, well-read lawyer, and is throughly posted in legal practice. In January of this year she formed a law partnership with Miss Nellie Carlin under the firm name of Hirtzel & Carlin. Miss Hirtzel has been a member of the Illinois State Bar Association since 1898. For sketches see 29 CHICAGO LEGAL

CORA B. HIRTZEL.

NEWS p. 341, and 32 CHICAGO LEGAL NEWS p. 185.

29.—MISS CATHERINE E. WALLACE.

Miss Catherine E. Wallace, daughter of ex-Judge M. R. M. Wallace, of Chicago, after graduating from the Union College of Law was admitted to the Illinois bar June 9, 1891.

30.—LAURA M. STARR.

Laura M. Starr, after graduating from the Union College of Law, was admitted to the Illinois bar June 9, 1891. See 28 CHICAGO LEGAL NEWS, p. 244.

31.—SARAH N. KNAPP.

Sarah N. Knapp was admitted to the Illinois bar October 22, 1891.

32.—LOUISA DENNERT.

Louisa Dennert was admitted to the Illinois bar March 16, 1892.

33.—MISS MARY LEE COLBERT.

Miss Mary Lee Colbert, of Chicago, (Chicago College of Law, LL.B., 1893,) graduated from the Chicago College of Law in 1893, attaining an average of ninety-eight in the law college, standing third highest in a class of 125; received honorable mention, and was admitted to the Illinois bar June 14, 1892, LL.B. degree in 1893; secretary of the Alumni Association in 1894-5, and first vice-president of the association and a member of the executive committee for the past three years. Also a member of the Chicago Bar Association.

Miss Colbert has been a clerk in the law office of Julius Rosenthal (later of Julius & Lessing Rosenthal) for more than ten years, attending mainly to probate work, to wills, conveyancing, etc. We knew Miss Colbert's father as a thrifty business man of Chicago.

34.—MARION H. DRAKE.

Marion H. Drake graduated from the Chicago College of Law in 1892, and was admitted to the Illinois bar June 14, 1892,

and was in the law office of Moran, Kraus & Mayer about three years. At the commencement exercises of the Chicago

MARION H. DRAKE.

College of Law in 1895 Miss Drake delivered a paper upon "The Lawyer as a Philanthropist." For copy of this address see 27 CHICAGO LEGAL NEWS, p. 351.

35.—MISS EFFIE HENDERSON.

Miss Effie Henderson, (Illinois Wesleyan University, LL.B., 1892,) of Bloomington, was admitted to the Illinois bar June 14, 1892. She is a woman of ability and her legal work since her admission has been such as to gain the respect of her professional brethren. See 24 CHICAGO LEGAL NEWS, p. 358.

36.—MRS. MARY M. NEGUS.

Mrs. Mary M. Negus, of Chicago, (Northwestern University, LL.B.,) was admitted to the Illinois bar June 14, 1892. See 24 CHICAGO LEGAL NEWS, p. 341.

37.—ALICE M. ALBRIGHT.

Alice M. Albright (Northwestern University, LL.B., 1892,) was admitted to the Illinois bar June 14, 1892. See 24 CHICAGO LEGAL NEWS, p. 341.

38.—MRS. CHARLOTTE C. HOLT.

Mrs. Charlotte C. Holt studied law for two years in the law office of Higgins & Parker, and after passing the examination before the Appellate Court, was admitted to the Illinois bar March 28, 1898. Soon after, Mrs. Holt opened an office in the Chicago Opera House Block, but subsequently gave up the practice of law for family reasons.

Mrs. Holt is a woman of culture and broad sympathies, and an active member of the Chicago Woman's Club. In 1886 Mrs. Holt was appointed agent of the Protective Agency for Women and Children, which position she filled with great ability for five years. She then served as director in this organization for six years and is at present a director on the board.

Mrs. Holt is specially gifted as a lecturer and has been very successful in conducting study classes. She is now giving lectures on law to classes and clubs of women. These lectures are practical subjects to the laity and designed to assist women in a knowledge of those fundamental principles of the law which are needful to save them from avoidable mistakes in the administration of their own affairs.

39.—MINERVA K. ELLIOTT.

Minerva K. Elliott, of Chicago, was admitted to the Illinois bar June 15, 1893.

40.—MISS CECELIA HEDENBERG.

Miss Cecelia Hedenberg, of Chicago, (Northwestern University, LL.B., 1893,) was admitted to the Illinois bar June 15, 1893. See 25 CHICAGO LEGAL NEWS, p.

364. Miss Hedenberg is now engaged in educational work.

41.—MISS ZETTA STRAWN.

Miss Zetta Strawn, of Ottawa, (Northwestern University, LL.B., 1893,) was admitted to the Illinois bar June 15, 1893. Miss Strawn studied law in the office of Miss Ellen A. Martin; is a good business lawyer.

42.—MARY KENNEDY BROWN.

Mary Kennedy Brown was admitted to the Illinois bar January 15, 1894; married Lieut. Bosworth Smith, and is now living in England.

43.—MISS IDA PLATT.

Miss Ida Platt is the first colored woman ever admitted to the Illinois bar. She was born in this city, graduated from the high school at the age of sixteen and from the Chicago College of Law in 1894. In 1892 she entered the law office of Jesse Cox as stenographer and began the study of law in the Chicago College of Law. In July, 1893, she established herself in the Ashland Block as general stenographer and law reporter. She is proficient in German, French and music. Miss Platt has been teaching shorthand and typewriting in one of the city evening high schools for the past five years. She was admitted to the Illinois bar

IDA PLATT.

June 15, 1894, and has been ever since and now is, in the law office of the well-known lawyer, Joseph W. Errant, practicing law. For sketch see 26 CHICAGO LEGAL NEWS, p. 352.

44.—MISS MARY MARGARET BARTELME.

Miss Mary Margaret Bartelme (Northwestern University, LL.B., 1894,) was admitted to the Illinois bar, June 15, 1894. She was born in Chicago; graduated from the West Division High School with honor at the age of sixteen; when nineteen she began teaching in the Chicago public schools, and continued teaching until the year 1892, when she consulted Myra Bradwell, who took a great interest in her welfare, and under her advice commenced the study of law and entered the law school in the class with which she graduated. For sketch of Miss Bartelme see 26 CHICAGO LEGAL NEWS, p. 337. Miss Bartelme's thesis upon graduation was upon "Spendthrift Trusts" which was published in 26 CHICAGO LEGAL NEWS, p. 335.

The *American Law Register and Review* of Philadelphia, offered a prize of $75 to the students of all law schools in the United States, graduated in June, 1894; for the best annotation of a case decided that year. Many contended for the prize, which was awarded Miss Bartelme on her annotation of Synge v.

Synge, 1 Q. B. 466 (1894), in an article on "Contracts to Make Wills." CHICAGO LEGAL NEWS, Vol. 27, p. 70.

(Continued from page 344.)

Miss Bartelme was appointed to the responsible position of public guardian of Cook county by Governor Tanner in

MARY M. BARTELME.

1897, which office she now holds, and has not only shown great ability in disposing of the legal questions connected with that office, but a warm heart and untiring efforts in personally looking after the welfare of the children committed to her official care. Miss Bartelme has been a member of the Illinois State Bar Association since 1896.

She has been professor of medical jurisprudence in the Woman's Medical School of the Northwestern University for several years.

45.—EMMA S. CORRINGTON.

Emma S. Corrington was admitted to the Illinois bar June 15, 1894.

46.—MISS LOISE FOSKETTE.

Miss Loise Foskette was admitted to the Illinois bar June 15, 1894. Graduated from the Cook County Normal school in 1886, and taught school for seven years. Miss Foskette attended the public schools as a teacher in the daytime for two years, and the evening classes of the Law College; learned the legal lessons assigned her by the professor and not only maintained her standing in the

LOISE FOSKETTE.

class, but graduated eleven ahead of the required number. Such continued application and perseverance undermined her health. For sketch see 26 CHICAGO LEGAL NEWS, p. 352.

(Continued on page 344.)

WOMEN LAWYERS OF ILLINOIS.

By James B. Bradwell.

(Continued from page 341.)

Miss Foskette opened an office in the Ashland Block and practiced law for nearly three years with success, but was taken ill with consumption and went South, hoping to regain her health, but died there, lamented by a host of friends, March 6, 1897. For an account of her life, see 29 CHICAGO LEGAL NEWS, p. 243.

47.—MISS FLORENCE E. JAQUES.

Miss Florence E. Jaques, of Ottawa, was admitted to the Illinois bar October 22, 1894, on certificate from the Appellate Court of the Second District, having passed the examination before that court in May, 1894. Florence is a sister of Jeannette, who was admitted on the same day. See 27 CHICAGO LEGAL NEWS. p. 93.

48.—MISS JEANNETTE A. JAQUES.

Miss Jeannette A. Jaques, of Ottawa, was admitted to the Illinois bar October 22, 1894, on certificate from the Appellate Court of the Second District, having passed the examination before that court in May, 1894. See 27 CHICAGO LEGAL NEWS, p. 93.

49.—ARISTA B. WILLIAMS.

Arista B. Williams was admitted to the Illinois bar October 24, 1894. See 27 CHICAGO LEGAL NEWS, p. 93.

50.—MRS. MABELLE THATCHER LITTLE.

Mrs. Mabelle Thatcher Little (Northwestern University, A. B., LL.B., 1895,) was admitted to the Illinois bar January 11, 1895. See 27 CHICAGO LEGAL NEWS, p. 361.

51.—MRS. FLORENCE E. EMBREY.

Mrs. Florence E. Embrey (Kent College of Law, LL.B., 1895,) was admitted to the Illinois bar June 6, 1895.

Mrs. Embrey and her husband were classmates in the law college.

Mrs. Embrey devoted several years in Chicago to the practice of patent law. See 27 CHICAGO LEGAL NEWS, p. 344.

52.—NORA PALMER.

Nora Palmer (Kent College of Law, LL.B., 1895,) was admitted to the Illinois bar June 6 of that year. See 27 CHICAGO LEGAL NEWS, p. 344.

53.—MRS. FLORENCE KELLEY.

Mrs. Florence Kelley (Cornell University, A. B., 1882, Northwestern University, LL. B., 1895,) was admitted to the Illinois bar June 12, 1895. See 27 CHICAGO LEGAL NEWS, p. 361.

Mrs. Kelley has been a resident of Hull House for many years and has been actively engaged in sociological work. She has made many investigations in Illinois for Carroll Wright of the National Labor Bureau and Henry D. Lloyd. She was appointed factory inspector by Gov. Altgeld and performed the duties of this position with great ability. She is a clear, convincing speaker, and has done signal service in the crusade against sweat shops. She is at present secretary of the National Consumers League with headquarters in New York City.

54.—MISS MARY EVA MILLER.

Miss Mary Eva Miller (Chicago College of Law, LL.B., 1895,) was born in Michigan; graduated from the Marshall High School, and the Ypsilanti State Normal School; taught in the High School of Portland, Michigan, the year following her graduation from the Normal school; came to Chicago in 1889, pursuing a course of stenography and typewriting. She entered a commercial house as stenographer; after a little more than a year she entered the office of Charles H. Aldrich, ex-Solicitor General

of the United States, and from that time until July, 1895, was employed in law offices, her duties ranging from stenog-

MARY EVA MILLER.

rapher pure and simple, to general office manager. In the fall of 1893 she entered the Chicago College of Law, graduating therefrom with honor in May, 1895, and was admitted to the Illinois bar June 12, 1895. Since her admission Miss Miller has devoted herself to both civil and criminal practice.

Miss Miller was secretary of the Alumni Association of the Chicago College of Law.

55.—MISS MARGARET TAYLOR SHUTT.

Miss Margaret Taylor Shutt was admitted to the Illinois bar November 21, 1895.

56.—MISS NELLIE B. KESSLER.

Miss Nellie B. Kessler was admitted to the Illinois bar January 16, 1896.

57.—MRS. HELEN H. TUNNICLIFFE CATTERAL.

Miss Helen H. Tunnicliffe, now Mrs. Catteral (Vassar, A. B. '89), was examined before the Appellate Court in Chicago, in March, 1896, passed a creditable examination, and was admitted to the Illinois bar March 28, 1896.

Mrs. Catteral is a talented woman. She pursued a post graduate course in political economy at the University of Chicago, and in 1893-95 had the honor of holding a fellowship in political economy in that university. She is a daughter of Ex-Judge Tunnicliffe. See 28 CHICAGO LEGAL NEWS, p. 343-344.

58.—MISS MILDRED ELWELL TREMAINE.

Miss Mildred Elwell Tremaine was born in Chicago; spent some time in Oberlin College, is a young woman of culture, graduated from the Chicago College of Law in 1896 and was admitted to the Illinois bar June 10, 1896. Her pur-

MILDRED ELWELL TREMAINE.

pose in studying law was "to grow" as she said, and better to fit herself for any line of work she might thereafter adopt. See 28 CHICAGO LEGAL NEWS, p. 339.

59.—MISS NELLIE CARLIN.

Miss Nellie Carlin graduated from the Chicago College of Law in 1896 and was admitted to the Illinois bar June 10 of that year.

Miss Carlin was educated in the public schools of this city; took a course of instruction in the Chicago Athenæum Business College of stenography and book-keeping. She held a position as stenographer and book-keeper in one office for five years, and for some time held a position in the law office of C. S. Darrow of this city. Miss Carlin is an independent, original thinker, and is not afraid to express her views upon any

NELLIE CARLIN.

subject. For sketch of Miss Carlin see 28 CHICAGO LEGAL NEWS, p. 339.

Miss Carlin is an expert in the preparation of lawyers' briefs, and is at home in the trial of a suit. In January of this year she formed a law partnership with Miss Cora B. Hirtzel. See 32 CHICAGO LEGAL NEWS, p. 183.

60.—MISS JESSIE L. DAVIS.

Miss Jessie L. Davis (Kent College of

JESSIE L. DAVIS.

Law, LL.B., 1896,) was born on a farm near Stirling, Ill.; finished the course of the Stirling High School and a course at a business college; taught school for two years and then entered Kent College of Law and was admitted to the Illinois bar June 10, 1896. See 28 CHICAGO LEGAL NEWS, p. 331.

61.—MISS GENEVIEVE MELODY.

Miss Genevieve Melody was born and educated in Chicago; after graduating from Northwestern University she took a post graduate course in Lake Forest

University; taught mathematics and literature in the Hyde Park High School; graduated from the Kent College of Law in June, 1896, and was admitted

GENEVIEVE MELODY.

to the Illinois bar June 10, 1896. See 28 CHICAGO LEGAL NEWS, p. 332.

62.—MISS EVA MAY REYNOLDS.

Miss Eva May Reynolds (Chicago College of Law, LL.B., 1896,) was a skilled stenographer for several years before her admission to the bar. She is intellectually able, and a persistent student; she graduated from the law college, third in the class of 128 members, and received honorary mention. This speaks well for the ability of women to compete with men in the study of the law. She

EVA MAY REYNOLDS.

was admitted to the Illinois bar June 10, 1896. See 28 CHICAGO LEGAL NEWS, p. 339.

Miss Reynolds has been for some time in the office of the legal author, James D. Andrews.

63.—MISS GRACE REED.

Miss Grace Reed (Chicago University,

GRACE REED.

A. B., Kent College of Law, LL.B., 1896,) is a Chicago girl and the product of the Chicago public schools. After her college course at the University of Chicago, she prepared herself specially for scientific work at Harvard annex; taught school a number of years in the Chicago public schools; was principal of the Calumet avenue Grammar School when she was admitted to the bar. June 10, 1896. See 28 CHICAGO LEGAL NEWS, p. 330.

64.—J. PYLE BOWEN.

J. Pyle Bowen (Kent College of Law, LL.B., 1896,) was admitted to the Illi-

J. PYLE BOWEN.

nois bar June 10, 1896. See 28 CHICAGO LEGAL NEWS, p. 332.

65.—MRS. ANNA M. MULLIN.

Mrs. Anna M. Mullin, of Chicago, (Chicago College of Law, LL.B., 1896,) was admitted to the Illinois bar June 10, 1896. She studied law, not with a view of practicing at the bar, but to educate herself generally. She believed that a knowledge of the principles and rules of law was essential to a broad understanding of business relations.

Mrs. Mullin, at the time of her admission and for several years previous, conducted a large commission business on the West Side. She taught in the Chicago schools several years and is a fine Latin scholar as well as a thorough student of English literature. In fact, this quiet, unassuming woman is a living refutation of the old fallacy that a woman loses her womanliness by entering man's sphere (so called), and proves conclusively in her life that experience and responsibility

ANNA M. MULLIN.

enrich all, and that the more one has in himself or herself, the more he or she can give the world. See 28 CHICAGO LEGAL NEWS, p. 339.

66.—MRS. LILLIE C. SPINK.

Mrs. Lillie C. Spink was the only woman examined in the class of 1895 before the Appellate Court. She was admitted to the Illinois bar June 16, 1896, and is now practicing law with her husband under the firm name of Spink & Spink, with offices at 59 Clark St., Chicago.

67.—EMMA SMITH.

Emma Smith was one year in the Chicago College of Law, took the examination before the Appellate Court, and was admitted to the Illinois bar November 6, 1896.

68.—EDITH MAY CORK.

Edith May Cork was admitted to the Illinois bar May 7, 1897. See 29 CHICAGO LEGAL NEWS, contents page, following page 312.

69.—MISS VIRGINIA DIXON.

Miss Virginia Dixon (Kent College of Law, LL.B., 1897,) was admitted to the Illinois bar June 5, 1897. She is a daughter of a Methodist minister. Miss Dixon stood very near the head in examination marks in her law class and was a popular member. See 29 CHICAGO LEGAL NEWS, p. 333.

70.—VICTORIA A. DESALLIOUD.

Victoria A. Desallioud graduated from the Chicago College of Law in 1897 and was admitted to the Illinois bar June 16, 1897. See 29 CHICAGO LEGAL NEWS, p. 340.

Miss Desallioud has a fine mind, is a studious, careful worker, and since her graduation has been engaged with the

VICTORIA A. DESALLIOUD.

well-known law firm of Shope, Mathis & Barrett. The senior member of the firm is S. P. Shope, ex-judge of the Supreme Court of this State; the junior member is Elmer E. Barrett, secretary of the law college from which she graduated, and for whom she has acted as private secretary and assistant for some time.

Miss Desallioud is especially to be commended because of the neat and methodical manner in which she prepares her papers and transacts business.

71.—MRS. ALICE ST. CLAIR LENAGHAN SHOREMAN.

Mrs. Alice St. Clair Lenaghan Shoreman, of Chicago, graduated from the Chicago College of Law in 1897 and was admitted to the Illinois bar June 16, 1897. See 29 CHICAGO LEGAL NEWS, p. 340.

Immediately after her graduation she became a member of the law firm of Ellis, Ellis & Lenaghen.

Mrs. Alice St. Clair Lenaghen Shoreman was in the office of Hugh A. White, a prominent lawyer of this city, for many years prior to his death, and after his death took charge of his estate and acted as business manager for Mrs. White, who at her death left Mrs. Shoreman $50,000 in her will.

72.—MISS ELIZABETH L. KENNEY.

Miss Elizabeth L. Kenney (Northwestern University, LL.B., 1897,) was ad-

ELIZABETH L. KENNEY.

mitted to the Illinois bar June 16, 1897. See 29 CHICAGO LEGAL NEWS, p. 356.

73.—MAE ISABELLE REED.

Mae Isabelle Reed was admitted to the Illinois bar November 4, 1897.

74.—CARRIE LIBBIE RAPP.

Carrie Libbie Rapp was admitted to the Illinois bar November 4, 1897.

75.—EMMA BLOOD.

Emma Blood was admitted to the Illinois bar November 4, 1897. See 30 CHICAGO LEGAL NEWS, p. 5.

76.—HELEN M. KEARNS.

Helen M. Kearns passed a successful examination before the Appellate Court at Mt. Vernon, Illinois, August 28, 1897. See 30 CHICAGO LEGAL NEWS, p. 5. She was admitted to the Illinois bar November 4, 1897.

77.—MINNIE MAUD HALLAM.

Minnie Maud Hallam was admitted to the Illinois bar February 15, 1898.

78.—MISS MARION E. GARMORY.

Miss Marion E. Garmory, of Rockford, in response to our letter at the time of her admission said among other things: "Out of respect to the founder of your paper, Mrs. Myra Bradwell, who made it possible for me to obtain admission to the bar of this State, I gladly comply with your request. My life has been uneventful; I was born in Rochelle, Illinois, July 7, 1872, and graduated from the High School at that place in 1889. Nearly six years ago I became connected with the law office of R. K.

MARION E. GARMORY.

Welsh as stenographer, and all the success I have had in my life I owe to one thing—environment. I studied systematically for three years and in a desultory manner for some time previous to that, not from any belief or hope that I would ever obtain fame or fortune as a lawyer, but as a means of education and advancement in my work, and because of the enjoyment and satisfaction I derived from it." Miss Garmory was admitted to the Illinois bar April 20, 1898. For letter, see 30 CHICAGO LEGAL NEWS, p. 238.

79.—MISS ISABELL A. HELMICH.

Miss Isabell A. Helmich graduated from the Chicago College of Law in the class of 1898 and was admitted to the Illinois bar October 15, 1898. See 30 CHICAGO LEGAL NEWS, p. 339.

Miss Helmich is the present secretary of the society of women lawyers known as the Chicago Lawyers' League.

80.—MRS. ANTOINETTE L. FUNK.

Mrs. Antoinette L. Funk, of Bloomington, passed an excellent examination and stood high in the class before the State Board of Law Examiners at Springfield in October, 1898, was admitted to the Illinois bar October 15 of the same year, and is now practicing her profession. See 31 CHICAGO LEGAL NEWS, contents page, following p. 66.

81.—MINNIE ROSS POWERS.

Minnie Ross Powers was admitted to the Illinois bar in February, 1899.

82.—MISS ESTELLE V. PEASE.

Miss Estelle V. Pease, of Chicago, (Chicago College of Law, LL.B., 1899,) was

ESTELLE V. PEASE.

admitted to the Illinois bar October 14, 1899.

At the commencement exercises of the law college in 1898, Miss Pease delivered an address upon "Equity," which will be found in 30 CHICAGO LEGAL NEWS, p. 339.

Miss Pease is now engaged abstracting chancery records with the Chicago Title and Trust Company.

83.—MARIE RAWSON.

Marie Rawson, of Princeton, Illinois, (Northwestern University, LL.B., 1899,) was admitted to the Illinois bar October 14, 1899. See 32 CHICAGO LEGAL NEWS, p. 72.

84.—MARGARET C. WICH.

Margaret C. Wich, of Irving, attended the Chaddock College Law School three years; also read law under the tuition of Charles A. James from June 14, 1898, to August 31, 1899, and after passing a successful examination before the State Board of Law Examiners was admitted to the Illinois bar October 14, 1899. See 32 CHICAGO LEGAL NEWS, p. 72.

85.—JANE C. TRULL.

Jane C. Trull, of Chicago, (Chicago College of Law, LL.B., 1899,) passed a successful examination before the State advertise brands of flour, corsets, soap or, mayhap, cheap cigars. Departed statesmen and philanthropists may or may not have any effective means of defense against this form of outrage, but surely the private woman—and, of course, the private man—still in the flesh and capable of suffering from "guying," should have some legal means of preventing the appropriation of their features for such ignoble uses against their will, in order that thereby some enterprising tradesman may swell his profits by enlarging the sales of his articles.

THE LEGAL PROFESSION FOR WOMEN.

BY CATHARINE WAUGH MCCULLOCH, OF THE CHICAGO BAR.

[From the Woman's Journal, of Boston.]

A recent decision of the Supreme Court of Tennessee, excluding women from the practice of law in that State, has called forth severe criticisms from the leading journals of the country. The ground of exclusion was that lawyers were officers of the court: that women were not allowed by the law of that State to hold any office, and therefore could not be lawyers. Miss Marion Griffin is the woman whose application has just been refused.

The State of Maryland is agitated by the same question. Miss Etta H. Maddox has lately been graduated from the Baltimore Law School, and now discovers that only those are admitted to the bar who, in the language of the State, are "male citizens."

These States are still in the midst of their medieval history in holding that women are ineligible for these places of honorable employment. It is true that there have been many ancient and renowned examples of similar sex injustice but most of them were in the dark ages, before the twentieth century had opportunity to illuminate the path of justice.

Friends of women's equality had hoped that women lawyers had reached the end

CATHARINE WAUGH MCCULLOCH,
Of the Chicago Bar.

of their struggles, and that they might be allowed to succeed or fail according to their ability and not their sex.

IN FORMER AGES.

While in a majority of instances in the past, women have not been allowed to act as attorneys, it is interesting to notice that in spite of objections, codes, and decrees in various countries, women have occasionally become skilled in legal science, and some of them have finally received judicial approval for their entrance into the profession.

Jewish teachers did not advise teaching law to women, yet some Jewish women named in sacred and profane history attained renown for their legal ability. Among them were Deborah, the judge; Beruria, in the time of Hadrian; Mijiram Shapirim, in the twelfth century; Sara Coppia Sullam, Bella Falk Cohen, and Mirjam Lovia, in the seventeenth century.

Grecian women were, as a rule, kept in ignorance of legal matters, yet Aspasia pleaded causes before the Athenians.

Roman women were generally kept in legal inferiority, but they were occasionally admitted to the judicial inclosures as representatives of others. The names of Amesia, Sentia and Hortensia are preserved as among those who thus appeared in the Roman forum. But, alas for the rights of women, there appeared at last one Afrania or Cafrania, known also as Calpurnia, who was so bold and loquacious that the scandalized judges thereupon forbade her and all other women to speak before them. She died in the time of Cæsar, far enough in the past to be forgotten, but her reputation lived after her, and she was specified in Roman law as the cause of the exclusion of all women from arguing in court. The code of Justinian continued this prohibition because "a woman, like a slave, can not take part in the administration of justice."

Still women could study law, and they did. The renowned University of Bologna in Italy in the time of its greatest prosperity, when the number of its pupils reached 10,000, was so liberal as to even employ women lecturers in law. One of these, Novella, who lectured in the fourteenth century, was said to have been so beautiful that she was obliged to deliver her lectures from behind a curtain, in order that the attention of the students might not be distracted. In the eighteenth century there were two other women lecturers who won renown. Shakespeare's Portia might well have been one of these attractive lecturers, for from time of the thirteenth century Padua, the university from which she was said to have come, was renowned for its law classes.

A MODERN INSTANCE.

Within the last few years Lydia Poet, who received the highest law degree conferred by the Turin University, began practicing law in Italy just as though she had never heard of Calpurnia. But, alas! others had, and decrees of court were issued in 1883 and 1884 forbidding women to practice as advocates and referring them for reasons to the old Roman law. So the evil done by loquacious Calpurnia lived after her.

Under the feudal law women were allowed to be attorneys and judges, with certain restrictions if they were married.

In Germany, Austria, Hungary and Scotland, though there were no specific prohibitions upon women being attorneys, yet the law schools being closed to them virtually debarred them from the profession.

Among the ancient Celts the Druidess as well as the Druid had the right of sitting as judge of murder.

Cæsar tells us that the women of ancient Britain had power in court and council and that no distinction of sex was made in places of command or government. Women sat in the ancient Witenagemot for the framing of laws. Woman landowners held courts of their own in the times of Edward I., Henry I. and even down to the seventeenth century. In the reign of Henry VII. the Countess of Richmond was made justice of the peace.

CUSTOMS OF TO-DAY.

The English common law did not forbid women acting as attorneys. Modern

WOMEN LAWYERS OF CHICAGO.

There is yet a question in the minds of some as to whether the law is a proper or useful field for women. This question was mooted at the last annual meeting of the American Bar Association held at Denver. The following fine tribute was paid to the women lawyers of Chicago, by James DeWitt Andrews. The conservative tone of the remarks adds to their weight.

While it is quite plain that this distinguished jurist regards the home as the highest and best field for women, yet if inclination or business policy leads her to choose employment, the legal field is fitted for her, and she is in no way disqualified from distinguished service in that field. The women lawyers of Chicago have honored the profession and the profession has honored them. Mr. Andrews had the honor of representing in the American Bar Association a city that has more women lawyers than any other city in the world. No man in a single address, can do justice to the merits of the able lawyers found among the more than one hundred women lawyers of Illinois.

We take the following from page 474 of the report of the American Bar Association:

"James D. Andrews, of Illinois:

I thought while Dr. Rogers was speaking that I would take the opportunity, not of debating any question which he has raised, but of giving to you the result of my own observations, because, after all, that is about all that we can now do in this matter. The question of their admission is a foreclosed one. We glean what we can from observation and facts. As a resident of Chicago, I have had an opportunity to observe the practice of law by women as well perhaps as any one this side of New York at least. Now the name of the honored woman who was first mentioned, Mrs. Myra Bradwell, who made the fight for admission, does not afford the opportunity of knowing precisely what a woman in active practice might do, but I think my brethren from Chicago will agree with me that Mrs. Bradwell has done as much to elevate the standard of the law in Illinois as any man. And I think her business career coupled with her domestic career is one of the finest illustrations of the fact that a woman may engage very actively and successfully in business, and that business connected with the law, and lose nothing of the tenderness of women or nothing of the respect and admiration of her husband, because there never was a sweeter couple than Mr. and Mrs. Bradwell.

Mrs. McCullough, I think, must be taken as an illustration that a woman may practice law side by side with her husband and yet never lose anything of dignity or purity or of the respect of those who are acquainted with her, or the admiration and affection of her husband. Mrs. McCullough I knew before she was admitted to the bar. During her study I knew her, and since her marriage; and I have taken especial pains to observe and reflect upon the career of that noble woman. She has been a successful practitioner, and yet, as I consider that she is the mother of a family, and that the duties of her employment were interrupted by the higher duties of motherhood, I believe that if I were to choose her career, with the knowledge of what I have known, I should have preferred that when she became the wife of Mr. McCullough she had ceased to practice law.

Take Mrs. Ahrens, a dignified woman, who has received the respect of the bench and bar.

Miss Cora B. Hirtsel has occupied the office of assistant corporation counsel and has performed all of the duties with ability—signal ability.

Of course, the principle has long since been exploded that, so far as mental ability is concerned, women are not the equals of men.

I became much more closely acquainted with a Miss Reynolds and several others that I could name. Out of all of them that I have known in Chicago, I think there is but one against whom even a breath of scandal was ever raised, and I do not believe there was any foundation even for that.

So my observation and contact with a number of women assure me that our profession is one which may justly and properly be opened to them. And, in fact, I am happy to state the other side of the proposition, that we may congratulate ourselves, so far as my observation goes, upon the fact that the respect and forbearance and the assistance of the lawyers has been a subject of self-congratulation to the women, and we may congratulate ourselves, I think, that the bar has always treated women lawyers with the greatest respect."

THE WOMEN LAWYERS AND THE CHICAGO BAR ASSOCIATION PRIMARY.

The resolution of the Chicago Bar Association provided that the primary for the selection of candidates for judges should be open to the members of the Cook County Bar. This of course included the women lawyers of this county and they were not slow to exercise this right of voting.

Miss Ellen G. Roberts, a prominent member of the Chicago Bar, was much interested in the primary, and wrote to a number of the women lawyers calling their attention to the fact that they had the right to vote. Miss Roberts received from Miss Florence King, a patent lawyer of this city, the following:

CHICAGO, April 22, 1902.

Miss Ellen G. Roberts, 81 Clark St., City:

DEAR MADAM: Yours of the 19th inst. duly received. My ballot received from the Bar Association has already been sent in. It had not occurred to me that any woman receiving one of these ballots would fail to send it in. I know, as you say, too many women are indifferent in these matters, but surely a woman lawyer ought not to be. I am sure no opportunity to vote ever passes me unexercised. This taxation without representation business is one upon which I always get in my word when it is possible. I am a taxpayer, and the idea of paying out money every year without a word to say regarding its expenditure is, in my mind, worthy of a good deal of consideration. No women are in a better position to keep the ball rolling than the women lawyers are, and I feel that they should never be placed in a position where it might be said they ever neglected the privilege. At least I do not propose to.

Very truly yours,
FLORENCE KING.

Mrs. Catharine Waugh McCulloch, a lawyer since 1886, wrote:

April 28, 1902.

Miss Ellen Gertrude Roberts, 145 La Salle St., Chicago, Ill.

DEAR MADAM: I was pleased to see by your letter of April 19 that you were awakening the women lawyers to their duty. I voted as soon as the ballots reached me and presented the matter to others. I hope many women voted.

Yours truly,
CATHARINE WAUGH MCCULLOCH.

The following are the names of some of the women lawyers who voted at the bar primary:

Ellen G. Roberts.	M. Isabelle Reid.
J. Clara Breese.	Miss Grace Reed.
Mary M. Bartelme.	Catharine Waugh McCulloch.
Marion H. Drake.	Jane C. Trull.
Cora B. Hirtzel.	Mary E. Miller.
Bessie Bradwell Helmer.	Charlotte C. Holt.
Antoinette L. Funk.	Miss Florence King.
Mrs. M. E. Squire (nee J. Pyle Bowen).	Miss Nellie Carlin.

Never in the history of the world did so many women lawyers vote at a bar primary, as voted at the bar primary last week in the city of Chicago.

"The jury of the future—One that might temper justice with mercy."—Life Publishing, 1902.

"Studies in Expressions—When women are jurors."—Collier's Weekly, 1908. (Both courtesy Judge Ronald Olson, Circuit Court of Cook County, IL)

The Evanston Daily News, June 16, 1913

Illinois Suffrage Struggle Succeeds After 58 Years

Mrs. Catharine Waugh McCulloch Tells of Success After Years of Failure.

FAIRNESS TO PREVAIL

They Will Study Important Questions and Decide Them According to Their Own Viewpoint.

By Catharine Waugh McCulloch.
The awful thirty years' war in Germany for religious liberty was a brief affair compared to the fifty-eight years of peaceful warfare in Illinois for woman's political liberty. In 1855, in Earlville, was organized the first suffrage association here of which we have any record.

the Mississippi to grant woman suffrage in a presidential election. Women immediately ran for office. The campaign which attracted the greatest attention was that of Marion Drake, suffragist and attorney. She ran for alderman against Bathouse John Coughlin. Although she lost, 95,000 women did come out to vote.

In June 16, 1913 the *Evanston Daily News* headlined: "Suffrage demonstration was greatest in Evanston's History", saying "thousands gathered in Fountain Square Saturday night to take part in Jubilee...Mrs. McCulloch's wit and clever comment on words of speakers kept the great crowd happy". The citizens turned out en masse to pay tribute to the victorious suffrage leaders and rejoice with them over their great victory of last week. The street was packed with thousands of men, women and children anxious to get a close glimpse of Mrs. McCulloch and other leaders.

In 1914, the Women's Bar Association of Illinois (WBAI) was organized by nine women lawyers practicing in Chicago.

The early WBAI, like many other women's organizations at that time, worked for a passage of the U.S. constitutional amendment granting women the right to vote. In the years which followed, WBAI would mirror the progress of women lawyers throughout the state. Its activities were divided between the burning contemporary social and political issues and the practical need to help its members gain employment.

WBAI's original charter was applied for by Alice C. Edgerton, Martha Elvert, Mary M. Epperson, Elizabeth L. Hoffman (Buchhalter), Eunice D. Martin, Ella Zoelzer, Mae L. Minock, Nettie Rothblum and Charlotte D. White, and the charter was issued June 23, 1914, Nettie Rothblum being the first president. Its purpose was "to promolgate, promote, advance and protect the interests of women lawyers in the state of Illinois..."

The plans for the organization were formulated at a meeting of the charter members in Lincoln Park. In the early days of the Association, its most active work was in connection with an auxiliary organization known as the Public Defenders League for Girls.

WBAI member, Alice McClanahan, admitted to Illinois practice in 1915, recalled in her book, *Her Father's Partner*, the public's negative attitude toward woman lawyers. Her father, by making it clear to clients she would be handling their cases as well as he, risked losing many clients, but he believed in women's suffrage and the equal ability of women.

WBAI's second president (1915-16) was Miss Nellie Carlin. She wrote, in 1934, "The women lawyers of to-day who share prestige of their brothers in civic and political affairs should not forget the early struggles - the antagonisms and ridicule heaped upon those who declared for equal suffrage...foremost in this struggle was Myra Bradwell, wife of the editor of the *Legal News*, who made a valiant fight for the right of women to practice law. Then came Catharine Waugh McCulloch and others, making their fight for equal suffrage. Great credit is due her and Grace Wilbur Trout for their untiring fight in this cause. Without the granting of this amendment to our Constitution, all progress for women in civic and political life would not now be enjoyed..."

(Editor's Note: When the Nineteenth Amendment finally was passed, Illinois became the first state to ratify it, on June 10, 1919.)

"Of course the pioneer women lawyers had to overcome the prejudice of the Bench and Bar, and were often termed with an indulgent though cynical smile: "The lady lawyers." The great objection was that women should take up a criminal practice, and when a lawyer named Kate Kane undertook to practice criminal law and was forced to use the same tactics and language as her brother practitioners, their sense of propriety was shocked and a great cry was raised that this was what should be expected by a woman's participation in the sacred practice of the Law. The usual salutations many years ago when a woman graduate announced that she intended to practice law was: "Oh, you are going to be a lawyer like Kate Kane."

"All honor to Kate Kane, whom I did not know; but this much I do know, that she was one of the pioneer lawyers who brooked insult and ridicule from the unthinking crowd and who made possible, today, the presence of the woman lawyer on our Circuit, Municipal and Appellate Benches of the United States...

"Now that Equal Suffrage is an assured fact with no danger of the repeal of this amendment to our Constitution, there is great opportunity for the woman lawyer. She can make her influence felt for much good in a worthy cause or causes. There is still great need for the protection of women and children in our Courts...

"From this nucleus of nine women the organization has now grown to a membership of well over two hundred women lawyers. Not many records are now available as to the earlier activities of the Association, as those women, little realizing the proportions to which their little organization would grow, were more interested in results accomplished than in leaving a history of their deeds". (WBAI 20th Anniversary Journal and Directory).

The Journal and Directory then highlighted WBAI's history to that date, noting: (in part)

"Following Miss Carlin's term as President, Mrs. Catharine Waugh McCulloch took over the destinies of the organization and served as its President for four successive, and we might add, successful, years....

"Mrs. McCulloch was most gracious during her terms of office in throwing her home open for annual picnics and outings, which occasions are treasured in the memories of all those attending."

(Editor's Note: In 1917 Mrs. McCulloch was appointed Master in Chancery of the Superior Court where she served until 1925.)

The scarcity of women on the bench was blamed on the fact that women, not having the vote, were unable to garner political support. As the suffrage movement gained momentum, the view that women should be considered for Judgeships gained popularity among women and women's organizations, and led to an increasing number of women on the bench, though mostly in divorce and children's courts.

In 1917, Ada Cartwright was appointed assistant Attorney General of Illinois and reappointed in 1925.

In 1919, Matilda Fenberg became the first woman to attend Yale Law School. She graduated in 1922 and became a well known attorney in Chicago.

"Succeeding Mrs. McCulloch's regime, Esther Dunshee (Mrs. Bower) became President for the year 1920-1921. It was during this year, chiefly through the efforts of Miss Dunshee and Mrs. McCulloch, that a bill was for the first time introduced in the Illinois Legislature providing for service on juries by women."

(Editor's Note: By the end of 1921, 20 state legislatures had granted women that right; Illinois was not among them.)

"The annual banquet that year was a singular success, there being over 250 persons in attendance." (Editors note: This is the first mention of WBAI's annual banquet, commenced in 1914. In 1932 it was changed to a dinner dance. In the 1940's it became a Party for Judges, including dinner. In 1975 it became the annual Judicial Reception as it continues to this day).

"The President of the Association for the year 1921-22 was Charlotte D. White, one of the Founder members of the Association. The annual banquet, the eighth, was held on the same date as the first banquet given by the Association - Washington's Birthday. This banquet was tendered to the Judges of the United States Circuit Court of Appeals...many outstanding lawyers and Judges also attending. The principal speaker was Mabel Walker Willebrandt, who was then Assistant Attorney General of the United States in charge of Prohibition enforcement. The Judges of the Circuit Court of Appeals made brief remarks, as well as the Presidents of the Illinois State and Chicago Bar Associations. The Chicago Bar Association Chorus furnished its usual fund of comic melodies, and Miss Geraldine Vance, harpist, rendered several selections.

Alice Greenacre, noteworthy civil practitioner, served as President for the year 1922-1923.

(Editor's Note: The Nineteenth Amendment had not eliminated the sexual division of labor. Even aspiring career women were limited to positions traditionally set aside for females. Law schools placed strict quotas on the number of female students they would admit, and some refused to admit them. Law firms frequently denied women the opportu-

CERTIFICATE FOR CORPORATION NOT FOR PECUNIARY PROFIT.   Form No. 688.   Printed by the Chicago Legal News Co.

State of Illinois,
COOK COUNTY.

PAID JUN 23 1914 $10

To James A. Rose, Secretary of State:

We the Undersigned, ALICE C. EDGERTON, MARTHA ELVERT, MARY M. EPPERSON, ELIZABETH L. HOFFMAN, EUNICE D. MARTIN, MAE L. MINOCK NETTIE ROTHBLUM, CHARLOTTE D. WHITE, ELLA ZOELZER

Citizens of the United States, propose to form a Corporation under an act of the General Assembly of the State of Illinois, entitled, "An Act concerning Corporations," approved April 18th 1872, and all acts amendatory thereof, and that for the purpose of such organization we hereby state as follows, to-wit:

1. The name of such Corporation is "WOMEN'S BAR ASSOCIATION OF ILLINOIS"

2. The object for which it is formed is to promulgate, promote, advance and protect the interests of the women lawyers in the State of Illinois, and to do all other and necessary things in connection therewith, including the publishing, printing, or circulating pamphlets or journals in relation thereto;

3. The management of the aforesaid Association shall be vested in a Board of five (5) Directors, who are to be elected annually.

4. The following persons are hereby selected as the Directors to control and manage said Corporation for the first year of its corporate existence, viz:— Charlotte D. White, Alice Edgerton, Mae Minoch, Eunice Martin and Nettie Rothblum.

5. The location is in the city of Chicago in the County of Cook in the State of Illinois, and the postoffice address of its business office is at No. 1709 - 139 No. Clark Street, in the said city of Chicago.

SIGNED:

[signatures: Alice C. Edgerton, Martha Elvert, Mary M. Epperson, Elizabeth L. Hoffman, Eunice D. Martin, Ella Zoelzer, Mae Minock, Nettie Rothblum, Charlotte D. White]

nity to compete for positions held by men. Women regularly received less pay and fewer promotions than men when they did secure a position. The proportion of women lawyers remained almost constant from 1910 to 1930, at less than 3 percent. Women's inequality was embedded deep in the social fabric. Occasionally, an outstanding woman would prove an exception to the general role into which women were thrust. One such woman was Mary Bartleme, a protege of Myra Bradwell. An 1894 Northwestern Law School graduate, she became in 1923 the first Illinois woman attorney elected to a judgeship other than justice of the peace. She presided over the juvenile court for 10 years, attaining world-wide fame. She was noted for her concern with the problems of young women and helped establish three homes for girls.)

"Following Miss Greenacre as President, was one of the most widely known and best beloved of our members, the late lamented Ada M. Cartwright, former Assistant Attorney General of Illinois. It was through her influence and strategy that women lawyers were admitted to membership in the American Bar Association. All these things have long since become accepted facts, but it is well to note in passing that it was this early work in this organization which helped it attain the high position which it now occupies and which we are too prone to take as a matter of course.

"Pearl Hart was the next President, serving in the year 1924-1925. Miss Hart, one of the most outstanding members of the local bar, has long been known for the social aspects of her work.

(Editor's Note: In 1925 Ada H. Kepley died in St. Anthony's Hospital in Illinois, having become a broken woman and impoverished, according to Karen Berger Morello in *The Invisible Bar*.)

(Editor's Note: The travails of women

Chicago Legal News—1918

seeking to become attorneys were documented and published in a 1925 Chicago-Kent Law School article. There, the author noted that even though women had proven their scholarship was as high as that of men, there were still law schools which refused to admit women.)

"In 1925-1926 the Association President was Edna E. Barnett, the membership then having increased to 103 members. Up to that time but three of our members had been lost by death. Since then several have passed away, among them Ada Cartwright. This year marked Miss Cartwright's last real active work in the organization. It was her idea to publish a book of the organization. Her zeal and enthusiasm were irresistible and the book was published. It was hoped to make the book an annual publication and in fact many colleges and universities which received complimentary copies wrote requesting subsequent issues. Meetings were held at the Brevoort Hotel.

"During this year the organization was almost disrupted due to the fact that at the annual picnic held at the Cartwright Farm on the banks of Rock River near Oregon, headed by that capable legal pathfinder, Edna Barnett, several members - who could blaze a trail through the densest of legal entanglements - were, however, unable to find their way back from a hiking party in the woods, but fortunately for themselves and the organization were eventually rescued. Probably that is the first, last and only time the Women's Bar Association was or will be 'lost.'

"In October, 1926, Mary D. Bailey, who for many years was and is still Assistant United States Attorney, took up the duties of President. The principal endeavor for the year was activity to secure passage of a bill providing for women on juries in Illinois, which bill, however, failed of passage." (Note: 1926 Minutes confirm each meeting's concentration on the association's campaign to make women eligible to serve on juries).

"The following year (1927-1928), Honorable Mary Bartelme was President of the Association. (An 1894 graduate of Northwestern University Law School, she was later known as "Suitcase Mary." She insisted young girls leaving detention homes were to be provided with a satchel of clothing to assist them in making a fresh start.)

Alice McClanahan's book recalled 1927. It recounts her experiences, after trying cases to an all-male jury, of lobbying with WBAI for the jury bill. The senators seemed to think women's plea for the right to jury service was nothing more than a demand by a neurotic few who had a yearning for importance. Some explained that men needed to protect "lady folk" from the soiling influence of the law courts.

In 1927 WBAI's 13th annual banquet was held at the Congress Hotel. Speakers included U.S. Senator Charles Deneen, Congresswoman Mary Norton of New Jersey, National Democratic Committee woman Emily N. Blair and Judge Mary Bartelme.

In June, 1928, Rebecca Willner Liss, general civil practitioner, was elected President of the Association. During her regime, active work to procure passage of the jury bill was again resumed." (In 1928 Kathryn Barasa

(Rinella) joined the City Attorney's office in Chicago as a lawyer).

"In January, 1929, Honorable Daniel P. Trude, then Municipal Judge, spoke to the Association advocating that women should serve as Judges, particularly in Morals Court, Boys Court and Domestic Relations Court. Also as a speaker during the year was Honorable Henry Horner (now Governor), at the time Judge of the Probate Court, the largest court of its type in the world, who spoke on the need for housing insane and feeble-minded persons. Following this talk the Association appointed a committee to further the passage of a bill appropriating more funds for housing the insane people of Illinois. A later speaker was Honorable Robert E. Gentzel (now Deceased), Judge of the Superior Court, as to the need for a public defender in Cook County.

"During this year, through the efforts of the Association in conjunction with other organizations, a bill was passed in the Illinois legislature providing jury service for women but with a referendum clause to submit the question to the people in the 1930 general election. Much credit is due to Esther Dunshee (Mrs. Bower) for her tireless work on the jury bill.

"During this year also a placement bureau was organized by the Association to endeavor to further employment of women lawyers and women aspiring to the Bar.

"Irene V. McCormick, long known for her sincere and able work in the Legal Aid Bureau was elected President of the Association in June, 1929-1930. During the year a State-wide campaign was carried on to secure a favorable vote on the Jury Bill Referendum, and in this connection the Association maintained a speakers' bureau from its members to fill requests for speakers on the subject throughout the State." On March 8, 1930, a newspaper report noted, WBAI held its 16th Annual

Helen M. Cirese, 1925, attorney at Oak Park, sought election as justice of the peace. The Herald and Examiner ran a story headlined "Portia's Smile to Test in Vote" which ended with "Her winning smile has proved too captivating to most of Oak Park's male voters to permit them to say 'no.'"

EDNA E. BARNETT
President

Admitted to Illinois Bar, October 8, 1918.

Chicago Kent College of Law, L.L.B.

Practice—General.

Member: Women's Bar Association of Illinois, Chicago Bar Association, Illinois State Bar Association.

MARY D. BAILEY

Admitted to Illinois Bar, October, 1920.

Tutored by Edwin L. Pray.

Practice—General.

Assistant U. S. Attorney, Northern District of Illinois, Eastern Division. (Appointed June, 1921.)

Member: Women's Bar Association of Illinois, Chicago Bar Association, Kane County Bar Association, Illinois State Bar Association.

MARY D. BAILEY
1st Vice President

ELLEN M. YOCKEY

Admitted to Illinois Bar, October 13, 1915.

Tutored by Arthur Yockey.

Practice—General.

Member: Women's Bar Association of Illinois.

ELLEN M. YOCKEY
2nd Vice President

EDITH M. GABEL

Admitted to Illinois Bar in 1917.

John Marshall Law School, L.L.B.

Practice—General. Abstracts.

Member: Women's Bar Association of Illinois, Chicago Bar Association, Illinois State Bar Association.

EDITH M. GABEL
Secretary

IRENE V. McCORMICK

Admitted to Illinois Bar, April 14, 1921.

Chicago-Kent College of Law, L.L.B.

Practice—General.

Member: Women's Bar Association of Illinois.

IRENE V. McCORMICK
Treasurer

Board
of
Directors

ADA M. CARTWRIGHT

ADA M. CARTWRIGHT

Admitted to Illinois Bar, October 13, 1915.
John Marshall Law School.
Tutored by James H. Cartwright.
Assistant Attorney General of Illinois. (Appointed February, 1917; reappointed January, 1925.)
Practice—General.
Member: Women's Bar Association of Illinois, Illinois State Bar Association.

PEARL M. HART

PEARL M. HART

Admitted to Illinois Bar in 1914.
John Marshall Law School, L.L.B.
Practice—General.
Member: Women's Bar Association of Illinois, Chicago Bar Association, Illinois State Bar Association.

CATHARINE WAUGH McCULLOCH

CATHARINE WAUGH McCULLOCH

Admitted to Illinois Bar, November, 1886.
Union College of Law, L.L.B.
Master in Chancery, Superior Court of Cook County 1917 to 1925. (Appointed.)
Practice—General.
Member: Women's Bar Association of Illinois, Chicago Bar Association, Illinois State Bar Association, American Bar Association.

CORA B. GREEN

CORA B. GREEN

Admitted to Illinois Bar, October, 1912.
Chicago - Kent College of Law, L.L.B.
Practice—General.
Member: Women's Bar Association of Illinois.

1925
and
1926

CHARLOTTE M. STEVENS

Admitted to Illinois Bar in October, 1914.
Chicago - Kent College of Law, L.L.B.
Practice—General.
Member: Women's Bar Association of Illinois, Chicago Bar Association.

MARY M. BARTELME
Judge of the Circuit Court of Cook County.

Admitted to Illinois Bar in 1894.

Northwestern University. L.L.B.

Public Guardian of Cook County, 1897-1913. (Appointed.)

Assistant to the Judge of Juvenile Court, 1913-1923. (Appointed.)

Judge Circuit Court of Cook County. Elected November 6, 1923.

Member: Women's Bar Association of Illinois, Chicago Bar Association, Illinois State Bar Association, American Bar Association.

MARIE O. ANDRESEN.
Admitted to Illinois Bar December 14, 1922.

Northwestern University, University of Illinois, L.L.B.

Assistant State's Attorney of Cook County, Illinois. Appointed September 15, 1923.

Engaged in prosecution of criminal cases.

Member: Women's Bar Association of Illinois, Chicago Bar Association, Lawyers' Association of Illinois, Illinois State Bar Association, American Bar Association.

JEANETTE BATES.
Admitted to Illinois Bar in 1908.

University of Chicago; Northwestern University, L.L.B.

Assistant Attorney General of Illinois, January 8, 1917-July 1, 1921. (Appointed.)

Examiner of Titles, Torrens System; Recorder of Deeds. (Appointed 1921.)

Practice—Examiner Real Estate Titles; Statutory Duties.

Member: Women's Bar Association of Illinois, Chicago Bar Association, Illinois State Bar Association, American Bar Association.

JEANETTE BATES

MABEL F. BARCKLEY.
Admitted to Illinois Bar April 2, 1919.

Chicago Kent College of Law, L.L.B.

Practice—Corporation, Real Estate, Blue Sky.

Member: Women's Bar Association of Illinois.

MABEL F. BARCKLEY

ELIZABETH H. BUCHHALTER
Admitted to Illinois Bar April, 1914.

Chicago Kent College of Law, L.L.B.

Webster College of Law.

Practice—General.

Attorney for West Park Board, appointed July, 1924.

Member: Women's Bar Association of Illinois, Illinois State Bar Association.

ELIZABETH H. BUCHHALTER

BERTHA D. BAUR
Admitted to Illinois Bar, June, 1908.

Chicago-Kent College of Law, L.L.B.

Practice—General.

Member: Women's Bar Association of Illinois.

BERTHA D. BAUR

FANNIE ADELE BIVANS
Admitted to Illinois Bar, October, 1912.

University of Chicago, L.L.B.

Practice—General.

Member: Women's Bar Association of Illinois, Decatur Bar Association, Illinois State Bar Association, American Bar Association.

FANNIE ADELE BIVANS

OLIVE NEVILLE BARTON
Admitted to Illinois Bar, April 13, 1922; to Iowa Bar, June, 1924.

University of Michigan, J.D.

Practice—General.

Member: Women's Bar Association of Illinois.

OLIVE NEVILLE BARTON

INA M. R. CAMPBELL.
Admitted to Illinois Bar in 1918.

Chicago-Kent College of Law, L.L.B.

Practice—General.

Member: Women's Bar Association of Illinois, Lawyers' Association of Illinois.

INA M. R. CAMPBELL

MARTHA L. CONNOLE
Admitted to Illinois Bar, October 9, 1917.

St. Louis University, St. Louis, Mo., L.L.B.

Practice—General.

Public Administrator of St. Clair County, Illinois.

Member: Women's Bar Association of Illinois, East St. Louis Bar Association, Illinois State Bar Association.

MARTHA L. CONNOLE

MARY SELLERS CONNERY
Admitted to Illinois Bar, October 18, 1909.

Chicago Kent College of Law, L.L.B.

Practice—Common Carriers and Interstate Commerce.

Member: Women's Bar Association of Illinois, Chicago Bar Association.

MARY SELLERS CONNERY

HAZEL BLACK CHERNEY
Admitted to Illinois Bar, October, 1911.

Illinois College of Law, L.L.B.

Practice—General.

Member: Women's Bar Association of Illinois.

HAZEL BLACK CHERNEY

AGNES B. CLOHESY
Admitted to Illinois Bar in 1922.

Chicago-Kent College of Law, L.L.B.

Practice—General.

Member: Women's Bar Association of Illinois.

AGNES B. CLOHESY

NELLIE CARLIN

Admitted to Illinois Bar in 1896.
Chicago College of Law. LL.B.
Practice—Probate and Chancery.
Assistant State's Attorney. (Appointed August, 1917.)
Member: Women's Bar Association of Illinois, Chicago Bar Association, American Bar Association.

NELLIE CARLIN

KATHARINE S. CLARK

Admitted to Illinois Bar in 1911.
Chicago-Kent College of Law. LL.B.
Practice—General Probate.
Justice of Peace, Oak Park, for three terms.
Member: Women's Bar Association of Illinois, Chicago Bar Association.

KATHARINE S. CLARK

HELEN M. CIRESE

Admitted to Illinois Bar in 1921.
DePaul University. LL.B.
Practice—Real Estate and Criminal Law.
Member: Women's Bar Association of Illinois, Chicago Bar Association, Illinois State Bar Association, Lawyers' Association of Illinois, Justinian Society of Advocates.

HELEN M. CIRESE

HERMENA BELLE DEICHES

Admitted to Illinois Bar, June 12, 1924.
Chicago-Kent College of Law. LL.B.
Practice—General.
Member: Women's Bar Association of Illinois.

HERMENA BELLE DEICHES

ESTHER A. DUNSHEE

Admitted to Illinois Bar in 1902.
Chicago-Kent College of Law, Lake Forest University. LL.B.
Practice—General Civil Practice.
Member: Women's Bar Association of Illinois, Chicago Bar Association, Illinois State Bar Association.

ESTHER A. DUNSHEE

JOANNA E. DOWNES

Admitted to Illinois Bar, December, 1917.
Hamilton College of Law. LL.B.
Practice—General.
Member: Women's Bar Association of Illinois, Lawyers' Association of Illinois, Chicago Bar Association, American Bar Association.

JOANNA E. DOWNES

MARGARET MARIAM DOWNES

Admitted to Illinois Bar, April, 1921.
Hamilton College of Law. LL.B.
Practice—General.
Member: Women's Bar Association of Illinois.

MARGARET MARIAM DOWNES

ALICE CRAIG EDGERTON

Admitted to Illinois Bar in 1910; to Wisconsin Bar, March, 1926.
Chicago-Kent College of Law. LL.B.
Practice—General, specializing in Probate.
Member: Women's Bar Association of Illinois.

ALICE CRAIG EDGERTON

ELIZABETH M. FIHE

Admitted to Illinois Bar, February 15, 1923.
DePaul University. LL.M.
Practice—General.
Attorney for Sanitary District, Chicago. (Appointed May, 1925.)
Member: Women's Bar Association of Illinois, Chicago Bar Association, Illinois State Bar Association.

ELIZABETH M. FIHE

MARGUERITE RAEDER GARIEPY

Admitted to Illinois Bar, October 15, 1919.
Northwestern University. LL.B.
Practice—General.
In charge of Legal Aid Bureau.
Member: Women's Bar Association of Illinois, Chicago Bar Association.

MARGUERITE RAEDER GARIEPY

SUSAN M. HASSELL

Admitted to Illinois Bar, February, 1911.
Chicago-Kent College of Law. LL.B.
Practice—General.
Member: Women's Bar Association of Illinois.

SUSAN M. HASSELL

MARY CLINTON HOWE

Admitted to Illinois Bar, February 4, 1920.
Kent College of Law. LL.B.
Practice—General.
Member: Women's Bar Association of Illinois, Illinois State Bar Association, American Bar Association.

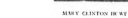

MARY CLINTON HOWE

MATILDA FENBERG

Admitted to Ohio Bar, July 11, 1922; Illinois Bar, October 11, 1923.
Yale University School of Law. LL.B.
Practice—General.
Member: Women's Bar Association of Illinois, Chicago Bar Association, Illinois State Bar Association, Hancock County Bar Association, Ohio.

MATILDA FENBERG

MARGARET L. FAY

Admitted to Illinois Bar in 1916.
Chicago Law School. LL.B.
Practice—Probate.
Member: Women's Bar Association of Illinois, Lawyers' Association of Illinois.

MARGARET L. FAY

ANNA G. FLORENCE

Admitted to Illinois Bar, February, 1924.
DePaul University. LL.B.
Practice—General.
Member: Women's Bar Association of Illinois, Chicago Bar Association.

ANNA G. FLORENCE

PEARL FRANKLIN

Admitted to Illinois Bar.
Chicago-Kent College of Law. LL.B.
Practice—General.
Member: Women's Bar Association of Illinois.

PEARL FRANKLIN

Women Lawyers Guests Here

Judge Francis B. Allegretti of Boys' Court chatting with Helen M. Cirese, who occupied the position of public defender in his court for a day. The position is filled in rotation by lawyers who have volunteered their services to defend youths, unable to hire counsel. The defenders' aim, they say, is not simply to get people out of jail, but to sift the facts and get the truth in each case. Mar. 28, 1930.

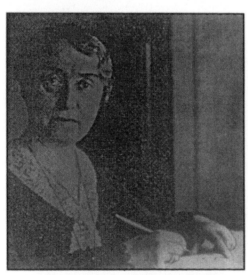

Judge Genevieve R. Cline, the only female Federal jurist at the time, addressed the WBAI annual banquet in 1930. She told them sex is no barrier to a job.

Banquet. Genevieve R. Cline (Judge at the U.S. Customs in New York) the first and only woman federal judge in American history was one of the speakers.

"Helen Cirese, notably successful criminal and civil lawyer, was elected President of the Association in June, 1930. The outstanding work of that year was an active campaign for a successful referendum on the jury bill. The activities of the campaign savored much of the women's suffrage movement of 15 years before, with torchlight parades, stump speeches and newspaper propaganda. The efforts were rewarded by a successful referendum, the jury bill receiving the approval of the populace by the necessary majority of all votes cast at the election. The success was short-lived due to the fact of a test case being taken to the Supreme Court of Illinois, which court held that passage of the bill with the referendum attached was an illegal delegation of legislative powers. Esther Dunshee was requested by the Circuit and Superior Court Judges to represent them in the test case. During this year, prosperity having not yet rounded the corner, the Association felt the call to do something for the needy rather than to expend money for an elaborate annual banquet as had been the custom. To this end a large card party was held at the Chicago Bar Association and a considerable sum was realized for charity.

"In June, 1931, Mary G. Kelly, an outstanding woman lawyer and attorney for the City Council Committee on Streets, Alleys and Public Industries, became President of the Association. The outstanding event of the year was the dinner-dance held at the Bal Tabarin, which gala affair will long be remembered as a social triumph, being the first affair of its kind ever held by the organization. Much of the activity of the Association in this year was centered upon the candidacy of Pearl M. Hart for Associate Judge of the Municipal Court. Because of the decision of the Supreme Court holding invalid the jury bill previously passed, much attention during this year was again given to procure passage of a new law providing for women on juries, which bill, however, failed of passage by two votes. An Association Journal was also published in this year."

Except for 1926, 1931 is the first year from which we have WBAI meeting minutes. They show that year's first general meeting was held at the Brevort Hotel, 120 W. Madison, Chicago, on October 1. Judge William Lindsay of the Superior Court spoke on "Probation and Parole." Dinner cost one dollar. A January Dinner Dance took the place of the 1932 annual banquet, WBAI members danced with Justices of the Illinois Supreme Court.

The 1932-33 WBAI Journal notes:

"Mrs. M.B.R. Shay, now 84 years of age, residing at Streator, Illinois is believed to be the first woman to graduate from an accredited law school. She graduated in 1879 from the Wesleyan at Normal, Bloomington, Illinois, with the honors of her law class. She is the author of *Students Guide to Common Law Pleading*, the first law book written by a woman."

However, we now know the first woman law graduate was Ada Kepley in 1870.

In January, 1933, a Chicago Newspaper asked:

Are women who work to blame for the Depression? That's not proven, said Hoover's commission. Helen Cirese was noted as one of the few women in the professions.

By 1933, the Honorable Mary Bartelme had retired and moved out of Illinois and was no longer eligible for WBAI membership under then existing by laws. (Our by laws permit and we now have members from coast to coast). It was proposed that Bartelme be made an honorary member. Two members voted no, one explaining that she was opposed because Bartelme had failed to recommend or comment favorably on other women for the office of Judge of the Juvenile Court. However the motion passed and Judge Bartelme was made their first honorary member of the Women's Bar Association of Illinois.

On January 4, 1934, WBAI passed a resolution urging that Justice Florence Allen, of Ohio, be appointed to the United States Circuit Court of Appeals. WBAI sent letters to the President and the Attorney General of the United States. In 1935, President Franklin D. Roosevelt appointed Florence Allen to the U.S. Court of Appeals for the Sixth Circuit. She was the first woman to serve on the U.S. Court of Appeals.

The Journal & Directory states that, "in June, 1934, Edna Devlin, well known attorney in insurance circles, was elected President of the Association." Again it was voted to concentrate the energies of the Association for the enactment of a bill providing for women on juries and to maintain a lobby in Springfield for that purpose, which work is still continuing. In October a very hospitable housewarming was held in the Chicago Bar Association lounge at which past and present officers poured tea and new and prospective members were welcomed. During this year the President, Edna Devlin, and the Treasurer Kathryn M. Barasa, became brides. At the November monthly dinner, a reception was held for the brides, a beautiful large wedding cake gracing the table. This was sponsored by Beatrice Hayes Podell and Eleanor Ruth Borgmeier. The Association gave the brides sterling silver carving and steak sets as wedding gifts.

The Depression made the 1930s especially hard for women to succeed in the practice of law; and in Illinois, women were still prohibited from jury service. A quest for jobs and women on juries would dominate that era.

Minutes of meetings of the Women's Bar Association of Illinois dating back to the early 1930s document debates over tactics to achieve passage of the controversial Women's Jury Bill, simultaneously with discussion about funding customary social events in view of the Great Depression.

One month saw an emergency decision since 50 percent of the members were in arrears, to reduce all outstanding dues to $1.00. Nonetheless, in another meeting, WBAI members in 1935 voted to spend what ever sums necessary to get the jury bill introduced including sending the Jury Bill Committee Chair downstate by railroad to lobby for it and spending $35.00 for correspondence urging 400 club women in the southern part of Illinois to pressure their senators and representatives in favor of the jury bill.

BERTHA L. MacGREGOR

President

Admitted to Illinois Bar, October, 1915.

Chicago Kent College of Law, LL.B.

Practice: Patent, Trademark, Copyright and Corporation law.

Member: Women's Bar Association of Illinois, Chicago Bar Association, Illinois State Bar Association, American Bar Association.

BERTHA C. CARLSON
Vice-President
Admitted to Illinois Bar, October, 1928.
Chicago-Kent College of Law, LL.B.
Practice: General.
Member: Women's Bar Association of Illinois.

BEATRICE HAYES PODELL
Second Vice-President
Admitted to Illinois Bar in 1919.
DePaul University, LL.B.
Practice: General and Real Estate.
Member: Women's Bar Association of Illinois.

ANNA FLORENCE NELSON
Treasurer
Admitted to Illinois Bar, February, 1924.
DePaul University, LL.B.
Practice: General.
Member: Women's Bar Association of Illinois, American Bar Association, Chicago Bar Association.

ELSA C. BECK
Secretary
Admitted to Illinois Bar, January, 1930.
Northwestern University Law School, J.D.
Practice: General.
Member: Women's Bar Association of Illinois.

KATHRYN M. BARASA
Admitted to Illinois Bar, October, 1928.
DePaul University, LL.B.
Practice: General.
Member: Women's Bar Association of Illinois, Chicago Bar Association, Justinian Society of Advocates.

ELIZABETH M. FIHE
Admitted to Illinois Bar, February 15, 1923.
DePaul University, LL.M.
Practice: General.
Member: Women's Bar Association of Illinois, Chicago Bar Association, Illinois State Bar Association.

GRACE H. HARTE
Admitted to Illinois Bar in 1912.
Practice: General, specializing in Real Estate Law.
Member: Women's Bar Association of Illinois, Lawyers' Association of Illinois.

NELLIE MacNAMARA
Admitted to Illinois Bar, October, 1917.
Northwestern University, LL.B.
Practice: General.
Member: Women's Bar Association of Illinois, American Bar Association, Illinois State Bar Association.

ELLEN L. NYLUND
Admitted to Illinois Bar, January, 1928.
University of Michigan, LL.B.
Practice: Trust Work.
Member: Women's Bar Association of Illinois, Chicago Bar Association.

BOARD OF DIRECTORS
1932-1933

MEMBERS
OF THE
WOMEN'S BAR ASSOCIATION OF ILLINOIS

ANDERSON, MISS ESTHER C.,
105 S. LaSalle St., Chicago.

ANDERSON, MISS GRACE,
1037 E. Main St., Galesburg, Ill.

ANDRESEN, MISS MARIE O.,
643 Barry Ave., Chicago. Gra. 3339.

BAILEY, MISS MARY D.,
827 Federal Bldg., Chicago. Har. 4700.

BARASA, MISS KATHRYN M.,
10 N. Clark St., Chicago. Ran. 2620.
2228 Dayton St., Chicago. Lin. 5758.

BARNETT, MISS EDNA E.,
720—110 S. Dearborn St., Chicago.
Sta. 7020.

BARTELME, JUDGE MARY M.,
Juvenile Court, 2246 Roosevelt Rd.,
Chicago. See. 8400.

BATES, MISS JEANETTE,
1012 County Bldg., Chicago.
Fra. 3000—Local 25.

BAULD, MISS KATHARYNE E.,
1610—100 N. LaSalle St., Chicago.
339 S. Oak Park Ave., Oak Park, Ill.

BAUR, MRS. BERTHA D.,
1511 Astor St., Chicago. Del. 1511.

BEALL, MISS MARIE BRADLEY,
205 W. Monroe St., Chicago. Sta. 1901.
7350 Ridge Ave., Chicago. Rog. 5894.

BECK, MISS ELSA C.,
105 E. Delaware Place, Chicago.

BENNETT, MISS ESTELLE B.,
29 S. LaSalle St., Chicago.
525 Arlington Place, Chicago.

BERNSTEIN, MISS LENA M.,
30 N. LaSalle St., Chicago. Sta. 7271-7268.
722 Independence Blvd., Chicago.
Ked. 5155.

BEST, MRS. ANN BROWN,
77 W. Washington St., Chicago.
Dea. 7966.
300 S. Hamlin Ave., Chicago.

BINKS, MISS VERA M.,
436 E. Pine Ave., Kewanee, Ill.

BISSELL, MRS. CUSHMAN B.,
111 W. Monroe St., Chicago. Ran. 0470.
1507 Oak Ave., Evanston. Evan. 7029.

BISSELL, MISS HARRIET WHITE,
6700 S. Union Ave., Chicago.

BITHER, MISS LUELLA M.,
127 N. Dearborn St., Chicago. Cen. 8344.
1027 E. 46th St., Chicago.

BLASZENSKI, MISS STEPHANIE X.,
1836—160 N. LaSalle St., Chicago.
Dea. 1575.
3826 Barry Ave., Chicago. Ave. 5228.

BOGUSIEWICZ, MISS ANNA R.,
3235 Lockwood Ave., Chicago.

BORGMEIER, MISS ELEANOR RUTH,
5100 N. Long Ave., Chicago. Kil. 2058.

BUCHHALTER, MRS. ELIZABETH H.,
123 W. Madison St., Chicago.
Ran. 5877 or Bit. 3800.

BURROWS, MISS ANNE,
221 N. LaSalle St., Chicago. Sta. 6257.

BUSENBARK, MISS WILMA,
5944 W. Ohio St., Chicago. Aus. 3052.

CARDWELL, MISS MARTHA E.,
1 N. LaSalle St., Chicago. Sta. 5577.

CARLIN, MISS NELLIE,
123 W. Madison St., Chicago. Ran. 5877.

CARLSON, MRS. BERTHA C.,
7221 N. Paulina St., Chicago. Hol. 3812.

CHAYES, MRS. EDWARD,
1414 Hollywood Ave., Chicago. Sun. 7076.

CHERNEY, MRS. HAZEL BLACK,
Fox River Grove, Ill.

CIRESE, MISS HELEN M.,
221 N. LaSalle St., Chicago. Sta. 6257-8.

CLOHESY, MISS AGNES B.,
506 S. Wabash Ave., Chicago.
Har. 7042 or Aus. 9319.

COLBERT, MISS MARY LEE,
1906—139 N. Clark St., Chicago.
Cen. 3659.

COLEMAN, MISS FERN,
69 W. Washington St., Chicago.
Dea. 7700.
659 Grace St., Chicago. Bit. 9764.

COLLINS, MISS VIRGINIA,
69 W. Washington St., Chicago.
Dea. 7700.
7815 Burnham St., Chicago. Sag. 8212.

CONNERY, MRS. MARY SELLERS,
301—236 N. Clark St., Chicago.
Fra. 1807.

CUPPAIDGE, MISS HELEN V.,
Federal Building, Chicago. Har. 4700.
5748 Dorchester Ave., Chicago.

CZACHORSKI, MRS. HELEN FLEMING.
1309 N. Ashland Ave., Chicago.
Bruns. 2525.
13304 Brandon Ave., Chicago.
So. Chi. 9648.

DAVIS, MRS. HELEN T.,
1649—228 N. LaSalle St., Chicago.

DEVLIN, MISS EDNA,
1248—29 S. LaSalle St., Chicago.
Cen. 3954.
6433 Greenview Ave., Chicago. Rog. 3037.

DeWOLF, MISS BLANCHE L.,
913 Union Ave., Belvidere, Ill.

DORSEY, MISS BERNADETTE L.,
7064 Sheridan Rd., Chicago. Rog. 0816.

DOWNES, MRS. JOANNA E.,
29 S. LaSalle St., Chicago. Ran. 4711.

DOWNES, MISS MARGARET M.,
941—29 S. LaSalle St., Chicago.
Ran. 4711 or Cen. 7691.
145 Bertling Lane, Winnetka. Win. 2394.

DUNAKIN, MRS. CHARLOTTE BUETHE.
408 W. Jefferson St., Wheaton, Ill.

DUNSHEE, MISS ESTHER A.,
1601—231 S. LaSalle St., Chicago.

ELVERT, MISS MARTHA,
539—30 N. LaSalle St., Chicago.
Dea. 2846.

ELZER, MRS. KATE ZOOT.
661 Sheridan Rd., Chicago.

ERB, MISS RUTH ANNA,
160 N. LaSalle St., Chicago.
Sta. 4371-8965.

EVANS, MRS. JEAN SMITH,
1422—160 N. LaSalle St., Chicago.
Cen. 4470.

FAY, MRS. MARGARET L.,
815—139 N. Clark St., Chicago.
Dea. 1964 or She. 6298.

FENBERG, MISS MATILDA,
1303—120 S. LaSalle St., Chicago.
Cen. 1972.
5401 Cornell Ave., Chicago. Fai. 8000.

FIHE, MRS. ELIZABETH M.,
901—111 W. Monroe St., Chicago.
Ran. 7682 or Bit. 0252.

FITZGERALD, MISS MARGARET,
6526 Woodlawn Ave., Chicago.

FLYNN, MISS MABEL E.,
10723 Calhoun Ave., Chicago.
So. Chgo. 7401.

FLYNN, MRS. MARGARET McGINNES,
1553 W. 91st St., Chicago. Crd. 1793.

FOLTZ, MISS PEARL E.,
904—203 N. Wabash Ave., Chicago.
Sta. 7160.

FRANKLIN, MISS PEARL,
1216—19 S. LaSalle St., Chicago.
Ran. 0876 or Mid. 7308.

FRY, MISS HAZEL M.,
19 S. LaSalle St., Chicago. Ran. 5161.
5200 W. Chicago Ave., Chicago.

GABEL, MISS EDITH M.,
7133 Bennett Ave., Chicago.

GILMER, MRS. MARY ELIZABETH,
38 S. Dearborn St., Chicago.
400 Deming Place, Chicago.

GINNANE, MISS AGATHA,
6511 Greenview Ave., Chicago.

GLEASON, MISS CLAIRE,
203 N. Wabash Ave., care Legal Aid,
Chicago. Sta. 7160.

GREEN, MISS CORA B.,
605 Federal Bldg., Chicago. Har. 4700.

GREENACRE, MISS ALICE,
822—38 S. Dearborn St., Chicago.
Cen. 2102.

HALLGREN, MISS FLORENCE,
8858 Cottage Grove Ave., Chicago.

HAMSMITH, MISS MARY,
Sycamore, Ill.

HART, MISS PEARL M.,
30 N. LaSalle St., Chicago.
Sta. 7271 or Whi. 7382.

HARTE, MRS. GRACE H.,
310—163 W. Washington St., Chicago.
Dea. 3418.

HASSELL, MRS. SUSAN M.,
2249 Winnemac Ave., Chicago. Rav. 7477.

HATHAWAY, MISS ALBERTINE,
Care Amer. Bond & Mtge. Co., 127 N.
Dearborn St., Chicago.

HELLENTHAL, MISS GERTRUDE H.,
69 W. Washington St., Chicago. Dea. 7700.
1000 Lake Shore Dr., Chicago. Sup. 1183.

HENRY, MISS FLORA M.,
139 N. Clark St., Chicago. Dea. 3335.
2425 Lawrence Ave., Chicago.

HEPTIG, MRS. BESS SULLIVAN,
422 Melrose St., Chicago. Bit. 4106.

HIRTZEL, MISS CORA B.,
Hotel LaSalle, Chicago. Fra. 0700.

HOLMOS, MISS IRENE,
166 W. Jackson Blvd., Chicago.
Har. 9481.
646 Fullerton Parkway, Chicago.
Div. 0940.

HOWARD, MISS CELIA M.,
656 Federal Bldg., Chicago. Har. 4700.

HUITT, MISS GERTRUDE,
106 N. Main St., East St. Louis, Ill.

HURSEN, MISS EVANGELINE C.,
160 N. LaSalle St., Chicago.
Fra. 1815, Nor. 4148 or Col. 7387.

IZDEBSKI, MISS ISABELLE,
3019 Milwaukee Ave., Chicago. Pens. 2323.
3805 N. Tripp Ave., Chicago. Pens. 2323.

JACKSON, MISS FRANCIS R.,
7521 Coles Ave., Chicago.

JACOBSON, MISS LEAH,
6 N. Clark St., Chicago. Fra. 7960.
1455 N. Ashland Ave., Chicago.

JACOBSON, MRS. PEARL HOFFMAN,
111 W. Washington St., Chicago.
Sta. 1616.
1216 Madison Park, Chicago. Ken. 0083.

JOHNSON, MISS ANNA D.,
6724 Calumet Ave., Chicago. Eng. 4513.

JOHNSON, MISS HILDAH A.,
500 N. Dearborn St., Chicago. Sup. 8121.
1245 Winona Ave., Chicago.

KEHOE, MISS KATHERINE,
77 W. Washington St., Chicago. Cen. 4752.
2167 Wilson Ave., Chicago.

KELLY, MISS CYNTHIA R.,
804—29 S. LaSalle St., Chicago.
Fra. 6085.

KELLY, MISS MARY G.,
2644 N. Troy St., Chicago.
Bel. 3175 or Ran. 8000—Ext. 290.

KING, MISS ELIZABETH R.,
6529 Greenwood Ave., Chicago.
Hyde Park 5342.

KOGAN, MRS. ESTHER R.,
825 N. Oakley Ave., Chicago. Arm. 7658.

LAPHAM, MISS OLENE,
4920 Winthrop Ave., Chicago. Edg. 8849.

LARDNER, MISS KATHERINE R.,
Trust Dept., 1st Union Tr. & Sav. Bk., 33
S. Clark St., Chicago. Fra. 6800.

LEE, MISS PORTIA MARY,
203 N. Wabash Ave., Chicago.
7649 Eastlake Terrace, Chicago.

LEFKOW, MRS. IRENE M.,
601—58 W. Washington St., Chicago.
Sta. 3243.

LEWIS, MRS. MARCIA EISNER,
1514—38 S. Dearborn St., Chicago.
Cen 2150 or Dre. 2291.

LINK, MISS DORA E.,
305—111 W. Jackson Blvd., Chicago.
Wab. 2310 or Dre. 6642.

LISS, MISS REBECCA WILLNER,
5240 Sheridan Rd., Chicago. Coh. 5073.

MacGREGOR, MRS. BERTHA L.,
2620—105 W. Adams St., Chicago.
Sta. 1661.

MACHUTT, MISS MARY C.,
3654 Kimball Ave., Chicago. Jun. 3441.

MacNAMARA, MISS NELLIE,
203 N. Wabash Ave., Chicago. Sta. 7160.

MADDEN, MRS. LOUISE ERB,
160 N. LaSalle St., Chicago.
Sta. 4371.

MAGUIRE, MISS VITA,
4226 W. Adams St., Chicago.

MARCUS, MISS DOROTHY J.,
310 S. Michigan Ave., Chicago. Wab. 1100.
3647 W. Flourney St., Chicago. Van. 7783.

MARSHALL, MISS MARION,
33 N. LaSalle St., Chicago. Ran. 6277.

MASON, MRS. JANE WHITLOCK,
1519 Hinman Ave., Evanston.

MATELSON, MISS ROSE A.,
2411 Lincoln Ave., Chicago.

MAZAC, MISS MARIE,
1847 S. 56th Court, Cicero, Ill.

MAZUR, MRS. ANNE,
203 N. Wabash Ave., Chicago. Sta. 7160.
4448 W. Adams St., Chicago. Man. 8516.

McCABE, MISS ALMA L.,
422 S. Hamlin Ave., Chicago. Nev. 4452.

McCARTHY, MRS. MARGARET,
1400 Lake Shore Dr., Chicago. Whi. 4180.

McCORMICK, MISS IRENE V.,
904—203 N. Wabash Ave., Chicago.
Sta. 7160.

McCULLOCH, MRS. CATHERINE
WAUGH,
231 S. LaSalle St., Chicago.
Cen. 2386-7-8 or Uni. 1126.

McCREADIE, MISS ESTHER,
4123 Belle Plaine Ave., Chicago.

McGOORTY, MISS FLORENCE,
929 E. 45th St., Chicago. Oak. 6261.

McLAUGHLIN, MRS. MARY,
224 N. Menard Ave., Chicago. Aus. 3573.

MEDER, MRS. LEONORA Z.,
812—139 N. Clark St., Chicago.
Dea. 1964 or Buc. 4132.

MELNICK, MISS ESTHER,
709—77 W. Washington St., Chicago.
And. 4421.

MILLER, MISS RUBY S.,
821 Sixteenth St., Moline, Ill.

MINOR, MISS EVA L.,
703 N. Schuyler Ave., Kankakee, Ill.

MOLLER, MRS. BERTHA C.,
Prosecutor, Women's Court, Chicago.

MORICI, MISS MARIE,
203 N. Wabash Ave., Chicago. Sta. 7160.
12 Jackson Blvd., Oak Park, Ill.

MURRAY, MRS. GRACE COOPER,
53 W. Jackson Blvd., Chicago. Har. 1624.
1242 Elmwood Ave., Evanston.

MYERS, MRS. JOSEPHINE MELVILLE,
2959 Michigan Blvd., Chicago.
3547 Grand Blvd., Brookfield, Ill.

NELSON, MRS. ANNA FLORENCE,
11100 S. Michigan Ave., Chicago.
Pul. 1217.

NEWMAN, MISS HELEN K.,
511 City Hall, Chicago.
5608 Adams St., Chicago.

NYLUND, MISS ELLEN L.,
Trust Dept., 1st Union Tr. & Sav. Bk.,
33 S. Clark St., Chicago. Fra. 6800—
Local 869.

O'MARA, MISS HELEN A.,
714—110 S. Dearborn St., Chicago.

O'NEILL, MISS BESS,
5664 Washington Blvd., Chicago.

OSTROM, MISS GWEN,
189 W. Madison St., Chicago. Fra. 2545.
5711 W. Campbell Ave., Chicago.

PERRATON, MISS EDNA G.,
203 N. Wabash Ave., Chicago. Sta. 7160.
6934 Glenwood Ave., Chicago.

PERRY, MISS ELIZABETH,
1130 County Bldg., Chicago.
Fra. 3000—Local 7600.

PFLUEGER, MISS NANCY M.,
228 N. LaSalle St., Chicago. Dea. 7801.
948 N. Crawford Ave., Chicago. Bel. 7439.

PIERCE, MISS MARCIE,
1445 Highland Ave., Chicago. Hol. 7047.

PIERCE, MISS MARGARET,
644 Roscoe St., Chicago. Bit. 7858.

PISHA, MISS CONSTANCE,
139 N. Clark St., Chicago. Ran. 5440.
4729 Greenwood Ave., Chicago.

PODELL, MRS. BEATRICE HAYES,
1910 Bradley Place, Chicago. Buc. 1094.

PROBST, MISS VIRGINIA,
310 S. Michigan Ave., Chicago.
Wab. 7788.
2316 Estes Ave., Chicago. Rog. Pk. 2434.

QUINN, MRS. MARY BERKEMEIER,
160 N. LaSalle St., Chicago. Ran. 3229.

RABE, MRS. OLIVE H.,
835—11 S. LaSalle St., Chicago.
Sta. 7067 or Dor. 3440.

RAITER, MISS FRANCES E.,
North Am. Accident Ins. Co.,
Rookery Bldg., Chicago.
Orrington Hotel, Evanston, Ill.

RAITHEL, MRS. ALICE McCLANAHAN,
160 N. LaSalle St., Chicago. Ran. 3229.

RATHJE, MISS MARION,
3500 Sheridan Road, Chicago.

REED, MISS GRACE,
638 Groveland Park, Chicago. Doug. 4370.

REITZ, MISS MAY E.,
900—203 N. Wabash Ave., Chicago.
Sta. 7160.

RICE, MISS CORRINE L.,
1605—1 N. LaSalle St., Chicago.
And. 1588 or Sag. 8011.

ROTHBLUM, MISS NETTIE,
33 N. LaSalle St., Chicago. Ran. 7010.

ROTHBLUM, MISS RUTH,
19 S. LaSalle St., Chicago.
Fra. 5826 or L. B. 2741.

ROWE, MISS RUTH,
5550 Kenmore Ave., Chicago. Lon. 9160.

RUSSELL, MISS VESTA M.,
Pentwater, Michigan.

SCHILLER, MISS ESTHER,
965 Milwaukee Ave., Chicago.

SILVERMAN, MISS MARY,
1216—19 S. LaSalle St., Chicago.
Ran. 0876.

SINGER, MRS. ESTHER C.,
360 Park Ave., Highland Park.
540 Central Ave., Highland Park, Ill.

SLATIS, MRS. JESSIE COHN,
3436 Douglas Blvd., Chicago. Roc. 3770.

SLAVITT, MISS CHARLOTTE,
188 W. Randolph St., Chicago. Dea. 3680.
St. Clair Hotel, Chicago.

SMUKLER, MRS. FREDA WIEMAN,
771 E. 88th St., Cleveland, Ohio.

STACK, MRS. MARY SOLON,
1801—105 S. LaSalle St., Chicago.
Ran. 2350 or Moh. 3200.

SPOONER, MISS FRANCES E.,
905—19 S. LaSalle St., Chicago.
Dea. 3978 or Dre. 8686.

STALEY, MISS JENNIE B.,
1926 Keyes Ave., Madison, Wis.

STARR, MISS EVELYN,
160 N. LaSalle St., Chicago. Cen. 5885.
3654 Lexington St., Chicago.

STEVENS, MISS CHARLOTTE M.,
1 N. LaSalle St., Chicago. Cen. 1736.

STONE, MISS ZITA J.,
10 S. LaSalle St., Chicago. Fra. 1494.

SULLIVAN, MISS BRIDGET H.,
Public Guardian, 908 County Bldg.,
Fra. 3000—Local 44 or Div. 5610.

SULLIVAN, MRS. ELLA ZOELZER,
1501 W. Center St., Park Ridge.

SVATIK, MISS ANNA,
822—38 S. Dearborn St., Chicago.

THOMPSON, MISS RUTH,
900 Rush St., Chicago.

TIFFANY, MISS EDITH DEVERE,
Freeport, Illinois.

TODD, MISS EMMA B.,
1576—38 S. Dearborn St., Chicago.
Ran. 0236.

TUCKER, MISS BERTHA FAIN,
105 N. Clark St., Chicago. Cen. 8729.

VINER, MISS LUCY MAE,
1600—160 N. LaSalle St., Chicago.
Cen. 3987.

WAGNER, MRS. VIVIAN,
456 Washington Blvd., Oak Park.

WEAVER, MRS. FRANCES,
140 S. Dearborn St., Chicago. Ran. 2491.

WELDON, MISS ISABEL H. R.,
1340 Greenwood Ave., Wilmette.

WELLMAN, MRS. HELEN GOLTRA,
228 N. LaSalle St., Chicago. Sta. 2331.

WELLNER, MISS EFFIE SEEDS,
6738 Dorchester Ave., Chicago. Dor. 2766.

WELLS, MISS ESTELLE M.,
160 N. LaSalle St., Chicago. Dea. 0089.

WHITE, MRS. CHARLOTTE D.,
38 S. Dearborn St., Chicago. Ran. 6543.

WILLIAMSON, MISS JESSIE A.,
4641 N. Lincoln St., Chicago.

YOCKEY, MISS ELLEN M.,
Taylorville, Ill.

YOELIN, MRS. MATILDA SCHACHTER,
1631—160 N. LaSalle St., Chicago.
Dea. 0089.
1442 N. Maplewood Ave., Chicago.
Hum. 7945.

ZEISLER, MISS IRENE,
11 S. LaSalle St., Chicago.

NEW MEMBERS 1932-1933

Katharyne E. Bauld .... 100 N. LaSalle St., Chicago
Marie Bradley Beall .... 205 W. Monroe St., Chicago
Lena M. Bernstein .... 30 N. LaSalle St., Chicago
Virginia Collins .... 69 W. Washington St., Chicago
Helen Fleming Czachorski .... 1309 N. Ashland Ave., Chicago
Bernadette L. Dorsey .... 7064 Sheridan Road, Chicago
Margaret M. Downes .... 29 S. LaSalle St., Chicago
Florence Hallgren .... 8858 Cottage Grove Ave., Chicago
Gertrude H. Hellenthal .... 69 W. Washington St., Chicago
Isabelle Izdebski .... 3019 Milwaukee Ave., Chicago
Rose A. Matelson .... 2411 Lincoln Ave., Chicago
Anne Mazur .... 203 N. Wabash Ave., Chicago
Josephine Melville Myers .... 2959 Michigan Blvd., Chicago
Matilda Schachter Yoelin .... 160 N. LaSalle St., Chicago

Some lawyers' estates had no money to pay funeral expenses. On October 3, 1935, WBAI voted to assume and immediately pay a $150.00 funeral bill for the burial expenses of one of the WBAI members.

In the 1930s a woman law student often found herself the only woman in the class. Law programs that accepted women were still an oddity, even in 1935, as shown by an advertisement from Chicago-Kent College of Law, touting the law school as "co-educational."

In the 1930's, WBAI had no nominating committee. There was great competition to be nominated as President. Kathryn Rinella recalled one meeting where there were three WBAI members contending for that position. Despite numerous ballots, there continued to be a tie. The meeting had to be adjourned to another date so that the election could be held again.

Rose Matelson Adelman, another 1930's WBAI member, also recalls that phenomenon. She herself was treated to a WBAI membership so that she could be eligible to vote in one of the hotly contested WBAI Presidential Elections.

The 1934-35 Journal and Directory notes: "A further major work of the year was the preparation and publication of this Twentieth Anniversary Journal and Directory, which we hope may in some small measure chronicle and preserve a record of the activities and remarkable growth and progress of this Association which had its humble beginning just twenty years ago and may prove in the years to come an inspiration to greater growth and

Chicago Bar Association gives play, Oct. 6, 1932. L to R: Vilma Busenbark, Leon Desprez, Morton Bernard, Jerome Weiss, Dean Terrill, Kathryn Barasa, Don Hatmaker, Leo Stone, Lawrence Dahlgren and Evelyn Laird. (Chicago Tribune)

In 1933, the younger members of the CBA lampooned their elders in a play called "Felonies of 2933." L to R: Vivian Wagner, Portia Lee, Elsa Beck, Hildah Alden Johnson and Kathryn Barasa.

EDNA DEVLIN
President

BEATRICE HAYES PODELL
1st Vice-President

ELSA C. BECK
2nd Vice-President

KATHRYN M. BARSA
Treasurer

MARION LEE MARSHALL
Secretary

JEAN SMITH EVANS
Director

ANNA FLORENCE NELSON
Director

ALICE McCLANAHAN RAITHEL
Director

ZITA J. STONE
Director

ANNA SVATIK
Director

EDNA E. BARNETT

MARY L. BERKEMEIER

LENA M. BERNSTEIN

WILHELMINA K. BORGMEIER

ESTHER DUNSHEE BOWER

HARRIET WHITE BISSELL

LUELLA MARY BITHER

WILMA ELIZABETH BUSENBARK

MARTHA E. CARDWELL

ELIZABETH H. BUCHHALTER

LILLIAN N. BLASZCZYNSKI

ANNA R. BOGUSIEWICZ

ELEANOR RUTH BORGMEIER

NELLIE CARLIN

BERTHA C. CARLSON

ANNE M. CHAWK

KITTY TORCH CHAYES   HAZEL BLACK CHERNEY   AGNES L. CHERRY

MARY SELLERS CONNERY   GRACE COOPER   HELEN F. CZACHORSKI

HELEN M. CHROMCZAK   HELEN M. CIRESE

JOANNA E. DOWNES   MARGARET M. DOWNES

AGNES B. CLOHESY   FERN COLEMAN   CECIL COHEN

RUTH ANNA ERB   EVANGELINE HUBSEN FADY   MATILDA FENBERG

MARGARET FITZGERALD   MABEL E. FLYNN   PEARL E. FOLTZ

PEARL M. HART   GRACE HARTE   MARION S. HARWAS

HAZEL M. FRY   CLAIRE L. GLEASON

SUSAN M. HASSELL   GERTRUDE H. HELLENTHAL

FRANCES B. GREGALUNAS   FLORENCE HALLGREN   IRENE HALMOS

BERNICE HOFFMAN   CELIA M. HOWARD   FRANCES ALDINE HUTCHISON

23

ISABELLE IZDERSKI   LEAH L. JACOBSON   PEARL HOFFMAN JACOBSON

MARY G. KELLY   ELIZABETH R. KING   EVA KOSH

ANNA D. JOHNSON   HILDA A. JOHNSON   HELENE CECILE LEACH   PORTIA M. LEE

SARA KAMIN   MIRIAM HAMILTON KEARL   CYNTHIA R. KELLY   IRENE M. LEFKOW   REBECCA WILLNER LISS   BERTHA E. McGREGOR

LOUISE ERB MADDEN   VITA MAGUIRE   JANE WHEELOCK MASON   EVA L. MINOR   JOSEPHINE MELVILLE MYERS   DORIS E. NOHREN

ROSE A. MATELSON   MARIE K. MAZAC   GERTRUDE E. NORMAN   LILLIAN M. NOVAK

CATHARINE WAUGH McCULLOCH   IRENE V. McCORMICK   ESTHER MELNICK   ELLEN L. NYLUND   MARY PAYTON   FANNIE X. PERRON

NANCY M. PFLUEGER

 EVA ROSE POLLACK

 RUTH ROWE

 KATHERINE KEHOE RUNKEE

 ETHEL E. SCHIETER

 MAY E. REITZ

 MIRIAM POLISHECK REITER

 ESTHER C. SINGER

 CHARLOTTE SLAVITT

 LAURA REYNOLDS

 FRANCES C. BAUER

 ORETA ROMEI

 FRANCES E. SPOONER

 MARY SOLON STACK

 MARY K. STRETCH

 STELLA STRINGI

 BRIDGET H. SULLIVAN

 ELLA ZOELZER SULLIVAN

 ISABELLE H. WELDON

 EFFIE SEEDS WELLNER

 BERTHA VAN ECKER

 MARJORIE VAN HORNE

 ESTELLE M. WELLS

 HELEN E. WILLETT

 LUCY MAE VOYER

 VIVIAN WAGNER

 LOUISE WALTHER

 MATILDA S. YOELIN

 ELLEN M. YAGKES

LEONORA Z. MILDER

A QUICK LOOK AT THE FACTS

ABOUT THE MARY BARTELME CLUB

The purpose of the Mary Bartelme Club is to provide the right kind of home, the right social environment and the right care and attention to girls who need these things, who cannot get them for themselves and who can profit by them.

•

The Club was founded in 1914 by Judge Mary Bartelme, the only woman Judge of the Juvenile Court of Cook County, who was able to see the need and wanted so much to meet it that she gave her own home in Austin for the purpose.

•

There are now three homes serving a limited number of selected girls—one home in Evanston and two in Chicago (on Lakewood Avenue; and Judge Bartelme's original home).

•

Only girls with distinct behaviour problems and recognized potentialities for development are accepted — in other words, only girls who need the facilities most and who can profit by them best.

•

Each home is as much like a real family home as possible—with all the care, education, supervision, love, sympathy and understanding that this implies.

•

The problems of each girl, whatever they may be, receive expert attention from doctor, dentist, consulting psychiatrist, social case worker, recreational and vocational supervisor and others.

•

Girls come to the homes from the Juvenile Court of Cook County—the Chicago Orphan Asylum—the Family Service Bureau of the United Charities—the Illinois Children's Home and Aid

• • •

Maybe you answered this appeal as far back as 1935. With the help of people like yourself, the Mary Bartelme Club has been providing opportunities for deserving girls for the past 31 years, and the need for your help is greater now than ever before. So please give generously.

Society—the Bobbs Roberts Hospital, University of Chicago — St. Mary's Home for Children—the Institute of Juvenile Research and elsewhere.

•

The Club is endorsed by the Chicago Association of Commerce and is a participating agency in the Community Fund of Chicago—a member of the Chicago Council of Social Agencies, the Social Service Exchange, the Joint Service Bureau and the Evanston Council of Social Agencies.

•

Financial support comes from four sources—1) partial reimbursement of board for some girls by the court, other agencies, and families—2) dues from members—3) interest from investments —4) voluntary contributions. More than 75 percent of the club's income comes from the source last mentioned.

•

Voluntary contributions come from the Community Fund of Chicago, the several auxiliaries of the Mary Bartelme Club, Tag Day, the Service Club of Chicago, the Suburban Guild of Oak Park, Welfare foundations, small groups and individuals.

•

The need for funds is greater now than ever before. The Clubs have never yet been able to serve all girls who could profit by the club facilities and who need these facilities desperately. The Lakewood Home is new, and funds are urgently needed to pay for this new home.

•

Please give as much as you can. Your contribution -- however large, however small—will be deeply appreciated—not only by the girls themselves but by all who are giving their time and money to provide a chance for these girls who need it and deserve it so much.

•

Mail your check to

THE MARY BARTELME CLUB

MRS. ROY L. DAVIS, President

30 North Dearborn Street, Chicago 2, Illinois   **Phone Franklin 2325**

"DECENCY, INDEPENDENCE, SELF-RESPECT - -"

These are the qualities named by Judge Mary Bartelme in a recent article as essential for the girl who has her living to earn . . . Easy enough for the girl to attain who steps out of a sheltered home . . . difficult, almost impossible for the girl whose home is unfit or who has no home at all.

These are the vital qualities which THE MARY CLUBS aim to instill and to foster in the girls who are placed in their charge by the Juvenile Court.

Since 1914 these homes, one in the city and the other in a suburb, have been proving their worth by sending out girls who have made good, both in the business and domestic world and in their own homes.

Won't you help us to sustain them?

As little as a dollar will help a lot!

Gratefully yours,

Harriet Borland, President.

Florence Dibell Bartlett
Chairman Finance Committee.

OFFICERS OF THE MARY CLUBS

JUDGE MARY BARTELME, Honorary President
MISS HARRIET BORLAND   MRS. THOMAS R. KING   MISS FRANCES BACON FORD
President   Vice-President   Secretary
MISS FLORENCE DIBELL BARTLETT   MRS. CLAIRE STUART
Treasurer   Executive Secretary

BOARD OF DIRECTORS

DR. PHYLLIS F. BARTELME	MRS. F. A. HILL	MISS HELEN MILLER
MRS. A. G. BECKER	MRS. F. A. HILL, JR.	MRS. L. W. OLIPHANT
MISS ROBERT M. CUTTING	MRS. GRANT LAING	MRS. LESLIE B. OLMSTED
MISS ELAINE BLACKMAN	MRS. CYRUS MARK	MRS. HAROLD SIPPY
MRS. CHARLES A. FORD	MRS. H. W. MARKWARD	MRS. ARTHUR I. STEPHENS
MRS. HARRY HART	MRS. GEORGE V. McINTYRE	MRS. DUDLEY TAYLOR

Endorsed by The Chicago Association of Commerce Subscriptions Investigating Committee for the regular period ending November 30, 1935.

1935

Members of National Association of Women Lawyers   **August 24, 1936**

Standing, Left to Right—Miss Emily Hass of Albany, N. Y.; Mrs. Percilla L. Randolph, President; Florence K. Thacker of Indiana; Mrs. Ida D. Rosenthal of Birmingham, Ala. Seated, Left to Right—Miss Helen Cirese of Chicago; Miss Lilian Schlagenhauf of Quincy, Ill.; Miss Darden Moose of Arkansas; Miss Frances Spooner of Chicago

---

finer achievements." (Editor's note: We hope the same for this WBAI History).

In 1935, a telegram was sent to Jane Adams in honor of her 75th birthday. The annual banquet was held at the Union League Club.

On July 2, 1935, following a "cordial" invitation to WBAI members, a buffet supper musicale was held at the home of Catherine Waugh McCulloch at 6:00 p.m. The invitation promised "a very delightful time is in store for all of those who attend. Her garden is one of the showplaces of the North Shore and the guide who will show you through the Labyrinth of Riotous Floral Beauty will none other than Mr. McCulloch, most charming husband of Mrs. McCulloch." This was one of many parties.

At one of these festivities, Rose Matelson Adelman, who was smoking a cigarette, noticed that the women with whom she had been conversing had disappeared. It turned out that Mrs. McCulloch, the hostess, was member of the Women's Christian Temperance Union (WCTU) and did not allow the drinking of alcoholic beverages or smoking of cigarettes on her premises.

Great effort was expended by WBAI to obtain employment for its members. In 1935, its records report, a delegation of WBAI members sought to meet with Chicago's Corporation Counsel Barnett Hodies. After having been kept waiting a considerable time, the group was forceably ejected from his office by Police Lieutenant Mike Mills and his squad of men. A resolution expressing disapproval over such treatment was immediately issued. In 1936, WBAI sent representatives to meet with Governor Henry Horner urging him to recommend women for existing vacancies; he was cordial, but indicated little hope. Undaunted, the group met with the Cook County State's Attorney, Thomas J. Courtney, who advised the delegation that he was not in favor of women on the prosecutor's staff and did not feel women were qualified for that sort of work in that he did not care to discuss certain evidence with a woman assistant and did not like to ask them to go to various police stations at all hours of the night and did not feel they would be able to deal with the police in all instances. Also, if a woman lost a case which should have been won, there would be more criticism than if a man had done the same thing. He did feel women should be in almost any other phase of law, except the prosecution of criminal cases.

The committee further reported that it had personally called upon Michael Rosinia, City Prosecutor of Chicago, who had been very friendly to the cause of women and stated that he already had a woman on his staff, who was doing very fine work. However, Mr. Rosinia noted that with 15 Assistants and 50 Ward committeemen to satisfy, he did not believe he could add any more women to his staff at the time.

At the same meeting, Frances Spooner moved, and it was unanimously adopted, that the Women's Bar Association hold no further meetings at the Chicago Bar Association, "in view of the attitude of the Chicago Bar Association concerning their regular monthly meeting of the association." A committee was appointed to meet with the CBA. On January 9, 1936, the minutes report that the CBA had expressed regret over the conflict at the December WBAI meeting, and recommended that, "When a woman guest was invited to the CBA meeting, the President of WBAI be invited to sit at the speaker's table and that more members of the WBAI be placed on various CBA Committees."

In 1936, WBAI voted to make Nellie Carlin the second Honorary Member of the Association. In her response to this honor, Carlin recalled having been the first Assistant State's Attorney in Cook County and serving as Public Guardian from 1913 to 1916. She stated, "I have always felt that the credit was reflected on the WBAI, for these achievements."

In her President's Report of 1935-36, Elizabeth H. Buchalter reported the tables were turned and the judges of the Superior Court gave a dinner for the WBAI members on June 27, 1935, at the Chicago Athletic Club. Kathryn Barasa Rinella had begun a Glee Club which had performed splendidly at the Dinner Dance. There had also been a dinner on October 3, 1935 honoring past presidents, meetings discussing constitutional and general legislative issues, a skit by Pearl Hart, and a Spring Tea on March 27th in the CBA Lounge to meet the newer members. There had also been an elaborate pageant presented in which 15 WBAI members participated.

The WBAI continued in its effort to achieve passage of the jury bill. In 1936, it prepared and distributed a leaflet "in the nature of a rallying call to arms, not only to our members but to women in other organized groups throughout the state to enter the fray." A "sort of flying squad of speakers to go before assemblages of women desirous of obtaining enlightenment on a subject peculiarly within the knowledge of women lawyers" was created. The membership agreed to "continue to keep a mind single toward making jury service of women our major objective...."

WBAI also provided sociability. On July 11, 1936, WBAI had an outing at the Shawnee County Club in Wilmette where 79 members and guest enjoyed the luncheon, card party and swimming. But to continue to be actively engaged as lawyers, women lawyers needed jobs.

On December 3, 1936, at the regular WBAI meeting, the Public Office Committee noted it had sought appointment of a woman lawyer as Public Defender in Women's Court. Two months later, the appointment of Zita Stone as the first paid Public Defender in Chicago, was reported. She was assigned to Women's Court. WBAI, "Rejoiced in the appointment" and gave a luncheon in her honor. Stone expressed her appreciation to WBAI for making the appointment possible.

In 1937 WBAI adopted a resolution opposing passage of resolutions which concerned the Equal Rights amendment to the U. S. Constitution. On February 1, 1937, in a letter to a member of the U.S. House of Representatives, WBAI explained why:

"The grounds for our opposition to the bills are not that we do not desire equal rights for men and women, but that we believe that these bills will not accomplish their purpose. We believe that the amendment (1) would prove actively injurious to women, rather than a help to them, and (2) would cause great confusion in existing law.

"The injurious effect on women would be the automatic annulling of all protective state legislation for women, which has been secured only by the tireless effort of a large number of social and labor organizations for many years....

"It is a matter of common knowledge that women need protective legislation more than men do because of the physical differences of women and because of their disinclination to unionize and bargain collectively with their employers.

"The confusion which would be caused by the adoption of the amendment is almost ludicrous. In many states a woman of eighteen years is emancipated and may marry without her parents' consent, but a man is not so emancipated until he is twenty-one. Under the amendment, if a woman of eighteen has the right to marry, would the man of eighteen have the same and equal right? Or wouldn't the marriage be valid unless both were twenty-one? This is one of many examples which were given of the endless confusion which would arise in the law of property, descent, domestic relations, sexual crimes, and other phases of established law of long standing."

On March 4, 1937, the Public Office Committee sent letters urging that a woman fill the next vacancy in the Superior Court of Cook County.

Statistics were presented to a 1937 WBAI meeting showing few women on the law faculties of accredited law schools. An effort to persuade law school deans to provide "responsible women" with positions was initiated.

WBAI's Placement Committee acted as a clearinghouse for employers and employees to assist the woman lawyer to "find her place," be she newly admitted to the bar or desirous of a more suitable position.

One issue debated by the members was whether stenographic training and secretarial work were, or were not, useful as a means for gaining entry into the legal profession. Elsa Beck, WBAI President 1936-37, took the position that stenographic training was not an impediment and that the woman lawyer who used such skills to gain a position would not remain a clerk forever. Based on their own experiences, many other WBAI members supported her view. Beck also argued that the "truly able women is impeded by naught."

A *Chicago Herald and Examiner* article probed the issue, "should married women work?" Superior Court Judge Rudolph Desort

This article appeared in a 1937 newspaper. It was contested by many women lawyers including Kathryn Barasa Rinella and Elsa C. Beck

Suit Career for Home, Judge Advises Wives

Desort Finds Outside Work Causes Divorces

There would be fewer divorces if women abandoned their business careers when they are married.

That was the answer yesterday of Superior Judge Rudolph Desort, who listened to the marital woes of several thousand couples during his term in the divorce court, to the question:

"Should married women work?"

At the same time, Kathryn Barasa Rinella, president of the Woman's Bar Asosciation of Illinois, wife of Attorney Samuel A. Rinella and mother of a young son, answered the question being debated throughout the city:

"Circumstances alter cases. Some women can handle both career and family capably. Others cannot."

PSYCHOLOGIST WARNS.

Since Dr. George Crane, Northwestern University psychologist, declared women should choose either marriage or a career and not attempt to mix them, the subject has aroused widespread interest in Chicago. To learn the opinions of its readers, The Herald and Examiner will publish each day a limited number of letters, restricted to 200 words each. For every letter printed a prize of $2 will be awarded.

Judge Desort, discussing the advisability of wives continuing in business, declared:

"For the first five years after marriage a woman should give up all thoughts of business and try

MRS. KATHRYN RINELLA
Devotes herself to her home.
Paul Stone Raymor photo.

to adjust herself to her husband and marriage. Then, if she cannot have children, she might return to work.

"If women followed this sort of schedule in their marriages the divorce rate in this country would be greatly diminished."

SOME MORE CAPABLE.

Mrs. Rinella, who has abandoned active pursuit of her career, although retaining her interest in it and in activities of the Bar Association, declared:

"There are women who are capable of handling both home and career, with the help of highly trained nurses for their children."

This is a topic on which all women should have opinions. Write yours in less than 200 words and send it to the Women's Work Editor of The Chicago Herald and Examiner.

was quoted as saying, "for the first five years after marriage a woman should give up all thoughts of business and try to adjust herself to her husband and marriage. Then, if she can not have children, she might return to work. If women followed this sort of schedule in their marriages then the divorce rate in this country would be greatly diminished."

However, Kathryn Barasa Rinella, president of the Woman's Bar Association of Illinois, wife of Attorney Samuel A. Rinella and mother of a young son, who has abandoned active pursuit of her career although retaining her interest in it and in activities of the Bar Association, declared:

"There are women who are capable of handling both home and career, with the help of highly trained nurses for their children." She concluded: "Circumstances alter cases. Some women can handle both career and family capably. Others cannot."

All women should have an opinion on the subject, said the newspaper. If yours of less than 200 words were published, a prize of $2.00 will be awarded.

The December 21, 1937 *Chicago Daily Law Bulletin* ran an article by Grace H. Harte noting, "Time was but a few short years ago when waitresses headed the group of women whose stock in the matrimonial market was highest, with trained nurses as runners-up. That was easily accounted for as the male of the past listed creature comforts first in his list of qualifications for a wife: and the waitress placing a juicy beefsteak and thick chunk of apple pie with cheese on the side before him at the table symbolized the acme of domestic bliss and joy to the innerman. The nurse, too, typified physical well-being: and while she patted and plumped the pillows behind his head and smoothed the sheets and performed a thousand and one little intimate services for him, the sick and happy male convalescent naturally fell into ruminating on the lines:

"Oh Woman, in our hours of ease uncertain, coy and hard to please; when pain and anguish wring the brow, a ministering angel thou!"

"But from a casual glance at the roster of members admitted to the bar and to our association during the last five or six years, and who have married since, one is forced to the conclusion that women lawyers, per capita, are more in demand as wives than any other group of women."

"Not so long ago a woman who attained a sheepskin or university degree of any kind, or was chosen as the valedictorian of her class, might as well have small-pox so far as her appeal to the would-be benedicts was concerned, unless she concealed the fact by affecting a "baby stare" or baby talk, a clinging vine manner or stooped to conquer in various ways to lure the unsuspecting male.

"But now a license to practice law, as evidenced by the experience of the Women's Bar, brings fan mail: and one by one its members change their names, so that at each monthly meeting, some one must be reintroduced under a new name. The young men of today laugh at their fathers and grandfathers' prejudice against the higher learning for their women folk: and they no longer leave the Portias or Minervas withering on the stalk.

"Well, one asks, after all the study and preparation for a professional career, are these women now going to merge their individualities into that of their husbands, and be content to spend their time experimenting with recipes out of the cook book so as to prepare three or four meals a day for one man? Not at all. One has only to look around to find the married women lawyers practicing their profession assiduously as ever: and many are partners with their fathers, brothers, husbands and even with their mothers. Among the latter may be mentioned Mrs. Joanna Downs with her son and two daughter lawyers, and Mrs. Catharine Waugh McCulloch with her husband and sons.

"President Kathryn Barasa Rinella, Vice President Marian Marshall, and 2nd Vice President Jean Smith Evans are all law partners of their husbands.

"Another surprising thing is that of all women in the world none is so well-informed on the existence of unhappy domestic relations and infelicity as the woman lawyer, into whose ears her clients pour what is vulgarly expressed as the "low-down" on the hymenal relation. But being wise in her own generation, she knows there is another side to the question; and feels herself quite competent to live in harmony with the more enlightened male of today; and is actually doing so."

But if the 1930's found women lawyers in demand as wives, the same was not true as lawyers. Kathryn Rinella recalled that most WBAI members were not actually practicing law but working in other fields such as school teaching. It was almost impossible for a woman to make a decent living practicing law.

Efforts continued for passage of the Jury Bill. It was stressed, at an April 1, 1937 meeting, that support from downstate women would be needed. An amendment to the Jury Bill had been proposed that women under age 25 and all mothers and nuns be exempt from jury service. The WBAI Jury Bill Committee voted to oppose these amendments as they would eliminate 50% of women who would be jury material.

Over 650 letters were sent to public officials soliciting their positions on this bill. The politicking involved was sophisticated and complex. One legislative snag was overcome when WBAI found that the President of the Illinois Federation of Democratic Women's Clubs was the sister of a state senator who was threatening to withdraw his support from the

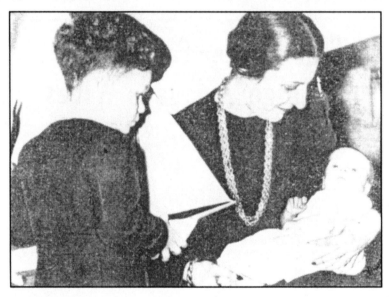

In the May 14, 1939 Herald-Examiner, Kathryn Barasa Rinella, assistant city attorney, illustrates that family and work can mix in a front page feature article.

MARY BERKEMEIER QUINN—6239 N. McClellan Ave.

Age 49. She was born in Port Chester, N. Y. She attended high school at Poughkeepsie, N. Y., Vassar College four years, University of Wisconsin one year, and summer courses at Cornell and Columbia Universities. She received her A.B. degree from Vassar and A.M. degree from the University of Wisconsin. She studied law at Yale Law School during 1919-1920 and 1921-1922, and at the University of Chicago Law School during 1920-1921, receiving the LL.B. degree from Yale. She was admitted to the bar in 1923 and has engaged in the general practice of law since that time. Prior to her admission to the bar she taught in elementary school one year and was an instructor in the department of history and mathematics for four years in high schools. In 1928 she was a candidate for nomination for judge of the municipal court; in 1932 was a candidate for ward committeeman, and in 1938 a candidate for judge of the municipal court. She is a member of the Chicago Bar Association.

She possesses an excellent background in education, a pleasing personality and an excellent reputation for integrity and fair dealing. She is likewise qualified for the office by professional experience, legal ability and capacity.

Jury Bill. Apparently, WBAI's reasoned arguments failed until the senator's sister put in a favorable word.

The Committee for Women on Juries reported in June, 1937 that the Chair made weekly trips to Springfield over a four or five month period. The Committee had published and distributed three different pamphlets, and its members had spoken to groups, made hundreds of phone calls and lobbied in Springfield.

Elsa Beck in her President's Report for 1936-37 reported that WBAI had gained 12 new members. The Emergency Fund had assisted several members in financial distress. Grace Hart, Chair of the Jury Bill committee, had worked tirelessly preparing and lobbying for passage of the legislation. Pearl Hart's Juvenile Court Committee had surveyed statutes related to jurisdiction of juvenile courts in other states and drafted legislation to raise the age of criminal responsibility from 10 years to 17 years old.

In May, some 365 members and friends supported the WBA card party held in the new CBA quarters and also had a booth at the ISBA Convention.

WBAI almost lost its not-for-profit-corporate status in 1937 when a Decree of Dissolution was entered for its failure to file annual reports in 1935-36. On payment of the appropriate fees, the WBAI was reinstated.

Meeting times presented a problem then, as now. One member resigned because, "I am not interested in keeping up my membership particularly since I am now married and cannot find it convenient to attend evening meetings." Kathryn Rinella recalled in an interview in the *WBAI News* that attendance by 25 members at WBAI meetings in the 1930s was a lot.

Echoing themes that are still relevant today, President Beck recommended a downstate meeting of the Association to make WBAI truly a state bar. She urged those who aspired to public office to get out and speak. To make public appearances would be good for business building as well as educate people that women attorneys were no longer a curiosity. She wrote, "We are a small group and need the support of every woman attorney if we are to gain recognition and the positions we seek such as judgeship. Let us all stand close together, forget self and join forces, that we may make it known that women attorneys are capable, competent and desirable public servants."

The first special downstate WBAI Meeting was held with the Illinois State Bar on September 15, 1937, at the St. Charles Country Club. Establishing association and friendship in the southern part of the State was valuable in order to obtain down state support for legislation on WBAI causes such as the Women's Jury Bill. Elsa Beck, Chair of the Down State Meetings Committee, observed that this pioneering venture would help establish women lawyers on an equal professional footing with men.

In October, 1937, "with a view of publicizing our Jury Bills", 52 members had attended the performance of "The Night of June 16th" at the Selwyn Theater.

In November, 1937, according to Grace Harte's column, WBAI members intently studied newspaper accounts of the demeanor and conduct of women jurors on a Cincinnati murder case. They concluded the women jurors were not as emotional as the average male, were able to comprehend the issues and did not exert a corrupting influence as the male jurors. They praised the women jurors for acting with dignity and not hesitating to bring in a guilty verdict.

Grace H. Harte's column which appeared in the 1930's in the *Chicago Daily Law Bulletin* announced that in February, 1938 more than 475 WBAI members and friends attended the 24th annual dinner dance. Red hatchets, tricornered hats & cherry tree favors complete with a playlet, "Bardwell vs Pickwick" which was described as "sidesplitting." The April 11, 1938 column detailed how in answer to a WBAI survey to legislators on women on juries, married male legislators had opposed jury service for women saying, "I have a wife," or "I have daughters. They do not want women jury laws. I am irrevocably opposed to having them subjected to the corrupting ordeal of being locked up with male jurors while deliberating on verdicts." But then the mood changed and legislators began saying, "I have a wife, of course I am for women jurors. My wife would consign me to the doghouse if I felt otherwise." And "This is still a free nation. Women have their own minds just as men have. I have a wife. I always respect her judgement. I am for your questions 100%."

For 1938 the Placement Committee concentrated on letter writing and the best approach to large corporations such as insurance companies, banks, and railroads. Two members were placed in jobs.

In December, 1938, Elsa Beck reported that 764 individually typed letters had been sent to members of the Chicago Real Estate Board. Fourteen replies were received expressing interest in a follow-up.

In 1939, WBAI endorsed a U.S. Senate Bill to prevent discrimination against graduates of certain law schools who sought appointment to government positions. The letter was sent to all members of Congress in Washington, D.C. On April 15, 1939 the annual dinner dance was held at the Congress Hotel.

At the June 1, 1939 general meeting, it was noted that the *Law Bulletin* had provided "fine" treatment to WBAI and "thrown its column open to us." The members voted to send a letter of appreciation to the *Law Bulletin*.

Finally, in 1939, after years of ceaseless lobbying, common sense prevailed. The Jury Bill passed the House 100 to 15 and the Senate 32 to 7. Governor Henry Horner signed the law giving women the right to sit on Illinois juries; it became effective July 1, 1939. The Illinois Supreme Court upheld its constitutionality.

WBAI decided to throw a "Victory Dinner" to celebrate. Because of the excitement caused by passage of the Jury Act, and the work entailed in preparation for the Victory Dinner, the Board of Directors on September 19, 1939, voted to defer all business until after the Victory Dinner had taken place.

The November 1939, Women Lawyers' Journal discussed the Victory Dinner as follows: "The Women's Bar Association of Illinois held a Victory Dinner Meeting on October 5th at the rooms of the Chicago Bar Association to celebrate DOUBLE TRIUMPH, i.e. the enactment of the law making women eligible for jury service and the upholding of its constitutionality by the Illinois Supreme Court.

"Twice before has the higher court handed down adverse decisions but now reason has finally prevailed...It was a jubilant and gleeful meeting; all the speakers were in a right merry mood. The judges told of their experiences with the newly qualified woman jurors in the court. While they stressed the novelty of the scene and touched on humorous incidents, all spoke highly of the woman's fairness, impartiality and efficiency, and said they were doing much to improve decorum in the courts, which was a good thing to preserve in the courts of justice."

(Honored guests included Governor Henry Horner and Mayor Edward J. Kelly. Dinner cost $1.25 per plate). "Among the dignitaries at the Victory Dinner was attorney Walter Dodd who, along with several WBAI members, had represented WBAI in a test case to prove the constitutionality of the Jury Bill. The question decided was whether the term "men" in the statute embraced "women."

Attorney Walter Dodd facetiously suggested that while the answer was that men embraced women, still-women sought the embraces!"

The Journal also had an article written before the Jury Bill passed, by Helen Cirese, the 1930-31 WBAI President, in support of the Jury Bill: "There are women lawyers, women Court attorneys, women Judges, therefore is it not absurd that women should be excluded in acting as jurors? Such exclusion is a lingering discrimination which does not belong in this century."

In 1939, the WBAI formed a Speakers Bureau to make Chicago women conscious of the existence of women attorneys and their capabilities. A letter was sent to all WBAI members stating, "the average women will say, "oh yes, there are women lawyers" but usually, she cannot give the name of one nor her particular kind of practice. She is usually very much surprised if she is told there are women lawyers who are experts in practicing any field of law." Other plans were made to give women lawyers new standing in the community and organizations were solicited to hear speeches by women lawyers.

The Women on Jury Information Committee reported that a brochure was being prepared to answer the many questions received from women about jury service.

The 1940's saw the Women's Bar Association continue to work for employment for its members. On February 1, 1940, the Placement Committee reported "happily" that it had run out of applicants. (By June 6th of the year, however, it reported that it had made efforts to place 36 job seekers. By October 3. 1940, the Placement Committee had succeeded in placing three women in legal jobs).

The early 1940's saw the Association busy giving talks and distributing leaflets informing women about their newly won rights to serve a jurors in Illinois. WBAI supplied 1000 names of women in nine counties for federal jury services. The Clerk of the U.S. Court reported that each of the women had been sent questionnaires and 500 had served or were serving on federal juries. WBAI also worked for legislation to insure that grand jury service was to be "regardless of sex", so that women could be assured of their rights there, too.

The April 4th 1940 WBAI minutes show a resolution was passed to look into the eight-hour law and see that the law stay on the Statute Books as it was, to protect the smaller bracket employee; but the law should be amended to protect the higher bracket employee, the executive; that she be not ousted from her place.

Elsa C. Beck, Chairman of the Placement Committee, made her report. She said that there was an opening for a woman lawyer and that applications would be considered.

On June 5, 1940, the following report was made on a tea for new members: "The tea was given in the lounge of The Chicago Bar Association from 4:30 to 6:30 in the afternoon on May 28, 1940. Sandwiches, small cakes, tea and coffee were furnished by The Chicago Bar Association dining room at sixty cents per person.

"The tea table was attractively arranged, and for beauty, distinction and elegance we are indebted to Mrs. Kathryn Barasa Rinella

for her silver tea service and to Miss Marion Rathje for her silver coffee service.

"All new members were invited as guests of the Association, and officers and representatives from the other bar association groups were invited as special guests, namely: Bohemian Lawyers Association, Decalogue Society of Lawyers, Justinian Society of Advocates, National Lawyers Guild, Nordic Law Club and Polish Lawyers Association. Responses were received to all invitations, and the representation from the other association groups was much more complete than had been anticipated.

"Tea was served to a total of 77, and many others were present who dropped in for a few minutes to visit but who were not served."

In her June 16, 1940, Notes of the Women's Bar Association column, Grace H. Harte noted:

"While the bar association throughout the country are showing real concern over the economic condition of lawyers, and especially of the younger group, women of the Illinois bar have been working with practical effectiveness to meet the financial problems of those of their own sex in or about to enter the profession of law, or to tide them over the first lean years which so frequently follow the bestowal of the coveted license to practice.

"Miss Elsa C. Beck, chairman of the Placement committee, presented the annual report at the meeting last week. It shows that during the year 38 applicants filed with the committee, of which nearly 50 per cent were non-members and advanced law students, the rest being members of the association.

"It also shows that 588 letters were sent to large business corporations in the Chicago area, state street department stores, insurance companies, mortgage bankers, railroad and credit men's organizations, and 50 law firms,

Chicago Tribune—1940

Miss **Frances D. Brown** of 6035 Eberhart avenue received her doctor of laws degree from the University of Chicago recently. Miss Brown, who plays the violin in the University of Chicago Symphony and the Florence Symphony orchestras, was the first woman to be elected secretary of the University Bar association.

apprising them that the committee was in a position to fill vacancies in such firms where legal training would be an asset.

"In response to these letters a number of openings were presented to the committee including positions for law clerks, combination attorney and secretary in law offices; legal editorial and publication service; one as attorney in real estate department of large mercantile establishment; another for combination attorney and office manager for printing corporation; and another as secretary in credit department of business concern."

In the 1940's women lawyers faced a new economic crisis. The jobs that had become available when male lawyers served in the armed forces during World War II were disappearing as the men returned to claim them. WBAI continued in its quest to locate jobs for its members.

A meeting with the president of the Chicago Park District produced his admission that he had not realized women lawyers had an association and, in fact, had never thought about them before. He had nine lawyers in his department, and all were men. But a letter to the same city of Chicago corporation counsel from whose office WBAI members had been forcibly removed five years earlier produced a report that he now had three women lawyers on his staff and would cooperate in efforts to obtain more. Meetings were also held with various candidates for public office.

The Dinner Dance Committee reported that the WBAI February 22, 1941 dinner dance, "was a most gala and festive occasion, based on a patriotic theme. It was attended by more than 60 members of the Women's Bar Association of Illinois, together with their friends and family of the Association....

"The program of the evening centered around the music of Don Pedro who provided specialty dance numbers. The dancers enjoyed an early number which was the formation of a circle and upon a break in the music, dancing partners were changed. Later in the evening our gracious President, Miss Nylund, welcomed the guests to the party and explained its motif and purpose. Shortly after her address, favors, consisting of red, white and blue canes and balloons were passed to the dancers and to those sitting at tables. The favors provided a chief source of amusement and pleasure to the party. Another specialty dance occurred late in the evening when 12 lemons were passed to the girls on the dance floor. The orchestra leader advised the dancers to pass the lemons to another girl on the floor as quickly as possible and to avoid being...."

President Ellen Whitsett's June, 1941 annual report stated, "Being president of the Women's Bar Association of Illinois has been one of the most surprisingly and remarkably pleasant experiences I have had. I am the more impressed by this for this was not an anticipated reaction. But it is a rare and pleasurable thing to have a Board of Directors composed entirely of women who were open-minded and willing to give of their time and best judgement of the administration of the organization and to find so many committee chairmen and members who worked diligently and tirelessly to accomplish the objectives we have set for ourselves. Without this, the year just ended would have been barren of results and a lamentable waste of your time and energy and mine.

"To give some logical sequence to this report it seems highly desirable to review briefly the purpose and function served by a women's bar association in Illinois. Two excellent professional organizations now exist in this same territory, the Chicago Bar Association and the Illinois State Bar Association. Women are freely admitted as members and participate in the work of their committees, attend their organization meetings, etc. To be sure, women have not been encouraged to take part in their golf tournaments or bowling leagues. But so far as can be ascertained at this time, this has not greatly handicapped us in our professional careers.

"The purpose of the Women's Bar Association is both social and practical. For this reason the activities have been varied and seemingly unrelated. But reduced to their simplest statement, they were intended to:

1. Increase our information on technical legal subjects;

2. Clarify our civic and social responsibilities;

3. Facilitate, if possible, the acceptance of women lawyers as a matter of course by our brothers in the law;

4. Keep women lawyers in a favorable light before the public;

5. Increase the active participation of more members in the work of the organization;

6. Establish contacts with as many young women entering the practice of law as was feasible;

7. Furnish a meeting ground for our members with other women lawyers who might chance to be in our city and to extend to them such courtesies as might be expected of an organization such as ours;

8. Widen our own horizons of interest; and

9. Derive as much pleasure from doing these things as possible."

On October 9, 1941, the WBAI held its first Joint Professional Dinner with the Chicago branch of the American Medical Women's Association. Dinner cost $1.35. The WBAI and AMWA met again in 1942 and in 1943, by which time the cost of the dinner rose to $1.65. The Joint Professional Dinner (expanded to include many other professions) has taken place each year since 1941.

On June 11, 1942, the Jury Committee reported that women jurors were being accepted as a matter of course and were no longer objects of curiosity. In fact, it was reported that women comprised a majority of those chosen to sit as jurors. The committee announced that it had received telephone call from women in Georgia and Alabama to aid in efforts to secure jury service for women in those states.

On November 5, 1942, WBAI resolved to endorse Florence Allen, a nationally recognized woman judge, to appointment to the United States Supreme Court. WBAI's repeated efforts in the 1940's were without success. In another first, a WBAI member was found guilty of a confidence scheme charge at the Criminal Court.

In 1942, WBAI became embroiled in controversy with the American Bar Association. The ABA's Special Committee on Law lists objected to WBAI's issuing a Directory of Members. The ABA's position was that under Canon 27, the only information that ethically could be provided in a Directory was the name, address and phone number of a member. However, WBAI proposed to include honorary memberships, public guardianships, degrees from several universities and other data. The ABA's representative wrote WBAI a letter which stated, "I believe you are transgressing on what may be included in a Bar Association Directory very heavily against Canon 27."

In June, 1942, President Tucker reported, "Through the good offices of Mayor Edward J. Kelly, we were granted the privilege of using the booth in the City Hall certain evenings a week for the purpose of giving free legal service to the men in our Armed Forces and to the members of their families. After Pearl Harbor, the City Hall was no longer open to the public in the evening so we discontinued services at the booth, but the individual members of the Defense Program Committee are continuing this very worthwhile and patriotic work.

"Another phase of the war work done by our Association has been carried on under the auspices of the War Savings Committee, of which Miss Helen M. Cirese is Chairman.

"The members of our Association have been zealous in the sale of War Savings Stamps and Bonds. For many weeks during the evening hours - six days a week - we manned a booth at the Drake Hotel, selling a substantial number of stamps. During the summer, Miss Cirese and the members of her Committee are to man a booth for the sale of War Savings Stamps and Bonds at the Selwyn Theater. In addition, many of our members served as Minute Men in the pledge campaign and as speakers.

"The work of both the Defense Program Committee and the War Savings Committee has been very arduous, necessitating the expenditure of many hours not only by the Chairmen but by the Committee members as well.

"No report of the war work done by the Association would be complete without mentioning the Red Cross Unit, organized by Antonia Rago with the assistance of Bess Sullivan Heptig. Many of our members took this Red Cross course and are therefore better equipped to serve their country in time of emergency.

"Our first social activity of the year was our annual summer outing. This year we had a steak fry and picnic at the Cabin in the Woods. The affair was highly successful.

"On April 11th, we held our dinner dance at the Edgewater Beach Hotel. This dinner dance was unique in that it was not only highly successful, but highly profitable as well. In a war year, this second factor is very gratifying to the Association. Mrs. Heptig and her associates deserve great credit for their handling of this affair, for as a result, the Association was able to make a contribution of $175.00 to the U.S.O.

"On May 28, in keeping with what is now

Women Lawyers Hold Annual Fall Outing at McCulloch Home

Ray Photo

Women lawyers from all parts of the Chicago area laid aside their law books last Saturday to assemble for the annual fall outing of the Woman's Bar association of Illinois at the home of one of their distinguished colleagues, Catharine Waugh McCulloch, 2236 Orrington avenue. Mrs. McCulloch is seated in the second row fifth from the right, and beside her are Miss Eva Pollack (left), president of the Woman's Bar association, and Mrs. Clementine Nicola (right), who was a candidate for one of the municipal court judgeships at the last election. Mr. McCulloch, also a lawyer, stands behind Mrs. Nicola, and the other two men in the picture are sons of two of the lawyer-mothers. The women during the afternoon made a tour of the Northwestern Technological institute, with Dean Ovid W. Eshbach as their guide, and after the tour returned to the McCulloch home for supper.

almost an established custom, we gave a tea in the Chicago Bar Lounge in honor of the new members of our Association and the senior members of the various law schools."

On April 1, 1943, WBAI adopted its first By Laws. They stated the object of the Association to be the following:

"Section 1: The object of this Association is to promote and foster, advance and protect the interests and welfare of women lawyers; to encourage a spirit of friendship and mutual helpfulness among its members; to aid in the enactment of legislation for the common good and in the administration of justice; to take such actions as this Association may deem advisable to promote its interests and the welfare of its members; and to maintain the honor and dignity of the profession."

A May 19, 1943 letter from the President reminded members that, "Our annual tea honoring the women members of the senior class of the law schools in the Chicago area, and attorneys admitted for membership in the association during the current year, will be held in the Lounge of the Chicago Bar Association, 29 South LaSalle Street, between the hours of 4:30 p.m. and 6:30 p.m., on Friday, May 28, 1943. The charge will be $.65. The following members of the association constitute the committee in charge of the tea:

Katherine Agar, Chairman, Mary Agnes Dolan, Eva R. Pollack, Frances Brown, Rosario Motto, Eva Charles, Alice Chellberg and Thelma Brook.

In 1943 the Dean of DePaul University Law School was quoted as saying, "The sacred domains of the law, for centuries closely cloistered against invasion by women, are about to surrender in a major way to modern Portias." This comment was made in the context of noting that DePaul Law School now had nine freshman women law students, one of whom was our member Frances Corwin.

On June 10, 1943, the Placement Committee reported 34 openings, a 36% increase over the previous years. Four applicants were placed in law offices. The Committee noted that 21 WBAI members worked in government agencies. Edna Parrington, the Chairman, stated, "We trust the Placement Committee will go on forever, but it is primarily our individual efforts as well as our collective

efforts that will ensure permanence in the field of law."

That same day, Charlotte Gauer, outgoing WBAI president included in her annual report the recollection of how the September 1942 steak fry and picnic had been rained out. On a more serious note, WBAI had sponsored a table for high school students at a vocational conference and war bond work continued.

In 1944 WBAI efforts continued to be World War II directed. On April 13, 1944, Jeanne E. Brown, Chairman of the Sub-Committee on mobilization of the Industrial Worker and Serviceman Post-War Committee Women's Bar Association of Illinois reported in part: "The demobilization of industrial workers and servicemen is a most vital question today.

"First, let us discuss the background for demobilization from previous wars. All through history, America's measures to change soldiers into civilians have been hit or miss. After the Revolutionary War, enlisted men were sent home with an $80 bonus, officers with five years' pay. Civil War veterans received bounties of up to $100 for those with three years' service.

"After the last war, soldiers were given a railroad ticket home and $60 mustering-out bonus. In 1936, the special bonus bills at the rate of $1.00 a day for service in the United States and $1.25 a day for service overseas were passed. A system of pensions for disabled soldiers and widows had been developed in the meantime.

"It was only after the last war that the nation attempted seriously to fit fighting men back into a peacetime economy and then it flopped miserably. Within five months of the Armistice, one-third of the men under arms had been thrown back into the labor market. Not all got their jobs back; those who did merely replaced the men who had substituted for them and thus eased the labor problem not at all.

"An interesting article on the *Public Attitude toward Ex-Servicemen after World War I* prepared in the Bureau of Labor Statistics, U. S. Department of Labor illustrates some of the problems that arose in connection with military demobilization at the conclusion of that war, as reflected in the press. The study brought

forth the point of view of the ex-serviceman himself toward each problems as his job and his employer, as well as the attitude of the employer toward the re-employment of the ex-soldier, - sailor, and -marine. The papers indicate also the type of events, regarding returned servicemen, that found their way into the public press at the time. Finally they reveal the major problems that attend demobilization during the post-war dislocation of the industry, some of the effects of the wholesale dismissal of hundreds of thousands of men accustomed to the discipline of Army and Navy life, and—more important—the obvious lack of an effective general re-employment policy involving the cooperation of labor, management, and government throughout the country.

"These episodes happened once, and may happen again at the conclusion of this war, unless effective steps are taken to prevent their recurrence.

"A word should be mentioned about the post-war role of American women. The Women's Advisory Committee of the War Manpower commission called upon Paul V. McNutt for positive and specific planning to preserve the jobs of women as well as of men. The Committee urged experimental programs of re-employment now during what it called the initial stages of reconversion. It stated its recognition of the fact that servicemen are to have their old jobs back if they want them when they return. It added, however, that all evidence so far shows that a relatively small proportion of women now at work will voluntarily withdraw from the labor market after the war and asked that full employment be defined to include all women now at work—those in uniform as well as civilian.

"As Mary Anderson, Director, Women's Bureau, U. S. Department of Labor said in a talk before the American Economic Association January 23, 1944, "We have the example of the last war to prove the need of present planning for future adjustment of women — if we are to keep history from repeating itself in bringing injustices and undue hardships to women. In World War I as in the present conflict womanpower became increasingly valuable— they stepped into the breaches and rendered efficient and indispensable service. Neverthe-

WOMAN LAWYERS SEEK DEMPSEY'S VIEWS
Delegation from the Woman's Bar Association of Illinois calls on John T. Dempsey, Republican nominee for state's attorney, demanding to know his ideas on a multitude of subjects with which he would have to deal if elected. Seated beside Dempsey is Helen W. Munsert, president of the group, standing (from left) J. Fain Tucker, Jeanne Brown, Mary (1944-5) Ramsey and Kathryn Baraso Finella.

Portias Break Masculine Barrier" proclaimed the headline alongside this photo Edna Brown, a DePaul law school senior in 1943.

HONOR AWARD
TO

WOMEN'S BAR ASSOCIATION OF CHICAGO

FOR GENEROUS SUPPORT OF OUR ARMED FORCES, OUR
ALLIES AND OUR HOME FRONT, THROUGH COMMUNITY
AND WAR FUND OF METROPOLITAN CHICAGO, INC.

FOR THE YEAR NINETEEN HUNDRED AND FORTY-FOUR

W.B.A. NEWS

DECEMBER 1945

Service Women....BEA FOX is home on terminal leave from the Coast Guard, looking fit and efficient as she handled the cash at the International Relations Dinner....SYLVIA ZELDEN has been discharged from the WAC and is at home, reported ill. Salute to BEA and SYLVIA for their active participation in the War!

Inter-American....KAY ADAR had a grand time at the Inter-American Bar Conference. She'll tell us all about it at the December meeting.

New Connection....IRENE MC CORMICK is as merry as a grig over her new connection with the firm of Cirese & Cirese. Best wishes for your well-deserved success, Irene!

International.... Congratulations to KAY ADAR and her International Relations Committee for a grand dinner meeting on November 16, 1945. NAWL joined with WBA for the occasion, happy to have our President LULU BACHMAN in town specially for a word of greeting. Tappan Gregory, the featured speaker, really tied the San Francisco Conference up in a bright blue ribbon for us. It was a rewarding evening for the goodly number attending.

Tea.... Your reporter had to miss the annual New Members Tea, but the grapevine tells us that CELESTE CRIST and her Committee turned in an effective performance.

Service Men....HELEN MUNSERT's "Ken" and ELEANOR GUTHRIE's "George" are back from the Wars. Tell us of other husbands' and friends' returning of interest to WBA members.

NAWL Convention.... Paste in your hat the date of the National Association of Women Lawyers Convention in Cincinnati, December 15 and 16, 1945. Plan to attend and make your reservation at once with the Gibson Hotel. Chicago and Illinois are far-famed for live women lawyers. Let's be at this Convention in full force.

Public Office.... Weren't we proud of our "public officers" on display at the November meeting! And wasn't Judge Binks' speech well-received? A fine meeting, everyone thought. Good work on the part of the Public Office Committee.

Member Away.... We have a newsy letter from BLANCHE SIMMONS now in New York City where her husband, Earl, is stationed with the Navy. She says that she will be back in Chicago around the first of the year. She and Earl "had a wonderful time on Navy Day. We saw the President review the fleet of 50 ships in the lower 7 miles of the Hudson River. In fact we spent the afternoon on the riverbank...." Thanks for the letter, Bach. We miss you and look forward to your return.

Sympathy.... We sorrow with ORPHA ROMPF in the loss of her Mother, with BERTHA CARLSON in the loss of her Father, with ANNA NELSON in the passing of her Mother, with MARGARET FITZGERALD in the loss of her Mother and with JOSEPHINE BIRONG, who has lost her Father. Our hearts go out to FANNIE PERRON whose husband passed away late this summer, to HELEN CIRESE on the loss of an Aunt and to EVANGELINE FAHY on the death of her brother. It is devoutly to be hoped that this sad record can be omitted in future issues -- its length at this time is due to covering the period since last summer.

News.... Help this News Sheet by sending items about yourself and your friends to the Secretary.

Thanksgiving.... Though the day will have passed when you receive this, your WBA officers and Board join you in the prayer that peace, now won, may be strengthened and preserved by men of good will throughout the world.

Diomedes.... Don't forget our adopted "brothers" of the U.S.S. Diomedes. Bring your gifts to the Christmas party.

---

less, no sooner had hostilities ceased than a reaction against women workers set in. With this background, let us look into some of the facts and factors of women's employment in the coming post-war period.

"Statistics have a significant story to tell of women in the labor force before, during and after this war. In spring of 1940, 11 million women were employed and an additional 2-1/2 million looking for work. Now there are approximately 16 million women at work with a possible peak of 18 million by the end of the war. That means about 4-1/2 million new women workers in the labor market since the beginning of the emergency. We can expect the flood tide to recede rapidly with the coming of peace to possibly 15 million. School girls, older women working from choice, housewives will gladly give up jobs—but not all. There will probably be more women in their forties and fifties in the labor market than before the war. War casualties and post-war training of servicemen will impose serious breadwinning responsibilities on many of these so-called duration workers.

"In general the unusual wartime opportunities that have opened up to professional women in their chosen fields will not shut down in the future. It seems safe to predict that many women who have performed with outstanding success will be retained in spite of male competition. The success of such women will create a growing demand for others in the new economy which we hope to achieve. Moreover, a larger number of highly trained and competent women will have leading roles on the national and international stage. The number has been deplorably small to date. I'm sure we all concur in her view."

On February 1, 1945, the WBAI sent a letter to Governor Green and Mayor Kelly requesting that a women be considered as a judicial candidate. Plans were made for a May dinner meeting to honor Municipal Court Judges at the Chicago Bar Association, at a cost of $3.00 per person. In April, 1945, there was a discussion about whether to permit individual WBAI members to select a judge to host or whether it was wiser not to have individual hostesses. The WBAI did not want a judge to be unaware that he was a guest of WBAI rather than of "The Particular Girl" who was acting as his hostess.

Helen Cirese was elected to Justice of the Peace. It was noted that the end of the war would restrict rather than enlarge the field of employment since soldiers returning to their former jobs displaced the women lawyers who had filled them. However, WBAI took an optimistic view and hoped that the many new problems coming out of the war emergency would call for the service of women lawyers. In fact Edna Parrington, of the WBAI Job Placement Committee, foresaw stimulating times ahead. She predicted that the next 50 years would be wonderful! In June, 1945, WBAI's membership unanimously voted to endorse U. S. Court of Appeals Judge Florence Allen for a vacancy in the United States Supreme Court. Miss Katherine Nohelty was installed as President at the Annual Meeting on June 7th. (She would later, in 1956, be the first woman to be nominated and elected as a Municipal Court Judge).

A 1945 article about the WBAI noted that the association had embarked upon a unique enterprise. WBAI had sponsored the USS *Diomedes*, a repair ship being converted in a Baltimore ship yard. As part of this undertaking, WBAI members would be "sort of fairy godmothers to the crew; and will send the boys many things that will give them pleasure and recreation. They will send games, cards, books, books and more books, magazines, papers, candies and other confections, any spare musical instruments, radios and so forth.

And to cap it all, they will send inspiring and encouraging letters to the individual members of the crew - letters which will revive the lost art of letter writing. And women lawyers are quite capable of doing just that".

WBAI's membership that year numbered about 181. WBAI sent a letter to Chicago Bar Association lawyers asking for contributions for a fund to be used to further the work on the Mary Bartelme Club. These clubs have provided homes for girls sent to them by the Juvenile Court and other social agencies.

In 1945, an Illinois woman attorney raised the right of a woman to use her maiden name. The issue came before the Supreme Court of Illinois when Antonia E. Rago challenged the right of the Board of Election to require her to register under her married name. The supreme court ruled a constitutional question was involved and remanded the cause for a hearing on the merits, and that year, Jeanne Brown Gordon (WBAI President 1949-1950) initiated the *WBAI News*.

The purpose of a "woman's" law association was then and continues now to be the subject of debate. In December, 1945, Rowland Shepard, an editor of a legal publication, addressed the National Association of Women Lawyers, of which Charlotte Gauer was second vice president and said: The subject assigned me is "Why a Women's Bar Association?" The very topic suggests that you, or in any event, some of the sisterhood of the Bar, entertain doubts as to whether there are compelling reasons for the existence of your organization.

"One of your number several years back, if I remember rightly, challenged the very expression "women lawyers." If a person is a lawyer, she remarked, what difference whether he is man or woman. To refer to a person as a man lawyer or a woman lawyer, she held, made no more sense than to refer to one as a fat lawyer or a skinny lawyer, a blue-eyed lawyer or a bald-headed lawyer.

"The point is not without merit. Yet I think you would be making a serious mistake if you overlooked the cogent reasons for forming an association of women lawyers, based on a community of interest and an area of service that is peculiarly your own.

"There are Bar associations organized on racial and religious lines - the National Bar Association for Negroes, for instance; the Decalogue Society, for Jewish Lawyers; the Guild of Catholic Lawyers. There are Bar associations representing a liberal political faith, as the National Lawyers Guild. There are Bar associations with what seems to me much less justification for existence-national extraction-as, for example, the Polish Bar Association. Then there are horizontal associations devoted to particular fields of law, such as, in New York, the Criminal Courts Bar Association, the Trade and Commerce Bar Association, and many others.

"Why a women's Bar association? I can name three excellent purposes and say to you in all sincerity that if you serve even one of them well, you will have brilliantly justified your organizational existence. These three purposes are: first, to serve the women of the Bar, both within and without your association; secondly, to inspire, to cajole, yes, even to irritate, the traditional Bar organizations; and third, to do for community, country and world what a woman's Bar can do better, perhaps, than any Bar group that comprises both sexes.

"Now, what can you do for the women of the profession? I say you have a stupendous job to do, and that is to lift your professional sisters out of that fog of inferiority that plagues so many of them- that leads them, after they have gone through the same colleges, graduated from the same law schools and passed the same Bar examinations as men, and often with a better scholastic record, to seek to work not WITH but FOR men lawyers, as typists, as secretaries, as a male lawyer's amanuensis but not as his professional equal."

In February, 1946, WBAI and Northwestern University established a fund to purchase books for the Northwestern University Law Library as a memorial to WBAI's third president Catharine Waugh McCulloch (1916-1920). Each book was to be inscribed with a specially designed book plate. WBAI donated $300.00 to Northwestern to fund the memorial, which continues to this day. However, the fund's establishment did cause controversy. Some felt the fund should have gone to Northwestern University and others felt the gift should have been larger. Others believed that a better idea would have been to establish scholarships for women lawyers at various law schools.

In honor of the Judges of the Municipal, County and Probate Courts. (WBAI News reported on May, 1946) the WBAI dinner committee was "working like beavers...the reception will be fun. The dinner will be good. There won't be any long winded speeches. You'll get acquainted with lots of interesting people. Husband, friends, family are welcome as guests..." The June, 1946 News stated: "It is obvious that the judges really appreciate our hospitality and that we are working toward a real tradition."

In July, the Joint Professional Committee

urged, "Promote our members for public office. Let's put a woman on the bench!" In October, the Joint Professional Dinner's charge had gone up to $2.25.

At the October WBAI monthly meeting, WBAI members rose to congratulate Katherine Nohelty on her appointment as Public Defender of Women's Court.

The January, 1947 WBAI News reported a contest between having a Judges' Dinner vs a Dinner Dance. "As we go to press, the Judges' Dinner is leading by a comfortable margin. Late returns may, however, change the results. Be sure and mail your postal card."

According to the April, 1947 WBAI News, "plans for our gala dinner honoring federal court judges are shaping up well under management of Eleanor Young Guthrie and her Ways and Means Committee". The June, 1947 News reported the affair was highly successful...thanks to Eleanor...and the members of her committee. "We believe that these dinners contribute to the advancement of our profession. One highly placed judge remarked to the WBAI president that 'women make just as good lawyers as we do' and he was always glad to have them appear in his court."

At the June 5, Annual Meeting, outgoing president, Dorthea Blender, posed a "serious question" that she wished to be considered: "Why a Women's Bar Association? We are, after all, a minority. It seems our function is to be social, cooperate with other Bar Associations, do our utmost to better the conditions of women and children everywhere. Unless we

carry out these functions, we have no reason to exist as a separate organization."

The year 1947 saw the Women's Bar Association of Illinois still seeking to "put a Woman on the Bench." WBAI president Katherine Agar (1947-1948) wrote all WBAI members noting the newly created Divorce Division and urged a women for one of the judicial spots. Dorthea Blender's Public Office Committee Report for 1947-1948 stated that the position of women attorneys relative to holding public office was "shocking." The report stated that the situation would be remedied eventually but only after rigorous and informed action as well as whole-hearted cooperation with both political parties and other women's groups. The committee urged that this was the time for WBAI to focus special attention on this problem.

On May 13th, it was announced that The Women's Bar Association of Illinois will entertain at a reception and dinner at the Chicago Bar Association's rooms for judges, assistants and clerks of the County Court and Probate and County Court Judges of DeKalb, DuPage, Kane, Lake, and County and Probate Courts.

The June, 1948 WBA News reported the dinner was "pronounced a success...The martinis were delectable, the roast beef delicious and our own lovely members were charming." There were no after dinner speakers. More than 200 guests attended.

The WBAI Placement Committee was still working hard to place WBAI members in jobs. The June, 1948 committee report stated that 42

NORTHWESTERN UNIVERSITY

EVANSTON · CHICAGO

March 23, 1946

To the Women's Bar Association
of Illinois:

ON BEHALF OF THE BOARD OF TRUSTEES AND

THE FACULTIES I ACKNOWLEDGE WITH SINCERE

THANKS THE RECEIPT OF YOUR RECENT GIFT

TO NORTHWESTERN UNIVERSITY.

Franklyn B. Snyder

PRESIDENT

NORTHWESTERN UNIVERSITY

ELBERT H. GARY LIBRARY
OWEN L. COON LIBRARY

SCHOOL OF LAW LIBRARY

Catharine Waugh McCulloch
Memorial Fund

1954

NEED A NICE LAWYER? No, this isn't a waiting room scene in theatrical agency . . . it's anteroom scene in State Supreme court. Gals have just been licensed to practice law in Illinois . . . and who's objecting? Left to right, front row: Helen I. Cohen, Elmhurst; Harriet M. Rosene, Lorraine L. Ring and Jane H. Francis, all of Chicago; back row: Emma H. Boye, Margaret P. Reichardt, Thelma S. Zinner, Margaret G. Baxter, all of Chicago; Monica A. Doyle, Barrington; Mrs. Stratford Rogers, Chicago; Jessie T. Smith, Springfield; Lorraine A. Jung, Chicago; Jeanette L. Stafford, Champaign; Mrs. Noreen G. Bengston and Sylvestern, Chicago. —AP Wirephoto attempts at placement had been made with six members placed and two placed temporarily. An advertisement had appeared daily in the *Chicago Daily Law Bulletin*, courtesy of that newspaper.

WBAI's Board of Directors called attention, on October 2nd, to the fact that the supply of membership cards was more than adequate for the number of applications being made so that it would be inadvisable to print new cards. However, a motion was made and passed that a line be drawn through the word "Race" that appeared on the application card.

WBAI's Board of Directors decided, on December 3, 1948, that any one who had joined WBAI between 1913 through 1921 should be made a life member, due to the poor condition of the records for those years.

A motion carried, on May 11, 1949, that the Public Office Committee be empowered to make endorsements of WBAI members for public office in the name of the association upon a two-third vote of the committee, consisting of not less than ten members. On November 3, 1949, WBAI's president Jeanne Brown Gordon wrote to the President of the United States advising him of WBAI's recommendation that Judge Florence Allen be appointed to the United States Supreme Court. WBAI member Helen Cirese was elected president of the West Suburban Bar Association which consisted of 380 attorneys. Because the organization was 99.44 percent male, the *Sun-Times* (as reported by Bea Fox, editor of the *WBAI News*) called her "the first powder puff prexy" in the history of that association.

One of the high points of 1949 was the annual Judges' party in March which was described as an "important and joyous event."

In the 1950's, Judge Carole Bellows recalls, when she was attending Northwestern Law School, a Chicago Bar Association recruiter for criminal lawyers prohibited women law students from attending the recruitment sessions.

A September, 1950 *Sun-Times* article featured Zenia Goodman as the only woman among 78 State's Attorney's in Cook County assigned to criminal cases. She was assigned to Juvenile Court. Most cases, she said, involved narcotics or sex.

The 1950's also saw efforts turned toward getting women into prominent positions and on the bench. Women lawyers began to toss their hats in the judicial ring. An April 4, 1950 article in the *Chicago Daily Tribune* noted: "Miss B. Fain Tucker and Mrs. Coula P. Butler, both past-Presidents of the Women's Bar Association of Illinois and practicing attorneys...contend they are as qualified for the judgeship as any masculine candidate, perhaps more so in fact."

The Democrats refused to slate a woman for the bench; the first women were slated by the Republicans. With the support of the Women's Bar Association and other organizations, Tucker was elected. She was quoted in the *Chicago Daily News* as giving the credit for her victory to all the women's groups who supported her. In honor of its 25th anniversary, WBAI had a reception and dinner at the CBA. Tickets were $5.50 and the occasion was "informal and business attire proper."

In June 1951, Eleanor Guthrie summarized her year as president with activities done in furtherance of each of WBAI's objectives. Amazingly, this document arrived in my hands in 1991, having been mailed to Eleanor in 1964 by Thelma B. Simon, and mis-laid at the post office until July 30, 1991. Part of the report reads as follows:

"Many of you know that our association has for some years contributed financially to the Mary Bartelme Clubs — founded by one of our members. This year Mary Johnson and I attended their annual meeting. We learned that the Mary Bartelme Clubs care for emotionally disturbed girls referred by the Juvenile Court, other public agencies, private so-cial agencies and private individuals. Emphasis is on helping each girl adjust better in her day by day living. They try to give her enough understanding of herself, her background, and her current problems to assure her of a happier present and a better future life.

"The club has three residences. They look like homes and are run like homes under the direction of a senior housemother.

"In future years it is believed the girls living there will be better homemakers and mothers. We believe they will lead happier lives through the help and understanding they have received in the club during their adolescence. The clubs are worthy of our continued support.

"Ann Goggin at an evening meeting of the Legislative Committee in October, led a discussion of the Subversive Activities Control Act of 1950.

"The Juvenile and Women's Court Committee has constantly blasted the manner in which women are incarcerated and tried and possibly convicted without even the police officer who made the arrest being present. Women tried in the police districts are repeatedly denied the right of having the Public Defender represent them. Our committee and the Committee on Women's Court and Detention Home on which Mary Quinn and Mary Johnson are active members, have done much towards having this situation corrected.

"Alice Chellberg reviewed disability benefit legislation. Richard McVey, Legislative Chairman of the Chicago Office of the Illinois Educational Association, spoke to the committee on educational program requirements.

"Katherine Stimson led a discussion on measures pending before the Illinois General Assembly.

"The Women's Bar Association has taken an active interest in improving the quality of our public servants.

BAR BANQUET--Women members of the bar were hostesses to judges of Cook County at their annual banquet Wednesday night. This banquet group includes (left to right) Judge Hugo M. Friend, appellate court; Attorney Coula P. Butler, president of the Women's Bar Association; Judge Thomas Lynch, circuit court; and Helen M. Cerise, magistrate of Oak Park. (Daily News Photo)

1948-49

NO MAN'S LAND

Stork Beats Former Bar Chief in Race for Bench

By Betty Walker

Chicago Sun-Times
March 3, 1950

CHICAGO BRIEFS

Home's The Place For Women, Judge Says

Is woman's place really in the home?

No doubt about it, said Judge Daniel A. Roberts of Circuit Court in a divorce ruling Monday. In fact, he added emphatically, "if I had my way I would drive all of them out of the factories and back into the home."

When the judge's words got around town, there was a fearsome outcry from some women who work. Mrs. Edna Perraton president of the Women's Bar Assn. summed up the opposition this way: "It would be ridiculous to drive all women out of factories and offices. It would cause a complete breakdown in our economic order. Most women would rather stay home, but have to go to work to help support themselves and their families."

In the divorce action, William

CHICAGO SUN-TIMES, TUESDAY, SEPTEMBER 16, 1952

JUDGE ROBERTS   MRS. EDNA PERRATON

Katherine Agar, a lawyer specializing in international law was named Chicago's "Woman of Distinction" in 1951.

Miss Tucker, Mrs. Butler Are Energetic Women

BY RITA FITZPATRICK

Justice is a lady. At least sculptors have always thought so and now the voters of Chicago will get a chance to decide for themselves in the April primaries. Two Portias are seeking nomination to the Municipal court on the Republican ticket.

They are Miss B. Fain Tucker and Mrs. Coula P. Butler, both past presidents of the Woman's Bar Association of Illinois, and practicing attorneys who contend they are as qualified for the judgeship as any masculine candidate, perhaps more so in fact.

Chicago Tribune—April 4, 1950

B. Fain Tucker is congratulated in 1953 for being the second women elected to to a Circuit Court judgeship.

"We have written letters to the leaders of the two political parties, Mr. Leonard East and Mr. Joseph Gill, requesting them to consider Helen Cirese and Katherine Nohelty for vacancies in the Circuit Court of Cook County. We wrote to Mr. Gill in connection with the appointment of traffic referee, urging the appointment of Katherine Nohelty and Ethel Schiller Zelden. Jeanne Brown, Chairman of the Public Office Committee, and Helen Cirese talked to Mr. Gill upon hearing he was opposed to appointment of a woman as traffic referee alleging certain lobbyists strongly opposed appointment of a woman.

"Letters were written to President Truman and Senator Douglas urging appointment of Helen Cirese as a Judge of the United States District Court for the Northern District of Illinois.

"Progress is slow. In this connection, however, your attention is directed to the record of Mary D. Bailey, a pioneer in women's rights.

"Mary D. Bailey — Assistant United States Attorney for 23 years — was known as one of the nation's most successful prosecutors. She was acting Recorder of Deeds of Kane County. After the death of Frank E. George, woman suffrage had not yet come — she was barred by a ruling of the Illinois Attorney General from becoming a candidate for office.

"Women have progressed. Our two members - B. Fain Tucker and Coula P. Butler - not only were placed on a judicial ticket and received Chicago Bar Association endorsement, but they made an excellent showing in the election for Judges of the Municipal Court. We are grateful for their personal sacrifices.

"Our joint meeting with women from the following fields: real estate, insurance, securities and banking was a kind of public relations. Marie Palumbo worked very hard on this function. 309 people were in attendance. We were proud of Dorothea Blender who without question gave the best speech of the evening.

"Contributions made by business and professional women to the development of Chicago were a feature of a pageant at the Chicago Lakefront Fair on August 22nd. Coula Butler, B. Fain Tucker and your President fulfilled secret stage ambitions. A portion of the pageant was devoted to the history, aims and ideals of WBAI. Our history was prepared with the help of Elsa Beck, Dorothea Blender and Alice Chellberg. It was fun to see how well the representatives of about 25 groups worked together and our Municipal Court candidates received some publicity."

In 1952, the *Chicago Sun-Times* quoted a circuit court judge as ruling that a woman's place is in the home and adding: "If I had my way, I would drive all of them out of the factories and back into the home." Edna Perraton, the president of the WBAI was reported as commenting that it was "ridiculous" and would "cause a complete breakdown in our economic order." However, the fact was that women still played only a tangential role in the legal profession. March, 1952 saw Lillian Kubicek joining the firm of Kirkland & Ellis.

In October, the Committee of Legislation and Constitutional Provisions gave a "Blue Ballot" tea honoring Ward and Township Committee women of the Democratic and

Republican parties. The purpose was to stimulate interest in the proposed Constitutional Amendments to be presented at the November election. Due to the tea and other efforts of the WBAI, the amendments passed.

The January 1953 *WBAI Newsletter* reported that Coula Butler was the sole female judicial candidate. Helen Munsert was the first woman appointed Assistant Commissioner of the Illinois Commerce Commission of Illinois and Grace Stripling was appointed Assistant Attorney for the Chicago Board of Education. Katherine Nohelty had been appointed the first woman traffic referee in Chicago.

In March, there was a police drive to ban unescorted ladies from Chicago bars. WBAI's president, Edna Perraton, stated the law should be thoroughly examined to ascertain if it were discriminatory but if it were not, it should be obeyed.

In April, Coula Butler was appointed by Governor Stratton as the first woman hearing referee in the Retailers Tax Division of the State Department of Revenue.

On May 4, at a Board of Directors Meeting, a letter was read from Governor Stratton acknowledging the WBAI resolution of the Public Office Committee urging appointment of the WBAI member for Public Guardian of Cook County. A letter was also read from the Republican Central Committee of Cook County stating that it would be happy to give women consideration to fill judicial vacancies when a committee had been appointed for that purpose.

The October, *WBAI News* reported that the B. Fain Tucker for Judge Committee included Monica Doyle Reynolds, who had just had her fourth baby a few weeks before but was "looking prettier than ever." The December 1953, *WBAI News* reported that B. Fain Tucker had won her election and that she was the first woman to win a seat in Chicago area election as a judge since Judge Mary Bartelme who had sat in juvenile court from 1923-1933, 30 years before. Judge Tucker, a Republican who was sworn in on November 20, 1953, credited WBAI for her victory. WBAI had distributed thousands of cards to commuters and shoppers calling themselves, "The Apron Brigade." They

had worn sandwich boards, going door-to-door campaigning, deluged the community with postcards and letters and released an avalanche of press releases. Marie Palumbo reported to the newsletter that, "our members promoted a historical victory."

In February, 1954, Myrtle Stryker was reported to be the first Negro woman appointed assistant Attorney General in Illinois and the First Negro woman so appointed in any state.

A 1954 *Chicago Daily Tribune* article reported on an exhaustive survey of the legal profession by the American Bar Association, which revealed that women lawyers must work twice as hard as men for half the pay and probably will have difficulty finding a position with a law firm.

A 1954 Chicago newspaper article featured a photo of several women advising, "No, this isn't a waiting room scene in a theatrical agency....it's the courtroom scene in the State Supreme Court. Gals have just been licensed to practice law in Illinois....and "who's objecting?" The headline read: Need a nice lawyer?

The *Chicago Daily News* reported Coula Butler managed to be both a successful business woman and a good homemaker and was giving a talk on that theme.

In 1954, Eleanor Guthrie made her Report of Delegate to Joint Committee on *Woman's Court and Detention Home*, noting in part:

"During the year the Committee urged appointment of a Public Defender to replace the able Miss Nohelty who, as you know, resigned to take a position as Traffic Referee. In addition, Mrs. Biederman and Miss Park stressed the urgent need for a Public Defender in the Court. To date none has been appointed.

"In April the members of the committee toured County Jail including the Woman's Department. The fact that narcotics may be sentenced to County Jail for five years and that many are sentenced on several offenses for a year for each offense—considered with the fact no rehabilitation or substantially no recreational facilities are available, was disillusioning and frightening to many of the observers. All, however, were impressed with the jail's cleanliness.

"It is felt by the writer that the Woman's

Bar Association of Illinois should never lack interest in conditions, their facilities and program for women sentenced in its penal institutions."

Lillian Kubicek, Chair, of the Public Office Committee reported they had recommended Helen Kelleher as Assistant to Probate Judge of Cook County. She was, in fact, appointed and Fannie Goodman as a school trustee for the Chicago Board of Education. Mayor Daley had acknowledged the recommendation.

In June, the Public Office Committee reported a crowning success: The election of B. Fain Tucker to Judge on the Republican ticket. Efforts to have the names of women lawyers appear on the Democratic ticket for Superior or Circuit Court had been made, but had been unsuccessful. The names submitted were Edna Devlin Bowens, Helen Cirese, Eve Costigan, Katherine Nohelty, and Margaret O'Malley. The committee had endeavored to have a WBAI member appointed to Public Defender for Women's Branch of Municipal Court to succeed Katherine Nohelty, who had been made a referee in traffic court. Names had been submitted to the Honorable Richard Daley, but no appointment had yet been made.

In October, the *WBAI Newsletter* reported that the Public Office Committee was urging WBAI members to affiliate with the political party of their choice to be prepared for the 1956 elections. In November, Winifred Maloney was the first woman attorney sent into a field office in the Department of Agriculture. The December, 1954 *WBAI Newsletter* reported an "All Out Drive" to secure appointment of Judge B. Fain Tucker to Family Court. In January, 1955, Helen Kelleher was the first woman appointed assistant Probate Judge in Cook County.

The May, 1955, *WBAI Newsletter* reported the election of Mary Neff as Alderman in a hotly contested election. WBAI had supported Neff and mailed 1,200 pieces of campaign material on her behalf. In May, Jewel S. Rogers was the first Negro woman to become an assistant U. S. Attorney and Jean Hurley became the first woman assistant state's attorney assigned to Felony Court.

In June, the Joint Professional Committee

Chicago Sun-Times,—March 2, 1953

Barred From Bar Stools, Ladies Table Issue

Eight prominent women greeted a recent police drive to ban unescorted ladies from Chicago bars in the following ways:

1—As an infringement of women's rights.

2—As nothing to get excited about.

3—As an occasion for laughter or for puzzlement.

The law is specific. "It shall be unlawful," it says, "for any licensee, his manager, or any other person in charge of the licensed premises to serve any female person unless she is seated at a table removed from any bar, counter, shelf or substitute therefor, or unless she is accompanied . . by a male escort."

MOST UNWORRIED

But the majority of the women are more worried about the probabilities of being seen unescorted in

MRS. COULA P. BUTLER   MRS. QUINCY WRIGHT

a bar than in the possible anti-feminine discrimination involved in the law.

Here's what they had to say:

Mrs. Coula P. Butler, twice a Republican candidate for the Municipal Court: "Under no circumstances should a woman want to sit at a bar unescorted, although as a

lawyer I can think of instances where such a law, if extended, would violate women's rights."

Lois Higgins, director of the Crime Prevention Bureau: "In their desire for equality women should take on the good habits of men, not their bad habits. We have enough problems now without adding this one. There are plenty of tables if a woman wants to drink."

Mrs. Quincy Wright, director of the Midwest office of the Institute of International Education: "I can't think of anyone getting excited about this, although I do think women look more graceful at tables."

"RIGHTS NOT INVOLVED"

Mrs. Clifton Utley, member of the Board of Education: "I'm afraid I have no serious answer. I'm feminine, not a feminist. I don't think

JESSIE FLORENCE BINFORD   HARRIET E. VITTUM

this has anything to do with women's rights."

Jessie Florence Binford, former executive director of the Juvenile Protective Assn.: "I think there may be a possibility that this violates women's rights. Think of the embarrassment if a decent woman is arrested in a reputable bar." Elaine Stritch, star of "Call Me

Madam": "I'm trying to get out of here after the show for a glass of beer. But I have an escort, thank you. If a couple of girls want to have a drink together, I see nothing wrong with it."

Harriet E. Vittum, long-time campaigner for women's rights and former resident head of Northwestern University Settlement: "In this day and age laws should apply equally to men and women. Women should make their own laws and not drink too much. Then their presence in bars would not be objectionable. And so should men."

Edna G. Perraton, president of the Women's Bar Assn of Illinois: "If we have a law we should obey it. If a law is thought to be discriminatory, we should thoroughly examine it to ascertain whether there is discrimination."

reported that it had held an October Dinner Meeting with women in education and medicine. The Placement Committee noted 13 inquires to hire women attorneys had been received. It recommended that the application form be changed to delete the reference to nationality, descent and religion of an applicant.

The President's report, stated that there were 305 WBAI members, it also reported that Mary Bartelme had died. In 1954-1955, WBAI obtained 18 new members. It hosted a cocktail party for the National Association of Women Lawyers at the Annual Meeting of the ABA.

In the fall of 1955, the WBAI Paternity Act Committee began its work. It wrote hundreds of letters, made numerous trips to Springfield and many appearances at legislative hearings. Mary Avgerin (Pappas) made a report about its activities. The committee's goal was to replace the "Bastardy Act" with a more enlightened Paternity Act. The Paternity Act would more adequately provide for the needs of unfortunate illegitimate children and place the burden of support where it belonged: on the natural parent and not government. In November, The *Chicago Daily News* reported Mayor Daley appointed "Edith Sampson (a Negro)" as the first woman Assistant Corporation Counsel in line with his policy of bringing women into city government. (However in 1928 Kathryn Rinella had worked for the City Attorney of Chicago).

On November 25, WBAI wrote to the Ethics Committee of the Chicago Bar Association, then located at Ten South LaSalle Street, asking whether WBAI would violate Canon 27 of the Code of Ethics of the Chicago Bar Association if WBAI furthered the interviewing of a WBAI member on a certain local television show aimed directly at housewives. The concern was that bringing out the fact that the particular woman interviewed was an attorney might be in violation of the Canons of Ethics. The Chicago Bar Association replied on July 21, 1956 that it would not be a violation of the Canons of Professional Ethics for the WBAI to so proceed so long as "no mention is made of the office address or firm of a person engaged

in the private practice of law. An interview should contain nothing which is laudatory of the person's professional qualifications. Any mention of experience in a particular field of law should be entirely casual and incidental to the remainder of the interview".

In March, 1956 the *WBAI News* reported, "It is still very much news when a large law firm takes a woman as a partner. Partnership seems to be one of the last doors opened to women." The News noted with "special pleasure" that Alice Bright had been made a partner of Sidley, Austin, Burgess and Smith that year. Other contemporaneous partners were Kay

Agar at McDermott, Will and Emery, Lillian Kubicek at Kirkland, Fleming, Green, Martin and Ellis, and Marie Palumbo at Eckart and Peterson.

In April, a Campaign Committee had been set up by the WBAI to elect Katherine Nohelty as Judge with WBAI members named treasurer, chair of radio and TV publicity, chair of newspaper publicity and chair of cocktail parties. In May she became a candidate of the Municipal Court in Chicago-the first woman ever to run with the endorsement of the Democratic Party. Our newsletter reported also that Jeanne Hurley had run ahead in the Demo-

In December 1956 Katharine Nohelty took the bench as the first Municipal Court judge. Top, She is honored by WBAI. Below, the Sun-Times covers the change, noting, "It was strictly ladies' day" in court. (Assistant State's Attorney Mary Ann Grohwih)

1954-1955 Democratic Lawyers Speakers Bureau. L to R: Jeanne Hurley, Helen Kelleher, Edna Perraton, Genieve Zaczek, Margaret O'Malley, Evelyn Laird, Evangeline Fahy, Katheryn Nohelty, Richard J. Daley, Edna Devlin Bowens, Esther Rothstein, Mary Hooton, Margaret McDowell, Mary Jane Lynch, Evelyn von Stein, Leah Brock, Mary Ann Grohwin.

cratic Primary election for State Representative, noting that she was the first woman lawyer, who as Assistant State's Attorney, had been assigned to a Felony Court. Jeanne still comments proudly that the WBAI's gift of $500 enabled her to participate in the campaign for the General Assembly.

In July, our summer outing included our first charterboat trip on Chicago's lakefront, followed by luncheon at the Chicago Yacht Club. Ann Bechly chaired that committee.

In October, the Joint Professional Dinner, under the chairmanship of Charlotte Hornstein, included not only doctor and dentists, but also educators. "Scientific Crime Detection" was the subject.

In that November election, Jeanne Hurley was elected from the Wilmette Evanston area as Representative in the Illinois General Assembly. There she met Paul Simon, a Representative from Troy, Illinois. Several years later they were married and reared a family, and with Jeanne's devoted help he continued his political career, eventually to become United States Senator from Illinois.

Judge B. Fain Tucker, a Republican, with the continued enthusiastic support of the Women's Bar Association and other women's groups, continued to get elected. WBAI also supported Katherine Nohelty, a Democrat. On her behalf, WBAI members addressed and mailed 16,000 cards, sponsored radio and TV publicity, and on election eve, wore sandwich signs and distributed 5,000 cards to the public. She was elected on her birthday, December 3, 1956, and the 50th anniversary of the seal of the Municipal Court of Chicago, which was fitting since she was the first woman to be elected judge in that court.

She wrote the WBAI thanking it for its assistance in financing and helping her campaign. Katherine Nohelty was subsequently installed as the first woman elected to the Municipal Court.

Our Holiday Party in December, 1956, included a puppet show entitled, "The Night Before Christmas" written by Etha B. Fox.

In January, 1957, member Mildred Giese of the Sonnenshein Law Firm presented an analysis of the Judicial Article of the Illinois Constitution at our monthly meeting. In February the WBAI launched the Paternity Act program under the chairmanship of Mary Avgerin (Pappas). The legislation was introduced in February, and with WBAI's backing and financial support and Mary's prodigious work it eventually passed. It was signed on July 6, 1957, by Governor Stratton, replacing the archaic Bastardy Act).

Our March, 1957, dinner meeting was devoted to "Women in Public Office." Fran Utley, a noted radio and television commentator moderated the panel discussion in which Mayor Richard J. Daley, as chairman of the Democratic party of Cook County, and Edward F. Moore as Republic county chairman, participated, as well as women leaders of both parties. The questions, posed, (but not the answers) are in the WBAI records. We honored all of our own members in public office and presented them to the presidents of some 40 leading women's organizations, who were our guests. We endorsed Lucia Thomas for appointment as Assistant States' Attorney, and also endorsed Judge Tucker and Helen Munsert for the next vacancy on the Federal Court Branch. Our president wrote letters on behalf of our endorsees.

On April 24, our president Thelma Brook Simon, formed a special committee for the re-election of B. Fain Tucker as Judge of the Circuit Court of Cook County, and Marguerite McNeil chaired that committee. It sent material to civic oriented clubs, sent press releases, presented a "Tea for Tucker" (actually a cocktail party) and had the use of $500 voted by our Ways and Means Committee. A vignette from Tucker biography: On November 3, 1953, she was the first woman to sit in the Criminal Court; and won re-election in 1957 as a Coalition Candidate of both the Democratic and Republican tickets. Later she sat in the Chancery Branch, which she loved. She was revered as our legal scholar.

April showers and fog in 1957 prevented Edward H. Corsi, Special Assistant to Secretary of State Dulles, and National Director of Immigration, from flying from New York to address our dinner meeting, arranged by the Current Law Committee under the co-chairmanship of Lillian Kubicek and Donna Klingbiel Simpson. Within hours that committee arranged a distinguished panel program of authorities on the subject of Immigration.

Our Younger Members Committee, chaired by Ann Lutterbeck and Catherine Vlachos, arranged in May a Cocktail and Ice Show Party for the membership. Lucia Thomas (subsequently Cook County Circuit Court Judge) and Mary Ann Grohwin (McMorrow) (now Justice of the Appellate Court of Illinois) presented a program on Juvenile Delinquency, in which distinguished members of the clergy and judiciary analyzed the problems. Our membership Committee, chaired by C. Lois Samuelson, in an effort to expand our membership, invited the women seniors of the various law schools to be our guests.

The WBAI Annual Dinner in June, 1957, arranged by Berenice Gremmels, as chairperson, with the major assistance of Katherine Agar, presented our honored guest speaker, Pauline Fredrick, the first distinguished National Broadcasting Company woman commentator. In June, 1957, the Membership Committee reported that letters to Illinois law schools had produced the names of 15 women seniors. Each was invited to the May dinner. There were 6 acceptances.

Throughout the 1956-57 year the WBAI maintained a Speaker's Bureau and Job Survey conducted by our Public Relations Committee, chaired by Leila Foster; and sent WBAI delegates to meetings of civic organizations, a practice which we hoped would enhance our visibility and stature.

In 1958 dues were $5.00 for lawyers admitted less than five years and $10.00 for lawyers admitted more than five years.

On January 8, 1959 WBAI amended its by laws. That year one WBAI member filed a grievance against another, charging her with "having consciously and knowingly assumed...distinctions to which she is not entitled" such as being the first woman to practice before the United States Supreme Court and the first of her sex to practice in the Criminal Court, etc. Teddy Gordon announced, in 1959, there had been several requests to the Placement Committee for the services of women attorneys. A memorial resolution was passed, honoring WBAI past President, Elsa Beck, who died June 15, 1959. She had established and for several years chaired the Emergency Fund Committee. The September, *WBAI News* reported that a woman had been named to the Chicago Bar Association Board of Managers for the first time: Helen Munsert. It was also announced that *Her Father's Partner*, written by Alice McClanahan Malik, had been published. Jeanne Hurley Simon was the only woman attorney in the State Legislature. She was also WBAI's president in 1959-1960. In December, *WBAI News* carried an article written by Francis Spooner reporting that Illinois had the distinction of having had the first woman lawyer elected to serve as National Committee Woman of either party. Her name was Bertha P. Bauer and she served as Republican Committee Woman in 1928. She was the second woman to

June, 1958, Charlotte Horstein, President WBAI. L to R Lucia Thomas, Esther Rothstein, Theodora Gordon, L. Berenice Gremmels, Lois Samuelson, Jean Harth, Helen McGillicuddy, Charlotte Hornstein.

serve in that post. (She had been a WBAI member, too.)

In 1969 the January, *WBAI News* reported efforts at reviving the old tradition of inviting Judges to guests at dinner. The September newsletter reported Jeanne Simon and Representative Paul Simon were the first husband-wife team in the Illinois House of Representatives. Television showed Jewel Stratford Rogers seconding a nomination at the Republican Convention. Soia Mentschikoff, Professor of Law at the University of Chicago, stated in the October News, that women are naturally attuned to the practice of law and have an instant understanding of the art of negotiation and persuasion, while it takes three years of law school to teach that to men. On October, 3, Marie Palumbo raised the question of long-term goals and projects of the association. The discussion was postponed until the January 3, 1961 meeting where the topic was discussed. It was agreed that projects which were important were as follows:

1. The study of problems of releasing unadoptable foster children for adoption.
2., To promote the Judicial Article
3. To study legislation on vote fraud.
4. To assist the Girl Scouts.
5. To reorganize the speakers bureau.
6. To cooperate for better Jury rooms.
7. To study Penal Institution Reforms.
8. To plan a Judge's dinner.

On June 20, the Public Office Committee reported that it had met with a representative of the *Tribune* newspaper, who had suggested an all-woman slate. The Public Office Committee also met with Mayor Daley urging including women on the slate for elective offices. In September, WBAI received an Award of Merit from the Illinois State Bar Association for its outstanding programs to the public in its Family Court Project.

In October, the League of Women Voters indicated it was "disturbed" over WBAI access to a list of LWV unit Chairmen since this list was intended for League use only. No reply was received to WBAI's response.

Judge-elect Helen McGillicuddy, attended the November Board Meeting and modeled her new judicial robe, a gift of WBAI. She personally thanked the board for WBAI's support of her candidacy and noted that WBAI president, Delores Hanna would be speaking on behalf of WBAI at her induction.

Even the 1960s did not provide a hospitable atmosphere for aspiring women lawyers. A 1963 law review article quoted law firm partners as admitting they discriminate against women lawyers and "the girls agree." Of all "deviant" groups, women were found the least desirable - blacks, minorities, rural, or blue-collar background lawyers were preferred.

Charlotte Adelman recalls that women students at the University of Chicago Law School, were prohibited from attending law firm job recruitment sessions.

In 1963 Etha B. Fox, Editor of *WBAI Newsletter*, noted in the January News that Judge McGIllicuddy's election to the bench was an "encouraging sign" for women law students.

A WBAI special candidate's committee report was filed on January 12, reporting that the committee had actively promoted the candidacy of several WBAI members: Jewel LaFontant for Judge of Superior Court, Helen McGillicuddy, for Judge of Municipal Court, Antonia Herbert for Suburban County Commissioner, Catherine Anagnost for Municipal Court Judge and Edith Sampson for Judge of the Municipal Court. The report noted that WBAI members had hosted 25 coffees for friends and neighbors, sent letters to 85 presidents of Women's Club, mailed 11,000 cards, issued publicity releases, obtained spot radio announcements and television coverage. As a result, Helen McGillicuddy had won and so had Edith Sampson. There had been a good showing for the rest of the candidates.

The chairs of the committee, Stella Cuthbert and Mary Hooton, stated that the effort showed the power of WBAI. Election results showed that those precincts which had been worked by WBAI had resulted in more votes for our candidates that those received elsewhere throughout the county and city.

The June president's report stated that Family Court Committee had assisted as counsel for parties requesting representation and had reported an immediate need for separate facilities for dependent children. In June, Matilda Fenberg, an Associate Attorney in the offices of Clarence Darrow, told the membership of circumstances attendant upon her receiving her law degree from Yale University, nunc pro tunc, as it were, after many years.

In October, the Public Office Committee was authorized to appear before the Central Committee of the Democratic Party of Cook County and urged that Margaret O'Malley be appointed Magistrate.

Joan Fleming organized a WBAI scrapbook. (Editors note: If you locate historical WBAI material, please turn it over to WBAI for

Women's Bar Unit Honors Judges

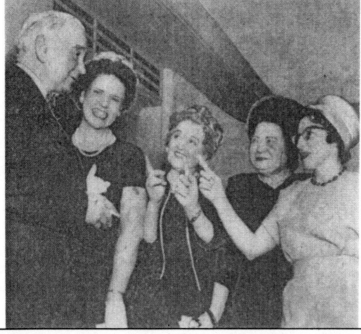

Chicago Tribune—1962. Augustine Bowe, chief justice of Municipal court, getting a "decision" at annual judge's dinner of the Women's Bar Association of Illinois. With him, from left, are Helen McGiullicuddy, Judge Helen Kelleher, Judge B. Fain Tucker, and Esther Rothstein, WBAI president.

our Chicago Historical Society collection.) The Christmas meeting featured a skit which Etha B. Fox wrote entitled. "The Case of the Concerned Will."

The Civil Rights Act, with its prohibition against discrimination in employment because of sex, among other categories, was passed in 1964. This was the turning point and gave women the incentive and right to enter the legal profession. They began to do so in large numbers. But attitudes about women as lawyers did not change with the same speed. Change did not become apparent until late in the 1960s and early in the 1970s.

In 1964 Margaret O'Malley and Marilyn Komosa were appointed Magistrates of the Circuit Court on June 1. Public Office Committee Chair Mary Hooton, conferred with Judge Augustine Bowe, head of the Municipal Court Division, regarding whether WBAI should recommend Edith Sampson as Associate Judge. He advised after serving on the CBA's Board of Managers and Judicial Evaluation Committee, that neither Judge

Sampson or B. Fain Tucker had received "Squares" to which they were entitled in the CBA poll. He said they had the strike of being a woman held against them. Noting that the CBA poll was little more than a measure of popularity, be urged the WBAI to act independently and not to rely on the poll of another organization, Mrs. Hooton also conferred with Chief Judge John Boyle. He confirmed the good job Judge Sampson was doing. He also urged the WBAI to rely on its own judgement and not be dependent on the CBA. The Public Office Committee then endorsed Judge Sampson by a vote of 8 to 1. It also endorsed Judge Tucker. The WBAI Board voted to concur.

On December 4, the WBAI contacted Governor Otto Kerner to request that Evalyn Walsh Laird be appointed Public Guardian. The Governor's assistant, Dawn Clark responded. WBAI prepared a letter to officials to contact WBAI for suggestions for qualified women to serve in public offices. In 1966 Governor Kerner declared July 26 to be Judge

'Mommy' Now 'Madame Magistrate' in Court

Mrs. Anagnost Files for Office

(1963)

50th Anniversary Celebration, Womens Bar Association of Illinois, April 21, 1964. L to R: Thelma Brook Simon, Chairperson 50th anniversary Celebration, Judge Helen Kelleher, Chief Justice Ray Klingbiel, Supreme Court of Illinois, Sylvia Cervenka, President.

41

Mary Bartelme Day On that day, the first recipient of the newly established Mary Bartelme WBAI Scholarship received her award.

Antonia Rago Herbert was quoted in *Woman's News* that summer as saying, "In order to succeed as a lawyer, a woman must work twice as hard as a man," in a full page feature article. In 1967 the WBAI endorsed proposed legislation to require gun registration. Two years later, members were urged to oppose repeal of the law.

In June, Mary Berkemeir Quinn died. WBAI passed a resolution in her honor, noting she was the Cook County Public Guardian for 1943 to 1959, and had run for Association Judge of Municipal Court in 1938 and 1938 and had run for Circuit Court Judge in 1939.

At the December general meeting, Esther Rothstein reported that the Judge Mary Bartelme Scholarship Committee would recommend the establishment of a WBAI Foundation, to give scholarships to deserving women law students The foundation was created that year and has continued even after to award scholarships to female law students.

In 1968 the February, *WBAI News* reported that Mary Pappas was the first woman to become an Illinois Institute for Continuing Legal Education faculty member, and in March, the News reported a contribution had been made to the Foundation in honor of Virginia Dunlap, who had died of burn injuries.

The WBAI committee on Opportunity for Employment for Women Attorneys surveyed job opportunities for women. It evaluated Sullivan's Law Directory to determine whether firms hired women attorneys. It considered ways to expand job opportunities for women lawyers. On April 19, 1968, each WBAI member was sent a questionnaire. It contained numerous questions.. Had any prospective employers stated a policy against hiring women attorneys, or expressed a favorable attitude toward hiring women attorneys? What were the obstacles or opportunities relevant to women in private practice? The questionnaire explored the role WBAI members wanted the organization to play relative to helping women lawyers obtain employment.

The June, the Public Office Committee Report recommended, and the Executive Board approved, a letter to the Governor urging the appointment of Jeanne Gordon to the Industrial Commission, and that WBAI members be appointed for Con-Con study. The Placement Committee Report noted 22 members had sought assistance. Three job requests from employers had been received, the Con-Con committee reported that its recommendation that Con-Con be endorsed had been approved by the WBAI.

The Con-Con Committee prepared a pamphlet to explain the importance of the Blue Ballot and distributed 5000 copies. Fifteen hundred postcards and many letters to the editor and press releases were sent. After the Blue Ballot passed, the WBAI approved the Committee's view that elections be non-partisan. The Membership Committee reported it had solicited 172 law students, 28 had joined as well as 11 new admittees.

In October, the *WBAI News* reported that on June 28, 1968, WBAI members had hosted

Hirsch High School girl students who wanted to observe a woman lawyer at work. On October 3, WBAI wrote to the County Commissioner to urge that the new Audy Home be used solely for delinquent children and to provide a separate facility for neglected and dependent children, as well as upgrading the attendant's salaries.

In 1969 on January 9, WBAI cast a resolution to advocate repeal of sanctions against abortions which licensed physicians perform. WBAI took the position that the individual should make her decision in light of medical advice received and her individual conscience. WBAI was authorized to publish the resolution, work for repeal of sanctions against abortion and establish a permanent committee to reform the abortion laws. On June 19, WBAI's Board endorsed the candidacy's of Odas Nicholson and Mary Pappas as delegates to the Illinois Constitutional Convention.

The 100th Anniversary of the Admission of Women to Practice Law in the United States was celebrated in Illinois in 1969, and proclamations were issued by Governor Ogilvie and Mayor Daley. That same year, women from two Chicago law schools charged their schools with sex discriminations. One charge concerned the law school's refusal to permit its female students to participate in the on-campus job interviewing process. Also that year, complaints were filed against two Chicago area banks for refusing to hire women attorneys. The polite resolutions of the 1930s had

been replaced by lawsuits. Responses to questionnaires sent to Chicago area firms indicated several firms felt that after having employed women attorneys, they would not hire another one.

The June, 1968 *WBAI News* reported the results of the 1968 questionnaire on employment for women attorneys. The report was prepared by Edith Graham and Helen Porter. Sixty had responded out of 350. It was concluded that there was considerable discrimination against women lawyers. Reasons given were unfavorable attitudes of clients, instability of the feminine temperament and excessive interference of family life. The report stated the objections were rooted in social and psychological attitudes, not because of any averment of lack of competence. Some respondents stated they felt discrimination was minimal and success depended on one's own attitudes and capabilities. Those in solo practice or with a partner appeared the happiest and least bothered by discrimination. They were also the most successful financially.

The report found members viewed WBAI's role to be providing effective job placement and central communication about appointments for women. Public relations efforts to sensitize the public about women attorneys' abilities and achievements were also suggested. A very few felt there was no justification for WBAI's existence. The question was not to disband but how to expand. Also urged was an interest in development of legal

Illinois Governor Richard Olgivie, Chicago Mayor Richard J. Daley and WBAI all recognized 1969 as the Women Lawyers Centennial because on June 18, 1869 Belle A. Mansfield of Mount Pleasant, Iowa became the first woman admitted to the Bar in the United states

education programs and increased participation in political and controversial issues. It seemed implicit that WBAI had an obligation to act with regard to voter education programs and perhaps as a pressure or lobbying group. The formation of a special committee to brainstorm WBAI's role was suggested.

In July, a member wrote a letter to the WBAI using her maiden name. She asked that in the future all mail to her be sent to her in her maiden name and not as Mrs. (for example) John Jones. She advised that she was known as Mrs. John Jones only after 5:00 p.m. and that the office staff didn't know Mrs. John Jones.

In November, WBAI approved a Northwestern law student's request to use the WBAI addressograph plate without cost to send a questionnaire on discrimination against women lawyers to the membership.

In December, WBAI's general membership passed a motion that WBAI write to the President of the Untied States urging that women be appointed to the Federal Judiciary and also to the United States Supreme Court.

The CBA sent WBAI a letter noting that it was "sad that .25 cents must be added to the basic price of new banquet menus. Drink prices will be increased only a dime....effective 11-15-69."

In 1969 the *Chicago Daily News* announced, "Bar Barriers Down". The article noted from 5% or less of the student body several years ago, women have grown to 10% or the new freshmen at John Marshall Law School and 16% of the University of Chicago Law School. Despite the headline, those interviewed indicated some prestigious firms still weren't hiring women, or at best, a token woman, and a few deans and professors still made women uncomfortable in class.

Lois Dierstein was WBAI President in 1969-70. In January, 1970, WBAI's Board voted to recommend to the membership that WBAI join in an amicus brief with the Committee on Medical Control of Abortion, in a test case challenging the Illinois abortion law. WBAI filed its own brief Amicus Curia in federal court in 1970. It was written by Helen Hart Jones, Sheli Z. Rosenbert, Patricia E. Mullin and Margaret M. Eisendrath, and urged that the present Illinois abortion statute violated the 14th amendment to the U.S. Constitution.

The January 1970 *WBAI Newsletter* reported on the origin of the WBAI Emergency Fund. It recounted that it had been formed in 1930-31, when Helen Cirese was WBAI president, because members were in financial need. The fund was empowered to make needy members loans. Instead of its usual annual banquet, WBAI had a card party that year to raise money for the fund. Six hundred and thirty four dollars was raised. It paid for burial expenses of some members who died penniless in the 1930s as a result of the crash.

Odas Nicholson was elected Secretary to the Illinois Constitutional Convention, and Mary Pappas was elected the first woman president of the Chicago Association of Immigration Lawyers.

That year Edith Graham presented WBAI's views on tax laws before the Constitutional Convention Revenue Committee, and WBAI endorsed the candidacies of Jeanne Brown Gordon for Cook County Board, Florence Dunbar for Tax Board of Appeals, and Jewel Lafontante for Federal Judge, with letters sent to President Nixon urging her appointment.

Edith Graham moved, on March 30, that WBAI be listed in the telephone book. The motion was seconded but defeated.

At the May 7, general meeting the membership approved WBAI's participation as an endorser of the CBA-ISBA joint plan for "merit selection" of judges.

In June, 1970, Lois Dierstein issued her outgoing president's report, noting that women from two Chicago law schools had charged their schools with sex discrimination, and that complaints had been filed against two banks, charging sex discrimination. Law school questionnaires had been sent to Chicago area firms about hiring women attorneys. Several firms indicated that after having employed a woman attorney, they would not hire another one. Numerous telephone inquires had been received by WBAI with questions ranging from WBAI's positions on abortion and Con-Con to information about women lawyers for their daughter's college papers.

The November 2nd Board Meeting, Helen Porter reported that 31 women had passed the Illinois Bar and were invited to our Holiday Party and Dinner Meeting in December as our guests. She also reported that Tala Engel had been excluded from participation in the CBA annual musical show, Christmas Spirits. WBAI voted to write the CBA President, copies to the Board of Managers, requesting an official statement as to women attorneys' participation in CBA committee work, the entertainment committee and attendance at summer golf outings.

Tala Engel filed a lawsuit in the United States District Court against the Chicago Bar Association to compel integration for its all-male cast. Her suit was dismissed, but in 1971, the cast was integrated by including Engel and Chole Arlan. Ever since, women lawyers have taken part in each of the productions.

Patricia Mullen was WBAI president in 1970-1971. In February, Carol Petersen, Chair of the Advancement of Women Committee, reported that placement directors from local schools were speaking on placement of women law students at a program entitled "Women Law Students and the Job Market". Also, WBA was filing an amicus brief in support of the federal lawsuit filed by the ACLU/NOW, handled by Charlotte Adelman and Sheribel Rothenberg. The suit challenged the major Chicago newspapers' practice of running sex segregated help wanted ads, stating that when they did so they acted as employment agencies and thus violated Title 7 of the Civil Rights Act. WBAI voted to file the amicus brief. WBAI's brief was written by Carol M. Petersen, Helen Hart Jones, Stephane Kanwit and Loretta Didzerekis, (now Douglas) and was also brought on behalf of the Illinois Federation of Business and Professional Women's Clubs and Womens' Equity Action League. Carol

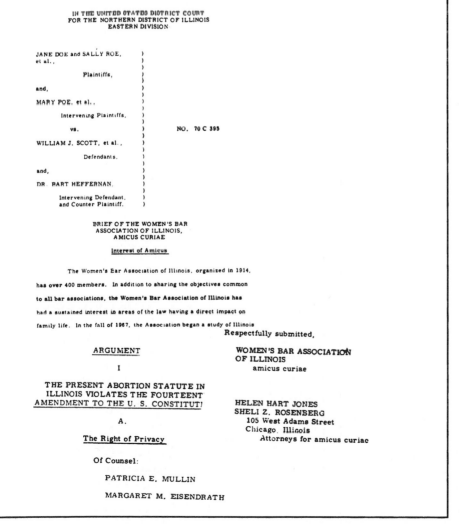

IN THE UNITED STATES DISTRICT COURT
FOR THE NORTHERN DISTRICT OF ILLINOIS
EASTERN DIVISION

JANE DOE and SALLY ROE, et al.,   )
)
            Plaintiffs,   )
)
and,   )
)
MARY POE, et al,,   )
)
        Intervening Plaintiffs,   )
)
            vs.   )   NO. 70 C 395
)
WILLIAM J. SCOTT, et al.,   )
)
            Defendants.   )
)
and,   )
)
DR. BART HEFFERNAN,   )
)
        Intervening Defendant,   )
        and Counter Plaintiff.   )

BRIEF OF THE WOMEN'S BAR
ASSOCIATION OF ILLINOIS,
AMICUS CURIAE

Interest of Amicus

The Women's Bar Association of Illinois, organized in 1914, has over 400 members. In addition to sharing the objectives common to all bar associations, the Women's Bar Association of Illinois has had a sustained interest in areas of the law having a direct impact on family life. In the fall of 1967, the Association began a study of Illinois

Respectfully submitted,

ARGUMENT

I

THE PRESENT ABORTION STATUTE IN
ILLINOIS VIOLATES THE FOURTEENT
AMENDMENT TO THE U. S. CONSTITUT?

A.

The Right of Privacy

Of Counsel:

PATRICIA E. MULLIN

MARGARET M. EISENDRATH

WOMEN'S BAR ASSOCIATION
OF ILLINOIS
amicus curiae

HELEN HART JONES
SHELI Z. ROSENBERG
105 West Adams Street
Chicago, Illinois
Attorneys for amicus curiae

Papers sued over 'male, female' ads

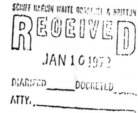

MEMORANDUM OF WOMEN'S BAR ASSOCIATION OF ILLINOIS,
THE ILLINOIS FEDERATION OF BUSINESS AND PROFESSIONAL
WOMEN'S CLUBS, INC. AND THE FIRST DISTRICT THEREOF,
AND THE WOMEN'S EQUITY ACTION LEAGUE IN OPPOSITION
TO DEFENDANT CHICAGO TRIBUNE COMPANY'S MOTION TO
STRIKE AND DISMISS AND DEFENDANT FIELD ENTERPRISES
INC.'S MOTION FOR A MORE DEFINITE STATEMENT

STATEMENT

Plaintiffs allege that defendants are violating the
provisions of Title VII of the Civil Rights Act of 1964, §§703(b)
and 703(c) (42 U.S.C. §§2000e-2(b) and 2000(c), hereinafter
called the "Act") by requiring that all help-wanted advertising
be classified on the basis of sex.

Carol H. Peters
231 S. LaSalle
Chicago, Illinois

Helen Hart Jones
105 West Adams
Chicago, Illinois

Stephanie Kanwit
135 S. LaSalle
Chicago, Illinois

Lorraine Dimoswskis
U.S. E.E.O.C.
Chicago, Illinois

Kipperman, counsel for the EEOC, also filed a brief in support of WBAI's position. In April, Patricia Mullen represented WBAI and spoke at the installation of Olga Jurco as Magistrate of the U.S. District Court.

In March, WBAI wrote to Senator Charles Percy, who was reportedly stalling on the appointment of a woman Senate page, whose appointment would be a first, urging her appointment.

In October, a letter from a member was read to the Board regarding an episode when she had been refused use of the women's restroom at the Chicago Bar Association. In view of the fact that she had received a letter of apology from Jack Fuller of the CBA, WBAI felt there was no need to act.

Georgia Lipke was WBAI president in 1971-72. The *WBAI News* reported that Judge McGarr had dismissed the suit challenging sex segregated help wanted ads. Thereafter, the *Tribune* decided to integrate the ads and the other newspapers were following suit.

In her president's report in June, 1972, Georgia Lipke noted that on September 10, 1971, the WBAI Foundation had presented its 6th scholarship award which had been given to Elaine Bucklo. WBAI had issued a letter which had been sent to every member of Congress urging support of the Women's Equality Act of 1971.

Helen Viney Porter was WBAI President in 1972-1973. WBAI voted to change its annual Holiday Party into an annual benefit for the WBAI Foundation Scholarship Fund. WBAI member Sara Kamin's death was noted and a memorial made for her. Her lawyer children included Carol Kamin Bellows.

On April 5, 1973, WBAI held a reception and dinner honoring the Judiciary at the CBA in honor of the Illinois Supreme Court, the Illinois Appellate Court (1st and 2nd district), the 12th, 16th, 18th, 19th Cook County Circuits of Illinois.

Odas Nicholson reported that a male attorney had inquired about membership. The Board decided men should be admitted and an application should be sent to him. It was pointed out that the San Francisco Women's Bar Association had benefited from admitting men because those men who joined were interested in promoting women's rights. The By Law Committee was instructed to prepare appropriate amendments to the By-Laws to enable men as well as women to be WBAI members.

In her President's Report, Helen Viney Porter reported she had only one disappointment: the ERA had not been ratified in Illinois. The records for that year show that committees were actively involved in planning ways to "fight sex discrimination".

Dorthea Blender died. A resolution was prepared by Thelma Brook Simon. Commerce Clearing House gave a scholarship in her memory.

Odas Nicholson (now a Circuit Court Judge) was WBAI President in 1973-1974. It was noted that WBAI members Stephanie Kanwit and Helen Hart Jones had sued private clubs for refusing to admit women. The theory was by so doing, private clubs violated the State Liquor License Law.

The Board opposed the Buckley Amendment which would prohibit abortion except to save a woman's life and extend equal protection to the unborn. The Board voted continued support to the Equal Rights Amendment and urged the membership to do so.

Robert Lyon's application for membership was received. Mary Hooton moved that the by laws be suspended for purposes of amending the by laws to permit men to join. It passed by over 2/3 vote. Katherine Abraham moved and it was seconded that the by-laws be amended to permit male membership. All present, except two, voted "yes". Thereafter, Lyon's admission to WBAI as a member was objected to on the basis that proper notice for changing the by-laws had not been given and thus men could not be admitted. It was noted that no objection was made as to Mr. Lyon's eligibility or qualifications. The parliamentarian said the by laws could not be suspended and that all action had been null and void. Because of WBAI's failure to admit Mr. Lyon, several WBAI members resigned. Several newspapers incorrectly reported WBAI had voted to permit male members.

WBAI member State Representative Adeline Geo-Karis wrote WBAI explaining she had been unable to attend a meeting because of obligations relative to running for re-election and she had won, leading the ticket. Watergate prosecutor Jill Wine Banks, (then Volner) had a name for male lawyers' comments about women lawyers such as: young lady, sweetheart: "sexual trial tactics".

Mary Ann McMorrow (now an Appellate Court Justice) was WBAI president in 1974-1975. Programs were presented to inform WBAI members how to become a more potent force in politics, to explain the operation of the court system under the new Constitution and to inform members about recent Supreme Court decisions. It was noted that Esther Rothstein had achieved the distinction of being nominated for 2nd Vice President of the CBA, putting her in line for the presidency. It was the first time in the 100 year history of the CBA that a woman had been nominated for that position. Another first was Carole Bellows, who became the first woman VEEP of the Illinois State Bar Association.

The Annual Reception and Dinner in honor of the Judiciary featured Judge James Parsons of the U.S. District Court. He spoke on women lawyers in Illinois. The chief judges of five courts: Robert Sprecher, Circuit Court of Appeals, Justice Daniel McNamara-Illinois Appellate Court, Judge Eugene Wachowski-acting Chief Judge of Circuit Court of Cook County were guests of WBA. Dinner was Prime Rib of Beef for $8.50.

Dr. Rowine Hayes Brown was WBAI president in 1975-76. WBAI voted to become a voting member of ERA Illinois. It was noted that WBAI had 350 members and 26 new members had joined.

For the April Judges reception, instead of a dinner, cocktails and hors d'oeurves were served. (Editors Note: and have been ever since) The *WBA Newsletter* found this more appealing that the traditional dinner for judges.

Entertainment: excerpts from Christmas Spirits.

In December, 1976, Helen McGillicuddy was the first woman elected to the Appellate Court.

Mary Hooton (now a Circuit Court Judge) was WBAI President in 1976-1977.

As late as 1977, the ISBA was still issuing its public education pamphlets, such as Know Your Lawyer, depicting attorneys exclusively as male, a practice to which Mrs. Hooton objected.

At the request of the WBAI, ISBA agreed to revise them and thereafter refer to attorneys as "he or she" instead of "he". That same year, both the ISBA and the CBA were headed for the first time by women attorneys, Carole Bellows and Esther Rothstein.

On June 23, 1977 it was voted to present a plaque to Carolyn Krause in recognition of her achievement in becoming Mayor of Mount Prospect.

WBAI urged that federal funding should be permitted for abortions for women who qualified for federal medical assistance. It also urged adoption of an amendment to the Civil Rights Act of 1964 banning discrimination against pregnant workers.

On October 20, 1977 Matilda Fenberg died. She was the first woman to receive a law degree from Yale University Law School, and had been closely associated with famed attorney, Clarence Darrow, and written numerous articles about him.

Katherine Abraham was WBAI President in 1977-1978. The Honorable Margaret O'Malley presented a WBAI position paper on "merit selection". Eleven of the 12 Board members polled favored election of judges instead of selection. WBAI also objected to the use of the term "merit selection" as accuracy would require it be termed a choice between the elective and appointive process of judicial choices. WBAI felt politics would never be completely eliminated from judicial choices,

The Bar News—May, 1974

(March, 1972)

Important Notice to Help Wanted and Employment Agency Advertisers and to those Seeking Employment.

Chicago Today Classified has combined most Help Wanted advertising into one classification. Classifications formerly headed "Help Wanted—Men," "Help Wanted—Women" and "Help Wanted—Men and Women" appear under the single classification "Help Wanted, Men and Women." Job offers are listed alphabetically for your convenience.

Similarly, other classifications which have been combined but appear separately from "Help Wanted, Men and Women" are "Employment Agencies, Men and Women," "Employment Service, Men and Women," Help Wanted, Part Time, Men and Women," "Help Wanted with Investment, Men and Women," "Help Wanted, Household Help, Men and Women" and "Help Wanted—Couples."

For your further convenience, you will now find many outstanding job offers listed alphabetically in the Help Wanted columns by Employment Agencies.

For complete classification listings, consult the Classified index.

Women's Bar Assn. Now Open To Men

CHICAGO — The 60-year-old Women's Bar Association of Illinois has opened its membership to male lawyers, the group announced. By-laws of the organization have been revised to provide that words of the feminine gender shall be construed to include the masculine gender, and the word "woman" shall also be deemed to include the word "man."

However, the purpose of the association, to promote and advance women lawyers will not be affected by the new decision, according to a statement by the group's president, Odas Nicholson.

regardless of the system used. "Merit selection" merely would shift the opportunity to influence and control, and the proposed method would lead to "panel stacking". WBAI favored election over selection.

Esther Rothstein became the first woman named to the Illinois Bell Telephone Company Board.

On April 3, 1978 WBAI's Board voted to support an amendment to the Illinois Marriage and Dissolution of Marriage Act which would provide for automatic enforcement of child support payments. WBAI members were urged to support the April 29th ERA march and attend an ERA party sponsored by the Illinois Women's Political Caucus.

It was noted that the lawsuit filed to prohibit private clubs from refusing to serve women had been ruled against by the Appellate Court.

Hon. Margaret O'Malley was WBAI President in 1978-79. Testimony was presented by WBAI members urging passage of the child support collection amendments to the Dissolution of Marriage Act.

Dawn B. Schulz was president in 1979-89. Her President's annual report recalled that in July, 1979, WBAI celebrated its 65th anniversary. WBAI's Foundation awarded $3,000.00 in scholarships. WBAI sponsored a Law Day Program with the Federal, State and Chicago Bar Association for new citizens. WBAI participated in filing two amicus briefs in Federal Court and financially supported an amicus brief submitted in State Court written by one of our members. WBAI wrote to the Chicago Law Bulletin about a discriminatory ad and it changed the ad's wording. WBAI had a registered lobbyist in Springfield, Paddy Harris McNamara. It had speakers available through its speaker's bureau. It formed a Law School Liaison Committee. WBAI marched for and financially supported passage of ERA, worked for child support collection legislation and on the issue of battered women.

At the April 5th - Judge's Reception, invited for the first time were all full Circuit Court Judges as WBAI's guests in addition to Judges from the Supreme, Appellate and Federal Courts.

Teresa Conway was WBAI President in 1980-81. In her president's letter in March 1981, Teresa commented that "many women seem discouraged by what seems to them to be a slow down in the improvement of the status of women." The *Chicago Tribune* had stated that women are underrepresented in the ABA. But she reminded WBAI members of Susan B. Anthony who overcame taunts and ridicule in her determination to seek equality for women.

The October, 1980, *WBAI News* ran an article entitled, *WBA's Splendid Victory* by Elsie Holzwarth chronicling WBAI's work on child support. Collection legislation starting with Charlotte Adelman's leading a conference in March, 1975 at the YWCA, the work of Charlotte, Jeanette Blum, Georgiana Daskais, Betty Gallo, Marcie Abrams, Elsie Holzwarth and Gabrielle Peiper and which culminated on September 12, 1980, by Governor Thompson signing into Law HB 24.

In her President's Report, Teresa Conway noted WBAI had presented a "Trial Practice Potpourri" demonstrating trial technique, a domestic violence panel of experts and a program updating progress in the child support law. The Law School Liaison Committee has met with a enthusiastic response from law students. WBAI had a group swearing in at the USSC.

Loretta Douglas (now Judge Douglas) was WBAI President in 1981-82. Ilana Rovner was the speaker at her June 4, 1981 Installation Dinner. Rovner noted how things have improved for women lawyers. She recalled how there were only three women in 1961 in her law school class at Georgetown: approximately the same numbers as in the late 1800's. Even in 1981 women partners were only 2% at the 50 largest firms, and 5% of the full law professors, when 11% of all lawyers were women. She urged using WBAI as a forum for discussion of the moral dilemmas and issues that face the bar, and to become leaders of the bar.

In her 1981-82 Report of President, Loretta noted, in part: The proudest accomplishment of this year is, in my opinion the establishment of a Lawyer Referral Service. The service has been operational since September of 1982 and by June of 1982 we had 25 participating member attorneys in almost all fields of practice. Over 210 calls (approximately 35 per month) have been handled by the service.

Also, for the first time this year, we were on the Steering Committee of the Illinois Women's Agenda and our member, Barbara Disko, attended regularly the meetings of this organization as our alternate delegate. I particularly enjoyed representing the organization on the Cook Court Bar Liaison Committee chaired by Judge Comerford, which met every other month at 8:00 in the morning in Judge Comerford's conference room and also the Chicago Bar Association's Bar President's Council meetings. In addition, I was honored to have been asked by Frank J. McGarr, Chief Judge of the United States District Court for the Northern District of Illinois to serve on the nine member Merit Selection Panel for the appointment of the new U.S. District Court Magistrate.

Honorable Marilyn Komosa was WBAI President in 1982-83. In 1983 Nina Appel was selected as Dean of Loyola Law School, maker her the fourth female dean of a major U.S. law school. Judge Komosa reported in her President's Report that in the 1982-83 WBAI year, certain events stood out. Among them were the by-law changes to admit men. Judge Allen Rosin became WBAI's first male member. WBAI became involved in Hishon vs King and Spaulding and filed an amicus brief in the USSC. Authored by Paddy Harris McNamara and Jacqueline Lustig, it opposed sex discrimination in partnerships. The ranks of women judges in Cook County swelled to 16, four WBAI members headed other bar groups. HB 24 sponsored and lobbied for by WBAI since the 1970s, took effect in 1982.

(Editors Note: This law enabled child support to be paid to the clerk of the court with automatic follow-up by the State's Attorney's upon delinquent payment.)

The question of women becoming partners, the most difficult hurdle faced by women lawyers, was addressed by the United States Supreme Court in 1984. In Hinson vs. King & Spaulding, the Court decided that partnerships, including law firms, must obey federal

ILLINOIS BAR JOURNAL

JULY 1977

Carole Kamin Bellows
President
Illinois State Bar Association
1977-1978

THE MAGAZINE OF ILLINOIS LAWYERS

Installation of the Honorable Margaret O'Malley as WBAI President in June, 1978. Back, Teresa Conway, Georgianna Daskais, Katharine Abraham, Loretta Douglas, Charlotte Adelman, Mary Hooton. Front, Judge O'Malley, Dawn Schulz.

L to R: Elzie Holzwarth, Rep. Herb Huskie, Jeannette Blum, Morgan Finley, Clerk of Circuit Court, Georgianna Daskais. Bottom, Charlotte Adelman, Gabrielle Pieper, 1980. WBAI Matrimonial Law Committee members met to celebrate passage, after years of hard work, of the Child Support Enforcement Act. Below, Chicago Sun-Times, January 12, 1981.

Help coming on child support

The Cook County Circuit Court is organizing a new seven-judge Child Support Enforcement Division to force (1) more fathers to reimburse the government for welfare payments made to their families and (2) more divorced parents to pay child support ordered by the courts.

It's high time.

Aid to families with dependent children is running at a billion dollars a year in Cook County, of which only about $12 million is recaptured from employed—but absent—parents. At last count, only 8 percent of the fathers required to pay support for children on public aid in Illinois did so. This compares, for example, with 50 percent in Michigan.

As for child support in divorce cases, about 15,000 orders are entered annually in the county courts. Of these, 85 percent fall into delinquency at some point in their average life of 7½ years.

The new judicial division will be armed with two much-needed new laws designed to put the burden of collecting support payments on state's attorney's offices and the courts:

• A federal law reinforcing requirements that public aid departments notify state's attorneys whenever parents who can afford it fail to pay support for children on welfare. Our Public Aid Department is remarkably slow-footed in meeting the requirement.

• A state law, effective next Jan. 1, requiring that child-support payments in divorce cases be made to the court clerk instead of the ex-spouse. Thus, without requiring the initiative of the ex-spouse, delinquents automatically will be summoned to court to explain or be jailed.

Taxpayers and mothers abandoned to support young children unassisted will be praying that a beginning can be made at last toward putting much more of their burden where it belongs—usually on the backs of irresponsible fathers.

Live and learn

As state's attorney, Richard M. Daley has a new perspective on the new mental health act he sponsored as a state senator.

Under the law as it stands, a man accused of killing four people and wounding 13 in four bombings and a shootout with police might have gone free last week after 11 years of mental care and without having been tried.

Pressed by Daley's aides, Judge Frank B. Machala strained to interpret the law in a way that would keep the man in custody.

Now Daley is drafting amendments to his own work to be sure confinement of dangerous criminals is assured by something more than strained law. And that's to his credit.

Law Bulletin— September 28, 1982.

9-28-82

Women's Bar scholarship winners

Five scholarships totaling $10,000 were awarded Sept. 10 by the Women's Bar Association of Illinois Foundation at their 17th annual awards luncheon at Chicago Bar Association headquarters. The winners, hometowns and law schools are (from left): Sharon R. Gromer of Buffalo, N.Y., Northwestern University; Susan M. Schurr of Chicago, University of Chicago; Laurie M. Judd of Carbondale, Ill., Southern Illinois University; Ruth Miller of Chicago, John Marshall; and Cheryl A. Johnson of Evanston, Ill., John Marshall.

anti-discrimination law in promoting women to partners or co-owners.

The annual Judicial Reception was held on April 6 at the CBA. Honorees: Chief Judge Harry Comerford. Also, Comerford's presiding judges

Mary Frances Hegarty was President in 1983-84. The Board approved the Public Office Committee recommendation that a Judge not be recommended by WBAI. WBAI created a Long Range Planning Committee and changed the look of its newsletter. It also planned a membership drive, unprecedented in its history, beginning with the publication of a new application form and brochure. It retained an Executive Director.

The Annual Judicial Reception on April 19th at the CBA honored all women judges in Illinois including federal and state circuit judges and U.S. Magistrates. This was to highlight the 70th anniversary of WBAI.

Charlotte Adelman was WBAI President in 1984-85. This year marked the 70th anniversary of WBAI's formation in 1914. Loyola Law School Dean Nina Appel spoke at the installation dinner, recalling when there were no female role models for women law students and lawyers. June Sochen, Northeastern University Professor, addressed the October Joint Professional Dinner on professional women's progress. On November 1st, Ilana Rovner was sworn in as a federal judge and invited the WBAI to participate in her ceremony, the first time WBAI had ever addressed a swearing in of a federal judge. The November meeting celebrated WBAI's birthday, honoring Federal Judge Ilana Rovner and featuring recollections by past WBAI Presidents Judge Odas Nicholson, Jeanne Brown Gordon and Thelma Brook Simon. Among the guests were our 1945-46 President, Judge Katherine Nohelty, whose 1956 nomination as a Democratic candidate for Municipal Court Judge shattered a 50 year tradition of not slating women, and Edna Devlin Bowens, who had been WBAI's president 50 years before in 1934-35.

WBAI's Public Office Committee, chaired by Susan Haddad, evaluated 32 Cook County Judges running for retention and 19 Judges running in contested elections. After reviewing the committee's report, WBAI's Board endorsed all but five associate judges seeking full judgeships, and issued press releases. The evaluation displeased certain judges, ignited the public's interest and added to WBAI's credibility and stature. The November, 1984, *Chicago Lawyer* ran an article as follows:

"Women's Bar Charges Judge Jordan abused power and prestige.

"The Women's Bar Association of Illinois has filed a complaint with the Illinois Judicial Inquiry Board charging that Cook County Circuit Court Associate Judge Michael S. Jordan tried to use the power and prestige of his office to intimidate the association's president and past president, *Chicago Lawyer* has learned.

"The board will investigate the charges - which Jordan vehemently denies- and decide whether to bring a formal complaint before the Illinois Courts Commission.

"The complaint alleges that attempts at intimidation occurred after Jordan learned several months ago that the Women's Bar, then headed by Park Ridge lawyer Mary Frances Hegarty, opposed his election to a full Circuit Court judgeship. Jordan is a Democratic candidate for a full judgeship in the November 6 election.

"The association's initial opposition to Jordan was based on statements he made when he appeared before an endorsement session of the association's Public Office Committee. Members of the committee inferred from his remarks that he did not want women personnel assigned to his courtroom.

"Jordan claims, however, that the committee members misunderstood what he said. He says he only said that he would not want the woman bailiff who had been assigned to the late Judge Henry A. Gentile's courtroom because she panicked and failed to call police or an ambulance when Gentile was assassinated in the Daley Center last year.

"Shortly after Jordan learned that the Women's Bar opposed him, Hegarty was succeeded as president of the Women's Bar by Chicago lawyer Charlotte Adelman. Jordan made several telephone calls and instigated several other calls to Hegarty and Adelman in an effort to get the association to reconsider its opposition to his candidacy.

"Hegarty and Adelman charge in separate signed statements submitted to the Judicial Inquiry Board that these telephone calls were attempts to intimidate them. Jordan denies there was anything improper about the calls.

"In an interview with *Chicago Lawyer*, Jordan said that Adelman, who has appeared before him in the Domestic Relationships Division, where he regularly sits, repeatedly assured him that she disagreed with the Women's Bar's decision to oppose his advancement to full judge.

"After Adelman told him this, Jordan said

he told her that he had received unanimously favorable ratings from other bar associations and thought that the Women's Bar evaluation procedure was unfair...

"Jordan said he then asked Adelman to consider issuing a public statement personally disavowing the evaluation. "Since I thought that the evaluation was unfair, inconsistent, and inappropriate," Jordan told *Chicago Lawyer*, "I said, "If it's going to be issued by you as the now-president, is there any way that you can announce, as an individual, not as the Women's Bar president, that you personally have the greatest confidence in me?"

"When she replied that it would be inap-

propriate for her to issue a statement, Jordan continued, "I said, 'Don't you think you're being inconsistent with yourself, telling me that you would do everything in the world, you have the strongest belief and confidence in me, and then on the other hand not being willing to do that? Doesn't that give me the belief that your words are not what your feelings are? If that's the split personality that you're displaying, then I just want to tell you I don't know if you're doing your clients a service coming before me and telling me things, because how can I believe you?"

"Sensing that he could not persuade her to issue a statement, Jordan said, he asked "mu-

President Hegarty visits with Edna Devlin Bowens (right), who was president of the Women's Bar Association in 1934-35.

Mary Frances Hegarty (right) takes the oath of office of president of the Women's Bar Association of Illinois from Chief Judge Harry G. Comerford during the annual installation dinner June 2 in the Chicago Bar Association.

tual friends" - leaders of the North Suburban Bar Association, in which Jordan and Adelman are both active - to call her "not to threaten her, not to coerce her, but to persuade her that she is inconsistent with herself."

A Chicago newspaper reported that Judge Thomas Maloney responded to WBAI's refusal to recommend him by saying WBAI members were "incompetent lawyers. Most don't even know where the criminal court building is." WBAI was alone among the bar associations to not recommend him.

In July the *Sun Times* wrote that the list of 13 newly elected Cook County Circuit Court Judges included no women. Two women were included in those sworn in as associate judges but 15 our of 338 still constituted pitiful underrepresentation said WBAI. The importance of increasing our membership was emphasized. An event was held at Jenner & Block, one planned at the Attorney General's Office, a letter sent by the president to all women alumni from her law school, a letter sent by Susan Haddad, members chair, to every female newly admitted to the Illinois Bar (over 500), the Law School Liaison Committee made presentations at all the local law schools and the by-laws were amended to enable WBAI to have affiliate chapters. (Sean Fox was By-laws Committee Chair).

WBAI hosted a brunch welcoming to Chicago the women attending the ABA Convention. The Women and the Bench Committee and the Rights of Women Committee presented programs on judicial selection and access by women to the bench. Other programs included Reproduction and the Law (test tube babies, surrogate mothers, etc.), legal ramifications of investigative reporting, flex and part-time and job sharing and the art of cross examination featuring Eugene Pinchon.

WBAI's Foundation gave $2,500 scholarships to women law students at Illinois law schools and raised $6,000 for 1985 scholarships at the Holiday Benefit Brunch.

Thelma Brook Simon, president in 1956-57 and Carole Siegel

WBAI director Jewel Klein and Teddy Gordon, WBAI Past President.

Judge Odas Nicholson, Cook County Circuit Court, WBAI president 1973-1974, addresses WBAI members and guests.

Mary Hegarty, Geraldine Brauneis, Carole Siegel, Elsie Holswarth .

Edna Devlin Bowens

Katherine Nohelty
Past WBAI Presidents

WBAI Marks its 70th

In honor of its 70th birthday, a WBAI committee composed of Charlotte Adelman, Elsie Hozwarth, Carole Siegel and Geraldine Brauneis created a 1985 Calendar, depicting important events in the history of Illinois women attorneys and WBAI. The calendar was made possible by the donation of the art and design work by Gerald Siegel & Associates (Carole Siegel's husband) and the donation of the printing and production by Commerce Clearing House, where Mary Ann Hynes was vice president. WBAI's president also initiated a special Illinois Bar Journal issue devoted entirely to women lawyers, which appeared in May, 1986.

New WBAI Committees were formed: Buddy System, Part-Time Lawyers' Network, Professional Women's Network (which initiated breakfast meetings) and the Humanitarian Treatment of Animals.

A special mailing under the president's signature was sent to each full Circuit Court Judge urging each to vote for Dawn Schulz as Associate Judge. However, none of the 13 new Associate Judges elected were women. WBAI supported an amendment to the Illinois Paternity Act, opposed mandatory arbitration, supported certain divorce related legislation, opposed the "Hyde Amendment" which aimed at restricting federal funds for abortion. WBAI voted to go forward with a documentary film and entered into a contract with a film producer, opposed a new federal tax law and undertook to become a clearinghouse for job opportunities for women attorneys. WBAI also obtained its own telephone number! A membership directory was issued, the first since 1934-35 to contain photographs.

The goal of maximizing WBAI's visibility to the legal community and the community at large was realized through much newspaper and other exposure, and the goal of financial solvency was reached. Soliciting donations from title companies and other entities for the annual dinner turned that into a money maker, as did advertising and fund raising pursued for the Directory. WBAI was recognized by the Chief Judge of the Cook County Circuit Court which appointed WBAI's president to the Special Commission on the Administration of Justice to make recommendations to improve the court system in light of the Greylord scandal. Robert Lyon, whose application to join WBAI ten years before had been rejected because the by-laws did not then permit male members, joined the WBAI. On February 14, 1985, the Chicago Historical Society and WBAI entered into a signed agreement whereby WBAI placed its non-current records with the Chicago Historical Society. Archie Motley, curator of archives and manuscripts wrote of WBAI's records, "They will be an important addition to our holdings and we are delighted to be chosen as their repository...our researchers will share our gratitude." Thereafter, records and memorabilia and materials from members were so placed and this project is on-going.

The honorees on April 18th at the CBA at the Annual Judicial Reception were Honorable Harry Comerford and Honorable John J. Ahern, for their contributions to the establishment and achievements of the Domestic Violence Court.

70th Anniuversary Calendar

Above, Charlotte Adelman, Chief Judge Comerford and Elizabeth Foran at the annual judicial reception May 18, 1985 which paid tribute to Judge John J. Ahern, below right. Below left, Adelman, president of WBAI, Deborah Gubin, Chair, Joint Professional Dinner and Professor June Socher.

June, 1985, Ilana Rovner was named "Woman of the Year." Below, sFrom left, Judges Blanche Manning, Sophia Hall, Donna Cervini and Odas Nicholson.

Judge Barbara Disko was WBAI President in 1985-86. The Installation Dinner took place at the new State of Illinois Building and had a record attendance of over 350 people. WBAI joined 46 other groups in an amicus brief opposing the Justice Department's effort to abolish affirmative action. Judge Mary Ann McMorrow's appointment to the Illinois Appellate Court was applauded by WBAI. Andrea Schleifer, WBAI's delegate to the Illinois Women's Agenda, reported success in efforts to pass the Spousal Health Insurance Rights Bill. The Past President's Roundtable was formed and the President appointed Charlotte Adelman to serve as WBAI archivist. Dues were increased form $50 to $55 for members participating five years or more. (Note: Our dues are a real bargain! In 1930, when WBAI dinner meetings cost only $1.00, WBAI dues

May, 1986

were $25.00)

For the first time, WBAI co-sponsored a seminar with IICLE (Women and Rainmaking) and started planning a second one entitled "Working Women as Clients". WBAI presented a workshop with the National Association of Bank Women. WBAI's Foundation awarded $25,000 in scholarships. WBAI joined in an amicus brief filed in the USSC, Thornburgh vs American College of Obstetricians and Gynecologists, to oppose the Reagan administration's efforts to undo Roe vs Wade and prohibit freedom of reproductive choice. To emphasize the discrimination sill existing against women academics at law schools, WBAI hosted a breakfast reception for women lawyers in academia. A letter was sent to Governor Thompson urging deletion of a provision in a bill which would discriminate against illegitimate children of firefighters in state operated pension programs. In response, Thompson used the amendatory veto to delete the offending provision.

On May 29, 1985, led by Carol Hallock, a group of Rockford, Illinois, women lawyers voted to form an affiliate of the WBAI. According to Hallock, the mere existence of the affiliate improved conditions for women lawyers in the Rockford area. Maryellen Provenzale was congratulated by WBAI on her appointment as the first woman associate judge in DuPage County.

The Law School Liaison Committee had wine and cheese receptions at local law schools and presented a seminar, resulting in several new student memberships. WBAI's Rockford Affiliate requested that WBAI video some of its Chicago programs so they could be shown at their meetings in other parts of Illinois.

It was reported that on February 3, 1986, the Cook County Child Support Collection Court was relocated form 13th and Michigan to the Daley Center after a two year effort by an ad hoc committee composed of various bar groups and other legal organizations, organized in 1984 by WBAI.

WBAI voted to oppose passage of the Marital Property Reform Act, (a form of community property) supported by the Illinois League of Women Voters, The Eagle Forum

March 12, 1986

More women needed on bench: WBAI

By CAROL McHUGH
Law Bulletin staff writer

The Women's Bar Association of Illinois, while not rating judicial candidates in the March 18 primary, is concerned "about the lack of women on the bench" and is urging support for female candidates.

The 1,000-member women's bar group noted in a prepared statement that only 3 percent of the 376 elected full circuit judges statewide in 1983 were women. "Women have added a new dimension to the

August 1985 by the nine law schools in Illinois showed only one school, Southern Illinois University School of Law, had less than 30 percent women enrolled for classes that began last fall. SIU had 28 percent women in its entering class while Loyola Univeristy School of Law, with 46 percent, had the highest percentage of women in any Illinois law school.

The WBAI noted that only one of the 42 elected members of the five state appellate courts is a woman while one other, 1st District

by the Chicago Council of Lawyers and "not recommended" by the Chicago Bar Association; 1st District Appellate Court Justice Mary Ann McMorrow, one of only two candidates found "highly qualified" by both the Council and CBA; and Diane Economou, who was found "not qualified" by the Council and "qualified" by the CBA.

The other candidates noted by the WBAI were Associate Judge Barbara J. Disko, who was found "qualified" by the Council and "highly qualified" by the CBA and

WBAI Past Presidents, September, 1986. Judge Marilyn R. Komosa, Esther R. Rothstein, Judge Margaret O'Malley, Judge Rosemary Duschene LaPorta, Justice Helen McGillicuddy, Susan Haddad, Thelma Broom Simon, Judge Barbara Disko, Charlotte Adelman.

and the Commission on Uniform State Laws. WBAI created an UMPA Task Force. In furtherance of its position, WBAI members debated the proposed law at various forums and spoke in opposition to it an a special Citizen's Council on Women's hearing in Springfield. WBAI joined with other bar groups to oppose the law.

WBAI debated the pros and cons of election or selection of judges at its February 18, 1986 meeting. In March, 1986, the *Chicago Tribune* reported a female partner at a big law firm who asked that her name not be used, maintained the issue of discrimination against women attorneys is one that's largely in the closet. This was in connection with a law suit against a prominent Chicago law firm for sex discrimination in not being made a partner. Marilyn Moats Kennedy spoke on office, law firm and corporate politics. WBAI presented awards to Judge Donald O'Connell and Judge Blanche Manning at the April 21, 1986, Judicial Reception, for their work to improve the First Municipal District in Cook County. For the first time, an Illinois Supreme Court Justice attended the reception: Justice Ben Miller was on hand and joined the WBAI!

The 1986-87 WBAI president was Susan Haddad. WBAI paid tribute to Justice Helen McGillicuddy, a WBAI past president and first woman ever elected to the Illinois Appellate Court, upon her retirement, and to Evalyn Walsh Laird for 60 years at the practice of law. The *WBAI Newsletter* continued to run its Law and Motherhood series featuring various members' perspectives on the subject. The WBAI UMPA Task Force debated the issue at Leagues of Women Voters forums. It presented testimony in opposition to the proposed bill and lobbied against its passage. WBAI's Board voted to send letters to all state legislators and all women's organizations in opposition to UMPA. Eventually, WBAI was successful in forcing UMPA proponents to substantiate their sweeping philosophical claims with practical answers. When required to do this, they came up short.

Due in great measure to WBAI pressure and persistence, UMPA proponents backed off, at least temporarily. In response to a request from Carol Hallock, of the Rockford chapter, WBAI wrote the Chief Judge of Winnebago County urging appointment of women to county judicial positions, in view of the total lack of women on the bench. Past President Helen Hart Jones wrote an item in the newsletter reminding WBAI members that WBAI has had a stand on abortion for 20 years, and she found it distressing that such a substantial effort was unknown to most present members. She noted that in the fall of 1967 WBAI began a study of Illinois laws pertaining to abortion and concluded in 1969 that sanctions against it should have no place in the criminal code and that individuals should be permitted to make decisions relating thereto in the light of medical advice and the dictates of their conscience. Further, in 1974 WBAI had opposed the "Buckley Amendment". WBAI's May newsletter ran a headline "Abortion Case to be Argued by WBAI Member". Colleen K. Connell, Director of the Preproductive Rights Project of the Roger Baldwin Fund of the ACLU challenged an Illinois criminal statute which would have required notification to both parents before a minor could receive an abortion.

The May 1986 *Illinois Bar Journal* was devoted entirely to women lawyers as a Special Issue. A membership survey was circulated on selection versus election of judges and WBAI's membership voted by a margin of almost two to one in favor of selection of state court judges. A cocktail party for prospective new members was held. The Judicial Reception honored Justices Mary Ann McMorrow and Helen McGillicuddy, both of whom gave much credit to the WBAI for its role in their attainment of their high offices.

WBAI's Public Office Committee made its recommendations regarding the 36 judges on the Cook County retention ballot and the Supreme and Appellate Courts. The Board considered the committee's report, voted and on October 10, 1986, issued a press release, and, as the *WBAI News* noted, "then the fun began". Several members of the Public Office Committee, some Board members and one WBAI member who was a candidate for associate judge were "pressured, insulted or downright threatened as a result of WBAI's stance on the retention ballot. Judges were angered that they were found merely 'qualified' and not 'highly qualified'. One disgruntled judge snarled, "Nobody does more for you people than I do."

In October, 1986 WBAI's Board voted to oppose wearing fur especially if the animal had not been ranch raised but caught in a trap, a position requested by WBAI's Humanitarian Treatment of Animals Committee.

The Trial Lawyers Committee presented a half day seminar on taking and defending depositions. The Lawyer Referral Service reported it was off to a good start as calls keep coming in and potential clients are referred out. The Newsletter began running the archivist's history of WBAI. The President reported that membership had grown from about 900 to 1060 members. She noted WBAI had co-sponsored formation of the Task Force on Gender Bias. In 1986 the Judicial Inquiry Board agreed to look into charges that Judge Cieslik made sexist remarks to a woman attorney who appeared before him.

On January 2, 1987 the *Chicago Sun Times* reported:

"The Illinois Judicial Inquiry Board filed complaints yesterday against two judges, accusing one of making racist and sexist remarks to people appearing before him and the other of making sexist comments to lawyers...

"Referring to Pierce as "young lady", Cieslik reportedly said, "Ladies should not be lawyers...and do not belong in court." He

Above, Carole Siegel and Jerry Seigel.

Right, WBAI's first married couple, Rhoda Davis and James Sweeney, They met at the 1986 banquet and were married May 15, 1987.

further is charged with saying that "ladies should be at home raising a family" and asking, "What does your husband think of you being down here [in court]?"

"And during another in-chamber proceeding in September of October, 1981, Cieslik allegedly told lawyer Lorna Propes, who was about six months pregnant, that he "would never allow a pregnant woman to try a case before him again."

"The complaint also accuses Cieslik of making improper remarks to lawyer Mary Jane Theis, who was also about six months pregnant, during a pretrial conference in of 1980. The judge reportedly said: "If your husband had kept his hands in his pockets, you would not be in the condition you are in."

On January 5, 1987, Mara Tapp, *Law Bulletin* feature writer wrote:

"The chief judge of the Cook County Circuit Court has transferred a judge who recently barred from his courtroom the partner of the president of the Women's Bar Association of Illinois, which found him unqualified in 1984. Judge Harry G. Comerford said that starting on Monday Judge Michael S. Jordan will be transferred from the Domestic Relations Division to the 2d Municipal District. Associate Judge James G. Donegan from that district will be transferred to Domestic Relations.

"Comerford called the move "an intercourt transfer," which he characterized as a frequent occurrence.

"However, some court observers said that the move reflects concern over whether Jordan should hear cases involving domestic relations.

"Jordan, who took the bench in 1974, declined comment.

"In response to inquiries concerning the matter, Judicial Inquiry Board Chairman Robert P. Cummins refused to confirm any board investigations. However, more generally, he noted, the board does investigate matters involving possible violations of the Code of Judicial Conduct.

"Jordan's transfer follows remarks he made in two separate hearings. When asked if the transfer related to these remarks, Comerford said he didn't "want to get into that."

"On January 20 and January 29, Jordan told Carole Siegel of Haddad & Siegel that he had "no respect" for her partner, Susan Haddad, the president of WBAI.

"Haddad was the head of the association's public office committee the year it found Jordan unqualified.

"When Siegel informed Jordan on January 20 of her recent partnership with Haddad, he "barred" her from "participating in the case" because he had "no respect" for Haddad's "conduct" and would not "allow her to be associated" in a case before him.

"Canon 3 of the Code of Judicial Conduct states in section C (1) that "A judge should disqualify himself in a proceeding in which his impartiality might reasonably be questioned, including but not limited to instances where (a) he has a personal bias or prejudice concerning a party or his lawyer..."

"Jordan also gave Siegel's client leave to seek new counsel within 21 days and appointed an attorney to represent the children in the matter.

"When Siegel asked for time to file a change of venue, Jordan denied it on the grounds that the time had "come and passed."

"However, he did grant Siegel's emergency motion for change of venue when she presented it to him...He preceded his order with a "statement."

"In the five pages of transcripts that followed, Jordan discussed his belief that Haddad had withheld information about him that he asked her to distribute to other committee members. Jordan also blamed Siegel and Judge Barbara Disko for circulating WBAI materials that were "not true" to news media, prompting him to tell the courtroom he was "led...to believe that [Haddad] is not a person whose representations were to be counted upon as being true."

"Disko, also a judge in the Domestic Relations Division, is the immediate past president of the WBAI.

"In the second hearing, Jordan told Siegel that he would grant the order transferring the case back to the division's presiding judge, Benjamin S. Mackoff, for random computer assignment. That, he noted, was "unlike the previous system," in which the presiding judge would "assign it so some judge that he felt the lawyers wished to be before."

"Jordan also talked in open court about the "great turnover" in the division and specifically mentioned the failure to retain one judge and the indictments and convictions of two others. he added that if his remarks appeared "intemperate," he believed that "further indictments" would show his "remarks will be borne out."

"Canon 2 of the Code of Judicial Conduct states in section A that "A judge should...conduct himself at all times in a manner that promotes public confidence in the integrity and impartiality of the judiciary."

"Mackoff said he had met with Jordan, Siegel and Haddad as part of his investigation of the matter, after it was brought to his attention last week. He declined to discuss those meetings.

"He did say that he had reported the matter to Comerford, although he also declined to discuss their meeting.

"Mackoff, who took over the division less than a year ago, said he had not discussed Jordan's remarks with Judge Disko. He also said he had not informed the Judicial Inquiry Board of the matter.

"When asked if he had contacted the board, Comerford said it was not his "place" to do so, especially since the matter had already been reported by the news media.

"Both Haddad and Siegel refused to comment on the matter."

Ina Winston was president in 1987-88. She noted in her installation remarks, "In the legal community, the workplace is structured on male experiences; the career commitment of the woman who has children is all too often viewed as suspect. The fact that inadequate maternity leave and the lack of flexible work arrangements may force women out of the workplace and make these suspicions a self fulfilling prophecy is rarely examined. "Thus we are challenged", she said, "to view childbearing and child rearing not merely as a matter of concern for women but also as a human issue and we must develop legislative approaches and litigation tools to move these issues out of the traditional equal rights framework and into a substantive rights framework."

The following is Ina Winston's Presidents year end report: "WBAI's major accomplishments during the 1987-88 were strengthening our working relationships with Legislature by holding our First Annual Legislative Reception. We increased our visibility in the political arena by appearing before and writing slatemakers and lobbying for the appointment of women to governmental boards. Befitting our stature as a major bar association, we exercised leadership by urging the appointment of Appellate Court Justice Mary Ann McMorrow to the Illinois Supreme Court. We supported a modified mandatory continuing legal education proposal; expressed concern over the nomination of Justice Bork to the United States Supreme Court; advocated passage of the Illinois Family and Medical Leave Act; and suggested changes in merit selection proposals.

"These outstanding achievements were made possible, in part, by the dedicated work of the officers and directors. The Program Committee, under the capable leadership of Pearl Zager, created interesting, well attended programs. The committees were highly productive. I am particularly appreciative to our past presidents for generously sharing their wisdom with us.

"Board Action: In July, 1987, pursuant to an earlier vote by the Board, WBAI filed a amicus brief in support of a petition for certiorari in Benzies vs. Illinois Department of Mental Health and Developmental Disabilities. The brief, written by Roslyn Lieb, challenged an opinion by the seventh Circuit Court of Appeals construing the paradigm for proof in the Title VII cases. Although the petition was denied, we are grateful to Roslyn for her work.

"In August, we sent letters to Senators Simon and Dixon and the members of the Senate Judiciary Committee setting forth questions to be asked of Judge Bork to properly evaluate his qualifications which would make them assets to the various Supreme Court Committees.

"In September, we voted to support the Family and Medical Leave Act and sent letters to all members of the Senate Executive Committee urging passage. The Act would allow an employee to take brief, unpaid leave upon birth or adoption of a child or the serious illness of a child or dependent parent.

"In October, the Board endorsed the concept of Mandatory Continuing Legal Education and sent a letter to the Illinois Supreme Court suggesting changes in the ISBA proposal. The change would make it possible for more women to serve on the MCLE Board, lower the number of hours required per year, and reduce the bureaucracy involved in administration of the program. We hope that WBAI will be able to provide low cost, high quality educational programs for our members and WBAI's MCLE Committee, capably chaired by Elsie Holzwarth and Ellen Hicks, with the help of Carol Siegel and Candace Gorman, are working towards this goal.

"In November, we reviewed the petition

Michael J. Howlett, Jr., Audrey Holzer Rubin (center), and Andrea M. Schleifer, members of the planning committee for the Illinois Task Force on Gender Bias in the Courts, met recently in Chicago to discuss the scope of the new task force.

Task force to be appointed: Gender Bias in the Courts

March, 1988

Rosaire Nottage and Eunice Ward were "fixed up" at a WBAI event and found they were so compatible they started their own partnership, with a twist. The studio photo at right accompanied the announcement of the opening of their family law firm and drew a large, positive response.

filed with the Illinois Supreme Court by the Chicago Council of Lawyers for adoption of a merit selection plan. While we affirmed our support for the concept of merit selection, we declined to endorse the plan because we objected to its blanket exclusion of all public sector attorneys, many of whom are women, from the Judicial Nominating Commissions.

"In December, on the motion of Jewel Klein, the Board voted to create a 501 (c) (3) corporation to fund legal research and the production of a film about women attorneys. Charlotte Adelman is presently talking with filmmakers.

"In January, `1988, WBAI sent a letter to the Illinois Supreme Court advocating that a woman be appointed to the vacancy left by Justice Simon and in March, we followed up by sending a second letter to the Court urging the appointment of Justice McMorrow.

"In March, WBAI sent a letter to the Chicago Housing Authority protesting the proposed termination of four women attorneys after they filed a sex discrimination suit.

"In April, the Board passed updated written rules governing the Public Office Committee and also voted to send a letter to members of the Circuit Court's Executive Committee advocating the appointment of our members as Associate Judges.

"Monthly Meetings and Committee Activities: In May, 1987, the Past President's Council gave a lovely luncheon for Susan Haddad, outgoing WBAI President, and myself. The council was capably chaired during the year by Theodora Gordon.

"The Annual Dinner, which was held on June 4, 1987, was chaired by Mary Frances Hegarty who as usual did a splendid job. Mary Frances has given generously of herself to WBAI for many years and we are most grateful. The keynote speaker at the dinner was Joan Beck, Chicago Tribune Syndicated Columnist, who gave an excellent speech. We owe a special debt of gratitude to Cornelia Honchar Tuite who contributed in many ways to the success of the dinner. It was an honor to be installed by Justice McMorrow.

"During the summer, we held an outing to a Cubs Baseball game and a night at Sportsman's Park. We thank Elizabeth Cutter for her work on these events as well as on the lovely September reception held at Leslie Hindman Auction Gallery. The reception was the brainchild of Liza Yntema.

"In September, the WBAI Foundation chaired by Esther Rothstein, outdid itself by awarding seven law school scholarships totalling $29,000 to deserving women students. The luncheon was a gala event and it has been a special pleasure for me to serve on the Foundation's Board in selection of the scholarship recipients.

"In October, Deborah Gubin, Mary Frances Hegarty, and Candace Gorman gave us interesting insights on starting private practice in their speeches at our monthly luncheon meeting.

"WBAI also held a cocktail reception for women in academia, which was co-hosted by Loyola University Law School. Dean Nina Appel spoke incisively about the need for women to be mentors to each other and graciously announced that the Law School would help defray the expenses of the event. The reception was a success and kudos also go to Rosaire Nottage who chaired the event.

"In October, the Rights of Women Committee, capably chaired by Roslyn Lieb and Barbara Greenspan, met with Senator Netsch to discuss strategy for passage of the Family and Medical Leave Act. During the year, the Committee arranged for WBAI to participate in a study by a doctoral student at Northwestern University on childbearing decisions by dual career couples.

"In November, over 150 women attorneys, physicians, architects, and others, attended the Joint Professional Dinner and heard Martha Seger, a Governor on the Federal Reserve Board speak on the economy. Liza Yntema together with Gayle Altur, Victoria Almeida, Jamie Miller, Susan Salita, and Pearl Zager did an outstanding job on the event.

"In December, the WBAI Foundation held a festive and financially successful Holiday Party auction at Alcott and Andrews.

"On January 28, 1988, 127 people braved a cold night to attend our First Annual Legislative Reception at which we honored the members of the Illinois House and Senate. Legislative Leadership Awards with Special Distinction in Women's Issues were given to Senator Dawn Clark Netsch for co-sponsoring the Family and Medical Leave Act and to Representative Grace Mary Stern. Legislative Leadership Awards were given to Senate President Phillip Rock, Senator Adeline Geo-Karis, and Senator Howard Carroll. Special plaudits go to Legislative Reception Chairs Marya Nega and Mary Farmar for the outstanding success of the event.

"In May, Kathryn Dutenhauer spoke on the United Nations and action taken by that body to combat sex discrimination. Kathryn also attended the April Board meeting and a committee was appointed to determine what role WBAI should take.

"As this goes to press we are looking forward to the Judicial Reception honoring Judge Rosemary LaPorta. Many people have worked hard to insure the success of the event and we especially thank co-chairs Elizabeth Foran, Patricia Vavra, and Carol McHugh, and members Laura Guzik, Ellen Hicks, Joan Riordan, Susan Condon and Victoria Almeida.

"This year also marked the establishment of several new committees including the Environmental Committee, which is off to a good start under the leadership of Johnine Brown, the 75th Anniversary Committee, Worker's Compensation Committee, which has met regularly under chair Barbara Sherman, and the Think Tank led by the creative Rosaire Nottage.

"We also continue our good relationship with IIT Chicago-Kent thanks to Sandra Ratcliff. In November, WBAI and IIT sponsored the third annual Women and Rainmaking Seminar, which included Johnnie Brown and Rosaire Nottage as speakers and with Jackie Lustig as moderator.

"The Part-Time Lawyers Committee under the leadership of Sheila Nielsen continued to work hard, as did the Goodwill and Memorial Committee under Theodora Gordon and Carole Siegel, and The Humanitarian Treatment of Animals led by Brigid McGrath

and Arline Swanson. We are looking forward to the Law Day activities which, as usual, will be memorable due to the efforts of Judge Marilyn Komosa. The Lawyer Referral Service, led by Penny Brown, continued to flourish as did the Legislation Committee chaired by R. Morgan Hamilton, the Matrimonial Committee chaired by Lee Witte and Margaret Benson, the Probate Committee headed by Patricia Hogan, The Real Estate Committee led by Gayle Altur and Barbara Miller, and the Trial Lawyers Committee chaired by Sheila Murphy. The Public Office Committee, chaired by Nancy Nicol, worked with dedication throughout the year.

"Our newsletter editors, Linda Kagan and Carol McHugh, deserve special recognition because their indefatigable efforts have made our newsletter an outstanding professional publication. Laura Guzik also worked with dedication to publicize our monthly meetings and committee activities. As a result of the newsletter and the publicity, WBAI has a much higher public profile and we are recognized by the legal community as a major bar association.

"We would like to express our appreciation to the Chicago Daily Law Bulletin and especially Stephen Anderson, former Associate publisher, for their consistent coverage of our activities which resulted in eight front page articles this year. Our activities were also reported by the National Law Journal and Chicago Sun-Times.

"Finances, Contracts, and other matters: Patricia Hegarty and Marya Nega have earned our appreciation by preparing our tax returns. Erika Palmer Rogers, chair of the Budget Committee, performed her duties admirably, with great integrity.

"We are especially grateful to Leslie Recht and Diane Stern who presented various options to the Board in our contract negotiations with Meerson Management. They unstintingly gave us the benefit of their legal skills and patience.

"I would also like to thank our parliamentarian, Eleanor Guthrie, for her generous help throughout the year.

"President's activities: In addition to answering correspondence, phone calls, newspaper inquiries and presiding at monthly Board and membership meetings, I had the pleasure of representing WBAI at many functions.

"On July 2, 1987, at the invitation of Chief Judge Comerford, your president spoke at the swearing in ceremony for new judges. I was also active in the Bar President's Council.

"In September, I gave a speech celebrating the Bicentennial of the Constitution at a ceremony presided over by Justice McMorrow and attended by the Appellate Court Justices and clerks. It was an honor for WBAI to have been invited to represent the organized bar at the function.

"In November, I, along with the presidents of other major bar associations, spoke at the swearing-in ceremony for new admittees to the bar. This was the first time the Illinois Supreme Court invited WBAI to participate in the ceremony and The Chicago Daily Law Bulletin marked this historic occasion by publishing my speech.

"In November, I appeared before the Cook County Democratic party slatemakers and

urged more women be slated for full Circuit Court judgeships. Your president pointed out that although women are 52% of the voters and 18% of all attorneys, we occupy a mere 7% of full Circuit Court judgeships in Illinois. I also wrote letters to all of the major state and local political leaders urging that more women be slated for office and appointed to boards and commissions.

"In January, I met with the presidents of the CBA and ISABA and we wrote a letter, appointing the members of the Gender Bias Task Force and describing the scope of the group's activities. It was a pleasure to work with Jack Jiganti, president of the CBA, and Don Schiller, president of ISBA.

"I also met with Jill Wine-Banks, Executive Vice President of the ABA, who was gracious and helpful in opening the lines of communication between our organizations.

"As of this writing, I am looking forward to speaking at a seminar on merit selection on April 25, and at the May 3, Law Day Ceremony.

"Recommendations: By the end of Fiscal Year 1987-88, June 30, we will have paid $38,650 to Meerson Management for executive director services. I recommend, as I did last year, that WBAI seek competitive bids this year so that we can be in a better position for contract negotiations and explore methods to reduce our costs.

"During my term, I tried to expand WBAI's activities so that we could meet the needs of women who practice in diverse areas. I recommend that we bring into our leadership ranks of women from the academic community and from large law firms as well as solo, small firm, and governmental practitioners.

"Today, feminist thought is not a monolithic set of ideas; feminists of good will may differ sharply on a wide range of issues. I recommend that we amend our by laws to allow for contested elections prior to the Annual Dinner with ample time to debate the important issues which face women and the legal community.

In 1988 women lawyers were elected to Cook County wide offices: Aurelia Pucinski, Clerk of the Circuit Court and Carol Mosley Braun, Recorder of Deeds.

Jackie Lustig was president in 1988-89. WBAI met with Judge Harry Comerford about the lack of women presiding judges and the lack of women presiding judges and the desire of WBAI for input into the selection process for associate judges. Mary Hooton, Supervising Judge - Personal Injury, a WBAI past president, reported that the 1988 Cook County Verdict Reporter states women lawyers represented 12.7% of jury clients in '88, up from 9.2% in '87. WBAI was involved in the campaign surrounding the impending U.S. Supreme Court review of the Webster decision on abortion rights. The Association sent a letter to ABA President Raven, strongly urging ABA to submit an amicus brief. Even though the ABA didn't, WBAI itself joined in a brief with several other bar associations. On March 20, 1989, Cook County Board President George Dunne sponsored a resolution, passed by the CCB, proclaiming June, 1989 Women's Bar Association Month. Jackie noted a dramatic increase in membership which has resulted in a change in character of the organization. We now have many members who join for the sole reason that they support our objectives and not in the expectation of actively participating. In effect, WBAI has two kinds of members to serve, we have the member who expects to benefit from programs, Lawyer Referral Service, professional development, etc. and we also have the member who supports the WBAI so that it can advocate for women and women attorneys. Fortunately, the WBAI can easily fulfill both roles.

Jewel Klein was president in 1989-90, the year which marked WBAI's 75th birthday. The following is her presidents' letter. "Dear Members: The concept of writing this last President's column terrifies me. WBAI tradition, manners and good taste dictate that I report on the year that's past and thank all the people that have contributed. There is no way that I can do either task properly. The joy of WBAI is that the whole is greater than the sum of its parts. Many people contribute in many ways. The president gets sent to ceremonial events, strategy conferences. She writes speeches and attends press conferences and she can not possibly be aware of all the activities of all of the members.

"In my April, 1990 President's letter, I named our members who had won their judicial primary elections. I failed to mention Judge Michael Gallagher. That omission makes me ever more nervous about this column. So with apologies in advance to those whom I am about to forget to mention, here goes:

"A president's year begins months before the installation with consideration of appointment of committee chairs and planning for the annual dinner. WBAI's 1988-89 president Jackie Lustig started then and continued through the year to serve as counselor and advisor, to remind me of things that needed to be done, to alert me to issues and problems. She represented WBAI at swearing in ceremonies in Springfield and on other boards and committees. I told Nancy Lischer that planning the annual dinner would be fun and easy. For the latter, she probably has cause of action against me for intentional and negligent misrepresentation. Nancy Lischer and Patricia Vavra organized, planned and promoted our annual dinner. We invited two speakers Anne Mollegan Smith of *Working Woman* magazine and Congresswoman Lynn Martin. We were fearful that congress would be in session and that Martin would have to cancel at the last minute. She didn't and we really had two speakers. Circuit Court Clerk Aurelia Pucinski served as M.C.

"Carole Siegel conceived that idea of an annual public service award and we honored the management team at Fel-Pro for its corporate concern for family issues and Sister Mary B. Breslin of Mundelein University for their innovative programs which allowed working people to attend college at night and on weekends.

"Victoria Almeida agreed to be program chair and scheduled a year of timely and informative activities (flag burning in October; the impact of abortion on the elections in November; women lawyers in politics in January; the state of affirmative action in March; and rainmaking in May).

"Past president, Thelma Brook Simon wanted the 75th Anniversary year to be special so she volunteered to have a picnic in her back yard on July 15, 1989. Thelma provided all of the food. Even if the weatherman had not cooperated, Thelma's warmth and hospitality made the sun shine.

"Starting almost two years ago, Charlotte Adelman, Elsie Holzwarth and Carole Siegel

WBAI honors Circuit Judge Sophia Hall, Chancery, Federal District Judge Ilana Rovner, Circuit Judge Monica Reynolds, Chancery, at the annual WBAI Judicial Reception, April 11, 1989. Left, Jackie Lustig, right, Jewel Klein)

WBAI Summer Outing—1989, Thelma Simon's house.

Olga Jurco, Judge O'Malley, Judge Reynolds and husband, Eleanor Guthrie.

Mr. LaPorta, Judge LaPorta, Arlene Swanson, Judge O'Malley, Justice McMorrow.

Front, Anne Sullivan, Lois Dierstein, Jeanne B. Gordon, . Rear, Pat Mullin, Joan Riordan.

Thelma B. Simon, Candace Gorman, Barbara Greenspan, Jackie Lustig.

Candace Gorman, Prof. S. Nahmoud, Judge Kenneth Gillis, Joel Daley, Susan Fox Gillis at "Flag Burning and Freedom of Expression" October, 1989, WBAI general meeting.

Carole Siegel, Elzie Holzwarth and Charlotte Adelman proudly show the first copies of the 1990 calendar.

ISBA President Leonard Amari, Jewel Klein, Mayor Daley and Laura Guzik at the 47th annual Joint Professional Dinner, November, 1989. (Photo by Stephen Anderson, ISBA)

Charlotte Adelman and Jewel Klein present a calendar to Eleanor Guthrie, WBAI parlimentarian. (November, 1989)

Justice Dan Ward, left and Jewel Klein with others.

WBAI 75

Portias Break Masculine Barrier

ANNIVERSARY

CALENDAR 1990

75th Anniversary Calendar Unveiled

1st Vice President Candace Gorman, County Recorder Carol Mosely Braun, County Clerk Aurelia Pucinski and Jewel Klein.

February 20, 1990—Elsie Holzwarth, Carole Siegel, Jewel Klein, Myra Bradwell photo, Charlotte Adelman, Victoria Almeida in 1914 costume.

Joan Riordan, Victoria Almeida, Kathryn Bigley lighting 75th anniversary cake.

Honored speakers—Judge Margaret O'Malley, Dean Nina Appel, State Sen. Dawn Clark Netsch.

Judge O'Malley, Dean Appel, Sen. Netsch, Deborah Gubin, Elsie Holzwarth, Charlotte Adelman, Carole Siegel and Jewel Klein.

Happy 75th WBAI

Jewel Klein, Bradwell, Kathryn Rinella, past WBAI presidents.

(Photos this page by Steve Anderson)

OFFICE OF THE MAYOR
CITY OF CHICAGO

RICHARD M. DALEY
MAYOR

P R O C L A M A T I O N

WHEREAS, the Women's Bar Association of Illinois, established in 1914, was founded to promote the interests and welfare of women lawyers and to aid in the enactment of legislation for the common good and administration of justice; and

WHEREAS, the Women's Bar Association of Illinois is celebrating its 75th anniversary with a luncheon at the Chicago Bar Association, 29 South LaSalle Street, on Tuesday, February 20; and

WHEREAS, the luncheon program will highlight 75 years of women's legal history, including women in law schools, in the judiciary, and the legislature:

NOW, THEREFORE, I, Richard M. Daley, Mayor of the City of Chicago, do hereby proclaim February 20, 1990, to be THE WOMEN'S BAR ASSOCIATION OF ILLINOIS DAY IN CHICAGO, in recognition of their fine efforts on behalf of women in our city.

Dated this 14th day of February, 1990.

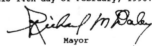

Mayor

began planning our 75th Anniversary Calendar. The calendar became a reality - a tribute to our glorious past and exciting present. Thanks to the generosity of Commerce Clearing House, and its general counsel, Mary Ann Hynes, the calendar was printed at no cost to WBAI. Carole Siegel's husband designed the calender and did the layout as his company's contribution.

"Taking on the task of the 47th annual Joint Professional Dinner, Laura Guzik told us that there was a chance that Mayor Richard M. Daley might be the speaker. When the word came, there were barely three weeks to publi-

Jeanne Hurley Simon and Odas Nicholson

cize the dinner and sell tickets. Liza Yntema's experience and thorough negotiating skills and Laura's super-human efforts paid off and Mayor Daley spoke. Several large law firms bought tickets. The dinner was a huge success.

"Having produced the calendar, Carole Siegel, Elsie Hozwarth and Charlotte Adelman turned their formidable energies to a 75th Anniversary luncheon on February 20, 1990. Over 200 people attended and heard Judge Margaret O'Malley, Dean Nina Appel, and Senator Dawn Clark Netsch speak on women in the judiciary, law schools, and politics. A birthday cake with 75 candles helped create an atmosphere of camaraderie and justifiable pride.

"Cook County Board President Dunne appointed me to the Judicial Advisory Committee and I participated (with a lot of help from Carole Siegel, Nancy Nicol and Teddy Gordon) in the joint effort by several bar associations in screening Democratic candidates for judicial positions. The process taught me a lot about politics and I am more convinced than ever that Illinois needs a merit system for appointed judges. Since judges will likely be elected for years to come, I have recommended to our Public Office Committee that we explore the possibility of joining with other bar groups to investigate and interview judicial candidates. Each association should reserve onto itself the right to evaluate the candidates but the joint nature of the effort would produce better investigations and be more respectful of the candidates' time.

"Outside events played a dominant role in shaping the events of this 75th year. In July of 1989, the U.S. Supreme Court sent their

issue of abortion back to the states and awakened a sleeping American majority. Women, and men, who had not written to their legislators, signed petitions, or participated in a demonstration in years turned out in record numbers to support a pro-choice position. Consistent with its 20 year old position, WBAI took a leadership role. Thanks to Barbara Greenspan and Penny Brown, we did a pro-choice workshop. The pollsters confirmed that the public wants the issue of abortion to be a women's decision.

"I was blessed as WBAI's President to serve during the same year as Leonard Amari was President of the Illinois State Bar Association. Len's commitment to improving the status of women and minorities in the legal profession is genuine and sincere. Thanks to Len (and Steven Anderson's trusty camera), WBAI was included in many bar events and my picture was in the paper so many times that I was embarrassed and my mother ran out of space on her refrigerator door.

"More importantly, WBAI has become a force to be reckoned with in the Illinois legal community. The larger firms are learning that the issues that concern women (maternity leave, part-time employment, care of elder family members) are also of concern to men. The firms are also learning that networking among women can produce clients and billings. It's no accident that over 200 judges agreed to attend the Judicial Reception in April. When WBAI talks, the legal community listens.

"There are others who deserve mention. Thanks to Elsie Hozwarth, the *WBAI News* is consistently fine, the best volunteer-produced bar newsletter in Illinois. Candace Gorman

April, 1991 Magistrate Joan Lefkow and Judge Mary Hooton, recipients of WBAI awards at the annual Judicial Reception with President Jewel Klein and Co-Chairs Laura Guzik and Lee Hugh Goodman. (Photo by Steve Anderson)

Esther Rothstein is inducted into 1990 Women's Hall of Fame.

Margaret Foster, Laura Gusik, _____, Susan Salita.

Justice Maryann McMorrow, Candace Gorman, president of WBAI, and Judge Sophia Hall at the Foundation Christmas party, 1990.

served on a federal panel which interviewed applicants for positions as U.S. Magistrate. Kathy Kintonis Hardesty, Carole Siegel and Mary Thompson got the idea of suburban meetings held in the southern suburbs. Barbara Miller started a group meeting in December in DuPage County. Carole Siegel and Charlotte Adelman devoted considerable time and energy to recruiting new members.

"Laura Guzik and Lee Goodman deserve special praise for co-chairing the 1989 Judicial Reception. Annual Judicial Reception honorees in April were: Circuit Court Judge Sophia Hall, Federal District Judge Ilana Rovner and Circuit Court Judge Monica Reynolds. Barbara Finesmith, Celeste Hammond, Gail Smith, Sharon Eiseman, Trudy McCarthy and Audrey Holzer took on special assignments and were able to fill in as needed. Through it all, WBAI's committees met regularly. Leslie Recht is putting together a membership directory.

"I have mentioned some of the WBAI board members above. They and the others - Lee Witte, Janet Gerske, Andrea Lyon, Ina Winston and Cathy Reiter - provided sage counsel and astute oversight to our organization in its 75th year.

"On June 7, 1990, I turn the gavel over to Candace Gorman. She's been involved in WBAI activities for years and will make a dynamic and exciting leader for the year to come. I leave WBAI in excellent hands. Very truly yours. Jewel N. Klein."

In 1990 in Cook County there were 46 women judges in (28 associate and 18 full) and three women appellate court justices.

On January 14, 1991 Dawn Clark Netsch became the first Illinois woman elected to a state wide office: Comptroller.

H. Candace Gorman was WBAI President in 1990-91. During her year, WBAI's motion to the Illinois Supreme Court to adopt the amicus curiae brief filed by the ISBA in the Kristen H. Fisher case was granted. Ms. Fisher was founded in direct civil contempt of court by a Judge in Champaign County, Illinois for refus-ing to provide information that Ms. Fisher claimed was protected by the attorney - client privilege. In addition to the reasons advanced by the ISBA, WBAI wanted to support Miss Fisher in honor of Myra Bradwell who, in 1869 was refused admission to the Illinois Bar because of a legal disability under which all married women were placed which was said to impair their ability to keep a client's confidence. In 1990 WBAI authored an amicus brief before the ARDC (Cornielia Tuite and Jewel Klein) arguing it is not okay for an attorney to threaten another attorney with sexual and physical harm. *WBAI's Newsletter*, first issued in 1945 with Jeanne Brown Gordon as editor, received the Chicago Woman in Publishing Award - 1st Place in the relevance to Women's Issues - Newsletters category. On June 11th, 1991 Elsie Holzwarth, *WBAI Newsletter* editor, accepted the award.

The probate committee developed a "durable power of attorney" WALLET CARD, a unique first. WBAI voted to oppose "Caller ID" without free call blocking. It sent written testimony to the Illinois Commerce Commission and issued letters to the editor, which sparked a spirited debate in the *Sun-Times*.

The 1990 annual Judicial Reception honored Honorable Joan Lefko and the Honorable Mary Hooton. A most glamorous person joined WBAI as a law student member: Miss America, Marjorie Vincent, a law student at Duke who lives in Oak Park, Illinois. The 1991 Judicial Reception honored Judges Marilyn Komoza, Barbara Disko and Sheila Murphy.

In conjunction with the preparation of this WBAI History book, the newly formed Illinois Supreme Court Legal History Society issued an enthusiastic note of support. It was signed by the officers of the society and Illinois Supreme Court Justice William G. Clark. At the Chicago Historical Society, WBAI has its own personal curator: Theresa McGill.

In 1991-92, under Carole Siegel's presi-

Judge Marilyn Komosa, new citizen Corey Ross, Candace Gorman, sister Mara Ross, father Chris Ross and Arnette Hubbard, Law Day, May 2, 1991.

Carole Siegel sworn in as president WBAI, 1992. R to L Judge Donegan, Judge Shields, Siegel, Judge Nowicki, and Judge Thomas.

dency, WBAI is continuing its leadership role. One of her first acts as President was to issue a press release announcing WBAI's endorsement of the Emergency Campaign to Overturn the Gag Rules, in keeping with WBAI's 21 year pro-choice position. In August President Siegel's letter to the Editor in *Today's Chicago Woman* was printed telling that, "The WBAI's Board of Directors voted unanimously to oppose caller ID without free blocking and has provided the Illinois Commerce Commission with written testimony on our position." Esther Rothstein has already mailed out the invitations for the WBAI Foundation's 26th Annual Scholarship Luncheon Award. Plans are being firmed up for the 50th annual Joint Professional Dinner. The October meeting will feature Kristen Fisher and others discussing attorney's Bill of Rights. In April, WBAI will entertain the judges at its 78th annual Judicial Reception. (Judge Susan Snow honored.)

A September 29, 1991 *Sun Times* article regarding the indictment of Judge Thomas J. Maloney on charges of taking bribes in murder cases noted that although the CBA regularly ranked him qualified and the Chicago Crime Commission recommended him in 1984, WBAI refused to recommend him citing his lack of respect for the courts.

Women are no longer a rarity in Illinois law schools; women judges are being appointed in increasing numbers, although none yet sit on the Illinois Supreme Court. Despite the 1936 state's attorney's opinion of women as prosecutors, today many women handle murder trials with ease. Law firms occasionally admit women to partnerships.

The question remains: Will women lawyers be able to progress further or even retain the gains they have achieved: Cynthia Fuchs Epstein, in her book *Women In Law*, notes that although men have "relaxed" their hold on the legal profession, they have not "released" it. Nonetheless, she predicts women lawyers will continue to do well.

In Unequal Access, Ronald Chester recalls George Santayana's warning: "Those who cannot remember the past are condemned to repeat it." He hopes that as women break into power positions they will remember their sisters and not "pull up the ladder." Noting that networks of women can help even the exceptional women lawyers, he believes they are vital for the advancement of those not so gifted. Exceptional women must realize, he reminds, that they did not achieve what they have sheerly by dint of their own efforts; the way was paved by women who struggled before them.

Unless women continue the struggle and, in great numbers, reach positions such as tenured professors in law schools, senior people in government and partners in important firms, the gains of the last few years may be less than secure.

In her wonderful 1986 book, *The Invisible Bar*, Karen Berger Morello says "It is tempting to point to these significant gains and to believe that the battle for equality is almost over. But history indicates otherwise. At nearly every stage of their development women attorneys incorrectly believed that once they themselves had proven their competence, acceptance for women in the next generation would be assured. As early as 1870 Chicago attorney Myra Bradwell was boasting that "the time will come, and shortly too, when women will not have to obtain legal knowledge and the right to use it under such difficulties..."Clearly the high expectations of these generations were never met. In part the problem was their belief that they had only to prove their worth in order to be welcomed by the bar. What they failed to realize, largely because they had no written history and far too few role models, was that they long ago had proven their competence and that there really were unspoken, undefined, invisible barriers that were keeping them from attaining positions of power and importance in the legal profession. As long as they continued to believe that proving their individual excellence was necessary, they would never be mobilizing the strength of their numbers to effect change."

Morello believes discrimination still exists but in far more subtle forms. Even though women enter the profession in substantial numbers, they are likely to be relegated to "second tier." Equality, she concludes, "is nowhere near completion."

In *Women in Law*, Cynthia Fuchs Epstein comments that women's bar associations in the past were oriented around "female" specialties: juvenile delinquency, domestic relations, probate. They have now expanded to deal with a wider range of women's interests and more self consciously act as a support group for women.

As this history goes to press, an August 21, 1991 *Chicago Sun Times* headline States: "Law Profs Discourage Women Litigators, Bar Chief Says." Roxanne Barton Conlin, President Elect of the Association of Trial Lawyers of America, was quoted as saying, "There are few litigators among attorneys but even fewer female litigators, and it starts at the law school level with the presumption and assumption that this is not something women should do or are capable of doing".

The always relevant question, Why a woman's bar association" is thus answered. Even as women progress in the profession, obstacles remain. Our association continues to work in furtherance of its purposes...the advancement and protection of women lawyers. There remain problems to overcome. We must protect the gains we have achieved. In unity there is strength.

Charlotte Adelman, Elsie Holswarth, chief editor and Kathy Bigley, news editors of the award winning WBAI News.

1991

CHICAGO WOMEN IN PUBLISHING

Awards Competition

AWARD OF EXCELLENCE

Presented to   *Women's Bar Association of Illinois*

For the publication   *Women's Bar Association of Illinois Newsletter*

Category   *First Place, Relevance to Women's Issues (Newsletters)*

Patricia M McCabe
President, Chicago Women in Publishing

Ana F. Rosa
Chair, Annual Awards Committee

History of the WBAI History Book

In 1988 the *WBAI News* carried my report of how it all came about, At that time I wrote: "It all started in 1984. I was preparing to serve as the seventieth WBAI President. WBAI's 70th birthday was an historic occasion, about which, I realized, I knew very little. I organized a 70th Anniversary Committee. We met repeatedly and agonized over how to dramatize this important occasion. One day, Jackie Lustig came up with the brilliant idea of a calendar. It was the perfect solution. It would provide a dramatic format for historical information plus be a daily reminder of WBAI for one full year.

"Next came work. For years, WBAI's records were contained in a battered old file cabinet on the Chicago Bar Association's 13th floor. It was locked and no one seemed to have a key. Fortunately, my letter to the manufacturer resulted in the prompt (and free) sending of two keys, which we carefully safe guarded. Elsie Hozwarth, Carole Siegel, Geraldine Brauneis and I formed teams to inspect the records. We copied important material on the CBA's frequently broken down copy machines.

"Mixed in with secretary's minutes, and treasurer's reports we found occasional gems: old newspaper clippings, handouts from long forgotten political campaigns, and photographs. Two albums full of newspaper clippings from the 1940's and 50's, carefully safeguarded by Judge Marilyn Komosa, proved to be "pay dirt". We also learned that, although WBAI was formed in 1914, no records existed (except for 1926) until 1931. We obtained photographs of Myra Bradwell, Alta Hulett, and Mary Bartleme from the Chicago Historical Society, and photographs of Audrey Hozer and Tala Engel in Christmas Spirits from the Chicago Bar Association and the *Sun-Times*. Carole Siegel, Elsie Holzwarth and I did the calendar's preliminary layout and wrote the history and captions. Carole Siegel's husband Jerry, donated the professional layout work and, through the good offices of Mary Ann Hynes, Commerce Clearing House donated the printing. The rest, as they say, is history.

"The 1985 WBAI calendar was a tremendous success. Using my office as headquarters, we mounted an ambitious advertising program where we solicited calendar purchases through items in the *Chicago Daily Law Bulletin*, and the publications of the National Association of Women Lawyers, The National Association of Women's Bar Associations and other organizations. My secretary filled orders from Hawaii to Florida. The project netted WBAI several thousand dollars.

"One day, Judge Howard Kaufman (one of our members) brought me a Florida Bar Association Journal completely devoted to women lawyers. Following up on this wonderful idea, I contacted the Illinois Bar journal and urged a similar issue. Isolde Davison, the editor, responded positively. The result was the May, 1986, Special Issue: *Illinois Women and the Law*. Among other important articles was the *Story of Women Lawyers in Illinois*, which I researched and wrote. Since WBAI's

history mirrored the progress of women lawyers throughout the state, much of the material used for articles was derived from the WBAI records.

"Preparation of the ISBA article was tantalizing, leading me to embark upon an even more thorough review of the WBAI file cabinet. Spending one or two hours at a crack., I made numerous trips to the 13th floor where I painstakingly went through the records, taking notes on my yellow pad. It was hot and stuffy up there, the isolation only occasionally broken by the arrival of CBA employees who used the area to watch television and eat lunch. Perusing the records was even more challenging because of the antiquated lighting available. I had to use a "hands-on" approach to the overhead light bulb. I was mollified only by the presence of volumes of Myra Bradwell's dusty, but nonetheless authentic, *Legal News*.

"Returning to the office with notes, I would immediately dictate them. The WBAI records were orderly (though incomplete) for the 1930s, 1940s and 1950s. However, after that, large gaps appeared and the records were completely out of order. Eventually, I completed my project. I was now in possession of a bulky typewritten summary. The WBAI Board resolved to donate WBAI's records to the Chicago Historical Society. The Chicago Historical Society has prepared an inventory of the records it received form the WBAI , as follows:

"Board of Directors Records, 1937-1939, 1969-1970, 1977-1978 (Box 1); Secretary's Records, 1960-1965, 1967-1969, 1971-1974 (Boxes 1-2); President's Papers, 1963-1964, 1969-1970 Box 2); General Administrative Records, 1954-1960, 1968-1969 (Box 3); Correspondence and Regular Meeting minutes, September 1931-1953, 1958-1959, 1970-1973, 1976-1977 (Boxes 3-4) 19256 Minutes; General Correspondence, 1957-1959 (Box 4); Newsletters, 1949-1956 (Box 4); Candidates Committee Report, 1963 (Box 5); Checkbooks, September 1948-June 1956 (Box 6); Dues Ledger, 1938-1956 (Box 6); Journal and Cash Book, 1936-1970 (Box 6); Treasurer's Reports, 1946-1957 (Box 6); Invoices and Bank Statements, 1956-1957 (Box 7); Vouchers, Cancelled Checks and Bank Statements, 1963-1967 (Box 7); Treasurer's Records, 1976-1977 (Box 7); Law Day Materials, 1970 (Box 7); Golden Anniversary Dinner Material, 1964 (Box 7); Annual Installation Dinner Material, 1964 (Box 7); Program, Women Lawyers' Centennial Dinner, 1969 (Box 7)

"Meanwhile, I'd been actively soliciting WBAI members for old records, newsletters, and other memorabilia. Many WBAI members responded generously with their time and energy and delivered precious irreplaceable materials. As I reviewed the materials, I was able to add information to the historical summary I had prepared. I also started a scrap book of current newspaper clippings, etc. It now numbers 16 volumes."

The next project was the 75th WBAI Anniversary Calendar. An article by Mara Tapp in the January 1990 *Merrill's Legal Times* pretty well describes it:

Admissible in court

Deidre Destia Cato now has the legal document to show she's been admitted to the state bar. Cato was one of 400 new lawyers sworn in in Chicago, and almost 300 took the oath at four other Illinois sites on Thursday.

Looking Back Three Quarters of a Century: WBAI at 75

"The women lawyers of Illinois ran up to their attics, emptied out their closets and dug into their pockets to rise to this occasion, and Charlotte Adelman and the Women's Bar Association of Illinois are grateful for what emerged.

"The fruits of these forays into the past are on view in the new WBAI calendar, which commemorates the association's 75th anniversary. On its cover, face earnest and arm outstretched in an oath, is Edna Brown. Next to her 1942 photo is a headline: "Portias Break Masculine Barrier."

"The guts of the calendar reveal a similar pot pourri of newspaper documentation of the history and ascent of Illinois female lawyers. The months, organized into subjects like "Judges", "Law and Marriage," Legal Aid," and "Gender Bias," feature an almost equal mix of older and more contemporary clippings.

"Most come from the personal files and belongings of WBAI members, according to Adelman who, along with fellow Calendar Committee members Elsie G. Hozwarth and Carole N. Siegel, put the calendar together.

" 'Some were waterstained but I was grateful nonetheless,' recalls Adelman who, besides her practice of law, is the WBAI's archivist and a former president. She recalls how one member, Petrina C. Penio, threw her clippings into the back of her car and hauled them down for Adelman's inspection.

" 'People really did that kind of thing,' Adelman says. 'That's why we were able to have this interesting old stuff'

"For example, Brown's cover shot came courtesy of her sister Frances B. Corwin, a lawyer with the Legal Aid Bureau. In fact, people were so happy to provide their materials to Adelman that she ended up with an office full - about 26 boxes worth - of materials to delight any archivist. That material has been turned over to the Chicago Historical Society where it's being preserved under the proper conditions.

"For the Calendar Committee and the two companies that designed and printed the calendar - Commerce Clearing House, and Gerald Siegel and Associates - it was a labor of what lawyers might call pro bono love. For Adelman, it was also the continuation of an older interest - pun intended.

" 'I got so involved when I was president in the history,' she says of WBAI. 'I've been collecting the stuff for five years now.'

"Now the WBAI members can collect her collections. And that way, history is sure to repeat itself."

In October, 1988 I read an article in the *Chicago Tribune* about Turner Publishing, a press providing an alternative for history books too small to attract major publishers. The article noted there would be no initial cost, just the price of the book. A sponsoring group would encourage its members to provide memories, biographies, photos and a list of its members.

In November, I contacted Turner Publishing to see if it would be interested in doing a WBAI History in honor of our 75th birthday. They were. WBAI's Board approved the project and we started publicity.

It hasn't been easy getting our members to send in their biographies. Even today, many haven't gotten around to it. Even though I'd done a lot of work researching our history, the more I did the more glaring became what I still had left to do.

So, here is a book. It contains many of our members biographies and pictures. It contains a lot of our history. There's a lot of both left out. I hope someone will pick up where we've left off and produce an updated more complete work.

WBAI's records and members' memorabilia have been donated to the Chicago Historical Society, where they are invaluable as an archive for historical research. Please help our collection grow; for information, contact Charlotte Adelman, 105 W. Madison, Chicago, IL (312) 263-2525.

Collection of WBAI memorabilia and records and members' personal recollections and photos, etc. . continues. Our collection at the Chicago Historical Society needs to be added to and replenished. So, please continue to search your closets, basements, for old files and the like and keep the materials coming.

Women's Bar Association of Illinois Foundation History

The Women's Bar Association of Illinois Foundation came into existence in 1966 as a WBAI Committee designated scholarships to deserving and qualified women law students in honor of Judge Bartelme and other distinguished women jurists. The Committee, with Esther R. Rothstein as Chairman and Dolores K. Hanna as Vice-Chairman, gave a $300 scholarship in each of the years 1966 and 1967, with funds contributed by the WBAI and its members.

In 1968 the Committee was reorganized and incorporated as the Women's Bar Association of Illinois Foundation, and Illinois not-for -profit corporation and was in due course granted an exemption from federal income

taxes under section 501 (c) (3) of the Internal revenue Code, so that contributions to it are deductible for income tax purposes as charitable contributions. The original Board of Directors as listed in the Articles of Incorporation consisted of nine members, including two ex officio members, then WBAI President, Helen Hart Jones and Vice President Elaine Strauschild Blatt, plus WBAI members Helen F. McGillicuddy, Esther R. Rothstein, Katharine D. Agar, Cary Ann Bechly, Sharon L. King, Mary Ann G. McMorrow and Mary Avgerin Pappas. The officers were Helen F. McGillicuddy, President, Esther R. Rothstein, Vice President, and Cary Ann Bechly, Secretary-Treasurer. The Directors are elected by the WBAI Board for three-year terms, with the terms of approximately one-third of the directors expiring each year.

The Foundation's stated corporate purposes are to provide scholarships for deserving and qualified women students in accredited Illinois law schools, and to honor the memory of distinguished women lawyers and judges by awarding such scholarships in their name and memory.; In accordance with its purposes, the Foundation has awarded scholarships each year at the end of 1989, in its 24 years of operation, first as the Bartelme Committee and then as the WBAI Foundation, it had awarded 87 scholarships totalling over $200,000, with the annual amount increasing from the initial $300 in 1966 to $32,000 in 1988 and 1989. The funds have come from individual contributions, fund-raising events, grants from Kraft, Inc. and Commerce Clearing House, a bequest from former WBAI President Alice M. Chellberg, and an endowment gift from WBAI member Ramona Hayes Healy, who died in 1988.

In 1983 the Foundation established an Advisory Council consisting of WBAI members who have shown special interest or been of special help in the Foundation's activities. Council members are invited to attend all Board meetings and give advise and counsel. Present Advisory Council members (as of May, 1990) are: Katharine D. Agar, Theodora Gordon, Mary Frances Hegarty, Honorable Olga Jurco, Honorable Rosemary LaPorta, and Honorable Lucia T. Thomas.

The 1990 Board of Directors of the Foundation consists of the following members: Esther R. Rothstein, President; Sharon L. King, Vice President,; Etha Beatrice Fox, Secretary; Cary Ann Bechly, Treasurer; Elizabeth C. Bannon, Laurel G. Bellows, Joanne R. Drsicoll, Dolores K. Hanna, Jacqueline S. Lustig, Patricia E. Mullin, Patricia Unsinn, Jewel N. Klein, (ex officio as WBAI President), Candace Gorman, (ex officio as WBAI 1st Vice President).

In June, 1990, when Jewel Klein's term as WBAI president ends, Carole Siegel will move up to the position of first vice president and become an ex officio member of the Foundation Board.

Two long-time Foundation Board members died in early 1990, Lillian K. Kubicek and Honorable Helen F. McGillicuddy, and the Foundation plans to dedicate a memorial scholarship to each of them.

The year 1990 was the Foundation's 25th scholarship year, and plans are under way for special celebrations at the 25th annual awards luncheon in September and the December Holiday party to mark this silver milestone of progress and achievement.

WBAI Foundation Board and Committee members — photo taken at Holiday Party committee meeting, April 5, 1990.

Seated, Cary Ann Bechly, Esther Rothstein, Sharon King. Standing, Patricia Mullin, Dolores Hanna, Patricia Unsinn, Elizabeth Bannon, Rosemary Shiels, Laura Bellows, Jacqueline Lustig. (Etha Beatrice Fox, Foundation Secretary was unable to be present at this meeting.)

INSTALLATION—1991

Esthel Allen

Victoria Almeida

Dean Nina Appel

Carroll Barry

Laurel Bellows

Helene Berger

Kathryn Bigley

Elaine Blatt

Geraldine Braundeis

Penny Brown

Carole Ann Budyak

Judge Ronald Davis

M. Lois Dierstein

Judge Loretta Douglas

Hon. Rosemary LaPorta

Barbara Finesmith

Susan Fox Gillis

Lee Hugh Goodman

Zenia Goodman

Theodora Gordon

H. Candace Gorman

Eleanor Guthrie

Laura Guzik

Dawn Haghighi

Mary Hamilton

Judge R. Morgan Hamilton

Delores Hanna

Idrienne Heymann

Linda Kagan

Beth Lehman

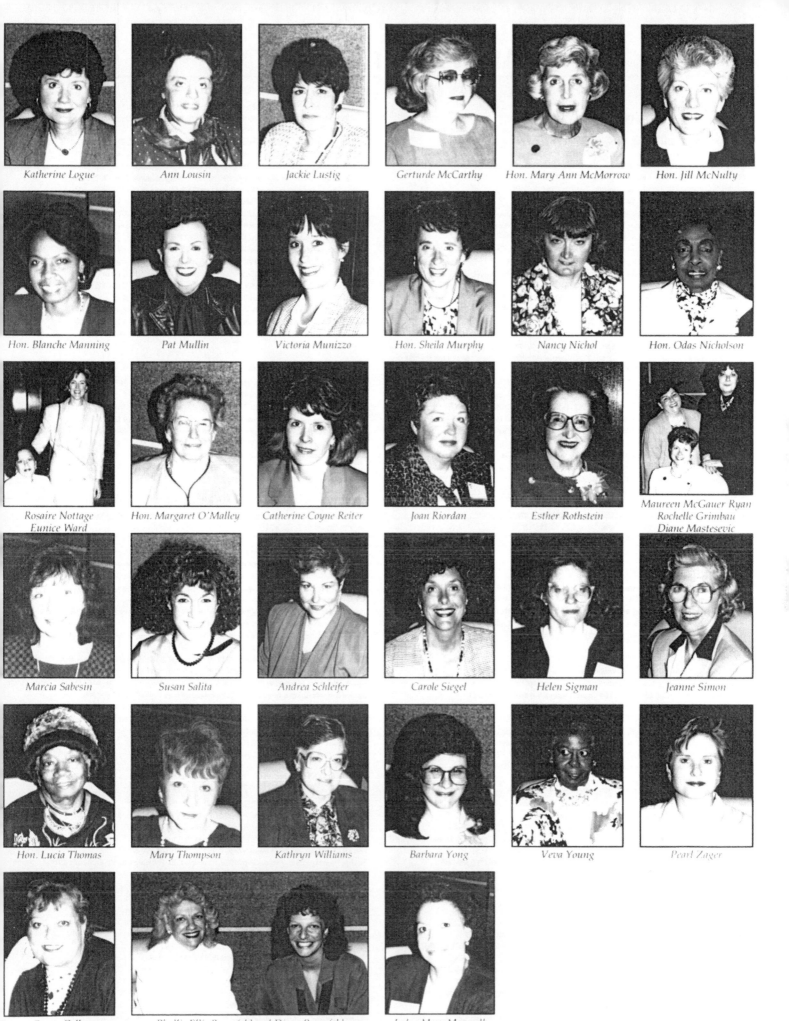

Katherine Logue

Ann Lousin

Jackie Lustig

Gerturde McCarthy

Hon. Mary Ann McMorrow

Hon. Jill McNulty

Hon. Blanche Manning

Pat Mullin

Victoria Munizzo

Hon. Sheila Murphy

Nancy Nichol

Hon. Odas Nicholson

Rosaire Nottage
Eunice Ward

Hon. Margaret O'Malley

Catherine Coyne Reiter

Joan Riordan

Esther Rothstein

Maureen McGauer Ryan
Rochelle Grimbau
Diane Mastesevic

Marcia Sabesin

Susan Salita

Andrea Schleifer

Carole Siegel

Helen Sigman

Jeanne Simon

Hon. Lucia Thomas

Mary Thompson

Kathryn Williams

Barbara Yong

Veva Young

Pearl Zager

Evette Zells

Phyllis Ellis Rosenfeld and Diane Rosenfeld

Judge Mary Maxwell
Thomas

LAW PRACTICE REPORT

Administrative

Lisa M. Aisner, Box 3297 RFD, Long Grove, IL 60047, (708) 438-7018
Carole J. Anderson, Lane & Waterman, 600 Davenport Bank Bldg., Davenport, IA 52801, (319) 324-3246
Bonny Sutker Barezky, 3311 Old Mill Rd., Northbrook, IL 60062, (708) 621-9700
Ann Breen-Greco, 4123 N. Maplewood, Chicago, IL 60618 (312) 539-8468
Nancy Brent, Nancy Brent Attorney at Law, 5445 N. Sheridan Rd. #1906, Chicago, IL 60640 (312) 728-3663
Patricia Bryant, 9050 S. Hoyne, Chicago, IL 60620 (312) 779-3555
Karen Michels Caille, 2211 Forestview, Evanston, IL 60201 (708) 328-3678
Gloria G. Coco, 339 W. Barry Ave. #14B Chicago, IL 60601
Terrance Diamond, Earl Neal & Associates, 111 W. Washington Ste. 1010, Chicago, IL 60602 (312) 641-7144
Joan M. Eagle, Schwartz & Freeman, 401 N. Michigan 34th Fl., Chicago, IL 60611 (312) 782-4115
Jodi Eisenstadt, Mayer Brown & Platt, 190 S. LaSalle, Chicago 60603 (312) 782-0600
Martha A. Garcia, Katz, Friedman, Schur and Eagle, 7 South Dearborn 1734, Chicago, IL 60603 (312) 263-6330
Lee Hugh Goodman, 2201 Center Ave, Northbrook, IL 60062 (708) 475-3744
N. Caroline Harney, Lewis, Overbeck & Furman, 135 S. Lasalle, Suite 1000, Chicago, IL 60603
Paula E. Hiza, 4052 N. Paulina, Chicago, IL 60613 (312) 248-2540
Marie Bellamy Johnson, 300 N. State #4525 E, Chicago, IL 60610 (312) 644-0171
Deborah Jones, Lord Bissell & Brook, 115 S LaSalle St., Chicago, IL 60603, (312) 443-1844
Susan Kaplan, Comm. Econ. Dvlpmt. Law Proj., 220 S. State St. #322, Chicago, IL 60604 (312) 939-3638
Jewel Klein, Holstein Mack & Klein, 250 S. Wacker 16th Fl., Chicago, IL 60606, (312) 906-8000
Judith Kolman, City of Des Plaines, 1420 Miner Street, Des Plaines, IL 60016 (708) 391-5302
Jacqueline S. Lustig, IL Dept. of Human Rights, 100 W. Randolph #10-100, Chicago, IL 60601 (312) 814-6234
Ofelia Manalang, 1731 Redman Ave., St. Louis, MO 63138 (314) 653-0329
Shirley Moscow Michaelson, 1840 1/2 Mohawk, Chicago, IL 60614 (312) 337-8055
Corinne McAlpine, IL Dept. of Empl. Security, 401 S. State St. 2nd Floor, Chicago, IL 60613 (312)-793-6947
Patricia E. Noble, 1455 N. Sandburg Terrace #2708B, Chicago, IL 60610 (312) 943-3612
Maria Pelaez Peterson, US Dept. Of Labor Off. The Soll., 230 S. Dearborn 8th Fl, Chicago, IL 60604 (312) 353-0890
Leslie Recht, Defrees & Fiske, 200 S Michigan Ave. Ste. 1100, Chicago, IL 60604 (312) 372-4000
Janice I. Rode, 7528 N. Bell Avenue, Chicago, IL 60645 (312) 465-6016
Evelyn Starr Rupert, 151 N. Michigan #2505, Chicago, IL 60601 (312) 861-1636
Terrie A. Rymer, Jewish Children's Bureau, 1 S. Franklin, Chicago, IL 60606 (312) 346-6700 Ext. 3053
Susan Salita, 1206 West Waveland #3, Chicago, IL 60602 (312) 433-3861
Barbara A. Sherman, 360 E Randolph #3306, Chicago, IL 60601 (312) 861-1130
Nancy M. Sherman, 2427 Chain Bridge Rd. NW, Washington, DC 20016 (202) 362-6229
Bridget M. Shovlin, 851 W. Margate Terrace, Chicago, IL 60604 (312) 561-0715
Nancy J. Smith, Sec., 219 S Dearborn Rm. 1204, Chicago, IL 60604 (312) 353-7454
Theresa M. Varnet, 1500 Carson Ct., Homewood, IL 60430 (312) 799-2270

Antitrust

Ellen M. Babbitt, Butler Rubin Newcomer Saltarel, 3 First National Plaza #1505, Chicago, IL 60602 (312) 444-9660
Virginia H. Holden, Illinois Bell, 225 W. Randolph #27B, Chicago, IL 60606 (312) 727-1486
Ellen G. Robinson, Robinson, Curley & Clayton, PC, 300 S. Wacker Dr. #1700, Chicago, IL 60606 (312) 855-0955
Marilyn J. Schramm, Law Dept. Quaker Oats Co., P O Box 9001, Chicago, IL 60604-9001 (312) 222-7407

Appellate

Cynthia Alexander, Attorney at Law, 305 Washington, Waukegan, IL 60085 (312) 662-9166
Lynne M. Baker, Holleb & Coff, 55 E. Monroe #4000, Chicago, IL 60603 (312) 807-4600
Joan S. Cherry, Asst. State's Attorney, 50 Daley Center, Chicago, IL 60602 (312) 443-5450
Geena Diane Cohen, Genson Steinback & Gillespie, 53 W. Jackson, Suite 1420, Chicago, IL 60604 (312) 726-9015
Colleen K. Connell, American Civil Liberties Union, 20 E. Jackson Blvd. 16th Fl., Chicago, IL 60604 (312) 427-7330
Cara Davis, Fraterrigo Best & Beranek, 55 W. Mopnroe #3400, Chicago, IL 60603 (312) 782-9255
Karen Fisher Di Monte, Fisher & Di Monte, 111 W. Washington #1860, Chicago, IL 60602 (312) 236-3280
Mary Ellen Dienes, Attorney at Law, 120 S. Riverside Plz. #1150, Chicago, IL 60606-3910 (312) 207-5454
Joanne Rouzan Driscoll, 7 Beechnut Dr., So. Barrington, IL 60010 (312) 359-0017
Debra DiMaggio, Johnson Cusack & Bell Ltd., 222 N. Lasalle Ste. 2200, Chicago, IL 60602
Lisa I. Fair, Law Offices of Michael J. Rove, 875 N. Dearborn St., Chicago, IL 60610 (312) 482-9100
Aviva Futorian, Legal Asst. Foundation Chicago, 343 S. Dearborn, Chicago, IL 60604 (312) 341-1070
Carol L. Gaines, 2133B N Magnolia, Chicago, IL 60614 (312) 871-8082
Janet Gerske, Attorney at Law, 542 S. Dearborn Ste. 1060, Chicago, Il 60605-1525 (312) 408-0329
Cynthia Giacchetti, Law Offices of Cynthia Giacche, 343 S Dearborn Suite 1510, Chicago, IL 60604 (312) 939-6440
Judith A. Griffin, 1st District Appell. Court, 2800 Daley Center, Chicago, IL 60602 (312) 793-2325
Patricia W. Hatamyar, Sonnenschein Carlin, 8000 Sears Tower, Chicago, IL 60606 (312) 876-7440
Diane P. Jackson, Diane Jackson & Associates, 1821 Walden Office Square, Schaumburg, IL 60173 (312) 397-2266
Linda S. Kagan, Attorney at Law, 10 N. Dearborn Penthouse, Chicago, IL 60602 (312) 263-2261
Karen Alice Klope, 256 N. Webster, Jacksonville, IL 62650 (309) 663-6911
Sharon G. Kramer, Attorney at Law, 205 W. Wacker #1515, Chicago, IL 60606 (312) 236-4946
Nancy G. Lischer, 4741 N. Paulina, Chicago, IL 60640 (312) 334-1576
Ellen Seavey Martin, Querry & Harrow Ltd., 135 S. La Salle St. #3600, Chicago, IL 60603
Mary Anne Mason, Kevin M. Forde Ltd., 111 W. Washington #1100, Chicago, IL 60602 (312) 641-1441
Carol McHugh, 1516 Hinman #209, Evanston, IL 60201 (312) 528-2933
Hon. Mary Ann G. McMorrow, Appellate Ct. 1st District, 30-58 Daley Ctr., Chicago, IL 60602 (312) 793-5432
Suzanne M. Metzel, Pope & John Ltd., 311 S. Wacker #500, Chicago, IL 60606 (312) 408-3390
Lora E. Minichillo, Schwartz & Freeman, 401 N. Michigan Ave. 3 #1900, Chicago, IL 60611 (312) 222-0800
Ayrie Moore, 5252 N. Wayne Ave., Chicago, IL 60640 (312) 784-6852
Kathleen Hogan Morrison, Jas. P. Chapman & Assoc. Ltd., 542 S. Dearborn St. Ste. 106, Chicago, IL 60605 (312)

408-0330
Ruth M. Moscovitch, 3901 N. Hamlin Ave., Chicago, IL 60618 (312) 463-1817
Cynthia L. McPike, IL. St. Labor Relations Bd, 320 W. Washington St. #500, Springfield, IL 62701 (217) 785-3155
Nancy J. Nicol, 1660 N. LaSalle St. 3909, Chicago, IL 60614 (312) 664-4235
Margaret L. Paris, Cotsirilos Stephenson Et Al, 33 N. Dearborn, Chicago, IL 60602 (312) 263-0345
Sharon Finegan Patterson, Lord Bissell & Brook, 115 S. LaSalle, Chicago, IL 60603 (312) 443-1733
Marilee Roberg, Pedersen & Houpt, 180 N. LaSalle #3400, Chicago, IL 60601 (312) 641-6888
Joseph V. Roddy, Attorney at Law, 77 W. Washington, Chicago, IL 60602 (312) 368-8220
Susan L. Satter, Attorney at Law; 123 West Madison #1500, Chicago, IL 60602 (312) 939-2070
Ricca Slone, Attorney at Law, 210 Twin Towers Plaz. 456 Fulton, Chicago, IL 61602 (309) 676-0335
Mary Jo Smerz, Lowrey & Smerz Ltd., 745 N. Waiola, La Grange Park, IL 60525 (312) 332-5433
Christine E. Smith-McMahon, Attorney at Law, 120 W. Madison #725, Chicago, IL 60602 (312) 782-4558
Lois Solomon, 150 South Wacker Dr., Chicago, IL 60606 (312) 782-2603
Abigail K. Spreyer, 3100 N. Sheridan Rd. #6D, Chicago, IL 60657 (312) 477-4949
Mary F. Stafford, Clausen Miller Et Al, 10 South LaSalle Street, Chicago, IL 60603-1098 (312) 855-1010
Joe Steinman, IIT Chicago-Kent College of LA, 77 S. Wacker Dr., Chicago, IL 60606 (312) 567-5006
Patricia Unsinn, Sate Appell Defender, 100 W. Randolph #5-500, Chicago, IL 60601 (312) 814-5472
Ruth E. Vandermark, Wildman Harrold Allen & Dixon, 225 W. Wacker Dr., Chicago, IL 60606-1229 (312) 210-2567
Katrina Veerhusen, Kevin M. Forde Ltd., 111 W. Washington #1100, Chicago, IL 60602 (312) 641-1441
Kathleen M. Krippner Watson, Clancy and Krippner, 7 S. Second Street, St. Charles, IL 60174 (312) 584-7666
Helen T. Wilson, Schiff Harden & Waite, 7300 Sears Tower, Chicago, IL 60606 (312) 876-7005

Arbitration/Mediation

Brigette S. Bell, Pretzel & Stouffer, One S. Wacker, Chicago, IL 60606 (312) 346-1973
Shirley L. Berngard, 2908 W. Pratt, Chicago, IL 60645 (312) 262-2883
Anne Wells Clark, Asher, Gittler Et Al, 2 N. LaSalle St. #1200, Chicago, IL 60602 (312) 263-1500
Susan Fox Gillis, Querrey and Harow Ltd., 135 S. LaSalle, Chicago, IL 60602 (312) 236-9850
Esther O. Keagan, Kegan & Kegan, 79 W. Monroe St. #1320, Chicago, IL 60603-4969 (312) 782-6495
Beth A. Lehman, Attorney at Law, 18 S. Michigan #1200, Chicago, IL 60603 (312) 332-5642
Carol G. Silverman, North Suburban Mdiation Service, 680 Bluff, Glencoe, IL 60022 (708) 251-5968

Banking

Jean A. Adams, Attorney at Law, 1350 E. Sibley Blvd. #400, Dolton, IL 60419 (708) 849-5577
Lynne M. Baker, Holleb & Coff, 55 E. Monroe #4000, Chicago, IL 60603 (312) 807-4600
Doris W. Bryant, (312) 352-3034
Melanie S. Carter, Citicorp Diners Club Inc., 8430 W. Bryn Mawr Ave., Chicago, IL 60631 (312) 380-5150
Patricia Sweeney Fisher, Amoco Corp., 200 E. Randolph #3206 B, Chicago, IL 60601 (312) 856-2579
Lynn S. Fradkin, Federal Depository Insurance Comp., 9525 Bryn Mawr, Rosemont, IL 60018
Ellen Beth Gill, Masuda, Funai, Eifert and Mitchell, One East Wacker Dr. Ste 32, Chicago, IL 60601 (312) 977-9500
Carol L. Gloor, Holstein, Mack & Klein, 250 S. Wacker Dr. Penthouse, Chicago, IL 60606 (312) 906-8000
Adorea Goodman, 309 Ferndale Rd., Glenview, IL 60025 (312) 724-7664
Sharon M. Henschen, Proffitt Law Offices, 110 E. Third St. P.O. Box 110, Pana, IL 62557 (217) 562-2151
Martha Hovorka, Central Feeral Savings, 10335 Milford Road, Westchester, IL 60154 (708) 656-5000
Laurie M. Judd, Kavanagh Scully Sudow Et Al, 301 SW. Adams Street Suite 700, Peoria, IL 61602 (309) 676-1381
Teri J. Kurasch, 1861 Larkdale Road, Northbrook, IL 60062 (708) 480-0990
Karen Drizin Levine, Novack & Macey, 303 W. Madison #1500, Chicago, IL 60606 (312) 419-6900
Carol S. McMahan, Carroll Hartigan & McCauley Lt., 1 N. LaSalle #3100, Chicago, IL 60602 (312) 236-3575
Lora E. Minichillo, Schwartz & Freeman, 401 N. Michigan Ave. #1900, Chicago, IL 60611 (312) 222-0800;
Maxine E. Noble, Baker & Mckenzie, 130 E. Randolph, Chicago, IL 60601 (312) 861-6589
Debra Price Prodromos, 1430 Hollywood Ave., Glenview, IL 60025 (708) 729-0277
Audrey E. Selin, Altheimer & Gray, 10 S. Wacker Dr. Ste. 4000, Chicago, IL 60606 (312) 715-4848
Vasiliki Tsaganos, 5701 N. Sheridan Rd. #14G, Chicago, IL 60660 (312) 334-3239
Michelle Becker Ventress, 17182 Hill Creek Ct., Orland Park, IL 60462 (312) 424-4900
Beverly A. Wyckoff, Sanwa Bank-Chicago Br., 10 S. Wacker Drive 31st Fl, Chicago, IL 60606-7401 (312) 661-6046

Bankruptcy & Reorganization

Kelly Anne Chesney, 4309 W. Sunnyside, Chicago, IL 60630 (312) 685-1918
Sara E. Cook, McKenna Storer Et Al, 200 N. LaSalle #3000, Chicago, IL 60601 (312) 558-3984
Linda Crohn, Shimberg and Crohn, 59 East Van Buren, Chicago, IL 60605 (312) 663-5575
Denise A. De Lauren, Holleb & Coff, 55 E. Monroe #4100, Chicago, IL 60603 (312) 807-4600
Mary Kathryn Duggan, 14459 Lincoln Ave., Dolton, IL 60419 (708) 841-3079
Patricia Sweeney Fisher, Amoco Corp., 200 E. Randolph #3206 B, Chicago, IL 60601 (312) 856-2579
Sharon Gromer, 2137 W. Montrose, Chicago, IL 60618 (312) 348-3833
Mary F. Hamilton, Law Offices of Mary Hamilton, 1104 Lake Ave., Wilmette, IL 60091 (312) 256-4259
Jacquelyn Haynes, Borovsky Erlich & Kronenberg, 205 N. Michigan 41st Fl., Chicago, IL 60601 (312) 861-0800
Cathy L. Hertzberg, Attorney at Law, 20 N. Clark Ste. 2550, Chicago, IL 60602 (312) 641-1051
Eileen R. Hurley, US Bankruptcy Court, P.O. Box 243, Springfield, IL 62705; (217) 492-4550
Elenie K. Huszagh, Robins, Kaplan Et Al, 55 W. Wacker Dr. Suite 900, Chicago, IL 60601 (312) 782-9200
Francine Green Kelner, 340 Redwing, Deerfield, IL 60015 (708) 541-9248
Gina B. Krol, Cohen & Cohen, 55 W. Monroe #920, Chicago, IL 60603 (312) 368-0300
Wendy R. Morgan, Law Firm of Wendy R. Morgan, 1301 W. 22nd St. #1007, Oak Brook, IL 60521 (312) 635-8442
Lauren Newman, 2100 N. Lincoln Park West, Chicago, IL 60614 (312) 248-5376
Alice M. Noble-Allgire, United States District Court, 301 W. Main, Benton, IL 62812 (618) 439-9513
Mary Sinclair Pearce, 724 Park Avenue, Wilmette, IL 60091 (312) 256-5968
Nettie R. Sabin, Nettie F. Sabin & Assoc., 6805 N. Sheridan Rd., Chicago, IL 60626-3897 (312) 274-8581

Lynn Sacco, 2548 W. Cortez, Chicago, IL 60622 (312) 525-2285
Leslie T. Shuman, Ross & Hardies, 150 N. Michigan Ste. 2500, Chicago, IL 60601 (312) 263-5100
Kathryn Somers, Attorney at Law, 33 N. LaSalle St. #3400, Chicago, IL 60602 (312) 332-1985
Sarah Stegemoeller, Defrees & Fiske, 200 S. Michigan Ave. #1100, Chicago, IL 60604 (312) 372-4000
Carolyn E. Winter, Mandel Lipton & Stevenson Ltd., 33 N. Dearborn, Chicago, IL 60602 (312) 236-7080
Jolene M. Wise, Sec., 219 S. Dearborn Room 1204, Chicago, IL 60604 (312) 353-7390

Civil Litigation

Marina Ammendola, Patricia Bobb & Assoc., Three First National Plaza, 66 Chicago, IL 60602 (312) 332-2350
Aimee B. Anderson, 260 E. Chestnut #4104, Chicago, IL 60611 (312) 943-0799
Joann Angarola, Ross & Hardies, 150 N. Michigan Ave., Chicago, IL 60601 (312) 558-1000
Debra R. Antone, Beermann Swerdlove Et Al, 69 W. Washington Room 600, Chicago, IL 60602 (312) 21-9700
Barbara Baer, 2800 N. Lake Shore Dr., Chicago, IL 60657 (312) 871-3258
Lynne M. Baker, Holleb & Coff, 55 E. Monroe #4000, Chicago, IL 60603 (312) 807-4600
Ana M. Bednar, Holstein Mack & Klein, 250 S. Wacker Dr. Penthouse, Chicago, IL 60606 (312) 906-8000
Laurel G. Bellows, Bellows & Bellows, 79 W. Monroe #800, Chicago, IL 60603 (312) 332-3340
Helaine L. Berger, Berger & De Paul, 20 N. Clark, Suite 1725, Chicago, IL 60602 (312) 641-2020
Patricia T. Bergeson, Pope Ballard Shepard & Fowle, 69 W. Washington St., Chicago, IL 60602-3069; (312) 630-4261
Patricia C. Bobb, Patricia C. Bobb & Assoc., 3 First National Plaza #660, Chicago, IL 60602 (312) 332-2350
Kathleen Bridgman, Connelly, Mustes & Schroeder, 208 S. LaSalle Ste. 1800, Chicago, IL 60604 (312) 726-5575
Penny Brown, Musch Shlist Freed Denenberg A., 200 N. LaSalle St., #2100, Chicago, IL 60601 (312) 346-3100
Myra J. Brown, Asst. States Attorney,500 Daley Center, Chicago, IL 60602 (312) 443-5669
Susan Davis Brunner, Attorney at Law, 2401 Simpson, Evanston, IL 60201 (708) 864-7974
Ann C. Buran, 1250 W. Grace 2F, Chicago, IL 60613 (312) 929-2048
Anne C. Burr, Thomas Mamer & Haughey, Box 967, Champaign, IL 61824 (217) 351-1500
Mary Ellen Cagney, 1100 N. Lake Shore Dr. Apt. 13B, Chicago, IL 60611
Gayle Tronving Carper, Attorney at Law, P. O. Box 790, Macomb, IL 61455 (309) 833-1702
Dewey Jeanne Caton, Quaker Oats Co., Law Dept., 321 N. Clark, Chicago, IL 60610 (312) 222-7802
Hon. Donna L. Cervini, 819 Linden Ave., Oak Park, IL 60302 (708) 383-5659
Joy L. Colwell, Beckman Kelly & Smith, 5900 Hohman Ave., Hammond, IN 46320 (219) 933-0482
Colleen K. Connell, American Civil Liberties Union, 20 E. Jackson Blvd.16th Fl., Chicago, IL 60604 (312) 427-7330
Clare E. Connor, Hinshaw Culbertson, 222 LaSalle, Chicago, IL 60601 (312) 630-4400
Darrah Desmond Cousino, Landau Omahana & Kopka, 8420 W. Bryn Mawr. #1030, Chicago, IL 60631 (312) 380-8800
Karen A. Covy, Querry & Harrow, Ltd., 135 S. LaSalle St., Chicago, IL 60603(312) 236-9850
Phyllis L. Crocker, The Texas Resource Center, 511 West 7th Street, Austin, TX 78701
Donna Del Principe, Kane Obbish Propes & Garippo, 100 W. Monroe Ste. 1900, Chicago, IL 60603 (312) 346-8355
Catherine Q. Delahunt, 827 Oakwood Ave., Lake Forest, IL 60045 (708) 615-9040
Ruthanne DeWolfe, Legal Assitance Fdn., 343 S. Dearborn 700, Chicago, IL 60604 (312) 341-1070
Karen Fisher Di Monte, Fisher & Di Monte, 111 W. Washington #1860, Chicago, IL 60602 (312) 236-3280
Marcia E. Doane, 210 E. Pearson St. Apt. 5A, Chicago, IL 60611 (312) 751-0619
Laura Dolin, Fritzshall & Gleason, 309 W. Washington #600, Chicago, IL 60606 (312) 236-6100
Karen M. Dorff, Gardner Carton & Douglas, 321 N. Clark #3200, Chicago, IL 60610 (312) 245-8698
Rochelle S. Dyme, Rosenthal & Schanfield, 55 E. Monroe, Chicago, IL 60603 (312) 236 5622
Melissa S. Ellison, Craig & Craig, 227 1/2 S. 9th Box 1545, Mt. Vernon, IL 62864 (618) 244-7511
Ruth E. Farbman, 2 E. Oak St. Apt. 3602, Chicago, IL 60611 (312) 263-0599
Mary Carol Farmar, Law Offices of Terry Sullivan, 60 Gould Ctr. 101, Rolling Meadows, IL 60008 (312) 228-1100
Ellen Barron Feldman, Dardick & Denlos, 737 N. Michigan Ave., Chicago, IL 60610 (312) 944-7900
Margaret M. Forenza, Baxter Healthcare Corp., 1 Baxter Parkway, Deerfield, IL 600165 (708) 948-4932
Susan Fleming, St. Francis Hospital, 355 Ridge Ave., Evanston, IL 60202 (708) 492-3340
Andrea Sykes Foote, Attorney at Law, 11 S. 2nd Street, Geneva, IL 60134 (708) 232-2290
Hon. Lester D. Foreman, State of IL, 2005 Daley Cntr., Chicago, IL 60602 (312) 443-5902
Susan Fox Gillis, Querry and Harrow Ltd., 135 S. La Salle, Chicago, IL 60602 (312) 236-9850
Sharon M. Gisselman, 1208 Gilber St., Wausau, WI 54401 (715) 845-6775
Judith Glaser, Rathje Woodward Dyer & Burt, 203 E. Liberty Dr. P. O. Box 786, Wheaton, IL 60189 (312) 668-8500
Lisa Ann Goldberg, 1341 West Waveland Ave. Apt. 2E, Chicago, IL 60613 (312) 929-6640
Lori A. Goldstein, 232 Hibbard, Wilmette, IL 60091 (708) 256-6640
Jannis E. Goodnow, Lord Bissell & Brook, 115 S. LaSalle, Chicago, IL 60603 (312) 443-1889
Barbara Greenspan, 2328 W. Farewell, Chicago, IL 60645 (312) 274-6980
Deborah Gubin, Deborah J. Gubin & Associates, 105 W. Adams 31st Fl., Chicago, IL 60603 (312) 201-9331
Elizabeth J. Guscott-Mueller, Attorney at Law, 3500 Three First National Plaz., Chicago, IL 60602 (312) 927-9249
Deborah A. Hill, Katten, Muchin & Zavis, 525 W. Monroe #1600, Chicago, IL 60606 (312) 902-5354
Sarah S. Hirsen, Cowan & Minetz, 180 N. LaSalle #2810, Chicago, IL 60601 (312) 236-9121
Barbara Levine Holcomb, Attorney at Law, 53 West Jackson #1220, Chicago, IL 60604 (312) 427-6050
Elsie G. Holzwarth, 1410 E. 55 St., Chicago, IL 60615 (312) 684-7627
Hon. Mary H. Hooton, 151 N. Michigan Ave., Chicago, IL 60601 (312) 565-1277
Linda K. Horra, Hinshaw Culbertson Et Al, 222 N. LaSalle St. #300, Chicago, IL 60601 (312) 704-3022
Leskie K. Horwath, Querry & Harrow Ltd., 135 S. LaSalle St., Chicago, IL 60603 (312) 704-2964
Burton Joseph, Barsy Joseph & Lichtenstein, 134 N. LaSalle, Chicago, IL 60602 (312) 346-9270
Jodi Landsman Kornfeld, Attorney at Law, 10 S. Wacker #4000, Chicago, IL 60606 (312) 750-6750
Rosemary Krimbel, 410 Webster, Chicago, IL 60614 (312) 327-9250
Judi A. Lamble, 2709 N. Mildred #2A, Chicago, IL 60606 (312) 871-1139
Anne Edelman Larsen, 688 West Irving Park Apt. D-6, Chicago, IL 60613 (312) 871-4648
Mary R. Lawton, Farley Industries, 6300 Sears Tower, Chicago, IL 60606 (312) 933-1718
Lori Lefstein, Robbins, Rubenstein Et Al, 25 E. Washington Suite 1000, Chicago, IL 60602 (312) 782-9000
Joyce Staat Lewis, Clausen Miller Et At, 10 S. LaSalle, Chicago, IL 60603 (312) 855-1010
Marjorie Press Lindblom, Kirkland & Ellis, 200 E. Randolph, Chicago, IL 60601 (312) 861-2254
Catherine E. Long, 6450 N. Magnolia Ave., Chicago, IL 60626-5306 (312) 743-6975
Peter H. Lousberg, Lousberg Kopp & Bonnett P. C., 1600 4th Ave. P. O. Box 4030, Rock Island, IL 61204-4030 (309) 786-7116
Theresa Murray Malysa, Attorney at Law, 9400 S. Cicero Ave. #304, Oak Lawn, IL 60453 (708) 425-1550
Diann Marsalek, 1108 W. Wellington, Chicago, IL 60657 (312) 472-0225
Mary Ann Mason, Kevin M. Forde Ltd., 111 W. Washington #1100, Chicago, IL 606002 (312) 641-1441
Gertrude L. McCarthy, Law Office/Solomon Gutstein, 180 N. LaSalle #3018, Chicago, IL 60601 (312) 368-4343
Maureen A. McGuire, Gorham Metge Bowman, 300 W. Washington #1500, Chicago, IL 60606 (312) 236-2713
Suzanne M. Metzel, Pope & John Ltd., 31 S. Wacker #500, Chicago, IL 60606 (312) 408-3390
Martha A. Mills, Attorney at Law, 221 North LaSalle St. #863, Chicago, IL 60601 (312) 609-6612
Nancy G. Minkes, Porzio Brombert & Newman, 163 Madison Ave., Morristown, NJ 07960-1997 (201) 538-4006
Susan M. Mongillo, Ross and Hardies, 150 North Michigan Ave #2500, Chicago, IL 60601 (312) 558-1000
Corinne McAlpine, IL Dept. of Empl. Security, 401 S. State St. 2nd Fl., Chicago, IL 606013 (312) 793-6947
Lauren Newman, 2100 N. Lincoln Park West, Chicago, IL 60614 (312) 258-5376
Grace Allen Newton, Robinson, Curley & Clayton P. C., 300 S. Wacker Dr. #1700, Chicago, IL 60606 (312) 663-3100
Jennifer T. Nijman, Coffield, Ungaretti Et Al, 3500 Three First National Plz., Chicago, IL 60602 (312) 977-4400
J. S. Nottingham, J. S. Nottingham and Assoc., 79 W. Monroe Suite 1324, Chicago, IL 60603 (312) 726-5355
Denise M. O'Malley, Corporation Council, 180 N. LaSalle St. Ste. 500, Chicago, IL 60601 (312) 744-7368
Lyne R. Ostfeld, Cowen Crowley & Nord P. C., 30 W. Monroe Ste. 1000, Chicago, IL 60603 (312) 641-0060
Margaret L. Paris, Cotsirilos Stephenson Et Al, 33 N. Dearborn, Chicago, IL 60602 (312) 263-0345
Beverly Susler Parkhurst, Holleb & Coff, 55 E. Monroe St. Suite 4100, Chicago, IL 60603-5803 (312) 332-0777
Michele K. Parthum, Lewis Overbeck & Furman, 135 S. LaSalle St. #1000, Chicago, IL 60603 (312) 580-1213
Sue Payne, Butler Rubin Et Al, 3 First Natl. Plz. #1505, Chicago, IL 60602 (312) 444-9660
Joann C. Pelka, 1218 N. Euclid, Oak Park, IL 60302
Joan Pennington, Mason Kolehmainen, 20 N. Wacker Drive S. 4200, Chicago, IL 60606 (312) 621-1300
Ann C. Petersen, Gen. Counsel. Dept. of Air Force The Pentagon, RM4E856, Washington, DC 20330-1000 (202) 697-0941
Elizabeth A. Pitrof, Bollinger and Ruberry, 500 W. Madison Suite 2300, Chicago, IL 60606-2511 (312) 781-6633
Kass Plain, Attorney at Law, 200 E. Randolph St., Chicago, IL 60601 (312) 861-1400
Carol A. Plogg, Carol A. Ploog and Assoc., 6446 W. 127th St. Ste. 201, Paolos Heights, IL 60463 (312) 371-9500
Susan M. Rentschler, Masuda Funai Et Al, One E. Wacker Dr. #3200, Chicago, IL 60601 (312) 245-7500
Ellen G. Robinson, Robinson Curley & Clayton, PC, 300 S. Wacker Dr. #1700, Chicago, IL 60606 (312) 855-0955
Jody B. Rosenbaum, Collins & Bargione, One N. LaSalle St #2235, Chicago, IL 60602 (312) 372-7813
Nancy G. Ross, McDermott Will & Emery, 111 W. Monroe Ste. #2400, Chicago, IL 60603 (312) 984-7743
Audrey Holzer Rubin, Covia, 9700 W. Higgins, Rosemont, IL 60018 (708) 518-3556
Terry Satinover, 155 W. Harbor Dr. #4207, Chicago, IL 60601 (312) 938-0987
Elizabeth Sitterly, Cassiday Schade & Gloor, 333 W. Wacker Dr. Ste. 1200, Chicago, IL 60606 (312) 641-3100
Nancy J. Smith, Sec., 219 S. Dearborn Rm. 1204, Chicago, IL 60604 (312) 353-7454
Letitia J. Spunar-Sheats, Sheats & Kellogg, 1636 N. Wells #406, Chicago, IL 60614 (312) 236-7855
Barbara W. Stackler, 200 W. Ohio, Chicago, IL 60610 (312) 871-0183
Pamela B. Strobel, Sidley & Austin, One First National Plaza, Chicago, IL 60603 (312) 853-2668
Suzan Sutherland, 4137 Lawn, Western Springs, IL 60558 (312) 246-8033
Cornelia Honcahr Tuite, 2314 N. Lincoln Park West, Chicago, IL 60614
Teresa Jacqueline Verges, 2827 N. Cambridge #202, Chicago, IL 60657 (312) 535-2229
Darlene Voracheck, Sidley & Austin, One First National Plaza, Chicago, IL 60603 (312) 853-7000
Ann Marie Walsh, Lord Bissell & Brook, 115 S. LaSalle #3300, Chicago, IL 60603
Margo Weinstein, Sonnenschen Nath & Rosenthal, 8000 Sears Twr 233 S. Wacker, Chicago, IL 60606 (312) 876-8000
Terry M. Weyna, Burditt Radzius Chartered, 333 West Wacker Suite 2600; Chicago, IL 60606 (312) 781-6633
Patrucua H, Whitten, Seyfarth, Shaw Et Al, 55 E. Monroe St. Suite 4300, Chicago, IL 60603 (312) 269-8515
Shelley L. Woodward, Ovlikoff & Flamm, 180 N. LaSalle #1515, Chicago, IL 60601 (312) 236-1515
Sandra Yamate, Sanchez & Daniels, 333 West Wacker Suite 810, Chicago, IL 60613 (312) 641-1555
Barbara L. Young, Siegan Barbakoff & Gomberg, 20 N. Clark Ste. 1000, Chicago, IL 60602 (312) 641 1155

Civil Rights

Vicki Lafer Abrahamson, Vicki Lafer Abrahamson & Assoc, 100 N. LaSalle St. #1700, Chicago, IL 60602 (312) 263-2698
Lisa M. Aisner, Box 3297 Rfd., Long Grove, IL 60047 (708) 438-7018
Colleen K. Connell, American Civil Liberties Union, 20 E. Jackson Blvd., 16th Fl., Chicago, IL 60604 (312) 427-7330
Karen Fisher Di Monte, Fisher & Di Monte , 111 W. Washington #1860, Chicago, IL 60602 (312) 236-3280
Karen Diamond, 8242 N. Merrill St., Niles, IL 60648 (708) 774-4546
Melissa S. Ellison, Craig & Craig 227 1/2 S. 9th Box 1545, Mt. Vernon, IL 62864 (618) 244-7511
Ann Hilton Fisher, 0126 South Grove, Oak Park, IL 60304 (708) 848-1654
H. Candace Gorman, Attorney at Law, 600 S. Federal #503, Chicago, IL 60605 (312) 427-2313
Roslyn C. Lieb, Chicago Lawyers Com. Civil Rights, 185 N. Wabash Ste. 2110, Chicago, IL 60601 (312) 630-9744
D. Rebecca Mitchell, 2101 W. Lunt, Chicago, IL 60645 (312) 338-4232
Grace Allen Newton, Robinson, Curley & Clayton P. C., 300 S. Wacker Dr. #1700, Chicago, IL 60606 (312) 663-3100
James M. Smith, 736 W. Aldine Apt. 1-S, Chicago, IL 60657 (312) 477-7801
Laura L. Sova, Broadlands Ltd. 1445 West Cullom Ave., Chicago, IL 60613
Dean Geoffrey R. Stone, U of Chicago Law School, 1111 E. 60th St., Chicago, IL 60637 (312) 702-9495

Commercial

Cathy K. Austin, 850 Eicher St., Keokuk, IA 52632 (312) 524-9047
Miriam Leskovar Burkland, Defrees & Fiske, 200 S. Michigan Ste. 1100, Chicago, IL 60604 (312) 372-4000
Melanie S. Carter, Citicorp Diners Club Inc., 8430 W. Bryn. Mawr. Ave., Chicago, IL 60631 (312) 380-5150
Joy L. Colwell, Beckman Kelly & Smith, 5900 Hohman Ave., Hammond, IN 46320 (219) 933-0482
Kay M. Crider, Hinsaw, Culbertson Et Al, 222 N. LaSalle, Ste. 300, Chicago, IL 60601 (312) 704-3141
Eileen Dittman, 405 N. Wabash, #3008, Chicago, IL 60611 (312) 421-4133
Catherine Elliott-Dunne, Law Office Catherine Elliott Dunne, One N. LaSalle St. Ste. #3950, Chicago, IL 60602 (312) 332-5535
Marta Farion, Redex Packaging Corp, 5050 Newport Drive Section 7, Rolling Meadows, IL 60008 (708) 398-1776
Janice R. Forde, Kevin M. Forde Ltd., 111 W. Washington, Chicago, IL 60602 (312) 641-1441
Idrienne Heymann, 2248 Linden Ave., Highland Park, IL 60035
Laverne R. Hosek, Follett Corp., 1000 W. Washington, CHicago, IL 60607, (312) 666-4300 Etx. 108
Elene K. Huszagh, Robins, Kaplan Et Al, 55 W. Wacker Dr. Suite 900, Chicago, IL 60601 (312) 782-9200
Kathleen E. Jacobs, Matuszewich & Foley, 150 N. Michigan Ave. #2810, Chicago, IL 60601 (312) 726-8787
Marianne Clay Lanuti, 415 N. Sheridan Rd. #1711, Chicago, IL 60640 (312) 728-6041
Karen Drizin Levine, Novack & Macey, 303 W. Madison #1500, Chicago, IL 60606 (312) 419-6900

Ann M. Lousin, The John Marshall Law School, 315 S. Plymouth Ct., Chicago, IL 60604 (312) 987-1434

Mary Anne Mason, Kevin M. Forde Ltd., 111 W. Washington #1100, Chicago, IL 60602 (312) 641-1441

Elizabeth Matich, Vedder, Price Et Al, 222 North LaSalle St., Chicago, IL 60601

Martha A. Mills, Attorney at Law, 221 North LaSalle St. #863, Chicago, IL 60601 (312) 609-6612

Mary C. Muehlstein, Pedersen & Houpt P. C. 180 N. LaSalle #3400, Chicago, IL 60601 (312) 641-6888

Sherry McFall, Hinshaw, Culbertson Et Al, 222 N. LaSalle Street, Chicago, IL 60602 (312) 703-4000

Lauren Newman, 2100 N. Lincoln Park West, Chicago, IL 60614 (312) 248-5376

Jane Hartley Pratt, Beal Pratt & Pratt, 57 SE. Public Sq. P. O. #10, Monouth, IL 61462 (309) 734-3193

Debra Price Prodromos, 1430 Hollywood Ave., Glenview, IL 60025 (708) 729-0277

Barbara J. Putta, Butler Rubin Newcomer, 3 First National Plaza #1505, Chicago, IL 60602 (312) 444-9660

Ellen G. Robinson, Robinson Curley & Clayton P. C., 300 S. Wacker Dr. #1700, Chicago, IL 60606 (312)-855-0955

Joy L. Sparling, Phelan Pope & John, 180 N. Wacker Dr., Chicago, IL 60606 (312) 621-0700

Jeanne M. Sylvester, Holleb & Coff, 5 E. Monroe Ste. 4100, Chicago, IL 60603 (312) 807-4600

Vasiliki Tsaganos, 5701 N. Sheridan Rd. #14G, Chicago, IL (312) 334-3239

Diane L. Yohnka-Jorstad, Hynds Rooks & Yohnka, P. O. Box 685, Morris, IL 60450 (815) 942-0049

Evette J. Zells, Attorney at Law, 405 N. Wabash #4003, Chicago, IL 60611 (312) 644-4441

Computer

Margo Lynn Hablutzel, Attorney at Law 135 S. LaSalle St., Chicago, IL 60603 (312) 220-9140

Susan A. Henderson, Law Offices of Susan Henderson, 500 W. Madison Suite 3800, Chicago, IL 60661-2511 (312) 876-1800

Laura Dickinson Lee, Altheimer and Gray, 10 S. Wacker Drive, Chicago, IL 60606 (312) 715-4985

Beverly Susler Parkhurst, Holleb & Coff, 55 E. Monroe St. Suite 4100, Chicago, IL 60603-5803 (312) 332-0777

Joan Pennington, Mason Kolehmainen, 20 N. Wacker Drive S. 4200, Chicago, IL 60606 (312) 621-1300

Barbara J. Putta, Butler Rubi Newcomer, 3 First National Plaza #1505, Chicago, IL 60602 (312) 444-9660

Audrey Holzer Rubin, Covia, 9700 W. Higgins, Rosemont, IL 60018 (708) 518-3556

Patricia Smart, Pattishall McAuliffe Et Al, 311 S. Wacker, Suite 5000, Chicago, IL 60610 (312) 554-8000

Ruth E. Vandemark, Wildman Harrold Allen & Dixon, 225 W. Wacker Dr, Chicago, IL 60606-1229 (312) 201-2567

Constitutional

Mary Becker, Univ. of Chicago School of Law, 1111 E. 60th St., Chicago, IL 60637 (312) 702-9596

Sharon Eiseman, Ancel Glink Diamond EtAl, 140 South Dearborn 6th Fl., Chicago, IL 60603 (312) 782-7606

Lisa B. Kauffman, Lisa B. Kauffman, 53 W. Jackson #1430, Chicago, IL 60604 (312) 986-0461

Rosemary Shields, 10425 S. Hale Ave., Chicago, IL 60643 (312) 779-4881

Christina M. Tchen, Skadden Arps. Slate Et Al, 333 W. Wacker Dr. #2100, Chicago, IL 60606 (312) 407-0518

Beryl White-Zerwer, Attorney at Law, 5600 Old Orchard Rd. Rm. 245, Skokie, IL 60076 (312) 470-7400

Corporate

Karen Blasingame, American Bar Association, 750 N. Lake Shore Drive, Chicago, IL 60611 (312) 988-5228

Shelby S. Boblick, McDermott, Will & Emery, 227 West Monroe St., Chicago, IL 60606 (312) 985-7503

Susan K. Bowen, Attorney at Law, 73 Cumberland Drive, Lincolnshire, IL 60069

Andrea Bryer, Cohon, Raizes & Legal, 208 S. LaSalle Ste. 1860, Chicago, IL 60604

Lyn Conniff, Shefsky & Froelich Ltd., 444 North Michigan Avenue, Chicago, IL 60611 (312) 527-4000

Susan Crane, Blue Cross Blue Shield of Illinois, 233 N. Michigan 12th Fl, Legal, Chicago, IL 60601 (312) 938-6803

Irene Clark David, Kantor & Apter Ltd., 650 Dundee Road #160, Northbrook, IL 60062 (708) 540-9600

Marie Eitrheim, Burke Wilson & McIlvaine, 500 W. Madison Ste. 3700, Chicago, IL 60606 (312) 715-5000

Joanne Elliott, Attorney Title Guaranty Fund, 29 S. LaSalle #540, Chicago, IL 60603 (312) 372-8361

Jean Grommes Feehan, Feehan & Grommes, 6525 N. Nokomis, Lincolnwood, IL 60646 (708) 677-2275

Patricia Sweeny Fisher, Amoco Corp., 200 E. Randolph #3206B, Chicago, IL 60601 (312) 856-2579

Sean Fox, Attorney at Law, 814 Commerce Drive #106, Oak Brook, IL 60521 (708) 574-0215

Susan D. Fox, Diane Gianos, Cohen, Wulfstat, Semer, Leff, 233 S. Wacker Dr. 99th Floor, Chicago, IL 60606 (312) 876-1100

Carol L. Gloor, Holstein, Mack & Klein, 250 S.Wacker Dr. Penthouse, Chicago, IL 60606 (312) 906-8000

Judith Anne Gold, Altheimer & Gray, 10 S. Wacker Suite 4000, Chicago, IL 60606 (312) 715-4925

Catherine A. Gryczan, Gottlieb & Schwartz, 4033 West Waveland, Chicago, IL 60641

Nancy Hablutzel, Attorney at Law, 135 S. LaSalle St. #1760, Chicago, IL 60603 (312) 220-9140

Julia Hagerty, Attorney at Law, 233 E. Wacker Dr., Chicago, IL 60601 (312) 236-2951

N. Caroline Harney, Lewis, Overbeck & Furman, 135 S. LaSalle, Suite 1000, Chicago, IL 60603

Susan K. Harold, Suzanne I. High, Renn & High Chtd., 4757 Main, Lisle, IL 60532 (312) 963-0110

Kathryn Rhode Ingrim, Lewis, Overbeck and Furman, 135 S. LaSalle St. Ste 1000, Chicago, IL 60603 (312) 580-1228

Deborah Jones, Lord Bissell & Brook, 115 S. LaSalle St., Chicago, IL 60603 (312) 443-1844

Helen Hart Jones, Attorney at Law, 122 S. Michigan #2050, Chicago, IL 60603 (312) 427-5100

Ruth E. Kim, Gallop Johnson & Newman, 101 S. Hanley 16th Fl., Clayton, MO 63105 (314) 862-1200

Christinia Kinton, Hlustik, Huizenga & Williams, 20 N. Wacker #2800, Chicago, IL 60606 (312) 372-1033

Teri J. Kurasch, 1861 Larkdale Road, Northbrook, IL 60062 (708) 480-0990

Karen Drizin Levine, Novack & Macey, 303 W. Madison #1500, Chicago, IL 60606 (312) 419-6900

Janice E. Linn, Chicago Osetopathic Health Systems, 5200 South Ellis Ave., Chicago, IL 60645 (312) 443-1733

Deidre R. Lloyd, Attorney at Law, P. O. Box 994, Park Ridge, IL 60068 (312) 692-6814

Kathleen S. Malloy, Malloy & Kleinman, 640 Pearson #206, Des Plaines, IL 60016 (312) 824-0990

Karen J. McCardle, Loss Management Service, 411 Aviation Way, Frederick, MD 21701 (301) 694-4295

Anita T. Molano, Keck Mahin & Cate, 8300 Sears Tower, Chicago, IL 60606 (312) 876-3595

Carol H. Morita, Masuda, Funai Et Al, One E. Wacker Dr. 32nd Fl. 3200, Chicago, IL 60601

Patricia E. Mullin, 3534 N. Lake Shore Dr., Chicago, IL 60657 (312) 871-0922

Maureen T. Mulville, Fort Dearborn Life Insurance Co., 233 N. Michigan Ave., Chicago, IL 60601 (312) 248-3082

Kwetra A. Mytich, Attorney at Law, 815 First National Bank Bldg., Peoria, IL 61602 (309) 673-1805

Mary Jo O'Donnell, 201-9th St., Wilmette, IL 60091

Beverly Susler Parkhurst, Holleb & Coff, 55 E. Monroe St. Suite 4100, Chicago, IL 60603-5803 (312) 332-0777

Beverly A. Pekala, Robins, Kaplan Et Al, 55 W. Wacker Suite 900, Chicago, IL 60601 (312) 782-9200

Fannie N. Perron, Asst. Corp. Council, 321 N. LaSalle #226, Chicago, IL 60610 (312) 744-482

Helen Viney Porter, Porter & Porter, 225 Maple Row, Northfield, IL 60093 (708) 446-2181

Debra Price Prodromos, 1430 Hollywood Ave., Glenview, IL 60025 (708) 729-0277

Debra Quentel, D'Ancona & Pflaum, 320 W. Illinois #1903, Chicago, IL 60610 (312) 580-2372

Linda R. Robison Esq., Shefsky, Froelich, Ltd., 444 N. Michigan, Chicago, IL 60611 (312) 836-4093

Marlene Schwartz Rothbardt, 6715 N. Kostner Ave., Lincolnwood, IL 60646 (708) 679-6715

Audrey Holzer Rubin, Covia, 9700 W. Higgins, Rosemont, IL 60018 (708) 518-3556

Marcia L. Sabesin, 641 W. Willow #145, Chicago, IL 60614(312) 944-0352

Anne Hamblin Schiave, McBride Baker & Coles, 500 W. Madison 40th Fl., Chicago, IL 60661 (312) 715-5700

Lynda Schultz, Malloy and Kleinman, 640 Pearson Suite 206, Des Plaines, IL 60016 (708) 824-0990

Eleanor F. Dein Sharpe, Lawyers Title Insurance Co., 20 N. Clark Street, Ste 1700, Chicago, IL 60602 (312) 558-5445

Julie Heisel Sullivan, Kirklan & Ellis, 200 E. Randolph, Chicago, IL 60601 (312) 266-1962

Bruno W. Tabis Jr., Anderson McDonnell, 200 S. Wacker #420, Chicago, IL 60606 (312) 906-8100

Sheery S. Treston, Sidley & Austin, One First National Plaza, Chicago, IL 60603 (312) 853-7116

Vasiliki Tsaganos, 5701 N. Sheridan Road #14G, Chicago, IL 60660 (312) 334-3239

Lisa M. Waggoner, Covey/Waggoner, 30 North Williams St. #A, Crystal Lake, IL 60014 (815) 459-0830

Barbara L. Wilcox, Wilcox & Grimbau, 120 W. Madison Suite #1108, Chicago, IL 60602 (312) 781-0177

Janet L. Witort, 828 S. Bodin, Hinsdale, IL 60521

Margaret F. Woulfe, Attorney at Law, 600 S. Federal St. #201, Chicago, IL 60605 (312) 236-2315

Pearl A. Zager, Vedder, Price, Et Al, 222 N. LaSalle St., #2500, Chicago, IL 60601 (312) 876-2100

Criminal

Linda S. Amdur, 1024 W. Oakdale, Chicago, IL 60657

Charisse A. Bruno, Attorney at Law, 6321 N. Avondale, Chicago, IL 60631 (312) 775-1672

Marianne Burke, 2318 N. Lakewood, Chicago, IL 60614

Mary Ellen Cagney, 1100 N. Lake Shore Dr. Apt. 13B, Chicago, IL 60611

Amy Patton Campanelli, 1033 W. Vernon Park Apt. C., Chicago, IL 60607 (312) 421-4391

Christine A. Campbell, Attorney at Law, 33 N. LaSalle #2200, Chicago, IL 60602 (312) 263-5151

Florence Marie Cole, Attorney at Law, 180 N. LaSalle St. Suite 1101, Chicago, IL 60601 (312) 704-8212

Diane Economou, 2836 W. 84th Street, Chicago, IL 60652 (312) 778-7166

Jean Bauer Fisler, 8036 Herb Farm Road, Bethesda, MD 20817 (301) 469-6475

Patricia M. Forestall, 324 N. Euclid, Oak Park, IL 60302 (708) 386-0751

Holly B. Fujiye, 1707AGeorgetown Dr., Champaign, IL 61821 (708) 295-1688

Deborah L. Goldberg, Law Office of Deborah Goldberg, 4343 W. Grand Ave. Suite 212, Gurnee, IL 60031

Meg Gorecki, 2 E Oak P.O. Box 106, St. Charles, IL 60174 (708) 584-6161

Kimberly Ann Griffith-Dunn, P. O. Box 6, 1123 Edgington Ave., Eldora, IA 62321 (217) 357-26746

Richard S. Gutof, Richard S. Gutof & Assoc. Ltd., 933 Lawler, #312, Skokie, IL 60077(708) 676-4880

Nancy A. Hala, Nancy A. Halas, Attorney at Law, 18225 Morris Ave., Homewood, IL 60430 (312) 799-6480

Julie M. Harmon, Attorney at Law, 2650 S. California 7th Fl., Chicago, IL 60608 (312) 890-3217

Patricia Brown Holmes, 1212 S. Michigan Ave. #2102, Chicago, IL 60605 (312) 427, 6763

Lisa B. Kauffman, Lisa B. Kauffman, 53 W. Jackson #1430, Chicago, IL 60604 (312) 986-0461

Kathleen Kavanagh, 63 S. Illinois Ave., Villa Park, IL 60181-3046 (312) 477-1434

Lynne Kawamoto, Cook Co. States Attorney Office, 1100 South Hamilton, Chicago, IL 60612 (312) 738-7027

Hon Bertina Lampkin, 317 W. 110th Pl., Chicago, IL 60628, (312) 928-0175

Mercedes Luque-Rosales, 1516 N. Monitor Ave., Chicago, IL 60651 (312) 889-3156

Andrea D. Lyon, Captial Resource Center, 600 Davis Street, 3rd Fl., Evanston, IL 60201 (708) 328-0698

Diana Mann, 3501 North Janssen, Chicago, IL 60657 (312) 281-0610

Patricia M. Martin, 10 Brookside Dr., Park Forest, IL60466 (708) 748-3588

Carol Pearce McCarthy, 706 McKinley, Hinsdale, IL 60521 (708) 655-2653

Helen D. Moorman, 445 S. Clevelan Ave. #301, Arlington Heights, IL 60005 (312) 255-3256

Wendy R. Morgan, Law Firm of Wendy R. Morgan, 1301 W. 22nd St. #1007, Oak Brook, IL 60521 (312) 635-8442

Ellen J. Morris, Attorney at Law, 5215 Old Orchard Suite 790, Skokie, IL 60077 (312) 470-9777

Kathleen O'Leary, State Bar of Nevada, 295 Holcomb Avenue, Reno, NV 89502

Dawn M. Overend, 5418 East View Park, Chicago, IL 60615 (312) 288-6561

Margaret L. Paris, Cotsirilos Setphenson Et Al, 33 N. Dearborn, Chicago, IL 60602 (312) 263-0345

Lynda A. Peters, 720 Gordon Terrace #3L, Chicago, IL 60613 (312) 348-5748

Judith B. Petrucci, Attorney at Law, 7949 W. Ogden, Lyons, IL 60534 (708) 442-0078

Hillary Sue Price, DuPage County States Attorney, 207 S. Reberst, Wheaton, IL 60134 (708) 682-7050

Nancy Scotillo, Attorney at Law, 1608 Colonial Parkway, Inverness, IL 60067 (708) 359-0333

Joane S. Shea, Attorney at Law, 2205 Enterprize Ctr. #511, Wstchester, IL 0153 (708) 531-0880

Gayle Shines, Office of Professional Standards, 1121 S. State St., Chicago, IL 60605 (312) 890- 3005

Victoria A. Stewart, City of Chicago, 121 N. LaSalle St. Rm. 302, Chicago, IL 60602 (312) 744-6510

Kimberly A. Sutherland, Attorney at Law, 180 West Washington #700, Chicago, IL 60603 (312) 726-0045

Hon Mary Maxwell Thomas, 1426 Mulford St., Evanston, IL 60202 (312) 869-1977

Diane N. Walsh, 8 Calle View Dr., LaGrange, IL 60525 (708) 891-1304

Kathryn Zenoff, Asst. States Attorney, 400 W. State St., Rockford, IL 61101 (815) 987-3160

Environmental

Mary C. Bryant, Rudnick & Wolfe, 203 N. LaSalle, #1800, Chicago, IL 60601 (312) 630-4232

Mary Ellen Cagney, 1100 N. Lake Shore Dr., Apt. 13B, Chicago, IL 60611

Joy L. Colwell, Beckman Kelley & Smith, 5900 Hohman Ave., Hammond, IN 46320 (219) 933-0482

Kay M. Crider, Hinshaw, Culbertson Et Al, 222 N. LaSalle, Suite 300, Chicago, IL 60601 (312) 704) 3141

Mary E. Doohan, 4338 Johnson Ave., Western Springs, IL 60558 (708) 246-5916

Andrea Sykes Foote, Attorney at Law, 11 S. 2nd Street, Geneva, IL 60134 (708) 232-2292

Lisa Gass, D'Ancona & Pflaum, 30 N. LaSalle, Chicago, IL 60602 (312) 580-2376

Jean M. Godlen, Cassiday Schade & Gloor, 333 W. Wacker Dr. #1200, Chicago, IL 60606 (312) 641-3100

Evalyn Walsh Laird, 47104 Pine Ave. Grand Beach, New Buffalo, MI 49117 (616)469-4586

Mary J. McElroy, 2100 Center Ave., Northbrook, IL 60062 (708) 480-1779

Molly McGinis, Lord, Bissell & Brook, 115 S. LaSalle, Chicago, IL 60603 (312) 443-0700

Suzanne M. Metzell, Pope & John, Ltd., 311 S. Wacker #50, Chicago, IL 60606(312) 408-3390

Katie Moertl, 341 S. Hickory, Bartlett, IL 60103 (312) 213-2468

Jennifer T. Nijman, Coffield, Ungaretti Et Al, 3500 Three First National Plaza, Chicago, IL 60602 (312) 977-4400

Rica Slone, Attorney at Law, 210 Twin Towers Plaza 456 Fulton, Chicago, IL 61602 (309) 676-0335
Ina S. Winston, Metro Sanitary District, 100 E. Erie, Chicago, IL 60611 (312) 751-6575

Estate Planning & Probate

Katharine Agar, 488 S. Soangetaha #A-28, Galesburg, IL 61401
Nancy D. Anderson, Chicago Title & Trust, 111 W. Washington, Chicago, IL 60602 (312) 630-2048
Chloe Arlan, 2040 N. Sheffield Ave., Chicago, IL 60614 (312) 348-6996
Lenita Aubuchon, Leniat Aubuchon Esq., 343 Spring Ave., Glen Ellyn, IL 60137 (708) 858-1155
Susan T. Bart, 702 S. Dunton, Arlington Hts., IL 60005 (708) 0710
Karyn Becker, Crowley, Christy & Ross, 200 West Adams, Suite 1101, Chicago, IL 60606 (312) 419-3899
Kathryn Godfrey Benish, Sachnoff & Weaver, Ltd., 30 S. Wacker, 29th Floor, Chicago, IL 60606 (312) 782-8300
Shelley Ballard Bostick, Attorney at Law, 723 Washington, Evanston, IL 60205
Marta Camafreyta Bukata, South Chicago Legal Clinic, 2938 E. 91st. Street, Chicago, IL 60617 (312) 731-1762
Sandra K. Burns, Attorney at Law, 348 Lathrop Ave., River Forest, IL 603305-2122 (78) 771-5252
Nancy Meehan Canafax, 2214 Greenwood, Wilmette, IL 60091 (708) 256-5805
Gayle Tronvig Carper, Attorney at Law, P. O. Box 790, Macomb, IL 61455 (309) 833-1702
Kelli K. Chase, Sugar, Freedberg, Felsenthal, 30 N. LaSalle #2600, Chicago, IL 60602 (312) 704-9400
Beth M. Hianik Clark, Sachnoff & Weaver, Ltd., 30 S. Wacker Dr. #2900, Chicago, IL 60606 (312) 664-4153
Mary Lynch Coleman, Rifis, Kucia, and Coleman 707 South Blvd., Oak Park, IL 60302 (78) 383-3000
Lyn Conniff, Shefsky & Froelich Ltd., 444 North Michigan Avenue, Chicago, IL 60611 (312) 527-4000
Sylvia O. Decker, First National Bank of Chicago Suite 0101, Chicago, IL 60670 (312) 732-4203
Eileen Dittman, 405 N. Wabash #3008, Chicago, IL 60611 (312) 421-4133
Ileana Dominguez-Urban, Schiff Hardin & Waite, 7200 Sears Tower, Chicago, IL 60606 (312) 876-1000
Rhea Dorsam, Borovsky Ehrlich & Kronenerg, 205 N. Michigan 41st Fl., Chicago, IL 60601 (312) 861-0808
Mary Kathryn Duggan, 14459 Lincoln Ave., Dolton, IL 60419 (78) 841-3079
Ruth Ehrlich, Attorney at Law, 4250 N. Marine Dr. #1801, Chicago, IL 60613 (312) 263-5215
Roberta Evans, Neal Gerber Eisenberg & Lurie 208 S. LaSalle, Chicago, IL 60604 (312) 269-8057
Cynthia R. Farenga, Law Office of Cynthia R. Farenga, 221 N. LaSalle #2600, Chicago, IL 60601 (312) 201-1222
Jean Grommes Feehan, Feehan & Gromes, 6525 N. Nokomis, Lincolnwood, IL 60646 (78) 677-2275
Joy D. Fisher, 567 Weidner Road, Buffalo Grove, IL 60089 (708) 537-7263
Frances Fox, 1221 Hunter Road, Wilmette, IL 60091 (312) 251-8674
Sean Fox, Attorney at Law, 814 Commerce Drive #106, Oak Brook, IL 60521 (78) 574-0215
Victoria Franzese, 220 S. Ninth Ave., LaGrange, IL 60525 (78) 579-9046
Betty Gallo, Attorney at Law 9150 S. Cicero Ave., Oak Lawn, IL 60453 (312) 425-0630
Ruth Goldman, Miller Shakman Hamilton & Kurt, 208 South LaSalle, Chicago, IL 60604 (312) 263-3700
Theodora Gordon, Attorney at Law, 8 S. Michigan #2000, Chicago, IL 60603 (312) 346-8243
Joan C. Grant, Grant & Grant, 180 N. LaSalle #2400, Chicago, IL 60601 (312) 641-3600
L. Bernice Grennels, 1100 N. Dearborn St. Apt. 811, Chicago, IL 60610 (312) 787-1000
Kathy Kintonis Hardesty, 10440 S. 75th Avenue, Palos Hills, IL 60465 (78) 598-1616
Sharon Harris, 116 Lake Shore Dr., Village of Oakwood Hills, Cary, IL 60013 (312) 516-1001
Mary Frances Hegarty, Hegarty, Hegarty & Kowols, 301 W. Touthy Ave., Park Ridge, IL 60068 (708) 692-3031
Antonia Rago Herbert, Attorney at Law, 1150 N. Lake Shore Dr., #13C, Chicago, IL 60611 (312) 787-0097
Patricia Hogan, 221 N. LaSalle Ste 2600, Chicago, IL 60601
Judith M. Kerr, 709 S. Stone Ave., LaGrange, IL 60525 (708) 354-9047
Hon Dorothy Kirie Kinnaird, 1508 Forest Ave., Wilmette, IL 60091 (708) 251-5345
Teri J. Kurasch, 1861 Larkdale Road, Northbrook, IL 60062 (708) 480-0990
Evalyn Walsh Laird, 47104 Pine Ave. Grand Beach, New Buffalo, MI 49117 (616) 469-4586
Alice S. Lonoff, Bell Boyd & Lloyd 70 W. Madison, Chicago, IL 60602 (312) 807-4314
Cindy Beth Lyons, 1155 S. Plymouth S. 1500, Chicago, IL 60305 (312) 431-1648
Andrea S. Mithchell, 1706 N. Riverside Drive, McHenry, IL 60050 (312) 831-3948
Susan Foley Moorehead, Lowe Moore Et Al, 1055 Citizens Bldg., Decatur, IL 62525 (217) 422-0235
Judith B. Mostovoy, 1346 Idelwild, Homewood, IL 60430 (78) 799-1792
Mary F. Murray, 6223 N. Navajo, Chicago, IL 60646
Regina G. Narusis-Firant, Narusis & Narusis, 213 W. Lake Shore Dr., Cary, IL 60013 (708) 639-5535
Katie Newsham, Rock Fusco Reynolds & Garvey, 350 N. LaSalle, Chicago, IL 60610 (312) 464-3500
Sandra G. Nye, Sandra G. Nye & Assoc., 151 N. Michigan Ave., Chicago, IL 60601 (312) 565-1666
Kathleen Julia O'Rourke, 10840 S. Kilpatrick, Oak Lawn, IL 60453 (708) 667-3527
Judith W. Olson, 3 S. 155 Blackcherry Lane, Glen Ellyn, IL 60137 (312) 858-7615
Carolyn Noonan Parmer, 9 Woodley Road, Winnetka, IL 60093 (708) 446-7454
Carol C. Pell, 1st National Bank of Chicago, 3 First National Plaza #0104, Chicago, IL 60670 (312) 732-8976
Mary C. Perisin, 1440 N. Lake Shore Dr., Chicago, IL 60610
Joan Riordan, Riordan & Robbins, 134 N. LaSalle St., Suite 2016, Chicago, IL 60602 (312) 372-0202
Deborah Sullivan Roberts, Sullivan & Sullivan, 188 W. Randolph, Ste 2400, Chicago, IL 60601-3005 (312) 332-5375
Janice I. Rode, 7528 N. Bell Avenue, Chicago, IL 60645 (312) 465-6016
Janice E. Rodgers, Burke Wilson & McIlvaine, 500 W. Madison Ste. 3700, Chicago, IL 60661 (312) 861-9239
Mary Stretch Root, 5815 N. Nickerson, Chicago, IL 60631 (312) 631-5280
Esther R. Rothstein, McCarthy & Levin, 100 W. Monroe #2000, Chicago, IL 60603 (312) 263- 1155
Marion H. Schenk, 1931 Bradley Pl., Chicago, IL 60613-3515 (312) 281-3750
Nancy Scotillo, Attorney at Law, 1608 Colonial Parkway, Inverness, IL 60067 (708) 359-0333
Judy A. Shawver, Shawver & Shawver, 40 Main St., Davenport, IA 52801 (319) 324-4182
Dorothy W. Spinka, Attorney at Law, 10412 S. Whiple St., Chicago, IL 60655 (312) 445-1223
Anne M. Sullivan, Sullivan & Sullivan, 188 West Randloph #2400, Chicago, IL 60601 (312) 332-5375
Arline Rusin Swanson, 123 Hidden Oaks, Barrington, IL 60010 (708) 381-3921
Valerie C. Swett, Deutsch Williams, 99 Summer Street, Boston, MA 02110-1235 (617) 951-2300
Mary Beth Taylor, Chicago Volunteer Legal Services, 205 W. Randolph #510, Chicago, IL 60606 (312) 332-1624
Nancy B. Thomas, 606 Kenilworth Ave., Kenilworth, IL 60043 (312) 256-3523
Amanda Toney, Amanda Toney Ltd., 542 S. Dearborn #580, Chicago, IL 60605 (312) 341-1314
Carol A. Tuman, 8024 S. Kirkland, Chicago, IL 60652 (312) 585-4123
Valerie Moehle Umholtz, Moehle Swearingen & Assoc., Ltd., 410 Broadway, Pekin, IL 61555-0875 (309) 347-4141
Laurie J. Wasserman, Westmoreland Building, 9933 Lawler Avenue Suite #312, Skokie, IL 60077 (708) 674-7324
Ellen Ann Yearwood, 380 Cambridge Road, Des Plaines, IL 60016 (708) 824-6716

Government

C. Victoria Almeida, Law Offices of Victoria Almeida, 201 N. Wells Suite 1900, Chicago, IL 60606-1364 (312) 444-1144
Nancy K. Bannon, 910 Western Ave., Joliet, IL 60435 (815) 727-9664
Theresa A. Barnett, Metra Metropolitan Rail, 547 W. Jackson, Chicago, IL 60606 (312) 322-6694
Mary Lou Boksa, City of Chicago-Corporation Councils City Hall Room 511, 121 N. LaSalle, Chicago, IL 60602 (312) 744-9826
Myra J. Brown, Asst. State's Attorney, 500 Daley Center, Chicago, IL 60602 (312) 443-5669
Ellen Cronin Craig, Illinois Commerce Commission, 100 W. Randolph 9th Fl., Chicago, IL 60601 (312) 8114-4790
John J. Cullerton, Fagel & Haber, 140 South Dearborn, Chicago, IL 60629 (312) 580-2232
M. Louis Dierstein, 1337 W. Fargo #11-B, Chicago, IL 60626 (312) 465-7376
Karen Dimond, 8242 N. Merril Street, Niles, IL 60648 (708) 774-4546
Zenia Sachs Goodman, Arbitrator, IL. Ind. Comm., 100 W. Randolph 8th Fl., Chicago, IL 60601 (312) 814-6516
Meg Gorecki, 2 E. Oak P. O. Box 106, St. Charles, IL 60174 (708) 584-6161
Sharon Gromer, 2137 W. Montrose, Chicago, IL 60618 (312) 348-3833
Julie E. Hamos, Julie E. Hamos & Assoc., 122 S. Michigan #1850, Chicago, IL 60603 (312) 427-4500
Hon Susan F. Hutchison, Assoc. Judge/19th Circuit, 2200 N. Seminary Ave., Woodstock, IL 60098 (815) 338-2040 Ext. 361
Jackie Kinnaman, Illinois Industrial Commission, 100 W. Randolph Soci 8-200, Chicago, IL 60601 (312) 641-6060
Donna M. Lach, US Court of Appeals, 219 S. Dearborn, Chicago, IL 60201 (312) 435-5798
Ofelia Manalang, 1731 Redman Ave., St. Louis, MO 623138 (314) 653-0329
Rea T. Markin, Asst. States Attorney, 32 W. Randolph St. #1204, Chicago, IL 60601 (312) 580-3200
Barbara Meyer, Village of Skokie Corporation Counsel, 5127 Oakton Street, Skokie, IL 60077 (708) 673-0500
Joann C. Pelka, 1218 N. Euclid, Oak Park, IL 60302
Hillary Sue Price, DuPage County States Attorney, 207 S. Reberst, Wheaton, IL 60134 (708) 682-7050
Shannon Sullivan, 625 W. Wrightwood #215, Chicago, IL 60614 (312) 477-0363
Elizabeth B. Yntema, Leo Burnett, Legal Dept., 35 W. Wacker 21st Fl., Chicago, IL 60601 (312) 220-4897

Hospital & Health

Marina Ammedola, Patricia Bobb & Assoc., Three First National Plaza, 66 Chicago, IL 60602 (312) 332-2350
Nancy K. Bannon, 910 Western Ave., Joliet, IL 60435 (815) 727-9664
Geraldine Brauneis, Legal Aid Bureau 15th Fl., 14 East Jackson, Chicago, IL 60604 (312) 986-4228
Nancy Brent, Nancy Brent, Attorney at Law, 5445 N. Sheridan Road #1906, Chicago, IL 60640 (312) 728-3663
Dr. Rowie Brown, 1700 E. 56 St., #3702, Chicago, IL 60637 (312) 288-2590
Myra J. Brown, Asst. States Attorney 500 Daley Center, Chicago, IL 60602 (312) 443-5669
Linda S. Consolo, Carrane Newman & Freifeld, 100 N. LaSalle #600, Chicago, IL 60602 (312) 372-2450
Rachel Dvorken, 1660 N. LaSalle #3611, Chicago, IL 60614 (312) 943-9853
Ann Hilton Fisher, 1026 South Grove, Oak Park, IL 60304 (708) 848-1654
Marcia Handler, Hinshaw & Culbertson, 222 N. LaSalle St., Chicago, IL 60611 (312) 704-3750
N. Caroline Harney, Lewis, Overbeck & Furman, 135 S. LaSalle Suite 1000, Chicago, IL 60603
Janice E. Linn, Chicago Osteopathic Health Systems, 5200 South Ellis Ave., Chicago, IL 60645 (312) 443-1733
Elizabeth M. Mills, McDermott Will & Emery, 227 W. Monroe #3100, Chicago, IL 60606 (312) 984-7555
Anne Murphy, Coffield Ungaretti Et Al, THree First national #3400, Chicago, IL 60602 (312) 977-4400;
Sandra G. Nye, Sandra G. Nye & Assoc., 151 N. Michigan Ave., Chicago, IL 60601 (312) 565-1666
Joyce Shanahan Rivers, Wm. M. Mercer Inc., 10 S. Wacker Dr. 15th Fl., Chicago, IL 60606-7485 (312) 902-7681
Janice I. Rode, 7528 N. Bell Ave., Chicago, IL 60645 (312) 465-6016
Linda M. Wakeen, American Dental Association, 211 E. Chicago Ave., Chicago, IL 60611 (312) 440-2813

Immigration & Naturalization

Goldie C. Domingue, Law Offices of Douglas Bristol, 20 S. Clark 710, Chicago, IL 60603 (312) 372-1991
Deborah L. Goldberg, Law Office of Deborah Goldberg, 4343 W. Grand Ave. Ste. 212, Gurnee, IL 60031 (708) 662-6147
Phylllis Lamb Goldman, 1113 Elmwood, Evanston, IL 60202 (708) 492-1942
Veronica M. Jeffers, Minsky Feiertag Et Al, 122 S. Michigan Ave. #1800, Chicago, IL 60603 (312) 427-6163
Linda S. Kagan, Attorney at Law, 10 N. Dearborn Penthouse, Chicago, IL 60602 (312) 263-2261
Margaret H. McCormick, Minsky Feirtag McCormick Et Al, 122 S. Michigan #1800, Chicago, IL 60603 (312) 427-6163
Carol H. Morita, Masuda, Funai Et Al, One E. Wacker Dr. 32nd Fl. 3200, Chicago, IL 60601
Joanne H. Saunders, Martin Craig Chester Et Al, 55 W. Monroe #1200, Chicago, IL 60603 *312) 368-9700
Michelle Wiznitzer, Attorney at Law, 1310 N. Ritchie Ct. #29 C, Chicago, IL 60610 (312) 337-5454

Insurance

Margaret M. Benson, Shand Morahan Co., Shand Morahan Plaza, Evanston, IL 60201 (708) 866-0868
Jill B. Berkeley, Cassiday Schade & Gloor, 333 W. Wacker Dr. Ste. 1200, Chicago, IL 60606-1289 (312) 641-3100
Goldie C. Domingue, Law Offices of Douglas Bristol, 20 S. Clark 710, Chicago, IL 60603 (312) 372-1991
Melissa S. Ellison, Craig & Craig, 227 1/2 S. 9th Box 1545, Mt. Vernon, IL 62864 (618) 244-7511
Ruth E. Farbman, 2 E. Oak St. Apt. 3602, Chicago, IL 60611 (312) 263-0599
Andrea Sykes Foote, Attorney at Law, 11 S. 2nd Street, Geneva, IL 60134 (708) 232-2290
Susan Fox Gillis, Querrey and Harrow Ltd., 135 S. LaSalle, Chicago, IL 60602 (312) 236-9850
Lee Hugh Goodman, 2201 Center Ave., Northbrook, IL 60062 (708) 475-3744
Elizabeth Walsh Gregory, 3 South Cypress Drive, Glen Ellyn, IL 60137 (708) 790-8421
Deborah Jones, Lord Bissell & Brook, 115 S. LaSalle St., Chicago, IL 60603 (312) 443-1844
Timothy M. Kelly, Beerman Swedlove, 69 W. Washington #600, Chicago, IL 60602 (312) 621-9700
Molly McGinnis, Lord, Bissell & Brook, 115 S. LaSalle, Chicago, IL 60603 (312) 443-0700
Joy Ann Perry, All State Insurance Company, All State Plaza North, North Brook, IL 60062, (708) 291-5942
Christine E. Smith-McMahon, Attorney at Law, 120 W. Madison #725, Chicago, IL 60602 (312) 782-4558
Dharon Stark Trowitch, Country Mutual Insurance, 1701 Towanda Ave. #2100, Bloomington, IL 61702-2100
Janet L. Witort, 828 S. Bodin, Hinsdale, IL 60521

Juvenile

Hon R. Morgan Hamilton, 1130 S. Michigan #4007, Chicago, IL 60605 (312) 922-1678
Sharon M. Henschen, Proffitt Law Offices, 110 E. Third St. P. O. Box 110, Pana, IL 62557 (217) 562-2151
Lisa B. Kauffman, Lisa B. Kauffman, 53 W. Jackson #1430, Chicago, IL 60604 (312) 986-0461
Mercedes luque-Rosales, 1516 N. Monitor Ave., Chicago, IL 60651 (312) 889-3156
Carolyn Noonan Parmer, 9 Woodley Road, Winnetka, IL 60093 (708) 446-7454
Helen R. Rogal, Attorney at Law, 180 N. LaSalle Suite 1101, Chicago, IL 60601 (312) 443-0008
Helen Sigman, Law Offices of Helen Sigman, 100 W. Monroe Suite 1310, Chicago, IL 60603 (312) 68-8441
Gail T. Smith, C.L.A.I.M., 205 W. Randloph #501, Chicago, IL 60606 (312) 332-5537
Frances Sowa, Asst. Pulbic Defender, Juv. Ct. 1100 S. Hamilton, Chicago, IL 60612 (312) 738-7047
Diane N. Walsoh, 8 Calle View Dr., LaGrange, IL 60525 (708) 891-1304
Kathryn Zenoff, Asst., States Attorney, 400 W. State St., Rockford, IL 61101 (815) 987-3160

Labor & Employment

Susan Brannigan, Asher, Gittler & Greenfield, 2 N. LaSalle St. #1200, Chicago, IL 60602 (312) 263-1500
Nancy Brent, Nancy Brent, Attorney at Law, 5445 N. Sheridan Road #1906, Chicago, IL 60630 (312) 728-3663
Anne Burke, Attorney at Law, 2650 W. 51st St., Chicago, IL 60640 (312) 436-9000
Patricia A. Collins, Asher Gittler Et Al, 2 N. LaSalle Suite 1200, Chicago, IL 60602 (312) 263-1500
Karen Dimond, 8242 N. Merrill Street, Niles, IL 60648 (708) 74-4546
Rochelle S. Dyme, Rosenthal & Schanfield 55 E. Monroe, Chicago, IL 60603 (312) 236-5622
Lori A. Goldstein, 232 Hibbard, Wilmette, IL 60091 (708) 256-6640
Laura L. Guzik, 655 W. Irving Park Apt. 3017, Chicago, IL 60613 (312) 935-4195
Linda K. Horras, Hinshaw Culbertson Et Al, 222 N. LaSalle St. #300, Chicago, IL 60601 (312) 704-3022
Jackie Knnaman, Illinois Industrial Commission, 100 W. Randolph Soic 8-200, Chicago, IL 60601 (312) 641-6060
Sara J. W. Larkin, 1357 Greenwood Ave., Deerfield, IL 60015 (312) 940-0704
Janice E. Linn, Chicago Osteopathic Health Systems, 5200 South Ellis Ave., Chicago, IL 60645 (312) 443-1733
Karen L. Mansfield, 204 S. Taylor, Oak Park, IL 60302 (708) 477-3149
Ellen Mayer, Syfarth, Shaw Et Al, 1730 N. Clark Apt, 1204, Chicago, IL 60614 (312) 346-8000
Carol H. Morita, Masuda, Funai Et Al, One E. Wacker Dr. 32nd Fl. 3200, Chicago, IL 60601
Corine McAlpine, IL Dept of Empl. Security, 401 S. State St. 2nd Floor, Chicago, IL 60613 (312) 793-6947
Jennifer Naber, 6651 W. Devon 2nd Floor, Chicago, IL 60631 (312) 594-9604
Grace Allen Newton, Robinson, Curley & Clayton, P. C. 300 S. Wacker Dr. #1700, Chicago, IL 60606 (312) 663-3100
Teresa Nuccio, 1031 South Aldine, Park Ridge, IL 60068 (708) 823-2082
Denise S. Poloyac, Katz Freidman Schurt Eagle, 7 S. Dearborn St. #1734, Chicago, IL 60603)312) 263-6330
Anita J. Ponder, Holstein Mack & Klein, 250 S. Wacker Dr., Penthouse, Chicago, IL 60606 (312) 906-8000
Andrea M. Schleifer, 1426 W. Farragut, Chicago, IL 60610 (312) 878-5533
Jane E. Shaffer, Laner, Muchin, Dombrow & Becke, 350 N. Clark Suite 400, Chicago, IL 60610 (312) 467-9800
Ann Shaw, 3840 North Seely Ave., Chicago, IL 60618 (312) 248-4457
Elinor P. Swiger, Robbins, Schwartz Nicholas, 29 S. LaSalle, Chicago, IL 60603 (312) 332-7760

Matrimony & Family

Michelle S. Abington, Chicago Sun-Times, 401 N. Wabash, Chicago, IL 606111 (312) 321-2177
Charlotte Adelman, 232 Lawndale, Wilmette, IL 60091 (312) 251-6726
Margaret C. Benson, Chicago Volunteer Legal Services, 205 W. Randolph #510,Chicago, IL 60606 (312) 322-1624
Kathryn Bigley, 7523 N. Karlov, Skokie, IL 60076 (708) 673-1453
Geraldine Brauneis, Legal Aid Bureau 15th Fl., 14 East Jackson, Chicago, IL 60604 (312) 986-4228
Charisse A. Bruno, Attorney at Law, 6321 N. Avondale, Chicago, IL 60631 (312) 775-1672
Diane M. Bruzas, 50 E. Bellevue #1506, Chicago, IL 60611
Anna Markley Bush, 249 W. Russell St., Barrington, IL 60010 (708) 382-1673
Nancy Meehan Canafax, 2214 Greenwood, Wilmette, IL 60091 (708) 256-5805
Gayle Tronvig Carper, Attorney at Law, P.O. Box 790, Macomb, IL 61455 (309) 833-1702
Lyn Conniff, Shefsky & Froelich Ltd., 444 North Michigan Ave., Chicago, IL 60611 (312) 527-4000
Frances Orwin, 9340 N. Hamlin, Evanston, IL 60203 (312) 673-1399
Linda Crohn, Simberg and Crohn, 59 East Van Buren, Chicago, IL 60605 (312) 663-5575
Lesly Datlow, 2140 W. LeMoyne, Chicago, IL 60622 (312) 276-3105
Lisa Lee Derr, Steffes, Schwefel, 108 North Lincoln Ave., Beaver Dam, WI 53916 (312) 845-3871
Marian A. Dixon, Rosenthal & Schanfield PC., 55 E. Monroe #4620, Chicago, IL 60603 (312 236-5622
Mary Kathryn Duggan, 14459 Lincoln Ave., Dolton, IL 60419 (708) 841-3079
Terri Edelson, 3703 W. Albion, Lincolnwood, IL 60645 (312) 677-9489
Kathryn D. Farmer, Rosenfeld Rothenberg Et Al, 221 N. LaSalle #1763, Chicago, IL 60601 (312) 372-6058
Joy M. Feinberg, Feinberg & Barry, 33 N. Dearborn Suite 2402, Chicago, IL 60602 (312) 444-1050
Barbara K. Finesmith, Pro Bono Advocates, 165 N. Canal, Chicago, IL 60606 (312) 906-8010
Adrienne M. Geary, Attorney at Law, 2650 W. 51st. St., Chicago, IL 60632 (312) 439-9000
Deborah L. Goldberg, Law Office of Deborah Goldberg, 4343 W. Grand Ave. Ste. 212, Gurnee, IL 60031 (78) 662-6147
Ilene Beth Goldstein, Schiller Ducanto & Fleck, 200 N. LaSalle #2700, Chicago, IL 60601 (312) 641-5560
Theodora Gordon, Attorney at Law, 8 S. Michigan #2000, Chicago, IL 60603 (312) 346-8243
Belle Lind Gordon, 1825 N. Lincoln Plaza #1401, Chicago, IL 60614 (312) 664-7741
Joan C. Grant, Grant & Grant, 180 N. LaSalle #2400, Chicago, IL 60601 (312) 641-3600
Nancy Hunter Griffin, Attorney at Law, 401 N. Adams, Hinsdale, IL 60521 (708) 323-7729
Anne B. Guinan, 9942 S. Walden Parkway, Chicago, IL 60643
Hon John W. Gustafson, 1660 N. LaSalle #601, Chicago, IL 60614-6008 (312) 951-9511
Susan C. Haddad, Attorney at Law, 3 First National Plaza #3600, Chicago, IL 60602 (312) 236-2298
Sharon M. Henschen, Proffitt Law Offices, 110 E. Third St. P. O. Box 110, Pana, IL 62557 (217) 562-2151
Lydia Gross Kamerlink, Attorney at Law, 221 N. LaSalle #2104, Chicago, IL 60601 (312) 855-0324
Ralla Klepak, Attorney at Law, 5158 N. Ashland Ave., Chicago, IL 60640 (312) 561-6568
Muriel Kuhs, Davis Freidman Et Al, 140 S. Dearborn, #1600, Chicago, IL 60603 (312) 782-2220
Michele F. Lowrance, Attorney at Law, 180 N. LaSalle #2416, Chicago, IL 60601 (312) 782-0653
Nora Mahaney-Turley, Attorney at Law, 205 W. Wacker Dr. #615, Chicago, IL 60606 (3120 236-9471
Earle A. Malkin, Attorney at Law, 180 N. LaSalle #216, Chicago, IL 60601 (312) 372-6150
Dorene Marcus, Grund, Marcus Et Al, 111 W. Washington #1861, Chicago, IL 60602 (312) 726-8400
Diana M. Matesevic, Maureen J. Mcgann-Ryan, 29 S. LaSalle #640, Chicago, IL 60603 (312) 782-3668
Veronica B. Mathein, Mathein & Rostoker, 134 North LaSalle St. #1108, Chicago, IL 60602 (312) 236-3062
Professor Peter J. McGovern, John Marshall Law School, 315 S. Plymouth Ct., Chicago, IL 60604 (312) 427-2737
Wendy R. Morgan, The Law Firm of Wendy R. Morgan, 1301 W. 22nd St. #1007, Oak Brook, IL 60521 (312) 635-8442
Victoria L. Munizzo, Nottage & Ward, 10 North Dearborn Penthouse, Chicago, IL 60602 (312) 332-2915
Regina G. Narusis-Firant, Narusis & Narusis, 213 W. Lake Shore Dr., Cary, IL 60013 (708) 639-5535
Rosaire M. Nottage, Nottage & Ward, 10 N. Dearborn, Chicago, IL 60602 (312) 332-2915
Judith B. Petrucci, Attorney at Law, 7949 W. Ogden, Lyons, IL 60534 (708) 442-0078
Joseph G. Phelps, Rinella & Rinella, One N. LaSalle, Chicago, IL 60602 (312) 236-5454
Gabrielle P. Pieper, Attorney at Law, 188 W. Randolph #2424, Chicago, IL 60601 (312) 263-2233
Joan Riordan, Riordan & Robbins, 134 N. LaSalle St., Suite 2016, Chicago, IL 60602 (312) 372-0202
Elizabeth Billie Rosenbloom, 1300 N. Lakes Shore Dr., #15C, Chicago, IL 60610 (312) 876-5244
Maureen J. McGann Ryan, Attorney at Law 29 S. LaSalle #640, Chicago, IL 60603 (312) 782-3668
Andrea M. Schleifer, 1426 W. Farragut, Chicago, IL 60610 (312) 878-5533
Mary C. Schlott, Mary C. Scholott,P.C., 750 West Northwest Hwy., Arlington Heights, IL 60004 (312) 259-8205
Ann Shaw, 3840 North Seely Ave., Chicago, IL 60618 (312) 248-4457
Carole N. Siegel, Attorney at Law, 3 1st. National Plaza #660, Chicago, IL 60602
Helen Sigman, Law Offices of Helen Sigman, 100 W. Monroe Suite 1310, Chicago, IL 60603 (312) 368-8441
Carol G. Silverman, North Suburban Mediation Service, 680 Bluff, Glencoe, IL 60022 (708) 251-5968
Susan B. Tatnall, Drendel Schanlaber Et Al, 520 Redwood Dr. P. O. Box 4010, Aurora, IL 60507 (312) 844-0800
Mary C. Thompson, Attorney at Law, 18115 Dixie Highway, Homewood, IL 60430 (708) 799-0051
Donna Anastazia Toulmin, Circuit Court of Cook County, 1901 Richard J. Daley Center, Chicago, IL 60602 (312) 443-5904
Joan Schiller Travis, Attorney at Law, 1550 N. Northwest Highway #401, Park Ridge, IL 60068 (312) 699-8686
Linda L. Walt, Northern Illinois Univeristy College of Law, De Kalb, IL 60115 (815) 753-1520
Grace E. Wein, Attorney at Law, 300 West Washington Suite 704, Chicago, IL 60606 (312) 372-1650
M. Lee Witte, Chicago Volunteer Legal Service, 205 W. Randolph, Chicago, IL 60601 (312) 332-1624

Municiple Law

Patricai Bryant, 9050 S. Hoyne, Chicago, IL 60620 (312) 779-3555
Sharon Eiseman, Ancel Glink Diamond Et Al, 140 South Dearborn 6th Fl., Chicago, IL 60603 (312) 782-7606
Anne L. Fredd, Earl L. Neal & Assoc., 111 W. Washington #1010, Chicago, IL 60602 (312) 641-7144
Virginia A. Prendergast, 5123 Caroline, Western Springs, IL 60558 (708) 246-0090
Ricca Slone, Attorney at Law, 210 Twin Towers Plaza 456 Fulton, Chicago, IL 61602 (309) 676-0335
Elinor P. Swiger, Robbins Schwartz Nicholas, 29 S. LaSalle, Chicago, IL 60603 (312) 332-7760
Valerie Moehle Umholtz, Moehle Swearingen & Assoc. Ltd., 410 Broadway, Pekin, IL 6155-0875 (309) 347-4141
Ilene M. Wolf, Wolf & Wolf, 1655 N. Arlington Heights Road, Arlington Heights, IL 60004 (708) 394-1713

Patents & Trademark

Amy Cohen, 3270 N. Lake Shore Dr., #12C, Chicago, IL 60657 (312) 327-2655
Dolores K. Hanna, Hill, Van Santen Et Al, Sears Tower 70th Fl., Chicago, IL 60606 (312) 876-0200
Esther O. Kegan, Kegan & Kegan, 79 W. Monroe St. #1320, Chicago, IL 60603-4969 (312) 782-6495
Dolores T. Kenney, Olson & Hierl, 20 N. Wacker Suite 3000, Chicago, IL 60606 (312) 580-1180
Doris Maroko, Willian Brinks Olds Et Al, NBC Tower 455 N. Cityfront, Chicago, IL 60611-5599 (312) 822-9800
Joan Pennington, Mason Kolehmainen, 20 N. Wacker Drive S. 4200, Chicago, IL 60606 (312) 621-1300
Hillary Sue Price, DuPage County State's Attorney, 207 S. Reberst, Wheaton, IL 60134 (708) 682-7050

Personal Injury

Marina Ammendola, Patricia Bobb & Assoc. Three First National Plaza 66, Chicago, IL 60602 (312-332-2350
Sen. Arthur L. Berman, Karlin and Fleisher, 111 W. Washington #1505, Chicago, IL 60602 (312) 346-8620
Mary Lynch Coleman, Rifis, Kucia, and Coleman, 707 South Blvd., Oak Park, IL 60302 (708) 383-3000
Donna Del Principle, Kane Obbish & Propes & Garippo, 100 W. Monroe Ste 1900, Chicago, IL 60603 (312) 346-835
Lisa Lee Derr, Steffes, Schwefel, 108 North Lincoln Ave., Beaver Dam, WI 53916 (312) 845-3871
Mary E. Doherty, 6024 N. West Circle Ave., Chicago, IL 60631 (312) 792-0026
Goldie C. Domingue, Law Offices of Douglas Bristol, 20 S. Claker 710, Chicago, IL 60603 (312) 372-1991
Theodora Gordon, Attorney at Law, 8 S. Michigan #2000, Chicago, IL 60603 (312) 346-8234
Margarita Gounaris, 5201 N. Washteaw, Chicago, IL 60625 (312) 769-8135
Patricia Hardiman, Hardiman & Hardiman, PC, 39 S. LaSalle #1212, Chicago, IL 60603 (312) 782-3090
Laurel S. Hickman, Attorney at Law, 5875 N. Lincolon Suite 230, Chicago, IL 60659 (312) 334-4242
Evalyn Walsh Laird, 47104 Pine Ave. Grand Beach, New Buffalo, MI 49117 (616) 469-4586
Carole J. Mallen, 1408 Lark Lane, Naperville, IL 60565 (8) 355-4164
Maureen A. McGuire, Gorham Metge Bowman, 300 W. Washington #1500, Chicago, IL 60606 (312) 236-2713
Lora E. Minichillo, Schwartz & Freeman, 401 N. Michigan Ave. #1900, Chicago, IL 60611 (312) 222-0800
Joann C. Pelka, 1218 N. Euclid, Oak Park, IL 60302
Judith B. Petrucci, Attorney at Law, 7949 W. OGden, Lyons, IL 60534 (708) 442-0078
Catherine Coyne Reiter, Pretzel Stouffer, One S. Wacker Dr. #2500, Chicago, IL 60606 (312) 346-1973
Ronnie Orzoff Robbins, Robbins & Robbins Ltd., 111 W. Washington #1901, Chicago, IL 60602 (312) 346-7227
Nettie F. Sabin, Nettie F. Sabin & Assoc., 6805 N. Sheridan Rd., Chicago, IL 60626-3897 (312) 274-8581
Ann Shaw, 3840 North Seely Ave., Chicago, IL 60618 (312) 248-4457
Sandra J. Slaga, Joseph A. Morrissey & Assoc., 3321 W. State St. Suite 1200, Rockford, IL 61101 (815) 965-5505
Christine E. Smith-McMahon, Attorney at Law, 120 W. Madison #725, Chicago, IL (312) 782-4558
Denise Y. Staniec, Attorney at Law, 134 N. LaSalle #300, Chicago, IL 60602 (312) 236-6951
Mary C. Thompson, Attorney at Law, 18115 Dixie Highway, Homewood, IL 60430 (708) 799-0051
Joan Schiller Travis, Attorney at Law, 15550 N. Northwest Hwy. #401, Park Ridge, IL 60068 (312) 699-8686
Ann Marie Walsh, Lord Bissell & Brook, 115 S. LaSalle #3300, Chicago, IL 60603
Janice A. Wegner, Larry L. Fleisher & Assoc. Ltd., 205 W. Randolph, Chicago, IL 60606 (312) 641-7117

Real Property

Esthel B. Allen, 4304 Cedarwood Lane, Matteson, IL 60443 (78) 748-1236
Ulana M. Baransky, Draper & Kramer Inc., 33 West Monroe, Chicago, IL 60603 (312) 346-8600
Gail Beesen-Swars, Katten Muchin & Zavis, 525 W. Monroe Suite 1600, Chicago, IL 60661 (312) 902-5398
Nancy Meehan Canafax, 2214 Greenwood, WIlmette, IL 60091 (708) 256-5805
Melanie S. Carter, Citicorp Diners Club Inc., 8430 W. Bryn Mawr Ave., Chicago, IL 60631 (312) 380-5150
Mary Lynch Coleman, Rigis, Kucia, and Coleman, 707 South Blvd., Oak Park, IL 60302 (708) 383-3000
Linda Crohn, Simberg and Crohn, 59 East Van Buren, Chicago, IL 60605 (312) 663-5575
Irene Cualoping, Chicago Title Insurance Company 111 W. Washington St., Chicago, IL 60602 (312) 630-2000
Diane H. Damico, 1552 Greenwood, Glenview, IL 60025 (312) 724-1696
Rochelle S. Dyme, Rosenthal & Schanfield, 55 E. Monroe, Chicago, IL 60603 (312) 236-5622
Jean Grommes Feehan, Feehan & Grommes, 6525 N. Nokomis, Lincolnwood, IL 60646 (78) 677-2275
Sean Fox, Attorney at Law, 814 Commerce Drive #106, Oak Brook, IL 60521 (708) 574-0215
Sharon B. Glazer, 414 Greenleaf St., Evanston, IL 602202-1329
Carol L. Gloor, Holstein, Mack & Klein, 250 S. Hacker Dr. Penthouse, Chicago, IL 60606 (312) 906-8000
June Wojtowicz Grady, 520 W. Roscoe #2E, Chicago, IL 60657 (312) 833-1744
Claudia M. Graham, Rodney C. Slutzky, 1 N. LaSalle #2015, Chicago, IL 60602 (312) 372-1104
Claudia Martin Graham, 536 W. Belmont #1A, Chicago, IL 60657 (312) 935-6630
Nancy Hunter Griffin, Attorney at Law, 401 N. Adams, Hinsdale, IL 60521 (708) 323-7729
Virginia M. Harding, Gould & Ratner, 222 N. LaSalle 8th Fl., Chicago, IL 60601 (312) 899-1627
Laurel S. Hickman, Attorney at Law, 5875 N. Lincoln Suite 230 , Chicago, IL 60659 (312) 334-4242
Katherin A. Ivanyo, Attorney's Title, 29 S. La Salle St #540, Chicago, IL 60603 (312) 372-8361
Camille A. Jaski, 2106 N. Lorel, Chicago, IL 60639 (312) 237-7238
Judith M. Kerr, 709 S. Stone Ave., LaGrange, IL 60525 (708) 354-9047
Amy L. Kurland, Masuda, Funai, Elbert & Mitchell, One E. Wacker Dr. Ste. 3200, Chicago, IL 60601 (312) 245-7500
Donna Mullen Leonard, 300 N. State St. #5323, Chicago, IL 60610 (312) 822-0558
Margarite Primozich Loew, Boorstein & Huszagh, 318 W. Randolph Ste. 600, Chicago, IL 60006 (312) 444-9600
Katherine K. Logue, 7043 S. Rockwell, Chicago, IL 60629 (312) 776-7998
Earle A. Malkin, Attorney at Law, 180 N. LaSalle #2416, Chicago, IL 60601 (312) 372-6150
Veronica B. Mathein, Mathein & Rostoker, 134 North LaSalle St. #1108, Chicago, IL 60602 (312) 236-3062
Barbara Miller, Valuemark Investment Services, 700 Ogden Ave., Ste #05, Westmont, IL 60559 (312) 323-3303
Regina G. Narusis-Firant, Narusis & Narusis, 213 W. Lake Shore Dr., Cary, IL 60013 (708) 639-5535
Nancy J. Nichol, 1660 N. LaSalle St. 3909, Chicago, IL 60614 (312) 664-5235
Mary G. Oppenheim, Korshak & Oppenheim, 3 First National Plaza #525, Chicago, IL 60602 (312) 346-2700
Mary C. Perisin, 1440 N. Lake Shore Dr., Chicago, IL 60610
Sandra K. Principle, 900 N. Lake Shore Dr., #913, Chicago, IL 60611 (312) 664-0264
Barbara J. Putta, Butler Rubin Newcomer, 3 First National Plaza #1505, Chicago, IL 60602 (312) 444-9660
Joan Riordan, Riordan & Robbins, 134 N. LaSalle St. Suite 2016, Chicago, IL 60602 (312) 372-0202
Deborah Sullivan Roberts, Sullivan & Sullivan, 188 W. Randolph Ste. 2400, Chicago, IL 60601-3005 (312) 332-5375
Esther R. Rothstein, McCarthy & Levin, 100 W. Monroe #2000, Chicago, IL 60603 (312) 263-1155
Nettie F. Sabin, Nettie F. Sabin & Assoc., 6805 N. Sheridan Rd., Chicago, IL 60626-3897 (312) 274-8581
Anastasia H. Schupp, 5425 S. Richmond St., Chicago, IL 60632 (312) 471-2775
Nancy Scotillo, Attorney at Law, 1608 Colonial Parkway, Inverness, IL 60067 (78) 359-0333
Dorothy W. Spinka, Attorney at Law, 10412 S. Whipple St., Chicago, IL 60655 (312) 445-1223
Joseph L. Stone, D'Ancona & Pflaum, 30 N. LaSalle Suite #2900, Chicago, IL 60602 (312) 580-2166
Mary C. Thompson, Attorney at Law, 18115 Dixie Highway, Homewood, IL 60430 (78) 799-0051
Deborah L. Toizer, Sonnenschein Nath & Rosenthal, 8000 Sears Tower, Chicago, IL 60606 (312) 876-8000
Carol A. Tuman, 8024 S. Kirklan, Chicago, IL 60653 (312) 585-4123
Valerie Moehle Umholtz, Moehle Swearingen & Assoc Ltd., 410 Broadway, Pekin, IL 61555-0875 (309) 347-4141
Marcia Banas Welcome, 714 Ashland, WIlmette, IL 60091 (708) 251-3817
Pearl A. Zager, Vedder, Price Et Al, 222 N. LaSalle St. #2500, Chicago, IL 60601 (312) 876-2100

Securities

Lee Hugh Goodman, 2201 Center Ave., Northbrook, IL 60062 (708) 475-3744
Anne Hamblin Schiabe, McBride Baker & Coles, 500 W. Madison 40th Fl., Chicago, IL 60661 (312) 715-5700
Nancy J. Smith, Sec., 219 S. Dearborn Rm. 1204, Chicago, IL 60604 (312) 353-7454

Social Security

Geraldine Brauneis, Legal Aid Bureau 15th Fl., 14 East Jackson, Chicago, IL 60604 (312) 986-4228
Terrie A. Rymer, Jewish Children's Bureau, 1 S. Franklin, Chicago, IL 60606 (312) 346-6700 Ext. 3053
Deborah E. Weiss, Katz Friedman Et Al, 7 S. Dearborn #1734, Chicago, IL 60603 (312) 263-6330

Taxation

Bonny Sutker Barezky, 3311 Old Mill Rd., Northbrook, IL 60062 (708) 621-9700
Bernadette M. Barron, Barron Financial Group, 720 Gordon Trace Apt. 19N, Chicago, IL 60613 (312) 348-0040
Cary Ann Bechly, 921 Verne Lane, Flossmoor, IL 60422 (312) 799-6628
Carole Ann Budyak, Philip Rootberg & Co., 250 S. Wacker Suite 800, Chicago, IL 60606 (312) 930-9600
Sharon Gromer, 2137 W. Montrose, Chicago, IL 60618 (312) 348-3833
Wendi Hangebrauck, 3334 Thornberry Dr., Glenview, IL 60025 (312) 729-3712
Laura N. Jasinsky, Altheimer & Gray, 10 South Wacker Drive Suite 4000, Chicago, IL 60606 (312) 715-4774
Sharon L. King, Sidley & Austin, 1 First National Plaza, Chicago, IL 60603 (312) 853-2664
Hon. Randye A. Kogan, 1311 Glenoak Lane, Northbrook, IL 6062 (78) 498-1904
Elizabeth M. Mills, McDermott Will & Emery, 227 W. Monroe #3100, Chicago, IL 60606 (312) 984-7555
Janice E. Rodgers, Burke Wilson & McIlvaine, 500 W. Madison Suite 3700, Chicago, IL 60661 (312) 861-9239
Dorothy W. Spinka, Attorney at Law, 10412 S. Whipple St., Chicago, IL 60655 (312) 445-1223
Barbara Christine Spudis, Baker & McKenzie, 2800 Prudential Plaza, Chicago, IL 6601 (312) 861-8633

Worker's Compensation

Lyne Bruggen Austin, 5815 El Paso Circle, Rockford, IL 611 (815) 397-7150
Cynthia Freund, 1715 Jasper Court, Wheaton, IL 60187 (708) 690-6480
Marianne Katz, Law Office of Michael L. Taden, 200 S. Wacker Dr. Suite 1800, Chicago, IL 60606 (312) 876-5799
Jackie Kinnaman, Illinois Industrial Commission, 100 W. Randolph Soic 8-200, Chicago, IL 60601 (312) 641-6060
Julia B. McCarthy, Wiedner & McAuliffe, Ltd., 111 W. Washington #1100, Chicago, IL 60602 (312) 855-1105
Carolyn B. Notkoff, 3652 N. Springfield Ave., Chicago, IL 60618

Other

Bonne Holtz Atkinson, 13529 South Erin Drive, Lockport, IL 60441 (708) 257-0443
Sara Joan Bales, 1716 W. Henderson St., Chicago, IL 60657
Shirley L. Berngard, 2908 W. Pratt, Chicago, IL 60645 (312) 262-2883
Karen Michels Caille, 2211 Forestview, Evanston, IL 60201 (708) 328-3678
Amy Cohen, 3270 N. Lake Shore Dr. #12C, Chicago, IL 60657 (312) 327-2655
Andrea M. Dudek, Sonnenschein Nath Et Al, 8000 Sears Tower, Chicago, IL 60606 (312) 876-8134
Dr. Florence Dunbar Ph.D., Attorney at Law, 642 Stanhope Dr., Casselberry, Fl 32707 (407) 830-5155
Catherine Elliott-Dunne, Law Office of Catherine Elliott Dunne, One N. LaSalle St. Suite #3950, Chicago, IL 60602 (312) 332-5535
Ann Hilton Fisher, 1026 South Grove, Oak Park, IL 60304 (78) 848-1654
Michael J. Gallagher, Circuit Court of Cook County, Rm. 2103 Daley Center, Chicago, IL 60602 (312) 443-4183
Bettina Gembala, 474 Uvedal Road, Riverside, IL 60546 (708) 447-4437
Theresa Gronkiewicz, 5S 527 Arlington, Naperville, IL 60540 (708) 745-1385
Cheryl Rich Heisler, Lawternatives, 203 N. LaSalle St. Suite 2100, Chicago, IL 60601 (312) 975-1229
Esther O. Kegan, Kegan & Kegan, 79 W, Monroe St. #1320, Chicago, IL 60603-4969 (312) 782-6495
Diana Mann, 3501 North Janssen, Chicago, IL 60657 (312) 281-0610
Victoria Martin, Associate Judge-Lake County 18 N. County, Waukegan, IL 60085 (708) 360-6360
Lucy Moss, National Clearinghouse for Legal Serivce, 407 S. Dearborn #400, Chicago, IL 60605 9312) 939-3830
Sandra G. Nye, Sandra G. Nye & Assoc., 151 N. Michigan Ave., Chicago, IL 60601 (312) 565-1666
Sally L. Park, 161 Chicago Ave. East 30 G., Chicago, IL 60611 (312) 944-1580
Mary McDonald Pascale, 2800 Lake Shore Drive #516, Chicago, IL 60657 (312) 528-5418
Lynda A. Peters, 720 Gordon Terrace #3L, Chicago, IL 60613 (312) 348-5748
Janice E. Rodgers, Burke Wilson & McIlvaine, 500 W. Madison Suite 3700, Chicago, IL 60661 (312) 861-9239
Terrie A. Rymer, Jewish Children's Bureau, 1 S. Franklin, Chicaog, IL 60606 (312) 346-06700 Ext 3053
Ann Slaw, Iicle, 304 S. State St., Chicago, IL 60604 (312) 726-5785
Elizabeth L. Snyder, Harcourt Brace Jovanovich, 176 W. Adams #2100, Chicago, IL 60603 (312) 853-3662
Joan Schiller Travis, Attorney at Law, 1550 N. Northwest Highway #401, Park Ridge, IL 60068 (312) 699-8686
Linda M. Wakeen, American Dental Association, 211 E. Chicago, Ave., Chicago, IL 60611 (312) 440-2813

Chicago Daily News 11-4-53

New Woman Judge Thanks The Ladies for Her Triumph

Miss Tucker 2d of Gentler Sex To Attain Circuit Bench Here

"The women obviously did it."

With these modest, sincere words B. Fain Tucker accepted her victory as the second woman to serve Cook County as Circuit Court judge.

"I will try to return the spirit of Mary Bartelme (Juvenile Court Judge for 20 years) to the Juvenile Court if I am given that assignment." Miss Tucker told reporters and woman friends who gathered Tuesday evening in her four-room apartment at 70 E. Walton.

She said she will request a bench seat in the Juvenile Court.

"I will put forth my best effort to merit the confidence expressed in me by the voters of Cook County," Miss Tucker pledged.

• • •

MISS TUCKER, a Republican, was humble in her election triumph. The women's organizations that had worked for her election deserved the praise, she insisted.

"Individually I was not particularly involved," smiled Miss Tucker, who is a pleasant-featured 54-year-old redhead.

"I was simply an agent for all of the women's groups who supported me—like an attorney for a client," she said.

She confided she had lost part of her name in the election. She had always been called B. because her mother's name was the same as hers, Bertha. If elected, she had promised friends she would drop the "B." and call herself simply Fain Tucker.

JUDGE MARY BARTELME (in 1922)

A new judge's inspiration.

• • •

HER TASTEFUL traditional living room buzzed during the evening with optimistic prophesies of woman backers. Several of them admitted to being Democrats who switched party colors to campaign for a woman in the Juvenile Court.

Miss Tucker was calm and relaxed during her evening's vigil. Only occasionally did she ask another visitor on arrival "Have you any late returns?"

Every so often she switched on her radio for an up-to-date count.

She made cheerful conversation with friends and even gave them a Hoosier recipe for persimmon pudding.

"You do the best you can, and then there's nothing you can do about it. So why be nervous?" she explained.

• • •

HER "BEST" was a diligent campaign that took her to the ends of the county, speaking to as many as six small groups a day.

Her two handicaps were a shortage of campaign money and no auto. Friends took turns driving her to rallies.

A past president of the state Women's Bar Association, she was the first candidate to be sponsored for office by the association.

Backing her were the National **Association** of Women Lawyers, the **Women's Share** in Public Service **and its 27 member organizations, the Women's** Republican Volunteers **and** the Cook County **Women to Elect** B. Fain Tucker.

Women's Bar Association

Dinner Dance

SATURDAY, APRIL 15th, 1939

Congress Casino

Congress Hotel

MENU

Fresh Crabmeat in Chilled Tomato
Sauce Ravigotte

Hearts of Celery   Mixed Olives

Cream of Fresh Mushrooms

Boned Squab Chicken Veronique
in Casserole
New Peas à la Francaise
Potatoes

Salad Surprise

Bombe Glacée Tutti Frutti
Petits Fours

Coffee

Women's Bar Association of Illinois

Marion Lee Marshall
President

Jean Smith Evans
First Vice-President

Vera M. Binks
Second Vice-President

Doris L. Nohren
Secretary

Agnes L. Cherry
Treasurer

EXECUTIVE BOARD

Kathryn Barasa Rinella   Wilma Busenbark

Elaine Eckerling   Esther Oswianza

Louise Erb Madden

All WBAI members were invited to contribute their story for this personal section of this history book. All which did so are included.

KATHERINE ABRAHAM, she received a A. in Political Science from the University of Illinois, d a J.D. from Chicago-Kent College of Law of the inois Institute of Technology in 1965. She is a ember of both the Illinois and Mississippi Bars. ior to attending law school, employment included ccounting with public accounting firms and Hotel anagement experience. She was in private practice d also an advisor and attorney for the U.S. partment of Housing & Urban Development for a mber of years. She was past president of the omen's Bar Association in 1977-78.

VICKI LAFER ABRAHAMSON, She is a 79 graduate of the University of Michigan School Law and has had her own law firm since 1985 ecializing in employment related matters. Ms. rahamson is a member of the Young Lawyers ction of the Labor & Employment Committee of e Chicago Bar Association, the Illinois State Bar sociation, and the Women's Bar Association of inois. She is also co-chair of the Trial Advocacy bcommittee, Subcommittee on Employee Rights d Responsibilities, Committee on Labor & nployment Law, of the American Bar Association, d is a member of its Section on Litigation. Ms. rahamson is a frequent contributor and speaker at minars on employment rights and is author of veral publications on that subject.

MARCY POHN ABRAMS, she attended Paul Law School and has been an Assistant State's ttorney. She chose Law as a career after eliminating terior Design and college teaching. When she rolled in DePaul Law School in 1975 she was the ly grandmother in the freshman class. She can still ar the cheers of her husband, children and andchildren when she received her J.D. In the 60's e was deeply involved in the Vietnam protest ovement. Her life has been filled with art, literature d law.

She is proud of the variety of accomplishments d associations she's enjoyed during her lifetime. e was an appointee to the Governor's Commission the Status of Women, and a member of the ISBA neral Assembly. She taught law courses at Oakton ollege and Mallinckrodt College. She is a member the WBAI and other bar associations, is involved drafting Domestic Violence legislation, and with e League of Women Voters. She was also invited to n the Honoratae and the National Mortar Board. ey say variety is the spice of life. What's ahead? n thinking!!!

CHARLOTTE ADELMAN, she graduated m the University of Chicago Law School in 1962, s admitted to the Illinois Bar on May 23, 1963, is f-employed, concentrating in domestic relations e was founding President of the Chicago Chapter the National Association of Women Business vners (NAWBO) (1978-79), served as 70th President the President of the WBAI (1984-85), and first man President of the North Suburban Bar sociation (NSBA) (1985-86). Bonuses of the WBAI esidency were being profiled in the June, 1984 day's Chicago Woman and September 1985 Chicago gazine, and appointment to the Special Commission the Administration of Justice, (Solovy

Commission). Charlotte is a Life Member and a former Trustee and Secretary of the Illinois Branch of The Nature Conservancy (TNC) and a life member of the British Royal Society for Protection of Birds (RSPB). She is proud of her efforts in drafting and working for passage of Illinois' first Child Support collection legislation, (HB24) which took effect in 1982, and has received several awards for her work in this area.

She finds ironic amusement in how the painful episodes of the past become today's amusing anecdotes. In law school, one professor told her not to continue law school but to be a housewife. A fellow law student publicly accused her of taking a man's seat and only being there to find a husband. Twenty-five years later she was invited to, and served, on the Law School's Visiting Committee. After passing the bar, she interviewed a large insurance company, to get trial experience. They had no women lawyers, and told her male lawyers could smoke at their desks but women employees had to smoke in the ladies room.

She worked for Jewel LaFontant for six months, then opened her own office in "space for services" where she exchanged legal services for a desk. She has been in private practice ever since. Her first case and many subsequent ones were tried in what used to be called "Women's Court". Men and women sat on opposite sides of the court room, supposedly to discourage solicitation since this was where prostitution charges were handled. Every time she went it, she had to battle a bailiff because the lawyers' bench was in the male section and she wasn't supposed to sit on that side. When she started out, older women lawyers were few and wore lady-like jewelry and little hats. Judges called her "young lady" and court clerks, unaccustomed to female attorneys, insisted she was a court reporter. Even in divorce court, women lawyers were a rarity. Male colleagues would say, "Stay as sweet as you are," which meant, of course, "Don't handle your end of the case". They used subtle pressure to capitalize on women's ambivalent feelings. Should we be assertive or sweet and nurturing? It was a conflict.

She and her husband Bernie Schwartz, collect Chicago "street person" Lee Godie paintings. They love their Wisconsin "nature preserve" surrounded by a marshy lake, where they attract birds and observe small mammals. And, as often as possible, they travel, always incorporating wild life viewing. She's also trying to write short stories.

ROSE MATELSON ADELMAN, her father encouraged her to be a lawyer so as to be independent. She graduated from DePaul Law School and started her career in 1932, the middle of the depression. When she applied for jobs she was told women weren't wanted and she should study shorthand and typing. She obtained practical experience by working as a volunteer for the Legal Aid Bureau and opened her own law office in 1933. She handled cases for those on relief and evictions when she started out and eventually worked into probate cases, workmen's compensation, and personal injury action and an occasional divorce. In her neighborhood practice, some-especially men - upon seeing the lawyer was a woman, would turn on their heels and tramp down the stairs. Since this was the deepest depression, she was sometimes paid in kind: knitted sweaters, an

Katherine Abraham

embroidered dress and even a bizarre table lamp of a nude female figure.

Rose notes her daughters, Charlotte Adelman and Lois Solomon, are both WBAI members.

KATHERINE D. AGAR, she attended Vassar College for three years before leaving to be married to Woodbury Agar. She later received her law degree by attending Chicago-Kent at night while working as a legal secretary during the day. After passing the bar exam, she was elected director of the National Association of Women. She became president of the Women's Bar Association, she also was a member of the American, Illinois and Chicago bar associations and sat on the boards of the Visiting Nurse Association and Three Arts League-Chicago Monroe Club. She was named Chicago's first Woman of Distinction by the Woman's Advertising Club. She was also chosen Woman of the Year by Chicago's Most Distinguished Alumni of the Chicago-Kent College of Law of Illinois. She died in 1991 at age 83.

LISA M. AISNER, she is a Staff Attorney for the Illinois Department of Human Rights. She was a Legal Writing Instructor at Northern Illinois University College of Law, Hofstra University School of Law and Long Island University, C.W. Post Campus. She has been the attorney for the Nassau County Coalition Against Domestic Violence, Inc.

She is involved in the National Organization for Women, pro-bono committee, Nassau Bar Association and Nassau County Coalition agaisnt Domestic Violence. Currently she is on the Board of Lifespan, a domestic violence agency.

ELLEN J. ALEXANDER, she received a J.D. degree from DePaul University Law School, a M.A. from the University of Illinois and a B.A. from the University of Michigan. She has been a Labor Arbitrator/Mediator on several different panels. She

has been in the legal profession since 1976. She is a member of the National Academy of Arbitrators, Labor Advisory Panel, American Arbitration Association, Chicago Bar Association, American Bar Association.

She has also received numerous awards on arbitration. As a child, she remembers finding her father's stories (he was an attorney/labor arbitrator) fascinating.

SUSAN J. ALEXANDER, she received her J.D., from Harvard Law School in 1967. Currently manager of associate development at McBride Baker & Coles, she has been an adjunct professor at San Diego Law School, an instructor at Michigan Law School and Northwestern Law School.

GERALDINE M. ALEXIS, she has been a partner of Sidley & Austin as a trial lawyer in the firm's Antitrust and Financial Litigation Group. Her practice includes antitrust litigation and counseling, contract and sales litigation, commodities and securities litigation, and other financial litigation. She received a bachelor of arts degree with high distinction from the University of Rochester in Political Science. She began the joint degree program in law and business at Northwestern University receiving a juris doctor degree (cum laude) and master of management degree (with distinction) in 1976.

She is a member of Beta Gamma Sigma, and served as staff member and notes and comments editor for the Northwestern Law Review. She served one year as law clerk to Chief Judge John F. Grady of the U.S. District Court of the Northern District of Illinois. She worked for two years as an associate at Sidley & Austin in Chicago. She served as an attorney-advisor in the Office of Legal Counsel of the United States Department of Justice for one year before returning to Sidley & Austin. She was appointed by the Chief Judge to chair the Magistrate Merit Selection Panel for the United States District Court for the Northern District of Illinois.

ESTHEL B. ALLEN, she spent her childhood in Saline County, and attended Southern Illinois University and Olivet Nazarene College receiving a B.S. degree, a Master Business degree from Governors State University and a J.D. degree from University of California, Berkeley, Boalt Hall. She was Affirmative Action Officer at Governors State University. She was the Assistant Vice Chancellor for Legal and Student Affairs and is currently serving as Dean of College of Business at Governors State University. She was inspired to go to law school by the broad involvement of her family in the legal profession. Her won legal work has inspired her children to succeed in their own careers.

CATHERINE COOK ANAGNOST, she was born in Greece in 1919 and came to the U.S. at age nine. In 1948 became an Attorney at law under Law Office Study Provision (no longer allowed, this provision requires remarkable self discipline inasmuch as no law school study is involved... for other examples, Albert Jenner and even Abraham Lincoln qualified under the Law Office Study Provision).

She has served as 1955 president of the Hellenic

Bar Association, (remarkable because in the 1950's women were not readily acceptable in legal associations, let alone one dominated by men of Greek descent.) West Suburban Bar Association, National Association of Women Lawyers. She was a Delegate to the Republican National Convention. She was on the Advisory Board of the New York World's Fair. She was a Delegate to the House of Delegates of the American Bar Association. She was actively involved in the practice of law, including divorce, criminal, corporate, probate and personal injury casework and litigation. She was a fellow of the Illinois State Bar and the Chicago Bar Foundation.

She was the Republican Candidate for Judge of the Chicago Municipal Municipal Court, Cook County Circuit Court Judge and Supreme Court of Illinois. At her death in 1991 her son commented, "She was truly a renaissance lawyer in an age marked by intensive specialization."

NINA S. APPEL, she was born in Prague, Czechoslovakia, and was forced to flee her homeland when the Nazis invaded in 1939. When Germany stormed France, her Jewish family made another narrow escape, this time arriving in Portugal. Then she came to the United States in 1940. She was a Phi Beta Kappa student at Cornell University. She attended Columbia University's Law school in 1956 and was one of 12 women in a class of 212. Upon graduation, she promptly was hired as one of the first women associates in law on the Columbia faculty. She joined the Loyola law school faculty some years later, teaching administrative law, evidence, products liability and torts. She served as chairman of the school's admissions and faculty recruiting committees. She also has been responsible for curriculum planning and development, as well as court scheduling. She was named associate dean in the spring of 1977. In that capacity, she established the school's orientation program and served as a faculty member on the committee for the future of the law school. In 1983 she was the first woman selected as dean of Loyola Law School.

As a child her lawyer father would ask her what she was going to do with her life. When she told him be a wife and mother, he answered, 'Yes, but what are you going to do?' She and her husband have two children.

CHLOE ARLAN, she graduated from De Paul University in 1969 specializing in trust and estate administration, now in private practice. She was the first female attorney (of two) to appear in CBA's "Christmas Spirits", she was the first female

chair of CBA Entertainment Committee. She is former editor of the WBAI newsletter.

She is a current member of WBAI, CBA, ISB and ABA. She is an Executive Board member of t Land Trust Council of Illinois. She is the director the Whirlwind Performance Company.

DOROTHY GRANT ARNDT, she graduat from Northwestern Law School in 1935, practici law from 1939 to 1980.

Her daughter, Judy Royko, remembers her loving the intellectual challenge of the law a the satisfaction of using her special skills to h others.

MIRIAM D. BALANOFF, she entered University of Chicago Law School in 1960 but w denied schloarship money because "you are primar a mother." After graduation was offered a job a loop bank but declined because male applicants w being paid more than she was offered. And after tl she opened her own practice. Because of experiel like being called at 2 a.m. by a husband whose w was just returning home with her lover, she does l recommend having your office phone ring at hor

She was elected as a Circuit Court Judge with being slated by any party. One of the reasons for l elections, she believes, is that she and her family ha been political and social activists for many years a have been involved in independent reform politi Neither position was handed to her. It was toul hard work.

SARA JOAN BALES, she became a law in Wisconsin before becoming a lawyer in Illin She was a staff attorney with a Civil Legal Serv Program in Milwaukee, before going into priv practice with an all woman firm she established, c of the first in Milwaukee. She was director o seventeen county Civil Legal Service program Green Bay, and served as Director of the Legal / Bureau in Chicago.

GLORIA J. BALLARD, she attend Elmhurst College and DePaul Law School. worked for Chicago Title Insurance Company dur and after law school. She is currently the manage a Chicago Title Insurance Branch and is responsi for some legal interpretations of Title Insurance Ru

She was encouraged to study law by her moth She is proud that she went to law school, worked time and raised three children, all at once.

SUSAN T. BART, she is with the law firm Hopkins & Sutter, she has specialized in Trusts a Estates since 1986. Her practice is diverse and exciti

She formulates and drafts sophisticated estate plans for owners of closely-held businesses, highly-compensated executives and wealthy individuals. As part of the planning process she assists owners of closely-held businesses to transfer control and ownership to younger generations. She also administers large estates, counsel fiduciaries on trust issues, and represent estates and charitable beneficiaries in contested matters.

She is a graduate of Grinnell College and the University of Michigan Law School and served as an Articles Editor for the law review and clerk for the Honorable Richard D. Cudahy on the Seventh Circuit Court of Appeals. In her free time she reads and discusses the classics of Western Civilization at University of Chicago's basic program.

MARY M. BARTELME, she was born in Chicago in 1866, and remembered seeing the Chicago fire. She began teaching school at the age of twenty and five years later defied the customs to the time by entering Northwestern University's law school. She was admitted to the bar in 1894 and was appointed public guardian three years later and served in that post until 1913 when she was named assistant to the juvenile Court judge. She was elected to the bench in 1923, the first Illinois woman elected to a judgeship. She gave her home in the Austin district to provide a home for dependent girls. It was the first of three clubs that have since cared for more than 1,500 homeless girls. She presided over Juvenile Court and was given the nickname of "Suit case Mary" because she gave a suitcase full of clothes to each girl she sent to a foster home. She also kept a stack of clean white handkerchiefs on her desk to pass out to sobbing children and parents. She was WBAI President in 1927-28 and died at the age of 88.

CARY ANN BECHLY, she was born in Watseka, Illinois in 1914 and received her under graduate and law school education at the University of Illinois in Champaign-Urbana, with law degree and admission to the Illinois State Bar in 1938. She was employed as an editor at Commerce Clearing House, Inc. prior to entering practice in the tax field with Kirkland & Ellis. One of her prize memories is being admitted individually and personally to the bar of the Supreme Court of the United States by Chief Justice Earl Warren. Her tax practice at Kirkland & Ellis led to a subspecialty in problems of tax-exempt organizations, and after retirement she continued in that field as Treasurer and Board member of the WBAI Foundation since its inception. The Foundation provides scholarships for women students in Illinois law schools. After retirement, she lives in the suburbs

and continues to commute frequently into the city to carry on WBAI Foundation activities.

She finds retirement very satisfying and enjoys traveling to England to visit friends. She recommends WBAI not only for its professional advantages but also for the many congenial and life-long friendships which develop from participation in its activities.

ELSA C. BECK, she was a lifetime member of NAWL and served as secretary, treasurer, regional director and assembly delegate. She brought energy and skill to all the duties assigned to her. Her consistent attendance at annual conventions and meetings of the Council of Delegates contributed to her wide acquaintanceship throughout the country.

She was a graduate of Vassar College and the Northwestern University School of Law. She practiced law in Chicago for a time immediately following her admission to the Illinois Bar. She also became a member of the legal staff of the Public Housing Administration in its Chicago office. In the course of her duties, she made a substantial contribution to the nation's war effort. Shortly after the Chicago Land Clearance Commission was established to acquire title to slum property, clear it and offer it for sale, she was appointed its Chief Attorney. She built a sound legal staff and handled its complex affairs with rare skill and competence. Her work with the Commission made important contributions to the development of housing law, both locally and nationwide. She also worked to advance in the interests of the American Bar Association, particularly through its Section of Real Property, Probate and Trust Laws. She was the first woman to be elected to membership on the Section's Council where she served with distinction. She was a past president of the Women's Bar Association of Illinois and an active member of both the Chicago and Illinois Bar Associations.

She died on June 15, 1959.

MARY E. BECKER, she is currently a Professor of Law at the University of Chicago. She has also been an Assistant Professor of Law at the University of Chicago, and a law clerk to the Honorable Lewis F. Powell, Jr., of the Supreme Court of the United States, and the Honorable Abner J. Mikva, United States Court of Appeals for the D.C. Circuit.

She received a J.D. cum laude, from the University of Chicago School of Law and a B.S. in mathematics cum laude from Loyola University in Chicago. She is a member of the Illinois Bar Association Advisory Board of Columbia Journal of Gender and Law and has written many scholarly publications.

PAULINE RICCI BECKER, she spent her childhood years in Chicago, and attended college and law school at DePaul University. She decided to attend law school after becoming a widow. She felt a tremendous discrimination toward women lawyers and also felt that she was well trained in the law but not in the practice of law. She was the House Attorney for a Radio and TV Corporation, then later went into private practice dealing mostly in real estate and probate. Before retiring, she was active in her husband's business, "Becker Medical Supply".

She is proud of getting through law school with two small children to tend to during the day and studying nights. She believes women are finally treated as equals by most right thinking male lawyers.

BRIGITTE SCHMIDT BELL, she is currently employed with McDermott, Will & Emery as a Litigation Associate in family law practice, handling all phases and types of divorce, adoption (including contested adoptions), prenuptial agreements, and post-decree matters. She has worked for several different firms during her employment years. She has a J.D. from the University of Chicago Law School (1979) and an incomplete M.A. from the University of Iowa, and a B.A. from Swarthmore College. In addition to her professional activities and memberships Brigette does volunteer mediation work.

CAROLE K. BELLOWS, she is a Circuit Judge, and she entered Northwestern School of Law in 1957 and those were the days when the four females in her class expected to be treated differently from their male counterparts. It never occured to them that exclusion from legal fraternities, access to lockers, law firm positions, and most judicial clerkships were anything but the ordinary course of business. She was fortunate, however, that Northwestern boasted the first female law graduate in the United States and a record of several female valedictorians or near valedictorians. She was thus spared from overt acts of hostility from faculty and students reported by her contemporaries around the country. These women often had to fight fierce parental opposition in addition to warring with faculty members and fellow students.

It wasn't popular to be "different" in the 1950's. When her mother, Sara Kamin, graduated from Kent Law School in the early 1930's, she had little hope of practicing law and didn't.

In 1977 Judge Bellows was the first woman to serve as ISBA President.

LAUREL BELLOWS, she is President of the Chicago Bar Association. She is a partner in the law firm of Bellows and Bellows, where she practices in the area of Commercial Litigation. She represents clients in investment fraud, commodity and securities matters on a nation-wide basis.

She is a lecturer and contributing author for the Illinois Institute of Continuing Legal Education and for the Chicago Bar Association. She received her B.A. from the University of Pennsylvania and a J.D. from Loyola University School of Law in Chicago.

She is a member of the Illinois, Florida and California bars.

In addition to being President of the Chicago Bar Association, she has served as Co-Chair of the Illinois Legal Needs Study; Secretary-Treasurer of the National Caucus of Metropolitan Bar Presidents; Board Member of the National Conference of Women's Bar Associations; and Past President of Women's Board of Travelers and Immigrants Aid Society.

She notes it's not easy balancing her CBA Presidency, her law practice and her role as mother of a young daughter but she and her husband Joel share a sense of humor about their lives and she enjoys the hectic pace.

JOSETTE BELVEDERE, she is a Chicago attorney and maintains a practice exclusively concentrated in Plaintiff's Personal Injury (including Products Liability and Professional Negligence).

She is a member of the Illinois State Bar Association Tort Section Counsel, Acting Chair of the Woman's Bar Association Tort Committee, a member of the Illinois Trial Lawyer Amicus Committee and the Association of Trial Lawyers of America as well as the Chicago Bar Association Tort and Insurance Law Committees.

A graduate of Northwestern University Law School with a B.S. from Loyola University of Chicago, she is a regular contributor to tort-oriented publications and has lectured and taught on various tort-related topics.

MARGARET C. BENSON, she was born in Jacksonville, North Carolina, the oldest of five children, and grew up in Grand Rapids, Michigan. She attended St. Thomas the Apostle grade school and Marywood Academy high school.

She graduated from Western Michigan University in Kalamazoo, Michigan and from Loyola University School of Law. After law school she was an associate to a solo practitioner. She joined Chicago Volunteer Legal Services Foundation, as Deputy Director. She worked with the volunteer attorneys. Because CVLS doesn't receive any government money, she also helped with fundraising. She is a member of the Illinois State and Chicago Bar Associations. She is in her second term on the ISBA's General Assembly. As a member of the Women's Bar Association, she co-chaired its Matrimonial Law Committee for two years, and she currently sits on the Board of Directors.

It was probably inevitable that she became a lawyer. Her maternal grandfather was and her father

is. She grew up listening to legal tales, tall and otherwise. The law is a noble profession and she is very proud to practice it. Though she sometimes fantasizes about being a full time mom she never will. She wants her daughter to grow up like she did, seeing, hearing, learning, knowing that the law is a noble profession.

HELAINE L. BERGER, she was born in Chicago, Illinois. Toward the end of her junior year at the University of Illinois, she decided to apply the law school with the sole purpose of gaining the knowledge to be able to "help people". After a year in law school at Washington University in St. Louis, Missouri, she transferred to IIT/Chicago-Kent College of Law where she became interested in trial work and criminal defense in particular.

It was through Kent's Legal Services Center that she was able to try her first case. After graduating from Kent with high honors, she started her career as an Assistant Public Defender for the County of Lake. There, she honed her skills as a trial lawyer. She later decided to learn about the civil side of litigation so she joined Purcell & Wardrope, Chtd. where she engaged in personal injury defense.

She eventually opened a law firm with Andrew DePaul. She finally achieved her goals of being able to represent both individuals and corporations, to help both the poor and the affluent, and to engage in both a criminal and civil practice. Maturity has taught her law is a business as well as a profession; women must learn to be comfortable in both the courtroom and the boardroom. She hopes by the 100th year a WBAI woman will have achieved total acceptance in the profession.

ARTHUR L. BERMAN, he is serving his 15th year in the Illinois Senate. Before that he served 8 years in the Illinois House of Representatives.

He is Chairman of the Senate Committee on Elementary and Secondary Education, a post he has held since being elected to the Senate. He also serves as Vice-Chairman of the Senate Committee on Finance and Credit Regulations. He is a member of the Senate Committee on Insurance, Pensions and Licensed Activities, the Senate Appropriations II Committee and the Senate Judiciary Committee. He is a member of the Executive Committee of the Conference of Insurance Legislators (COIL).

He was the principal sponsor of the Illinois Education Reform Act, the principal sponsor of the Chicago School Reform Legislation and the Chicago Reform Restoration Law. He is co-chair of the Illinois Task Force on School Funding, the committee charged with revamping school finance. He is a leader in issues of special concern to women, including freedom of choice; insurance coverage for mammography screening and fertilization programs; family leave; and wage parity.

In a poll of legislators and legislative observers, he was named one of the "10 Best,". He was named one of Illinois "Top Legislators", and was awarded an Honorary Doctorate of Public Service from the National College of Education. He is also the recipient of numerous other awards from civic and professional organizations.

ELAINE STRAUSCHILD BLATT, for as long as she remembers, she wanted to be a lawyer.

Her father was a lawyer and she remembers his pride in his profession. To him it was a special privilege which imposed great responsibilities in service and ethics. She graduated from Northwestern University Law School in 1951. Though there were women in other classes, she was the only one in the entering class who graduated. Her principal frustration as a young woman lawyer was exclusion from the then numerous men's guilds. Entertaining clients was not easy! After marriage and children, she practiced law part-time. She resumed full-time practice as a partner in the firm of Blatt, Hasenmiller, Flanagan, Leibsker & Moore. The Women's Bar Association has always been an integral part of her career. She became a member upon admission to the Bar. She has served as President, and now sits on its Board of Directors.

Though she cannot claim to be a pioneer - that title belongs to many others who preceded her - she has witnessed the transition of women lawyers from an almost invisible minority, through tolerance, to acceptance and to a potential majority. She is increasingly proud to be a lawyer and a woman.

DOROTHEA BLENDER, she was born and raised in Peoria, Illinois. She grew up in a family devoted to the medical profession, her father being a distinguished physician in the community, from whom she acquired at an early age, her values of integrity, loyalty and respect for each individual life, which characterized her conduct throughout her lifetime.

She attended, and was graduated from the University of Chicago, and thereafter from its renowned Law School. After her admission to the Illinois Bar, she initially worked on the editorial staff of Commerce Clearing House, a legal publishing company, and thereafter transferred to the management and executive areas of that corporation.

She became a member of the Women's Bar Association of Illinois and served on various committees, where her keen legal perception and decisiveness were valuable in analyzing and advocating passages of legislation.

She served as Treasurer of this Association, and a its President in 1947-48. Her presidency was characterized by a democratization in the membership of the Association. Her spontaneous wit and gift for terse pungent expression, manifested as she presided a meetings of the Association and with other Ba Associations, and at functions honoring the judiciary brought good will and respect of the Women's Ba Association of Illinois and its members. She served a Editor of the Journal of the Association of Women Lawyer and was elected president of that organization.

Ms. Blender is deceased.

PATRICIA C. BOBB, she attended Law School at the University of Notre Dame and received .D. Degree. She has also studied in foreign countries. e is currently President of Patricia C. Bobb & ssociates for plaintiff's personal injury emphasis on edical negligence cases. She was a partner in the w firm of Bobb, Kane, Obbish & Propes specializing civil and criminal litigation.

She has been a Trial Attorney for Philip H. orboy & Associates, P.C. specializing in plaintiff's ersonal injury litigation. She was also an Assistant ates Attorney, felony trial court supervisor. She is member of the Illinois Bar and admitted to the Bar the United States District Court and the Northern istrict of Illinois, and the Women's Bar Association.

She has served on numerous panels, speaks equently and is the author of many legal treatises.

EDNA DEVLIN BOWENS, she was an only ild. She was born in Canada, attended Toronto niversity and moved to the USA at age 21. She orked as private secretary for a multimillionaire, .A. Johnson, also known as "Death Valley Scotty". ventually, she had five secretaries working for her. e was the only woman in her night school class at yola Law School and became a lawyer in 1930. She so received a doctor of law degree. After becoming lawyer, she continued to work for Mr. Johnson, presenting him when, because of the Depression, s business went into receivership. Thereafter, she as a sole practioner handling whatever came in cept divorce, which she did not believe in. She rved as president of the WBAI in 1934-35 and she calls that as president she initiated inviting male torneys to attend WBAI dinner meetings. The rpose was two-fold: to make them aware of the fact at there were a number of woman attorneys, and to ovide WBAI members with the opportunity to eet male attorneys in a non-court setting. She called that WBAI had served as a nucleus for warm iendship over the years.

Her WBAI Presidency was devoted to seeking gislation to enable Illinois women to sit on juries.

CAROL MOSELEY BRAUN, she has been a iil blazer for more than a decade in Illinois government. native Chicagoan, she began her political career as a ember of the Illinois House of Representative. Trained a lawyer at the University of Chicago, and later as an ssistant United States attorney, her legislative career as marked from the beginning by an activist approach governmental reform.

She was the chief sponsor of the first minority id female set-aside law in Illinois; legislation

requiring divestment of Illinois pension funds from South Africa; election law reforms and the extension of voting hours; welfare and medical assistance reform and multi-million dollar capital budget allocations. She filed, and won, the important reapportionment decision which affirmed the "one person one vote" principle in Illinois.

She was the first sponsor of the Local School Improvement Act, which created the recently elected Local School Councils in the Chicago Public Schools. She served as the first African-American woman Assistant Majority Leader in Illinois history. Her career has been characterized by her sincere commitment to progressive, nonracial politics. She is the recipient of over one hundred prestigious awards for community and government service, including the Independent voters of Illinois/Independent Precinct Organization (IVI/IPO) Best Legislator Award, the Association of Commerce Industry Achievement Award, the Chicago Urban League Beautiful People Award and the Mexican-American Legal Defense Fund (MALDEF) Government Service Award.

She serves as Cook County Recorder of Deeds, Registrar of Torrens Titles. In March, 1992, she won the Democratic Primary for the U.S. Senate.

ANN BREEN-GRECO, she spent her childhood years in New York City living in housing projects. She graduated from high school when she was 16 and worked full time as a secretary. She attended night college classes at age 21 and worked during the day. She left school and work and moved to California. She left California and moved to Chicago with her husband and worked at the University of Chicago Hospital and the University of Illinois Hospital. She completed her undergraduate work and went on to graduate school.

She lived in Washington, D.C. for one year and decided to become a lawyer based on the need for advocates, and because of the impact law has on people's lives; she attended law school when she turned age 40 at Chicago-Kent, ITT. She worked for the Chicago-Kent Legal Service Clinic. After law school, she did not feel prepared to seek a fulfilling career; law schools emphasize test taking and job opportunities for top grad performers but do not assist the majority of students, but she says she will never regret becoming a lawyer and she encourages other women to do it.

She is an Administrative Hearing Officer on child abuse cases. She is also involved in legislative initiatives involving protection of children. She is a firm believer that women should be in the Women's Bar. She respects her colleagues in the WBAI and believe they are a positive force for women lawyers, remembering how WBAI supported her and her colleagues in a sex discrimination suit. She thinks the 1990's will be a battle ground for women as we refuse to let our hard won gains be stripped away by the Supreme Court and state legislatures.

PEG MCDONNELL BRESLIN, she is a State Representative and Assistant Majority Leader of the Illinois House of Representatives. She grew up on a farm north of Ottawa, graduating from Loyola University of Chicago with a degree in political science and law in the six year combined degree program.

Ann Breen-Greco

After law school she practiced in Chicago doing personal injury defense work and later as legal adviser to the State Board of Education in charge of litigation. But she always loved politics, so when a vacancy occured for state representative, she jumped at it and won. Politics and law are a great combination career for women. She recommends it.

ALICE M. BRIGHT, she graduated second in her class at the University of Chicago Law School in 1941. She had already accepted a position in military intelligence in Washington when she received a call from Paul Harper who, like other senior partners, was on the lookout for bright draft-exempt prospects. She was quite a rarity as one of only three women then at major Chicago law firms, although there were several who practiced alone or with one or two male partners. She was the first woman hired by Sidley & Austin, succumbing to a long illness in 1982.

She eventually worked with real estate, contract negotiations and other areas. She was made a partner and her practice became more diversified and ranged from child custody matters and complex divorce cases to drawing up wills and trusts. Later in her career, she enjoyed the role of a family counselor in working with second and third generations of clients she had served in her early days as the firm's first "lady lawyer."

(Editors note: See *Traditions and Challenges, the story of Sidley & Austin*, by: Kogan)

CHARISSE A. BRONO, she grew up in Chicago, Illinois and she attended Lawrence University in Appleton, Wisconsin and John Marshall Law School in Chicago, Illinois graduating in 1983. She went into private practice and she says the more she practices, the less glamorous is the profession. She works in the areas of divorce, minor criminal, and litigation.

She became interested at age 11 in becoming a lawyer. Her uncle was an attorney.

PENNY BROWN, she is an attorney with the law firm of Much, Shelist, Freed, Denenberg, Ament & Eiger, P.C.. Her principal areas of practice are Civil Commercial Litigation in federal and Illinois courts (with an emphasis in State Court Chancery matters). She is a member of both the Illinois and Federal Trial Bars. She is a 1979 graduate of Chicago-Kent College of Law and Roosevelt University with a B.A. in History. Her significant experience is litigation that primarily involves commercial matters, particular expertise in Chancery matters and equitable remedies. Former Assistant States Attorney.

She presently serves as chairperson of an inquiry panel of the Illinois Attorney Registration and Disciplinary Commission. She is a member of the Chicago Bar Association, Women's Bar Association of Illinois and Attorneys Registration and Disciplinary Commission.

ROWINE HAYES BROWN, M.D., she spent her childhood years in Harvey, Illinois and she attended Stanford University and the University of Illinois. She attended Chicago-Kent College of Law graduating in 1961. She became interested in becoming a lawyer while working with medical legal problems concerning children, such as child abuse, rape, and incest. She also teaches at Chicago-Kent College and is a past WBAI President. Her major career, however, has been in medicine.

CAROLE ANN BUDYAK, she is an Associate Partner in the firm of Philip Rootberg & Company, CPA's, and a part-time lecturer at IIT-Chicago-Kent College of Law teaching "Accounting for Lawyers". She has a J.D. from IIT-Chicago-Kent College of Law, a M.S. in Taxation from DePaul University, and a B.S. in Nursing from the University of Wisconsin in Milwarkee. She is a member of the Women's Bar Association, Illinois CPA Society, American Institute of Certified Public Accountants, Chicago Bar Association, Illinois State Bar Association, and the American Bar Association.

MARIANNE B. BURKE, she spent her childhood in Chicago, Illinois and graduated from the University of Illinois in Champaign. She attended DePaul University College of Law. She started her career as a Legal Aid Attorney and is now a Supervisor at the Office of the Cook County Public Defender.

BERNICE S. BURMAN, she spent her childhood in Chicago, Illinois and attended Central Y College. She attended George Washington University and Northwestern University. Her role model was her cousin, who still practices law. Her first position was with a very prestigious law firm (no longer in existence) Moses, Kennedy, Stein & Bachrach where she did research and writing. Their primary practice was in Constitutional Law. Then she spent 21 years with Legal Aid handling domestic relations law. She has helped to train other attorneys in management and handling of matrimonial law matters.

She feels strongly that being a woman and a lawyer are not mutually exclusive; one needn't act like one of the "guys" to obtain acceptance. Being reasonable and negotiable brings you respect and credibility.

ANNE MARIE CHRISTIAN BURR, was born in Lawrence, Massachusetts, the oldest of seven children. She graduated from Georgetown High School, Georgetown, Massachusetts, as valedictorian of her class. She received a B.A. in mathematics from Regis College, in Weston Massachusetts. She worked as a computer programmer after her marriage to Robert Eaton Burr. She began law school at the University of Illinois in Champaign in 1985 as one of the older members in her class.

She became a law clerk for the firm of Thomas, Mamer & Haughey in Champaign. In 1988 she joined the firm as an associate in defense litigation.

EDWARD R. BURR, (JUDGE), he spent his childhood in Chicago, Illinois and attended the University of Illinois in Champaign, Illinois. He attended Northwestern University School of Law. He is a retired Colonel from the United States Air Force, and is an adjunct professor of law at the John Marshall Law School. His late uncle, Morris was a role model. Judge Burr enjoyed law school; finding much of what had been abstract became real later in his career. He is proud of his marriage, family and pro bono work. He joined WBAI when membership opened to male attorneys to support the unique interests of female colleagues.

MARY ELLEN CAGNEY, she received a J.D. (cum laude) from DePaul University College of Law in 1976, and a B.A. from the Newton College of the Sacred Heart in 1972.

She is presently a State's Attorney with experience in appeals, traffic, misdemeanor trials, felony review, preliminary hearings and felony trials. She is a member of several different Bar Associations including the American Bar Association, Illinois State Bar Association, Chicago Bar Association Judicial Evaluation Committee, Woman's Bar Association, Association of Government Attorneys in Capital Litigation. Since May, 1991, she has served as Chief Deputy of the Sexual Crimes Prosecution Division.

NANCY M. CANAFAX, she is a sole practitioner in the area of general practice. She was an associate attorney with the firm of Borovsky & Ehrlich in the area of general practice, and a supervising attorney for Legal Services Benefit Plan. She received a J.D. from Georgetown University School of Law in 1968 and a B.S. in Chemistry from the University of Oklahoma in 1959.

She is a member of the Women's Bar Association, the Chicago Bar Association, and the Illinois State Bar Association. She has served on the Wilmette Board of Trustees since 1985. Husband Tom, a labor lawyer, and she have two children.

SYLVIA CERVENKA, she attended John Marshall Law School. In 1944 she graduated with honors. She remembers when WBAI debated whether or not to admit black women lawyers as members. She took the position that all women lawyers should be admitted regardless of race, creed or color. However, some WBAI members vehemently disagreed. There was quite a battle. Sylvia worked for General Electric for 45 years. She was WBAI president in 1963-64, WBAI's 50th Anniversary.

DONNA CERVINI (JUDGE)

ALICE M. CHELBERG, she was WB president in 1955-56. She graduated from t University of Illinois Law School at the top of t class and was inducted into the Order of the Coif. S specialized in health insurance law and worked member of the Chicago and Illinois Bar Associatic and past president of the Society of Chartered Prope and Casualty Underwriters. As WBAI president s initiated the practice of passing the gavel fro president to president. The gavel was donated her. This tradition continues to this day. Ms. Chelbe died in 1984.

ELLEN HOLDEN CLARK, she is the direc of the Disability and Elder Law Program at Chica Volunteer Legal Services Foundation. A senior citiz herself, she graduated from IIT Chicago-Kent Colle of Law in 1989. Having taught in the Chicago Pub Schools for many years, she went to law school prepare herself to meet some of the legal needs poverty-level people. She is delighted that she is al to do just that at CVLS.

Her duties at CVLS involve training a recruiting volunteer attorneys. Her work has be almost entirely in the Probate and Domestic Relatic Divisions. She assists volunteer attorneys guardianships of minors and disabled adults. S helped put together CVLS' Conference on Preventi Homelessness. Her sons are now young adults, free of family cares she can devote herself to law a her other love - travel.

ETTA J. COLE, she has been in private pract since 1969 with experience confined mostly to busine and/or corporate, probate, and divorce law; prior entering private practice, she was an Illinois Assista Attorney General. She was a Hearing Officer for t Illinois Fair Employment Practice's Commissi during her legal career. She was a member of the Jo Marshall Law School Faculty Lecturing in Fam Law.

Prior to entering the legal profession, she wa teacher in the Chicago Public Schools and a Sund School teacher. Her undergraduate work w completed at Northwestern University and s obtained her J.D. from John Marshall Law School

COLLEEN K. CONNELL, she has been Director and Chief Legal Counsel of the ACLU Illinois' Reproductive Rights Project. She supervi the Project's legal and educational work, and provic legal backup on reproductive freedom issues for ACLU's lobbyist in Springfield.

She specializes in litigation involving constitutional right of privacy and protecting rights of Illinois citizens to make decisions, concerni reproductive matters and child-bearing, witho undue governmental restriction. Her legal we includes litigation challenging governmen restrictions on abortion, contraceptives, and the of new reproductive technologies.

Under her direction, the Reproductive Rig Project has become the legal resource for women w are seeking to exercise their right of choi organizations and individuals who work reproductive rights issues and attorneys across the nation who need information on reproductive rights issues and strategies.

She is the attorney for Dr. Richard M. Ragsdale, a Rockford physician who challenged a restrictive Illinois abortion regulatory scheme. She was successful in having the state enjoined from enforcing the statutes and regulations in two federal courts. She has written several United State Supreme Court briefs, including an amicus in Webster vs. Reproductive Health Service. Prior to joining the ACLU's staff, she was a litigation associate at the law firm of Jenner & Block in Chicago. She is a native of North Dakota, and received her undergraduate degree from North Dakota State University and graduated with high distinction form the University of Iowa College of Law in 1980.

FRANCES CORWIN, she has a J.D. from the University of Chicago Law School, and a A.B. from the University of Chicago. She is a member of the Chicago Bar Association's Matrimonial Law Committee and a Past Chairman of the Mediation Subcommittee. She is a liaison to the Chief Judge of the Domestic Relations Division of the Circuit Court.

She first joined the Legal Aid Bureau in 1940, following her graduation from the University of Chicago Law School. She believes in Abraham Lincoln's advice to lawyers: Discourage litigation, encourage compromise.

MARY HAZEL CRAWFORD, she served on the WBAI Board and chaired several committees. Her legal career spanned over four decades, and included private practice with major law firms, followed by practice in the public sector, first as counsel and then as Head of the Legal division of the Bureau of Public Debt of the U.S. Treasury Department in Chicago.

She was the first and only woman to attain that post. She was also the first woman to be elected President of the Chicago Chapter of the Federal Bar Association. Her legal service was characterized by thoroughness and integrity, and her personal life and friendships reflected her sense of honor. She is warmly remembered by Anne Sullivan and Thelma Brook Simon.

IRENE CUALOPING, she was the 1990 Illinois State Bar Association Community Service Award recipient in the category of "Individual/Non Law-Related." She is an underwriting attorney at Chicago Title Insurance Company, and was nominated for the award by the Asian American Bar

Association of the Greater Chicago Area, of which she was a founding director.

Separately, she was one of nine recipients of the 1990 Asian Human Services Community Service Community Service Award. She is an active member of the Illinois Asian American Advisory Council to the Governor, the Illinois Minority and Female Business Enterprise council, the Asian American Bar Association of the Greater Chicago Area, the Asian American Journalists Association, Chicago Chapter, the Chinese American Service League and Angel Island Theater Company, of which she is a founding director. She is also a freelance artist and photojournalist.

STELLA ADAMS CUTHBERT, she has been the Illinois Commissioner of Unemployment Insurance. She graduated from John Marshall Law School and conducted a private law practice (mostly divorce), and served as an Assistant State's Attorney. She semi-retired to raise a family but when her husband died suddenly leaving her with two youngster to support, her temporary retirement ended abruptly.

She entered state government as an unemployment insurance hearings referee and received successive promotions to Chief Hearings Referee of Tax Hearings, Chief Attorney of Legal Services and Appeals, and eventually became the Unemployment Insurance Commissioner. Throughout the years she has taught evening law courses for paralegals and has maintained a small private part-time probate practice.

Her most memorable bar association activities include being chair of the public office committee of WBA, as well as serving as WBA Treasurer and editing the WBA Newsletter for three years, being chair of the CBA Administrative Law Committee and serving as President and Scholarship chair of the Hellenic Bar Association.

She almost passed up law for classical languages. Loula Butler urged her to go to law school. John Marshall Law School has awarded her its Distinguished Alumna Award.

LORETTA EADIE-DANIELS, she spent her childhood in Chicago, Illinois and graduated from Loyola University of Chicago and DePaul University School of Law. After graduation, she worked for the Chicago Transit Authority in the Tort Litigation Division as a Managing Attorney. She also worked for the Chicago Housing Authority in the Tort Litigation division as Deputy General Counsel of Tort Litigation.

Sylvia O. Decker

She is now in private practice in the area of personal injury. Married to a lawyer, they have two children.

SYLVIA O. DECKER, she is a Vice President with The First National Bank of Chicago and a Senior Trust Administrator in the Private Trust group. She is responsible for the bank's overall relationship with certain high net worth individuals who have trust and investment accounts as well as other banking ties with First Chicago.

Prior to her joining the bank, she was a partner and associate at a large national law firm, Sidley & Austin. She specialized in estate and financial planning, probate, adoptions and taxes affecting individuals such as income, gift, estate and inheritance taxes.

Her professional and civic work has included speeches and articles on estate and tax planning, such as life tenant-remainderman purchases. She is active in the local bar association, having recently served as President of CBA Television Productions, Inc. producing cable and broadcast TV shows on legal issues for the general public. She was on the CBA board of Directors, and was a member and sometimes the chair of committees on Finance, Probate, Federal Tax, Long Range Planning, Public Relations, Bicentennial Celebration, Operation of Circuit Court and Chamber Orchestra.

Her other work includes the Board of Directors of the Better Government Association, a Trustee of the Federal Defender Program, co-founder of the Neighborhood Legal Assistance Center, Founder and Incorporator of the Vietnamese Association of Illinois and counsel to various refugee groups, and President of the Yale Law School Association of Illinois.

She was graduated from Yale Law School, Wellesley College and New Trier High School. Married to Tom, an attorney, they have two teenage children.

DONNA DEL PRINCIPE, she grew up on the Near West Side of Chicago, Illinois. She attended college at the University of Illinois at Chicago Circle and night law school at John Marshall Law School, graduating in 1980.

After graduation she tried teaching and social work. Her first job was with a solo practitioner named Mark Bigelow, with a general emphasis on labor law. When her boss decided to give up general practice and work for a union, she found a job doing personal injury defense work for INA Insurance. She worked there for one and one-half years when she became pregnant. After the birth of her child she was not interested in going back to work full time, so she put an ad in the Women's Bar Association of Illinois newsletter asking for any attorneys interested in part-time work to give her a call. That ad was the beginning of the Part-Time Lawyers Network, a committee of the Women's Bar Association and the Chicago Bar Association. She was chairperson of the committee for two years. Once the legal community learned that there were lawyers who wanted to work part-time, many part-time jobs became available. She went to work for Kane, Obbish & Propes a small plaintiff personal injury firm. She handles all aspects of personal injury litigation, medical malpractice, and products liability cases. She has done pro bono work for Pro Bono Associates and is currently a Volunteer Lawyer for the Homeless.

RUTHANNE K. DEWOLFE, she didn't go to law school until she reached 40 years of age, before which she married, earned a Ph.D in psychology and raised three children. The decision to enter law school resulted from an increasing concern over the differences in resources - both kind and amount - applied to troubled poor inner city children and troubled affluent suburban children. She went to law school with a specific goal: to provide legal representation to delinquent juveniles. She changed direction during an externship with the State's Attorney. After law school, she served for three years as Regional Attorney for the now defunct Midwest Regional Office of the United States Commission on Civil Rights.

She is active in the state and local bar associations where she has chaired several committees relevant to her work. Her "free time" is largely devoted to playing chamber music with friends. She is grateful to the women-in-law who trailblazed before her.

MARY ELLEN DIENES, she spent her childhood in the Uptown district on Chicago's north side. She attended Loyola University and obtained a Bachelor of Science in Humanities (majoring in English Literature). She began law school at Northwestern University School of Law and obtained a J.D. in 1969.

She had always been interested in law. She has worked for the Illinois Defender Project (now the Office of State Appellate Defender). She was the Assistant Director of Defender Services, the Director of Research for NLADA, and finally the Director of the National Defender Survey. She opened her own practice in 1986, doing mostly appellate work, civil and criminal. Although she likes the freedom of private practice, she still gives 100% to the project she is working on.

BARBARA DISKO, she grew up in Chicago, attending Taft High School and the University of Illinois at Chicago with a degree in Sociology. Upon graduation, she enrolled at Kent night law school, while working at the Social Security Administration as a benefit authorizer. After graduation in 1973, she became an assistant State's Attorney assigned to the felony trial division. At that time, she and Patti Bobb were the only two women in the division. She left the State's Attorney's Office and opened her own practice doing criminal and civil work, including contract work with the Secretary of State's Office.

She was appointed as an Associate Judge and her first assignment was the child support division, where she became acting presiding judge. She was transferred to the Domestic Relations Division, hearing child custody and property trials. She was transferred to the Criminal Division where she hears felony jury and bench trials. She was elected Circuit Court Judge in 1988 and finds it very challenging. She enjoys participating in WBAI programs and served as WBAI president. Owner of three horses, she is a skilled rider and jumper. She is also a gourmet cook and world traveler. She is glad to see more women trying cases in court.

GOLDIE DOMINGUE, she spent her childhood in Baton Rouge, Louisiana, and attended Rice University in Houston, Texas. She attended law school at the University of Texas in 1986. She completed the Master of Library Science program at the University of Texas, and worked as the Director of Information Services for a Large Architectural/Engineering firm in Houston, Texas. She eventually became dissatisfied with the challenge of Library Science and decided to go into law, a decision she is glad she made.

She moved to Chicago immediately after graduating from law school. She had no contacts, and because her decision to relocate to Chicago was made late in her third year of law school, she has not interviewed with any Chicago firms. She spent the entire first summer preparing for and recovering from the Bar Exam. She later accepted a part-time job as a researcher for a solo practitioner. Within a year, this attorney invited her to join his practice. She is also a volunteer attorney for the Midwest Immigrant rights Center (MIRC), and she has handled two deportation/political asylum cases in that capacity.

JOHANNA DOWNES, she was Bess Sullivan Heptig's aunt. Ms. Downes graduated law school with her son and daughter and practiced law until she was 80 years old. The 1934-35 WBAI Journal shows Johanna and daughter Margaret Downes both as WBAI members.

LORETTA C. DOUGLAS, she is currently a Full Circuit Judge. She has a L.LM. from George Washington University National Law Center, a 1968 J.D. from Loyola University School of Law (Law Review), a B.S. from Loyola University in Chicago with majors in Psychology and Political Science.

She has had several appointments through the Illinois Supreme Court and the U.S. District Court and is involved in several Bar Activities. She was WBAI President in 1981-82.

HELEN V. DUDLEY, she was born in Chicago, Illinois and was educated in the Chicago school system. She attended Wilson Jr. College and John Marshall Law School. She was admitted to the Illinois Bar in June, 1946.

She served in the U.S. Army with overseas service in Egypt. She was active in the Women's Bar Association of Illinois, and the Chicago Chapter of the Federal Bar Association. She was employed as an attorney for five years by the U.S. Veteran's Administration, and for 23 years by the U.S. Railroad Retirement Board. While employed in the latter agency, she served in various capacities in Local 375 of the American Federation of Government Employees, and was awarded a life membership upon retirement.

When she retired in 1974, she moved to Wickenburg, Arizona and has lived there ever since. She served on the Wickenburg Town Council and has been president of an endowed non-profit charitable corporation, The Wickenburg Community Services Corporation.

She engaged in private practice for a time, and gave assistance to the Chicago Volunteer Legal Foundation, and for five years served part-time as an attorney on a volunteer unpaid basis at two clinics in the Chicago area.

FLORENCE WISSIG DUNBAR, she is the daughter of a Chicago physician and a registered nurse, and is a graduate of the University of Chicago, holding both the Bachelor of Arts and the Master of Business Administration from the School of Business of the University of Chicago. She received a J.D. in two years from DePaul University.

She entered the private practice of law in 1946, handling cases during the day and teaching nights in the Chicago City Colleges. She was invited by the Illinois Institute of Technology, to be their first PhD in Business/Economics, specializing in business arbitration. She was not only IIT's first woman graduate PhD in B./E. but also its first woman Industrial Engineer and Industrial Psychologist.

Taking an early retirement, she moved to Florida to pursue an avocation of working for animal welfare. She is an authority on the law in relation to animals, presents a lecture series each year at John Marshall Law School in Chicago, seminars at DePaul University, and has been made the only "Honorary Alumna" of the University of Illinois, where she holds workshops at the School of Veterinary Medicine of the University of Illinois, thus is considered an "Honorary Veterinarian."

She was voted one of the fifteen most prominent women lawyers of the Century by the Women's Caucus of DePaul University. She was the first woman president of the Orlando council of the Navy league of the United States, the first woman on the Board of the University Club of Winter Park, Florida and now serves on the USO Board at the Naval Training Center in Orlando, is Chair of the Sea Cadets, serves on the Board of the League of Women Voters of Seminole County, Florida, and on the Board of the Florida Hospitals. She is a lifetime member of the WBAI, a member of the Chicago Bar Association, the Central Florida Women Lawyers Association and serves as a commissioner on the Central Florida Commission on the Status of Women.

JENNIFER DUNCAN-BRICE, she became an attorney in 1976 and has worked for the Corporation Counsel's Office in Chicago since then. In 1985, she became the supervisor of the Torts Division. Prior to this, Gail Hagland had briefly served as the first assistant under Mayor Balandic and Jane Barnard had served under Mayor Washington. But Jennifer became the first woman responsible for the day to day operations and supervision of cases. Jennifer was the first woman supervisor. Now women compromise more than half of the supervisors.

LIBERTY PETRU DVORAK, she is one of the "oldies". She joined the Women's Bar Association of Illinois shortly after receiving her license. She was then practicing in Chicago with her husband and brother under the partnership name of Petru & Dvorak. She took over their practice during the war at which time she was active in the Woman's Bar and made many good friends. It certainly was a very close group and they all tried to help one another since they were the minority.

She retired in 1980 after practicing for forty years. Since then she became active in community affairs with the church and clubs in our village. However she will always remember the enjoyment she had being a member of the Women's Bar.

EMILIE CHADDOCK EGAN, "Dreams are tough". They don't die easily. In fact, they can go dormant for years, seemingly forgotten, only to pop up again and become a reality.

Her dad had always wanted her to be a lawyer and she did too. In eighth grade, she interviewed the Delaware Attorney General for a school report on her chosen career - lawyer. With an amused, indulgent smile she has never forgotten, he explained that there were only a few women lawyers in Delaware and one never saw them in court. In his opinion, she would be better off getting married and having a family.

Despite her dad's consistent encouragement, society's message was too strong for her. In college she realized that only the most brilliant and determined women could go on to law school. And, she was just an ordinary bright person, smarter than many of the men headed for law school but not part of that rarified group of top women. Despite the passage of the Civil Rights Act, the quota system for women and minorities remained intact at most universities, so she gave up what seemed to be, at the time, an impossible dream.

Women of her era married what they wanted to be and she, of course, married a lawyer. By the time law school admissions were truly open, she had three children and just figured it was too late for her. When, in 1979, Northwestern University School of Law offered a lecture series on various legal issues taught by its professors, she jumped at the chance to take it. There, the dream reawakened. It was a new era. Several of the professors encouraged her to apply to law school, and a few years later she did.

Two months after her fortieth birthday, she was a first year law student attending orientation at Northwestern. Sitting in the top row of Lincoln hall, she looked down upon a phenomenon she had never expected. Almost half of her fellow students were women - ordinary bright people just like she and her friends had been eighteen years before. It was a wonderful sight.

Her dream became a reality in 1986 when she graduated and was admitted to practice. The best part was her dad, who never stopped believing she should be a lawyer, lived to see her become one. Thirty years after that discouraging interview with the Delaware Attorney General, she was an Assistant Illinois Attorney General appearing in court several times every week. Dreams are tough. They survive. And, it's never too late to make a dream come true. Women do not have true equality of opportunity in the legal profession as yet and the struggle is not over but, as long as we continue to dream and refuse to give up, we'll get there.

TALA ENGEL, she was admitted to the bar in February, 1957, and has had a unique opportunity to practice law on a very high level. Moving to Chicago from her home state of Florida, and specializing in Immigration Law after working for the government for a few years, she was able to spend most of her career representing large corporate clients with an illustrious clientele, such as the Continental Bank, First National Bank, Sunstrand Corporation, Coca-Cola Bottling Co., Monsanto, Nalco Chemical Co., Beatreme Foods, Humbolt Wedag, Becker of Becker Radio, to name a few.

Her law school, the University of Miami, at Coral Gables, Florida, was more progressive than most schools. Her fellow law students were pleasant to her going through school. There were only a couple of acts of hostility by professors. When she wanted to donate a chair in Women's Rights she was told it would not be accepted and had to switch to Immigration Law.

Discrimination was open in that employers told you they did not hire women, including the government, and accepted in that women thought the reasons given by employers were valid. They must be valid, everybody was saying them.

In actuality most women never received the chance to get the experience needed to get ahead in most places and never received the opportunity to have access to clients.

Starting from nothing, and knowing no one, she became a self-made millionaire. Her field of practice gave her the opportunity to travel in about 55 countries. Having devoted her life to bringing about 30,000 people to America, she still practices law in the field of Immigration.

In 1970 she found herself the Plaintiff in a lawsuit against the Chicago Bar Association for discrimination against women in participation in the activities of the Chicago Bar. As a result of her lawsuit women were admitted to full participation in all aspects of the Association. The Association continued to treat her well and was a mainstay in the building of her practice.

EDNA SELAN EPSTEIN, she is in private practice concentrating in litigation. She is a 1973 graduate cum laude of the University of Chicago Law School, Law Review, Order of Coif. She has a PhD from Harvard University in Romance Languages and Literature, a M.A. from John Hopkins University in Romance Languages and Literature, and a B.A. from Barnard College , cum laude, Phi Beta Kappa.

She has been an Assistant Professor of French at the University of Illinois at Chicago, a member of the Faculty Senate, a Consultant to Illinois Bureau of the Budget, has been on the Illinois Institute for Social Policy, State's Attorney for Cook County, an Associate at Sidley & Austin concentrating in commercial litigation and a partner with the same firm.

She has been involved in many professional activities and served on several panels. She is a member of the American Bar Association, Chicago Bar Association, Chicago Council of Lawyers, International Bar Association, Women's Bar Association, and the Illinois State Bar Association.

Born in Yugoslavia to Jewish parents, Edna was among the few to escape the holocaust of World War II. She and her husband Wolfgang, have three children.

ROBERTA G. EVANS, she is the Assistant Dean and Director of Graduate Student Affairs at the University of Chicago Law School. She received her B.A. from the University of Connecticut with honors in government and was a member of Phi Beta Kappa when she graduated from the University of Chicago Law School.

After living in Japan for two years, she was associated with the Office of the Public Administrator of Cook County for seven years. Since 1973, she has been associated with the Chicago law firm of Neal Gerber & Eisenberg, where she specializes in estate planning and administration.

She served as chair of the AALS Section on Graduate Programs for Foreign Lawyers and has served on the ISBA Committee on Legal Education, Admission and competence for ten years.

RUTH E. FARBMAN, she spent her childhood in New York City. She received a B.A. magna cum laude from Smith College in North Hampton, Massachusetts. She received her J.D. from Northwestern University in 1987.

The "60's" opened the door. She needed a career, having raised three children. She was interested in Governmental law. With her friends and family's suggestions and support, she went to Law School.

It was very difficult to find someone to hire her in spite of her "B" average at Northwestern. She believes it was more because of her age rather than because of sex. She is a litigator for both insurance defense and subrogation. She took what she could get and adapted.

JEAN GROMMES FEEHAN, she has been a member of the Women's Bar since her graduation from Chicago-Kent College of Law in 1966. She was raised in Chicago, attended Foreman High School, The University of Wisconsin, and graduated with a Bachelor of Arts degree from Northwestern University. She became interested in law after learning that her paternal grandfather had attended Chicago-Kent. Though he never practiced law, he was a businessman, apparently utilizing what he had learned. Thus, her appetite began to grow as she read more and more about the law. She married fellow law graduate, James.

She did a term paper in high school on "Women in Law" and found that there were very few. All the more reason to go to law school. So, her goals became oriented toward the law and she achieved the degree, passed the Illinois and Florida State Bars.

Practicing law as a woman has changed drastically since she has gotten out of law school, due to the increase of women entering the profession. After graduation from law school, her first job was with The First National Bank of Chicago, where she learned about probate, trust and estate planning. She was able to get a law firm job with Hinshaw, Culbertson, Moelmann, Hoban & Fuller, where she worked until the birth of her first son in 1971. She now practices out of her home. All these many years, the one constant in her legal life is her association with WBAI and the friendships it helped her form.

MATILDA FENBERG, she entered the portals of Yale Law School in 1919 in fear and trembling, but after talking to the Dean's secretary she felt that she had come where she wanted to be. The secretary told her what subjects she would take, what books she needed, and she was duly registered. The secretary said there were no accommodations for women students in the building but that since Judge William Howard Taft, who taught constitutional law on Saturdays, came once a month only, it had been decided to let the women students use his office as their quarters.

The late Ms. Fenberg was thrilled at the thought of being the first woman to enter the office of William Howard Taft, who came from her native state of Ohio, and she decided then and there to take his course as soon as she was permitted. Ms. Fenberg was the first woman to matriculate at Yale Law School. In 1923 she associated in the practice of law with Clarence Darrow in Chicago.

BARBARA FINESMITH, she attended the University of Wisconsin Law School and IIT Kent College of Law graduating in 1986. She has taught legal writing. She worked for Frankel & McKay, Ltd. as a litigation attorney and as Assistant Corporate Counsel for the Department of Law in the City of Chicago doing litigation work. She is presently Executive Director, for the Pro Bono Advocate Volunteer Program, providing free legal service to poor people, especially battered women and children in Cook County. She proudly recalls Judge Ann Williams swearing in her daughter to the Northern District of Illinois and that her daughter received one of the WBAI scholarships.

JEAN BAUER FISLER, she spent her childhood in Santa Monica, California. She graduated from Santa Monica High School. During World War II, she entered UCLA where she majored in Psychology. She was Vice-President of the Student Body, graduated with Highest Honors, Phi Beta Kappa and Valedictorian of the class. That summer she studied at the University of Mexico in Mexico City.

She was employed by TIME, Inc. in New York City and then she worked for the United Nations Economic Commission for Europe in Geneva, Switzerland. She travelled in 23 countries of Europe and was one of the first Americans to journey behind the Iron Curtain. Upon her return to the United States she lectured extensively about her travels under the auspices of the Hollywood Artist Bureau.

She was honored in 1949 to be one of five women who along with forty five men were admitted to the very first class to start the UCLA School of Law. She worked for the Senate Internal Security subcommittee in Washington, D.C. and later worked for the City of Los Angeles.

After admission to the State Bar of California she practiced law from a home office while she raised three daughters. Her career as a lawyer has included private practice, working for the Legal Aid Office of the San Fernando Valley Bar Association and for the first Office of Economic Opportunity law office in the San Fernando Valley of California. After being out of law school 25 years, she moved to Illinois due to her husband's job transfer, and took and passed the bar. Since her husband retired, they have spent much time travelling the world and visiting their children and grandchildren.

MARTHA MARIE FITZSIMMONS, she was born January 14, 1952 in Chicago, IL. When she was 13, her family moved to Belize, Central America where she became fluent in Spanish. She attended Trinity High School in River Forest. Her fondest recollection is graduating. She graduated from Illinois Benedictine College in 1976.

She worked in banks, but decided that wasn't a good field for a woman so she went to DePaul Law School and graduated in 1983.

She was a Federal Public Defender in south Texas from 1984 to 1986 and has been a Cook County Public Defender ever since. She has handled 33 felony jury trials in state and federal court, involving everything from smuggling aliens to breaking into cars to burying a person alive.

Martha's criminal defense experience prepared her very well for raising her son Rafa singlehandedly. It takes a lot to gross her out.

MARGARET M. FOSTER, she attended the University of Arkansas and obtained a J.D. with honors, a M.A. with honors, and a B.A. in Speech-Language Pathology. She was also a visiting student at DePaul University College of Law. She has worked as a Law Clerk for Niblock Law Firm, Friday Eddredge & Clark, and Gable & Gotwals. She was an extern for the Organized Crime Strike Force for the U.S. Department of Justice, and a Research Attorney for the Illinois Appellate Court. She is a member of the American Bar Association, the Chicago Bar Association, the Illinois State Bar Association, and the Women's Bar Association of Illinois, where she serves as Program Committee Chair and Judicial Reception Committee Co-Chair.

ETHA BEATRICE FOX, she was born Chicago, Illinois in 1914 and attended the Chica Public Schools, Roosevelt University, A.B. Chicago-Kent College of Law, J.D. She was a Memb Round Table, Fellow of Honor Council, and receiv a M.B.A. from the University of Chicago.

She was admitted to practice in the Illino Supreme Court; U.S. District Court; Northern Distr of Illinois; U.S. Court of Appeals, 7th Circuit; U Supreme Court; U.S. Court of Military Appeals.

Her legal employment includes the Illinois Sta Bar Association Committee on Probate Law; Office Cook County Public Administrator; Office of R Stabilization, OPA; U.S. District Court, Northe District of Illinois, and U.S. Court of Appeals, 7 Circuit as Law Clerk to the Honorable Win G. Kno

She was a member of the American B Association; International Law, Legal Educatio Gavel Awards Committees; Federal Bar Associatie Board of Directors; Illinois State Bar Associatie Chicago Bar Association; Board of Manage International Law, Federal Civil Procedu Candidates Evaluation, Military Law, Continui Legal Education (chair), Professional Responsibil (Chair), Committee on Committees. She served the U.S. Coast Guard Reserve for 30 years and for years was editor of the *WBAI News*.

AVIVA FUTORIAN, she was the Director the Women's Law Project of the Legal Assistar Foundation of Chicago. The Women's Law Projec a special unit of the foundation that works to reso legal problems of poor women through class acti impact litigation, legislation and other law refo efforts, focusing on issues of government benef child care, reproductive rights, teenage pregnan paternity and child support, employme discrimination, custody problems and domes violence.

In 1988, she was inducted into the Chica Women's Hall of Fame for her contributions women's rights in the field of law. She is a foun and past chair of the Illinois Task Force on Ch Support and is a member of the steering committe the Illinois Task Force on Gender Bias in the Cou She has been on the Visiting Committee of University of Chicago Law School, and she serves the boards of the Emergency Fund for Needy Peo the Women Employed Institute and the Illinois Fan Support Enforcement Association. She is a mem of the Department of Public Aid's Child Supp Advisory Committee, and chairs its subcommitte review the state's child support guidelines.

She has been the treasurer and legislative ch

of the Women's Bar Association of Illinois and helped organize and conduct seminars for lawyers on legislative issues and on sex discrimination in the work-place.

She received the Civic contribution Award from the League of Women Voters of Chicago for her role in providing access for the poor to the legal system.

She received her law degree from the University of Chicago Law School, where she was on the editorial board of the Law Review in 1970.

BETTY GALLO

LAUREN GASH, she spent her childhood in Berkeley Heights, New Jersey and attended Clark University, in Worchester, Massachusetts. She attended law school at Georgetown University and Northwestern University graduating in 1987. She became interested in law through government and had a desire to "Make the world better" through law.

She dislikes the reputation lawyers have as non-caring, money-hungry, ambulance-chasing, unethical people. It really hurts her. She feels lawyers have an obligation to try to dispel this notion by showing that they don't fit it. She feels her accomplishments are being involved in worth while activities, public interest work, many volunteer organizations (especially women's rights-oriented). Her work has included being a full-time mom and Paul Simon's re-election campaign

CHARLOTTE E. GAUER, she was WBAI President in 1942-1943. She was born in Baltimore, Maryland (one of fraternal twins). The family moved to Chicago where her father was an independent petroleum dealer. She attended Chicago public schools, graduating from Lake View High School and enrolling in the College of Commerce at the University of Illinois. As a freshman, she had the highest grades of any woman in the Commerce School. She was awarded her B.S. degree with majors in accounting and economics and enrolled in the University's School of Law. She received her L.L.B. in 1935 and was admitted to the Illinois Bar.

Without political or professional connections, jobs in that depression year were less than scarce, particularly for women. She obtained a position in the Legal Department of Montgomery Ward & Co. working under the general counsel Stuart S. Ball. For two years she worked on criminal matters involving company employee defalcations and mail fraud against the company.

She was given the responsibility for defending charges against several of the company's more than 600 stores and 9 mail order houses for violation of OPA rationing regulations.

She was Illinois Vice President of NAWL and was elected president at the Association's Cleveland meeting. She received a letter from a Chicago lawyer, Foorman L. Mueller, telling her that the dean of her law school had recommended her for a position as Executive Secretary of the American Patent Law Association.

She accepted the position and became the first Executive Secretary of APLA with offices in the National Press Building. Due to the disabling effects of M.S., she retired from APLA in 1979 and retired to Arizona. On January 16, 1992 she had her 80th birthday.

BETTINA MARCHLEWSKI GEMBALA,

It was with the support of Frank, also known as the Honorable Francis A. Gembala, Associate Judge of the Circuit Court of Cook County, that she began law school at Illinois Institute of Technology, Chicago Kent College of Law.

After graduation, she began a private practice, her areas of interest were corporations, Real Estate, Civil Litigation, Business Law and Criminal Law. She accepted the challenge to work for Aurelia Pucinski, Clerk of the Circuit Court. Her assignment was Traffic Court.

It was a good decision. The division is complicated and interesting. New challenges are posed every day. She enjoys the problem solving, and the opportunity to work with her fine staff and city, county, and state agencies. Professional activities are also important to her. She is the first vice president of the National Advocates Society, the chairman of the Traffic Laws Committee of the Chicago Bar Association, on the Board of Governors of the Chicago based Advocates Society, a member of the Illinois Bar Association committee on Membership and Bar Activities and a member of the WBAI.

Gembala's motto: "Life is interesting".

ADELINE JAY GEO-KARIS, she was born on a farm in Tegeas, Greece. She was educated in the United States at Northwestern University, and received her L.L.B. from DePaul University in 1942, the only woman in her graduation class to survive law school. She served as Lt. Commander with the U.S. Naval reserves. She founded a law firm in Zion at a time when no firm would hire her because she was a woman, and is a former Municipal and Legislative Attorney for the Villages of Mundelein, Libertyville Township, and for the Long Grove School District, and is currently Village Attorney for Vernon Hills in Zion, Illinois. She is also currently serving as Mayor of the City of Zion. She was the first woman elected State Representative and State Senator in the history of Lake County, Illinois.

She was the first woman appointed to a leadership position from any party as Caucus Chairman in the history of the Illinois State Senate. She was also the first woman appointed Assistant State's Attorney and elected to the office of Justice of the Peace from Lake County. During her terms in the Illinois House, she was the Minority Spokesman for the Labor and Commerce Committee, the Environment, Energy and Natural Resources Committee.

She is currently a member of several committees.

She has devoted much of her time and energy to effect changes benefiting all citizens. She has also received numerous awards.

She successfully sponsored the repeal of the Illinois Inheritance Tax Law, which thus helped farm widows and widowers.

DIANE GERAGHTY

SUSAN FOX GILLIS, she received a B.A. from DePaul University and a J.D. from IIT Chicago-Kent College of Law in 1988. She is employed with Querrey & Harrow, Ltd. in the field of personal injury defense (auto, products liability, Structural Work Act and premises liability).

She is a member of the American Bar Association, Chicago Bar Association, Women's Bar Association of Illinois, Illinois Defense Counsel, Pro Bono Guardian Ad Litem work.

EVA GLASER, she was the first woman to practice law in Du Page county and was past president of the Women's Bar Association. She was born in Chicago, but moved to Downers Grove with her parents in 1914.

"She had a tremendous reputation as an attorney!" She was determined to go to law school and battled her way through. She graduated from Northwestern University Law School in 1932 and went to work for U.S. Representative Chauncey Reed of the 14th Congressional District. She then opened her own practice in Downers Grove and stayed at it for more than 50 years, except for the war years, when she worked on contracts for the federal government.

She was active in the Illinois and Du Page County Bar Associations and the Du Page County Professional and Business Women's Association.

She died in August, 1985.

CAROL L. GLOOR, she spent her childhood on the west side of Chicago and in Glenwood, Illinois. She attended Roosevelt University and obtained a B.A. In 1981 she received a J.D. from Northwestern University Law School. She decided to go to law school while working as a paralegal in a large firm and realized she was as smart as the lawyers. She has been working in litigation, general corporate and real estate law. She would like to become more involved with women owned businesses. Although her kids missed her when she was in law school and working for large firms, they respected her contribution to the family's finances.

DEBORAH G. GOGOLA, she is a Harper Trustee Scholarship Recipient and a graduate of

William Rainey Harper College. She attended DePaul University's College of Commerce as a Finance major, and graduated with a B.S.C. degree.

After completing one semester of paralegal training at Harper College, she enrolled in law school. While in law school, she received the IIT Chicago-Kent Class Award for Construction Law. She participated in Kent's Law Offices Program and was chosen for a legal externship with the City of Chicago in the Real Estate Division. She is a proud 1989 graduate of IIT Chicago-Kent College of Law.

She is presently an attorney for the City of Chicago. Expanded responsibility for the tutelage and supervision of the Traffic Division's Supreme Court Rule 711 Legal Extern Program has allowed her to ascend to a supervisory position. She is an active member of the Chicago Bar Association, and she serves on the Judiciary Committee. She is also a member of the Illinois State Bar Association and the Women's Bar Association of Illinois, and she has been admitted to the United States District Court. She is a published author of legal works.

DEBORAH L. GOLDBERG, she spent her childhood in Oak Park, Illinois and attended Oberlin College. She attended law school at John Marshall Law School. Her decision to enter law school was a last minute, impulse decision.

After graduation in 1984 she took a part-time litigation job before opening up her own practice. She is a litigator and handles a lot of domestic cases. She is happily married with one child.

LISA A. GOLDBERG, she spent her childhood in Houston, Texas. She received a B.A. degree from Washington University and was a member of Phi Beta Kappa. She spent a year abroad at Universite' de Caen, France. She attended law school at the University of Texas.

After graduation in 1986, she worked for Peterson, Ross, Scholerb & Seidel and Cowen, Crowley & Nord. She worked part-time and enjoyed the flexibility. She works in general civil practice and has served as an arbitrator in the new Circuit Court of Cook County Mandatory Arbitration Program. She is married and has a baby daughter. She appreciates WBAI's work in promoting women lawyers, women's rights and civil rights for all and has found the part-time lawyer's network a valuable resource.

PHYLLIS LAMB GOLDMAN, she attended and received a J.D. from the John Marshall Law School in 1985. She also attended the University of Notre Dame, Loyola University, and Grinnell College with a B.A. in history.

She has worked for the Illinois Department of Public Aid, Cook County States Attorney, and is presently in private practice. She has done Pro Bono Work and is a member of several legal organizations.

LORI GOLDSTEIN, she spent her childhood in Skokie, Illinois and attended the University of Illinois-Champaign where she received her law degree in 1984. She became interested in law through her pre-law classes and her media law teacher.

After graduation, she went to work for Holleb & Coff as a litigation and employment lawyer. Being a lawyer is both challenging and stressful.

ZENIA SACHS GOODMAN, she attended and received a B.A. cum laude, Phi Beta Kappa from Barnard College - Columbia University, received her J.D. cum laude from the University of Chicago Law School, Waves - Navy Reserve. She has been an Assistant States Attorney in the juvenile court.

She worked for Katz & Friedman and she is a Commissioner at the Illinois Industrial Commission.; a member of the Board of Directors Congregation AM Shalom, Trustee Village of Glencoe, Institute of Women Today, President of the Illinois Industrial Commission Arbitrator's Association. She is also a member of the WBAI, CBA, ISBA, and the NAALJ. Her law degree she notes, has added credibility to her community opinions and activities. She has loved everything about being a lawyer.

BELLE LIND GORDON, she is a specialist in Matrimonial Law with the Chicago law firm of Beermann, Swerdlove, Woloshin & Barezky. She received her J.D. in 1975 from Loyola University of Chicago, School of Law where she was a member of the Loyola University Law Journal. She was an Assistant Cook County State's Attorney and a felony trial assistant.

She is an elected member of the Assembly of the Illinois State Bar Association from the First Judicial District. She was previously elected and served on the Board of Directors, Chicago Greater Council, National Committee for Prevention of Child Abuse and the Board of Managers, Decalogue society of Lawyers. She was Chair of the Matrimonial Law Committee of ITLA, and is presently a member of the ISBA Family Law Section Council.

JEANNE BROWN GORDON, she is a graduate of the John Marshall Law School with degrees of LL.B.; J.D. with honors; LL.M. She was admitted to the Illinois Courts in 1936. She was an Assistant State's Attorney, Legal Technical Advisor and Hearing Officer in State License Violations, Illinois

Department of Registration and Education, (firs woman in said department); Private Practice in the area of Central Division Insurance Department of the American Can Company, which Division encompassed twenty states and was a self-insurer in Worker's Compensation cases.

She is a member of the American Bar Association Illinois State Bar Association; Chicago Bar Association National Association of Women Lawyers; and the Women's Bar Association of Illinois, of which she was president in 1949-50. Since 1964 she has served on John Marshall Law School's Board of Trustees Her hobbies are travel, symphony, opera, theatre and a doll collection.

THEODORA GORDON, she was born and brought up in the Bronx, New York. At that time, i was called the Borough of Universities. She graduated from Hunter College of the City of New York and immediately applied to the University of Chicago Law School graduating in 1947. She always knew that she wanted to be a lawyer, but recalls a job interviewer asking, "Why don't you go and have babies?" She went to work for the Harris brothers the founders of the Toni Company. The Harris brothers decided that since they made a woman's product, they should have women lawyers.

After 21 years, at the suggestion of her brother she went into private practice on her own. At that time, the only law she thought she would practice was product liability defense. It was a shock to discover that even though women has made progress in the field of law, if you were not one of the good old boys, you did not quite make it and receive the business. So since she enjoyed eating regularly, she became a general practitioner, whose first clients were the people she had worked with at Toni. She has never been bored and has found that she has become a family lawyer akin to the old fashioned family Doctor.

Teddie was the 1964-65 WBAI president.

MARY ELIZABETH GORECKI, (M.E.G.) she was born and raised in St. Charles, Illinois graduated from Rosary High School in Aurora Illinois. She received a B.A. in Political Science from Tufts University in Medford, Massachusetts Although she is only 23, her interest in the WBA originated over 100 years ago. You see during her senior year at Tufts University, she enrolled in a senior seminar entitled "The History of Women in the Professions".

After becoming extremely interested in Myra Bradwell's contribution to the profession, she noticed

t many legal achievements in Women's history curred in Illinois. During the course of the seminar e decided to focus on The History of Women in Law Illinois. While researching she found an article itten by Charlotte Adelman, past president and rrent historian of the WBAI. She contacted Charlotte d sent her a copy of her manuscript. Charlotte, in rn, sent the manuscript to the *Illinois Bar Journal* tich agreed to publish the article in conjunction with e WBAI 75th anniversary celebration.

Since that time she has become the president of e Women's Law Caucus at John Marshall. She has en named the first chair to the WBAI student mmittee and have been assigned to the WBAI ild Care task force. She has worked for Professor elvin B. Lewis of the John Marshall Law School as esearch assistant.

She is currently working for the Kane County te's Attorney. One day she hopes to join her father the practice of law. Her interests include golf, otography, Mickey Mouse and politics.

H. CANDACE GORMAN, she grew up on
e South Side of Chicago. She graduated from nwood Academy and the University of Wisconsin Madison where she was a Philosophy major. She rted John Marshall Law School and for three years as also a law clerk for her brother. She belonged to e Women's Law Caucus. During her last semester law school she worked in Juvenile Court where dge Odas Nicholson urged her to join WBAI.

She went into practice with her brother and gan slowly specializing in employment scrimination cases. The WBAI at that time held eakfast meetings. At one of them she gave a talk on iployment discrimination. As a consequence, she as referred to a client who in the ensuing years has, turn, referred her at least 15 other clients. She was commissioner and legislative chair of the City of iicago Commission on Women and WBAI president 1990-91. Due to her efforts, WBAI was included on e Task Force on Gender Bias. Her year emphazied e need for child care for working mothers.

FRANCINE GREEN-KELNER, she spent
r childhood in the southern suburb of Chicago. She ended the University of Illinois-Champaign/ bana and attended law school at IIT-Chicago Kent llege of Law. She has wanted to be a lawyer since e was in the 4th grade.

She has worked primarily as a general practitioner ncentrating in family law, real estate, and bankruptcy.

LLWELLYN L. GREEN-THAPEDI

A. (ALMA) ZOLA GROVES, she was born
on a farm near Golden, Illinois, and attended and graduated as valedictorian from Plymouth High School. She attended Western Illinois Normal, taught one year in Providence country school, then took a secretarial course at Gem City Business College in Quincy, Illinois.

She took a position as secretary to the President of the Illinois State Bank of Quincy which lasted 14 years and it ended when the opportunity came for her to work with the late Justice Loren E. Murphy of Monmouth. She moved to Monmouth where she remained for 8 1/2 years. During this time she studied public speaking and took American Institute of Banking courses. She studied law under the tutelage of attorneys in Judge Murphy's office and six years later was admitted to practice law in 1948.

She moved to Chicago and accepted a position in a Loop law office as a secretary. It was not what she had studied law to do. Her application for a position in the Law Department, office of I.A. Elliott, newly elected Attorney General of Illinois was favorably received and she became an Assistant Attorney General of Illinois in the Appeals Division. Although music was her first love, she also enjoyed golf, hats, books.

Ms. Groves is deceased.

CATHERINE COPELAND GRYCZAN,
she attended Tulane University School of Law and is in private practice concentrating in Corporate/ Business Law.

She would like to see WBAI continue to promote women attorneys in all of the legal career paths - public, private, education, pro bono, etc. Knowledge gives individuals the power to promote themselves. It would be helpful for younger attorneys to have access to a resource on typical salaries and benefits paid men in legal positions/ to have a job network or bulletin board/ to help women encourage their employers to adopt policies on maternity leave/ to have workshops on running for political office.

DEBORAH J. GUBIN, she was always
fascinated by the law and made the decision to become a lawyer her sophomore year of college. She attended John Marshall Law School at night and passed the bar in 1975. Since her concept of being a lawyer meant trying cases, she went to the Public Defender's Office. She went from the appellate division to the First Municipal to the Felony Trial Division. When she left she was in the On Going Representation Unit.

She became General Counsel for the Illinois Department of Financial Institutions, great title, but not an appropriate job for someone who loves trial work. Being in a non satisfying job gave her the push she needed to do what she wanted to do all along: HAVE HER OWN LAW FIRM. Building her own practice was a real challenge. It requires mixing legal training with business skills. Having chaired several committees and been on the board, she is aware of how important WBAI is for the advancement of women in the legal profession.

ELEANOR Y. GUTHRIE, she was born in
Annawan, Illinois and was raised in Geneseo, Illinois, graduating from Geneseo Township High School. She received a B.A. from the University of Illinois, an

L.L.B. from Chicago-Kent College of Law in 1940 and was admitted to the practice of law before the Illinois Supreme Court. She received a J.D. from IIT Chicago-Kent College of Law in 1971. She is admitted to practice before the Federal District Court, Northern District of Illinois.

She is a member of Zeta Phi Eta and Kappa Beta Pi. At the University of Illinois she was president of the Gregorian Literary Society, a member of the Women's Debate Team and participated with the men's team in debating the Oxford debaters. While attending law school at Chicago-Kent she participated one semester in radio debate.

She applied to and was employed by Commerce Clearing House working first in the Tax Department and then as Editor of the Trust Law and Legal Periodical services.

In 1950-51 she served as WBAI president. In 1952 she became a partner in Detrees and Fiske, the second woman to named a partner in a large Chicago law firm.

NANCY HABLUTZEL, Childhood was
spent in Chicago. Attended college at Northwestern University from 1957-1960 and law school at IIT Chicago-Kent from 1976-1980.

Nancy was high school debater and liked speaking and thinking on her feet. This is what interested her in law. Nancy first taught at Loyola, then ran a Legal Clinic for the Disabled. At present has returned to full-time private practice, but still teaches as an Adjunct Professor.

Nancy does a lot of work with children and families and with persons who have disabilities. She does lots of special education placements for children who need special services.

Nancy is married and has two children. Her daughter has just recently joined her in practice.

SUSAN HADDAD, was born in Chicago
and, except for attending school in the East, teaching in California, and working in the U.S. Congress in Washington, D.C., has always lived in Chicago. Susan has a B.A. in chemistry and a masters in English.

Susan wanted to found a health insurance company for animals, so considered attending business school. A lawyer friend pointed out that a law school background would provide the necessary skills and also other career alternatives. Susan attended night law school at John Marshall, while working as the speech writer for the then ABA president. Midway through law school, Susan became the assistant to the dean at the U of C Law School. Before graduation, Susan learned that her idea of health insurance for animals had already been done. She was faced with coming up with an alternative.

Immediately upon being sworn in to the Illinois Bar, Susan departed for a six week trek in Nepal, hoping for inspiration as to her future career path. None was forthcoming. She returned home and worked for a small law firm that did divorce. In 1980 she opened her own solo practice. She is now a successful divorce attorney.

A highlight of Susan's legal life has been her association with WBAI, of which she was president in 1986. Susan is a world traveler and her office walls are covered with photographs she took of people all over the world.

SOPHIA H. HALL, Judge of the Circuit Court of Cook County. Past President of the National Association of Women Judges. I joined the Women's Bar Association of Illinois after I graduated from Law School. I was inactive for a period of time when the Association refused to amend its bylaws to allow men to join. That has long since been rectified.

I was born and reared in Chicago. My mother, Beverly, was a native Chicagoan, and was active in community organizations. My father, Dr. John B. Hall, Jr. came from Boston to practice medicine and they married. He was the Director of the Cook County Public Health Department for over 25 years.

I graduated from the University of Chicago High School, University of Wisconsin in Madison, Wisconsin and Northwestern University Law School. After passing the bar exam, I joined a small law firm McCoy, Ming & Black. I was not their first woman lawyer employee. My mentor, William R. Ming, Jr., was an extraordinary attorney who was one of counsel for the N.A.A.C.P., accordingly, I was exposed to a wide variety of litigation, state and federal, trials and appeals. One of our specialities was election law. While in the practice, I was active in bar associations and the N.A.A.C.P. I was elected to the Board of Managers of the Chicago Bar Association. I also was elected first vice-president of the Cook County Bar Association.

Later in my career, I spent two and one half years as an administrative assistant to the Clerk of Cook County, during which I was appointed Deputy Clerk of the Cook County Board of Commissioners, the first woman, and the first African-American in that position.

A few years after my return to private practice, I ran for judge of the Circuit Court of Cook County and was elected November, 1980. My first assignment was to the Municipal Division. Then, in 1983, I was assigned to the Criminal Division at 26th and California. I was the first woman assigned there in 20 years. Four years later I became the first woman in 20 years to be assigned to the Chancery Division.

Being a black woman lawyer has not been an obstacle in obtaining opportunities because, at the time I was practicing, there were not as many as now. Also, the movement to bring more women and minorities into the profession and the bench was just beginning during the time I was qualified to be considered.

Now as a judge, I find that the profession of judging tends to be isolating, thus, I have continued my interest in professional organizations. They now provide an opportunity for collegiality with other judges and through them I can help to improve the administration of justice. The Illinois Judges Association and Illinois Judicial Council provides this opportunity on a local level, the National Association of Women Judges provides it on a national level, along with my activity in the Judicial Administration Division of the American Bar Association.

The Presidency of the NAWJ has been my most challenging experience. We have an extraordinary membership, and undertake cutting edge activities in the Association, with the help of its education and research arm the Women Judges Fund for Justice. Eradicating gender bias and racial bias in administration of justice has been one of our major

projects. I have learned through all of these activities that on most issues, change comes slowly, and we must work together to accomplish major change.

MARY HAMILTON, graduated from Chicago Kent College of Law in 1984. That was more than a few years after she had written a report entitled: "My Future Career: The Law" as a 6th grader in Bronxville, New York. Mary entered Northwestern University's special Pre-Law program in Evanston, Illinois, but after earning her B.S., got married, had four wonderful children, and taught school. When youngest child was a senior in college, Mary took the L.S.A.T. and within months enrolled at Chicago Kent as a night student. Three years later she left teaching when she had the opportunity to be part of Kent's Legal Service Center and had her first experience in Court as a 711. After graduation she joined Melvin Kaplan's Bankruptcy firm as an associate, and also started her own practice in Wilmette (evenings and week-ends.) Mel let her adjust her schedule so she could go to court with her own clients, and in two years her own practice had grown to be a full time practice.

Mary has found wonderful support from established attorneys through her bar association memberships...WBAI, CBA, ISBA, ABA and the North Suburban Bar Association, of which she is now president.

Her four children, their spouses and their nine children also supply support and encouragement. In fact one or two of her grandchildren are considering a career in the law along with Grandma!

R. MORGAN HAMILTON, has been an Associate Judge of hte Circuit Court of Cook County since December 1988. On March 9, 1992, she became Supervising Judge of Child Support Enforcement, Domestic Relations Division. She has presided in Domestic Violence Court, and Juvenile Court hearing child abuse, child neglect and dependency cases. She has been a member of the Commission on Minority Participation since 1988, a member of the Bench and Bar Section Council and the Committee on Juvenile Justice (serving as Chair and Vice Chair) since 1989, and a member of the Special Committee on Supreme Court Rules since 1991. She was involved in planning three ISBA Standing Committees on Minority Participation sponsored Women and Minority Attorneys' Conferences. At the 3rd Annual Conference, May 2, 1992, she will address The Road to the Bench, and Children's Rights/Rights and Responsibilities of Children and their Parents. At the 1992 Conference on Women and the Law she spoke

on Juvenile Offenders/Children in Crisis. She w planner and participant in the National Associati of Women Judges 1991 Annual Meeting, moderati Alternative Sentencing/the Crack-addicted Pregna Woman; planner and participant of the ISI Committee on Juvenile Justice sponsored 19 Juvenile Justice Conferencce; the Drug Affect Children (Cocaine Babies) Seminar at the 19 Midyear Meeting; and the ISBA Task Force on t Family 1988 Illinois Symposium on the Family.

Award from the Citizens Committee on t Juvenile Court, December 12, 1991, in appreciati for outstanding and dedicated work in the Co County Juvenile Court.

Employed as Supervising Attorney, Divor Division. The Legal Assistance Foundation Chicago, 1982-88.

J.D. 1976, Cleveland-Marshall College of La B.A., Biology, Hiram College, 1969.

JULIE E. HAMOS, Julie's firm specializ in lobbying and public policy. Her unique practi draws on sixteen years of experience in public servi

Julie grew up in Cleveland, where her fam located after escaping during the Hungari Revolution of 1956. Although Julie was only sev years old, the experience instilled in her a respect i risk-taking and change.

Julie received a B.A. from Washingt University (St. Louis), and a J.D. from Geor Washington University (Washington, D.C.). Fr her first legal position as Staff Counsel for the oversig Subcommittee of the U.S. house Ways and Mea Committee, she developed a serious interest in t working of government.

In 1976, Julie sought opportunities across t nation to lobby on behalf of low-income people. Illinois, she was hired as Staff Attorney for t Legislative Support Center, newly created by the fi legal services programs to advocate for issues interest to consumers, women, migrants a minorities. After authoring the first "Manual Public Interest Lobbying", she began a long career training on the art of lobbying.

Julie next served as Director of Legislation a Political Actions for the American Federation of Sta County & Municipal Employees of Illinois. In additi to lobbying on difficult issues affecting the pub employees labor union, Julie organized AFSCMI political action fund. As Co-founder of the Illino Coalition Against Domestic Violence, she develop policies of the criminal justice system for sexu assault victims.

Because of her combined skills in lobbying a crime victim issues, Julie was hired by the new elected Cook County State's Attorney Richard Daley. From 1981 to 1985, she served as the fi lobbyist for the State's Attorney's Office as well State's Attorney Daley's policy advisor on wome In this dual role, Julie engineered successf campaigns to enact the Illinois Domestic Violen and Illinois Criminal Sexual Assault Acts, to refo the Juvenile Court Act and to defeat the "prison ea release" program.

To learn first-hand about public administratio Julie served as Director of the Cook County Stat Attorney's Child Support Enforcement Division fro 1985 to 1988, with management responsibility over 300,000 child support and parentage cases, 150 staff and a $6 million budget. She was co-founder of the Illinois Task Force on Child Support and has participated in most legislative initiatives related to child support.

The firm of Julie E. Hamons & Assoc. was created in February, 1988 to provide lobbying and consulting services to clients with public policy objectives. Since its inception, the firm has been involved in a variety of important projects, such as: building a 150-organization coalition to defeat the 1988 Constitutional Convention referendum; serving as chief lobbyist for the successful campaign to enact the Illinois Affordable Housing Act; creating a legal services plan for the State's unemployment insurance system; and serving as the Chicago Regional Coordinator for the first court-supervised Teamsters International Election.

Julie lives in Chicago with her husband, Justice Alan Greiman. When she married, she was lucky to inherit three daughters, three sons-in-law and three grandchildren (now five)!

DOLORES K. HANNA,

Ms. Hanna served for many years as trademark counsel for Kraft, Inc., where she supervised its trademark operations.

She also served as president and as a member of the Board of Directors of the United States Trademark Association. Subsequently, she served as chairperson of the USTA Trademark review commission. The commission assisted in drafting and worked with congressional committees and bar and trade associations to insure passage of the Trademark Law Revision Act of 1988. This was the first comprehensive revision of the Federal Trademark Statue, The Lanham Act, since 1946.

She recently has been appointed by the Brand Names Education Foundation of the USTA as Executive Director of the Saul Lefkowitz National Moot Court competition. Also, she will continue to serve on the Executive Committee of the International Intellectual Property Association, the American Group of the AIPPI.

Her current board memberships include Cook County Court Watchers, Inc., Public Interest Law Initiative (PILI) and the Women's Bar Association of Illinois Foundation. Additionally, she has served as president of the Women's Bar Association and the Chicago Bar Foundation. She is a graduate of the IIT Chicago-Kent College of Law and received her undergraduate degree from Ohio University.

Her activities as a special trademark counsel will include consultation, alternative dispute resolution, expert witness testimony, counseling and seminars.

KATHERINE KINTONIS HARDESTY,

It had been my dream to be an attorney ever since I was in grade school.

I began the pursuit of that dream by attending college at the University of Illinois at Circle finishing with a major in Criminal Justice and a minor in English. I then applied to and was accepted by the John Marshall Law School, where I pursued the study of law.

Three years later, I took the Bar Exam (I couldn't believe I passed on the first try!) I then set up my own practice. I felt fortunate that I could rely on my spouse's income enough to venture out this way. I pursued this avenue for almost three years, until the time when I felt that a change was in order. (While business was growing, my expenses were making a dent into what I actually brought home.) I took a position with a general practice firm and am greatly enjoying the variety of cases I am working on.

Having realized my dream, I can only speculate on what other directions my life will take me based on the career choice I have made. How will a family fit into the picture? Will I change careers? All I know is how fortunate I am to be living at this time, how far women have come, yet how far we have yet to go!

VIRGINIA M. HARDING,

was born in Peru, IL in downstate Illinois. She attended the University of Chicago and graduated in 1972. She and 20 other women in her class were part of the first wave of women to go to law school.

She first became interested in the practice of law on her high school debate team. She looks back on law school as a dismal academic experience, but she made a lot of close friends. After graduating law school she knew she wanted to practice after working under rule 711 in a legal aid clinic but she also knew she did not want to represent people.

Her first job was in a newly formed corporate department. The law firm was "fired" and work came in house (an early version of the current trend). After 3 years she went to a firm — an unusual career move then because she did not like being employed by the client.

She in now with a firm as a partner doing real estate transactions. She was the first woman hired in 1975 and the first woman partner. She says that the job pays well and money makes the low points bearable.

She married a law school class mate. They have one daughter, Ellen, born in 1985. She had sufficient recourses and senority to smooth out the problems and reliable child care arrangments, so her job and family have merged.

The Vietnam war and the Civil Rights Movement played a major role in opening the profession. The greater numbers of women in law have made some issues go away. No one is unique anymore. The younger women do not really understand how hard it was to get jobs commenserate with our law school's reputation.

JEAN G. HARTH,

Retired Associate General Counsel, U.S. League of Savings Institutions. "Today, almost every familiar human condition boasts a 'support group.' Having been a law student at Northwestern University (1949-1952) and admitted to the bar in 1952, I happily attest that WBAI was a great support group for women attorney's in those days (as indeed it is today). That was a time when the male-female ratio in the legal field was glaringly one-sided; a female applying for a position as associate in a law firm might be asked whether she could type and take shorthand (not so a male applicant); and a judge in the old Chicago Municipal Court system could, with impunity, address a woman attorney representing a client before him as 'Girly'. How satisfying it has been to witness monumental changes for the better in these scenarios and to note that WBAI has been, and continues to be, a mighty instrument for such changes. I value my life membership in WBAI!

Corporate law departments offered an attractive alternative to women attorneys in those early days, and choosing this option proved satisfying for me. Most of my professional career was spent in the legal department of a national trade association that conducted many of its operations in Washington D. C. Over the years I met many individuals who were prominent in government, including Presidents Eisenhower, Johnson, Ford and Reagan; prepared briefs and legislative and regulatory proposals; and testified at Congressional and federal agency hearings. Much of my work centered on compliance in the area

of personnel law as well as the tax and labor law rules regarding pension and retirement plans.

In earlier years I found myself wishing for a daughter who, if she so chose, might become a lawyer like her mother. We had no daughters, but my wishes were fulfilled in a different, but equally satisfying way: We have two sons, and both have become lawyers. (I sincerely urged them to consider other disciplines, honest!). My husband and I shared a home-and-parenting career while pursing our separate and different careers, and it worked! We retired two years ago while in good health, to allow more time to travel, to enjoy our granddaughter and to pursue our interests in golf, cross-country skiing, reading, photography and researching family history.

For the sake of historical accuracy, I add this note about my years at Northwestern School of Law: A biographer of the late Harold Washington stated that Harold was the only black, and Dawn Clark Netsch the only woman, in the class of '52. We women were few but not that few; in fact we were three: Dawn, Barbara Blumenthal Miller and I.

Here's to the WBAI's next seventy-five years!

NEIL F. HARTIGAN,

Has a distinguished record as an attorney's, government official and businessman. Now a partner and Chairman of the Department of Public Law of of the nationally renowned firm of Gardner, Carton and Douglas, Neil served at the municipal level as the General Attorney, Chicago Board of Health; Deputy Mayor, City of Chicago; General Counsel, Chicago Park District; and 49th Ward Democratic Committeeman.

At the state level, Neil was elected the youngest Lt. Governor in the history of Illinois and created the first Department on Aging in America, a model for the United States. *Time Magazine* acknowledged him as one of the 20 future leaders of America, and he has received awards from more than 250 organizations for his professional, charitable and governmental contributions.

As Attorney General, Neil Hartigan pioneered more than 100 laws to protect the environment, consumers, senior citizens, persons with mental illness and developmental disabilities, farmers, veterans and crime victims. This approach brought to life the Comprehensive Health Insurance Plan, the Environmental Barriers Act, the Bill of Rights for Victims and Witnesses of Violent Crimes, the Freedom of Information Act, and the Illinois Grain Insurance Act, to name a few. Also, he created the first statewide system of regional and satellite offices and a network of Advisory Councils.

Prior to his election to Attorney General, Neil

was a Senior Vice President of the First National Bank of Chicago responsible for international banking in the Western Hemisphere. In this position he helped negotiate the first banking relationship with the Republic of China in 1979. He was also the President and Chief Executive Officer for Real Estate Research Corporation.

As a lifelong resident of Rogers Park, Neil's commitment to his community continues to be an active and strong one. He is a former member of the Board of Trustees for Mundelein College, of the Board of Directors of Georgetown University in Washington, D. C. He also serves on the Visiting Committee for the University of Chicago Department of Public Policy.

Neil Hartigan is a graduate of Loyola Academy and Georgetown University. He received his Juris Doctor from Loyola University in Chicago.

RAMONA HAYES HEALY, A life member of the WBAI, Ms. Healy is best remembered for her generosity. Past WBAI President, Lois Dierstein, one of Ramona's friends, spoke with us recently about Ms. Healy's accomplishments.

"Ramona liked people, loved to travel, loved to be on the go and didn't want to go to the same place twice," commented Ms. Dierstein. She related how Ms. Healy entered the travel business with her husband and founded Vanderbilt Better Tours and the Hayes Healy Travel Agency. Ms. Healy made Ms. Dierstein's reservations to Hawaii in 1961 and made travel arrangements for her ever since. Ms. Healy's tours were to interesting places, both near and far, such as the Holland Michigan Tulip Festival, the University of Indiana Madrigal Feast and Concert, and the New Orleans Mardi Gras.

Ramona Hayes Healy made substantial donations to her alma mater, DePaul Law School, and other educational institutions such as San Francisco State University, Notre Dame, Marquette University, Loyola Eye Clinic and to the WBAI Foundation, where she established an annual scholarship in her name. A successful attorney and businesswoman, Ms. Healy helped others achieve through her gifts to scholarship.

Active in many organizations, such as the DePaul University Women's Board, the Executive Board of Gordon Technical High School, the Chicago Women's Club, the Illinois Club for Catholic Women, the Chicago Travel Women's Club, Ms. Healy led an active life. Her Husband, John, died several years before her and she has one nephew who lives in California.

Ms. Healy is deceased.

MARY FRANCES HEGARTY, she attended and graduated from DePaul University College of Law and was admitted to the Illinois Bar in 1975. She has been admitted to practice before the U. S. Supreme Court, the U. S. District Court for Northern District of Illinois - Trial Bar, and the State of Illinois. She was 1983-84 president of the Women's Bar Association of Illinois, Women's Bar Association of Illinois Foundation, Illinois State Bar Association, Chicago Bar Association, Legal Assistant Foundation of Chicago, Chicago City Council, City of Chicago Sole Source Review Board, Attorney General Neil Hartigan's Committee on Professional Excellence,

Historic Pullman Foundation, and the Chicago Athletic Foundation.

She has been a partner in the law firm of Lannon & Hegarty, she has been Staff Council at Greenbaum & O'Brien, Inc., she was in private practice engaged in the general practice of law with special concentration in the areas of real estate, corporations and estates. She is currently a managing partner in the firm of Hegarty, Hegarty, & Kowols. Her greatest personal accomplishment is the restoration of a 15th century castle in Galway, Ireland.

SUSAN A. HENDERSON, has a broad client consulting and contract drafting practice in the marketing and technology law fields, with particular emphasis on computer law matters, but also including copyrights, trademarks, trade secret protection, licensing transactions, research and development agreements, unfair trade practices, publishing law, advertising law and antitrust law. Susan is a graduate of Stanford University (B.A. 1965; M.A. 1966) and University of Chicago (J. D. 1969).

Susan and her computer went "solo" in 1989. She finds this new, pressure-free way of practicing (which substitutes cheap, state-of-the art technology for expensive clerical and staff support) to be as much fun as practice in the early days when there was always time for lunches with friends and for keeping up with legal developments. Susan presently rents space form a patent firm, Wood Philips Mason Recktenwald & Van Santen, but is part of a loose network of solos who use computers to support their sophisticated legal practices. She was formerly a general partner in Altheimer & Gray, and has served as Chairman of the Chicago Bar Association's Antitrust Committee. As a volunteer for Lawyers for the Creative Arts, she incorporated and acts as general counsel to Bailiwick Repertory Company (a theater company which performs in the Lincoln Park area) and Lincoln Opera Company (a training ground for young opera singers which performs at Mundelein College). She also is a Director of Winnetka Family Service Organization. In their spare time, Susan and her husband Robert Cannon read, collect antiques, entertain friends, and attempt to train their child-substititue dog who sometimes comes to the name "Brenden."

BESS SULLIVAN HEPTIG, she was known to all of us as the president of WBA; she was known to many as a woman of wit and personality; and to still others she was known as a woman with a big and understanding heart. No matter what phase of her life you know, you realize it is only one side of her bright and varied interest.

She got an early start on her exciting life by being born the thirteenth child of a family of fifteen children in Marengo, Illinois. She learned early in life to defend her rights from any encroachments and developed a protective instinct for those less able to defend themselves. After graduation from high school, she entered the University of Illinois and took Public Speaking. To pay for college, she drove a horse and buggy to sell collapsible bathtubs to farmers.

Her professional career began as a teacher in Chicago, where she and six brothers and sisters set up housekeeping. She soon displayed the interest in

women's and children's affairs that was later to distinguish her by becoming a lobbyist for the Teachers for Women's and Children's Rights. She was instrumental in getting the Suffrage Bill signed into law in Illinois, and she was stumping for elections before she could vote. She enrolled in the evening classes at Hamilton-Loyola Law School and worked law classes and studying into a schedule of teaching, managing a household and an extensive social career. After her admission to the bar, she became the first woman State's Attorney. She left the State's Attorney's office to become a member of the firm of Sullivan, Sullivan, Sullivan and Sullivan, after which she married. Her husband and daughter both tragically died.

She traveled extensively and after seven years of leisure decided to return to public life. Her return was neither as a Republican of Democrat, but as a referee in the Juvenile Court. She heard all dependent cases and became known as "Aunt Bess." Her work was that of helping people in adjusting their lives and she exercised 5% law and 95% understanding. On November 14, 1991, Lilyan Nash, mother of Gordon Nash, CBA past president, recalled Aunt Bess as a champion of good causes. She would have been proud that her grandson was CBA president as well as of her lawyer grandniece's.

ANTONIA RAGO HERBERT, When I became a lawyer in 1938, women were not allowed to serve on juries, male law clerks were earning $10.00 a week, and I, as female, was offered only $5.00 a week. Feeling discriminated against, I opened my own office at 30 North LaSalle Street where I remained as a sole practioner for over 40 years, until the building was actually torn down. I moved my offices next door to the LaSalle Hotel, until it was torn down to make way for the present hi-rise office building.

Now representing third generation clients of the same families I first represented in the late 30's, I look back to a very gratifying career that has spanned over a half century.

After being admitted to the Federal District Court in 1940, I was appointed Amicus Curiae by Judge George Barnes and served in that capacity handling Federal, Civil and Criminal cases for 10 years, pro bono.

It was great experience and led to being admitted to the Supreme Court of the United States on January 5, 1942, with the distinction of being the youngest lawyer admitted.

Later, Chief Justice John Graber appointed me to represent defendants in murder cases, where the County paid the attorney's fees.

After marrying and later having a son and daughter, I left the criminal field to enter into international law. At various times I represented the Consulates of Mexico, Argentina, Panama, Uruguay, Guatemala, Equador, and Brazil.

During World War II, I was decorated by President Roosevelt for my work in the War Fund and Blood Donor Drives.

In August of 1948 I was sent to the Hague, the Netherlands, as a delegate to the peace Palace Conference to represent War Orphans and Displaced Persons.

Along the way, I was admitted to practice before the United States Treasury Department, I became a Real Estate Broker, and was appointed legal counsel to the Commission on the Status of Women.

In the 60's and 70's I served as an Arbitrator of the Illinois Industrial Commission, presiding over several thousand cases of men and women hurt or killed on their jobs.

After retiring as an Arbitrator and a lengthy trip round the world, I returned to private practice and to creative real estate activities.

The best part of all this is that my son has become a lawyer and my daughter teaches children with learning disabilities and I am the proud grandmother of five adorable grandchildren.

How was it all possible? Only because of having a terrific husband and very responsible and loyal live-in help. Yes - I know that after 50 years of great diversity and some adversity, I would do it all over again without any regrets.

IDRIENNE L. HEYMANN, lives in Highland Park, IL.

1940 to '42 - To Queens I went
Then UNC Law School was blue - heaven sent.
Found right tackle Bob Heymann and a law degree,
Three years at Carolina - what a spree!

'45 found me practicing with Tillett & Campbell.
Loved my law practice - what a gambol.
Corporate and Tax practice on my banner
Waved on behalf of Cannon, Mills, and Tanner.

But November '46 - life changed the tide
When Navy Lt. Bob Heymann made me his bride.
Moved to Chicago, in the cold Midwest,
Being the proper corporate wife was my next quest.

In 1950 and '53, after Caryl and Bobby arrived,
The law career took a decided dive.
Then came Tommy and Jeff - no more practice of law,
Instead, lots of the world I saw.

Travel plus charity and community work were next at bat.
Till '78, when for the Illinois Bar I sat.
This time around I became a Litigator,
A specialist in matrimonial law, much later.
1985 made me both a widow and grandma, too.
Jamie, then Scott, kept me from feeling blue.

"Regrets, I've had a few,
But then again, too few to mention.
I did what I had to do,
And saw it through without exemption.
I did it my way!!"

MARY WHITE HIRSEN, has a strong educational and professional background. She attended Northwestern University for her undergraduate degree and earned her law degree from DePaul University.

She attended a graduate program in medical technology at Northwestern University as well, a program which has helped make her uniquely qualified to work on cases with medical aspects.

Prior to her legal career she worked in laboratory medicine. To help keep her up to date in her field, Ms. Hirsen is involved with professional organizations such as the Illinois State Bar Association and the Chicago Bar Association.

Outside of work, Ms. Hirsen enjoys cooking, art, music, travel and a diverse range of activities with her husband and two children, including being a Cub Scout Den Mother. Her personal goals are to pursue her "roles as wife, mother and attorney to the best of my ability, with a strong sense of commitment and a high level of integrity."

Ms. Hirsen is a solo practitioner.

CAROL HOCHFELDER, Chicago, received her B.S. degree from the University of Wisconsin, did graduate work at the University of Chicago, received her J. D. degree from Northwestern University School of Law in 1963, and worked on her LL. M. in Taxation. She was a member of the law firm of Didzerekis Hochfelder Douglas Ltd., she was a member of various Bar Association Committees including the Trust Law Committee of the Chicago Bar Association and the Committee on Taxation Reform of the Chicago Council of Lawyers. Ms. Hochfelder was attorney and former Chairperson of the Illinois Women's Political Caucus and an organizer of the First Women's Bank of Chicago. She authored various articles published in Bar Journals and lectured in the areas of taxation and women's rights at numerous universities and law schools.

Ms. Hochfelder is deceased.

PATRICIA K. HOGAN, was born on March 1, 1943 in Waukegan, IL.. She graduated from Miami University in Ohio in 1965 and Chicago Kent-IIT in 1975.

She was admitted to the Illinois Bar on April 28, 1975 and has worked as a secretary, law clerk, and attorney from 1965 to 1982. In 1976 she became a Special Assistant Attorney General for the Illinois Department of Mental Health. She became an attorney with Bruce Lange, Lange and Lange in 1982 and since 1987 has been a sole practioner.

She is a member of the Illinois State Bar Association, the Chicago Bar Association. The Women's Bar Association, the National Guardianship Association, and the Guardianship and Protective Services Association of Illinois. Her other professional activities include work for the Little Brothers-Friends of the Elderly and being a panel member for seminars hosted by the North Suburban Bar Association, the Metropolitan Coalition on Aging, and the Chicago Volunteer Legal Services Foundation as well as being a volunteer consultant of the later two. She has chaired WBAI's Probate Estate Planning Committee.

BARBARA LEVINE HOLCOMB, was born in Long Island, NY. She attended the State University of N.Y. at Potsdam and graduated in 1958 with a degree in education. She received her M.P.A. at Western Michigan University in 1981.

Her law school career spanned over several years and several schools. She began in 1967 at the University of Arizona, then in 1968 at the University of Colorado. She finished the bulk of her studies at De Paul University, College of Law from 1981-1984. She graduated with honors in 1984.

The study of history turned her toward the study of law. She had a desire to be effective in society. When she started her law studies, she was the only female in her section of 75. When she went back in 1981 she enjoyed being a "day" student but was not prepared for being older (at 43) then many of her professors.

After law school she became less idealistic about the practice of law. She has worked for Katten, Muchin and Zavis; Vedder, Price, Kaufman, and Kamonholz; and Fox and Grove. Currently she is a sole practitioner as her own boss.

She has her likes and dislikes about the profession. She dislikes dealing with lawyers who do not have high ethical standards, and she dislikes the effect of stress in and around her. She does like the "people" contact and being her own boss.

She graduated law school at age 45. She is divorced and remarried (after law school) and has two grown children.

MARY HEFTEL HOOTON, was born on July 5, 1919 in New York, N.Y.. She spent her undergraduate years at Seton Hill College and West Virginia University. She graduated with a degree in Law from DePaul University in 1943. She has kept up to date on law practices by attending the John Marshall Law School, the Loyola University School of Law, the National Judicial College, and yearly Illinois Judicial Conferences.

She decided to be a lawyer when she was four years old. She wanted to be President of the U.S. but when people laughed at this she realized she had to be a lawyer first. She felt very secure about her law school years and after graduation she worked for a lawyer and in a private practice.

She has has been a Circuit Court Judge since 1976. As a judge she has had service in Juvenile Division and Domestic Relations Division, She is presently Supervising Judge of Personal Injury, Jury and Non-jury in First Municipal District.

She has liked all of her duties in the law practice, even the unpleasant adventures. She likes being able to help those less fortunate that she.

As 1976-77 president of WBAI she attempted to make women lawyers more known and accepted. She has one charge and that is for women to keep their heads up and keep going.

CHARLOTTE HORNSTEIN, graduated from the University of Chicago in 1933 and the John Marshall Law School in 1934. She was admitted to the Illinois Bar in March 1935 and to both the United States District and Supreme Courts in 1960. She has been employed by two firms in her career; Greenberg, Keele, Lunn & Aronberg, and Jenner & Block.

From 1958 to 1973 she was self-employed as a general practioner dealing with corporate tax, real estate, trusts, estate planning, and probate. Presently she is employed by the Cook County State's Attorney.

She was president of the Women's Bar Association from 1958 - 1959 and Chairman of the Committee on Professional Fees for the Chicago Bar Association from 1967 - 1968.

She has given several lectures, including "Legal Aspects of Retirement", "Legal Problems", and "Wills and Estate Planning".

First husband James A. Laird died in 1972. Second husband Edward Noble Lee died in 1986.

LAVERNE R. HOSEK, Corporate Counsel and Corporate Secretary, Follett Corporation, Chicago. Graduate of DePaul University Law School.

The entrance of significant numbers of women into law schools in the 1970's was very exciting to me. I admired and envied these women, and one day I decided to join them—at the age of 44, with full time job responsibilities, and with the responsibility of daily care for my disabled sister. The evolution of women's role in law, business, and government continues, sometimes at a discouragingly slow pace, but the effort has produced some extraordinarily talented women attorneys. I look forward to seeing the effects of their talent—in greater numbers and at higher levels in the future.

ARNETTE R. HUBBARD, throughout her career as an attorney at law, Arnette R. Hubbard has stood in the forefront of the legal profession working for the protection of individual rights and freedoms. She has served on important boards of public bodies and received honors and recognition both from her colleagues and from local and national civic organizations. Attorney Hubbard is in demand as a public speaker and regularly addresses organizations and educational institutions throughout the United States to talk on such topics as justice in the courts, women and law, issues of the 21st century, education for a democratic society, progress through free and fair elections, and strategies for overcoming racism and sexism.

She has appeared on Donahue, Chicago Tonight, Common Ground and various other television and radio talk shows to discuss these subjects and has herself hosted a weekly talk show.

Currently she serves as member and Secretary of three-member Chicago Board of Election Commissioners, which governs all elections in Chicago.

As commissioner, she is dedicated to the betterment of Chicago's electoral process and to insuring that all Chicagoians, regardless of political affiliation, receive equal treatment. She was instrumental in the inauguration of "Desert Fax," and innovative program to telefax absentee ballots to military personnel serving in the Middle East. Earlier, she spearheaded an aggressive voter recruitment program in which churches, food stores, shopping centers, fast food restaurants, high schools, colleges, trade schools, public transportation stations, and neighborhood festivals were utilized as voter registration locales to increase voter registration.

From 1985 to 1989, Commissioner Hubbard served the public as Commissioner of the Cable Commission, an appointment made by Mayor Harold Washington.

Commissioner Hubbard was admitted to the Bar in 1969 and has practiced both civil and criminal law. An active member of the legal community, Commissioner Hubbard presently is a member of the Committee on Character and Fitness of the Supreme Court of Illinois.

She was the first woman to serve as President of the National Bar Association and as President of the Cook County Bar Association, organizations in which she served in many capacities. Her professional affiliations also have included the American Bar Association, serving as member of the House of Delegates; The Chicago Bar Association, serving as member of the Committee on the Evaluation of Judges; and the Illinois State Bar Association, serving as Chair of the Section on human Rights and Responsibilities.

Her community interests include membership on the Board of Directors of the Alumni Association of Southern Illinois University; Leadership Greater Chicago; NAACP, NAACP-LDF; Operation PUSH; The Chicago Network, and the DuSable Museum of African American History.

Commissioner Hubbard received her undergraduate degree from Southern Illinois University at Carbondale and her Juris Doctor from the John Marshall Law School.

ELENIE K. HUSZAGH, spent her childhood in Portland, OR. She attended the University of Chicago from 1953-1957. She entered at the age of 16 as an "early entrant" in the Ford Foundation Program. She attended John Marshall Law School from 1960-1963.

She decided not to become a doctor in the middle of comparative anatomy class — she recalled the experiences of a couple of law school friends and decided to give law a try.

Her time in law school was not pleasant. She worked full time at the school and attended night classes. There was too much busy work and pressure. She would not care to relive the experience. After graduating she found it was good to be in the "real world" and to actually deal with problems, issues, etc. and get paid for doing so.

She has noticed more women in the profession, but too many lawyers with many attorneys lacking knowledge are becoming increasingly hostile and unpleasant.

After law school she found herself competing for work. She established her own firm in 1970, which still exists in Glenview, IL.. Presently she is a partner in a national law firm. She deals with commercial law, bankruptcy, and area dealing with "money" as a commodity. She finds that the job has its drawbacks in the pressures of time and the increasing complexities of the profession.

She describes herself as a survivor; raising her son as a fine person, having her marriage last, and keeping friendships. She describes home life as "confused". She and her husband met in law school and shared the family responsibilities before it became fashionable. It has been difficult and interesting and she would do it all again.

While a member of WBAI she was once the co-chair of the Judicial Candidates Commitee and at one time was one of the few members who did not wear a hat to meetings, (or even in court.)

MARY ANN HYNES, was born October 26, 1947 in Chicago, IL. and is married with 2 children. She attended Loyola University and the Lake Forest Graduate School of business. She received her law degrees from the John Marshall Law School in 1971. Presently she is Vice President and general counsel for the Commerce Clearing House (CCH).

She is chief legal officer of CCH, a Fortune 500 international company engaged in the publication of tax and business law information. International subsidaries of the company operate in Canada, Australia, England, Singapore, Japan and Mexico.

She has established an efficient communicatic pattern with top management of CCH companies business matters and in providing the various leg services. She is responsible for selecting and managi outside counsel and in-house legal services. H principal areas of concern include litigatio acquisitions, divestitures, contracts, compute technology transfers, leasing and licensing, real esta employee benefits and general employee relation

Her civic activites include being a memb patron, director, and president of sever organizations. These are: the Chicago Cri Commission, the Museum of Science and Indust the Midwest Council on National Security, the YWC the Chicago Symphony Chorus and Lyric Opera. United Way, the Chicago Archdiocesan Pasto Council, and the local School Board.

She is a member of the Chicago Club, the L. Club of the City of Chicago, the Legal Club of Chica the Executives' Club of Chicago, the DuPage Cl and the Forge. Her personal interests include scu diving, skiing, and film.

She was WBAI director and a WBAI Foundati Advisory Board member.

MARION MCCLELLAND JANOUSE
I was born and raised in Chicago and upon graduati from high school was awarded a one-year scholars to DePaul University where I enrolled in a liberal a course. Those were "depression" years and after t one year I found it necessary to take a short course business training and began working as a secretary a law office. Up to that time studying law was farthest thing from my mind, but the work was interesting that I completed pre-legal requireme in night school and enrolled at John Marshall L School, graduating as an honor student in 1938, a was admitted to practice in October of that year.

Although three years in law school were easy, I found the actual practice of law required ev more dedication, hard work and long hours, plus added responsibility of knowing that the interests my clients depended upon my handling of the ca I soon decided that I did not care for trial work, a since other lawyers in the office were eager for t work, they gladly turned over most of their prob work, which I enjoyed, to me, which practice I enga in until retiring in 1980, having maintained an off in my home since 1965.

I have found legal training to be of great valu everyday living, influencing almost every perso business transaction, and giving me confidence handling all kinds of experiences.

I have been married twice, both times to lawy and widowed twice. I have no children. My seco husband was Howard F. Janousek, whose first w Ellen, also a lawyer and known to many member WBAI, and a good friend of mine, had died while a trip to Russia in 1966.

Since retirement I have enjoyed having time social activities and travel, and in the past few ye have had trips to China, Russia, Greece and Turk Western and Northern Europe, as well as Hawaii a Alaska.

I have made some long-lasting friendships many new acquaintances during 50 years in the le profession, and I am surprised and pleased to how WBAI has grown, especially during the last years when I have not been active. This was not entirely my fault, as a foul-up by the postal system caused my name to be dropped from the mailing list, a situation which I am happy to say has now been corrected, and I wish WBAI many more years of success and growth.

EVELYN F. JOHNSON (JUDGE), was born in Chicago, Illinois, and is a product of its public schools. She holds the B. A. degree from The University of Chicago, and the Juris Doctor and Master of Laws from the John Marshall Law School of Chicago.

Judge Johnson was admitted to the practice of law by the Supreme Court of Illinois in 1950, and by the United States Supreme Court in 1958.

She is a former Executive Assistant to the Secretary of State of Illinois and served as the legal advisor to the Secretary on all internal matters. She was appointed Associate Judge of the Circuit Court of Cook County, Illinois, on January 3, 1983.

Judge Johnson is a member of the National, American, Chicago, Cook County, and Women's Bar Associations. She also holds membership in the World Peace Through Law; World Association of Judges; Alpha Kappa Alpha; YWCA; and NAACP. She is a former Trustee of Woodlawn African Methodist Episcopal Church of Chicago.

She is the wife of Justice Glenn T. Johnson of the Illinois Appellate Court for the First District. They have two children: Evelyn A., and Glenn Jr.

Judge Johnson is deceased.

MARIE C. BELLAMY JOHNSON, Born in Oklahoma Indian Territory; moved to Chicago, Illinois in 1928. Widowed in 1980; one son, two daughters and six grandchildren.

Attended John Marshall Law School in Chicago, Illinois received LL.B. in 1947 and J. D. in 1970.

Professional activities and memberships include some of the following: Founding member of the National Association of Administrative Hearing Officers, member of National Association of Administrative Law Judges, NAALJ Foundation Fellow, member of Illinois Hearing Officers Society, Board Member of Illinois Association of Administrative Law Judges, National Bar Association, Washington, D. D.; Women's Bar Association of Illinois; National Association of Women Lawyers; Illinois State Bar Association; International Association of Personnel in Employment Security, including the Illinois IAPES Chapter, and the American Bar Association.

Hobbies include gourmet cuisine cookery;

horticulture - plants and flowers; photography and reading.

Her most memorable law school teachers included Noble E. Lee, Constitutional Law. She became interested in law because of her father, Louis Cecil Taylor, of Indian descent, who was a lawyer.

MOIRA SUSAN JOHNSON, has been working in private practice since 1983 as a plaintiffs personal injury trial lawyer.

She would like to see the acceptance of women lawyers in all areas of legal work. She feels that Plaintiffs Personal Injury is still a relatively closed area for women. Defense work seems to be more integrated although perhaps not at the litigation level.

Ms. Johnson has been recognized as a leading female trial lawyer, and cited as one of the five busiest lawyers in Cook County in five years.

BURTON JOSEPH, grew up in the Chicago-Austin neighborhood. Attended the University of Illinois from 1947-1949 and attended law school at DePaul University from 1950-1952.

Was interested in the intellectual challenge of law, saw the chance to "do good".

Practices law in the area of litigation-first amendment. Just what he always wanted to do. He has held various positions starting out including slave, associate, partner (now accused of having slaves).

Enjoys the challenge, status and accomplishment of being in the law profession.

Burton Joseph is married with three children, two of which are lawyers, an one is a winemaker married to a lawyer. There is one grandchild.

Joseph feels that the more things change the more they remain the same - no battles are permanently won.

OLGA JURCO, graduate DePaul University, College of Commerce B. S. 1936 and College of Law, J. D. in 1938. When Congress created the new judicial office of United States Magistrate to assist the United States District Judges, she was one of three lawyers in the Northern District of Illinois appointed on March 12, 1971. She was the first female federal judicial officer to serve in the Seventh Federal Circuit. Prior there to she served as Senior Law Clerk to District Court Judges Richard B. Austin and Walter J. LaBuy. In 1973 she was recipient of the Milton Gordon Award given annually by the Chicago Chapter, Federal Bar Association to an outstanding government lawyer for excellence in federal legal service. In February 1973 the Chicago Bar Record published her article on "The United States Magistrate - A Transition Period." During her tenure she frequently spoke to bar associations and other groups to explain the position and function of her new office. She served as a member of the District Court's Planning Commission to implement the Federal Speedy Trial Act being Chairman of its Systems and procedures group. The Federal Center in Washington also asked her to participate as a faculty member at orientation and advanced seminars for Magistrates. Among the diverse work as Magistrate, she served as Special Master to supervise implementation of the District Court order in Gautreaux vs. C.H.A. the "historic" housing discrimination suit.

One of her most publicized security-screened hearings involved the extradition petition of Israel for a young Palestinian who opposed the petition claiming among other things, that the offenses were within the political exception to extradition provided in the treaty between the countries. Judge Jurco retired voluntarily in April 1985. She is a member of WBAI, Federal Bar Association, Bar Association, Seventh Federal Circuit, Judicature Society, Illinois State Bar Association, Chicago Bar Association.

LINDA S. KAGAN, I decided to become a lawyer after working as paralegal for three years in the mid 1970's. I realized that I had at least the same degree of intelligence and drive as the male lawyers for whom I worked and that being a paralegal was a dead-end. I began law school at Loyola University School of Law in Chicago, September, 1977, and was quite satisfied with that choice, as I had also earned my undergraduate degree there, (B.A., Spanish, magna cum laude, 1975).

Law school was very difficult the first semester, but after the initial shock subsided and I passed all the first semester exams, I began to enjoy the intellectual challenge and the exposure to how society shapes the law. There were about 40% women in my class when I graduated in June, 1980.

While studying for the Illinois bar exam, I met Jackie Lustig (WBAI, President 1988-1989.) She was already an attorney and took me under her wing. It was Jackie who encouraged me to join the WBAI, which I did in 1983. Jackie Lustig introduced me to Jewel Klein (WBAI President 1989-90) and in 1985 I began to co-edit the WBAI News with Jewel. I served as co-editor for about four years.

I have been a sole practitioner since 1986. I handle many types of civil litigation and civil appeals and also real estate transactions. I still find the practice of law a rewarding career, both financially and socially. I have made some wonderful friends and have handled some challenging cases over the years.

One outstanding memory I have is arguing a case, Brown vs. Tenney, 125 Il.2d 349 (1988), before the Illinois Supreme Court in May, 1988, with my then three and a half month old daughter, Chloe Brooks Pott, my husband David Brooks Pott and my mother, Cynthia Cooper Kaplan, watching in the courtroom. A photograph of us taken on the steps of the Supreme Court Building appears in the WBAI 75th Anniversary Calendar. Also, once as a young lawyer in 1981 an opponent referred to me as a "little lady" in court, and I demanded and received his written apology.

PENNY NATHAN KAHAN, a 1978 graduate of the University of California School of Law at Berkeley (Boalt Hall) has for the past nine years, limited her practice to employment law. In most cases, Ms. Kahan represents the individual employee in employment disputes, including wrongful discharge litigation. She also advises and assists employer clients in drafting and implementing personnel policies and procedures which minimize the risk of employee instituted lawsuits.

In addition to a very busy practice, active involvement in a number of Bar Associations including the National Employment Lawyers' Association in which she is a member of the Executive

Board and the Illinois State Bar Association in which she is currently a member of the Labor Law Section Council. She has several publications to her credit as well as lectures.

Bar activities include: American Bar Association, Labor Law Section, Employee Rights Committee; Chicago, Bar Association, Labor and Employment Law Committee; Illinois Bar Association, Labor Law Section, Member, Labor Law Section Council 1990 - to date; National Employment Lawyers Association, Executive Board - 1985 to date, Founder and Chair - Illinois Chapter, 1985 to date; Women's Bar Association of Illinois.

HOWARD R. KAUFMAN (CIRCUIT COURT ASSOCIATE JUDGE), born August 1, 1930 in New York City. High school education received in New York City. Undergraduate work was at Purdue University where he received a B.S. in Physical Education in 1952. Law school at Northwestern University School of Law, J. D., 1957. Military service as a Captain in the U. S. Marine Corp., active duty for two and one half years, 16 years reserve.

Judge Kaufman was admitted to the Illinois Bar in 1957, and joined the law firm of Schultz, Biro & Karmel; partner, Lane, Carment, McPolin & Kaufman. He was appointed Assistant United States Attorney for the Northern District of Illinois, and also served as Assistant Attorney General, Chief of the Consumer Fraud Protection Division. He has served as general counsel to the State Controller and Village Prosecutor for the Village of Elk Grove. Judge Kaufman was elected to the bench in 1981. His two daughters are Susan and Ilene. His hobbies include flying. He was Co-Chairman of the Reno-based anniversary banquet in the Chicago area on March 24, 1988 and he completed the Great Issues of Law course, July 24-29, 1988 at the Nation Judicial College.

Judge Kaufman leaves the bench after 10 exciting years dispensing justice. He will miss clerk Lisa and Baliff Ed and WBAI. He will reside in Naples, Florida and Ellison Bay, Wisconsin.

LYNNE KAWAMOTO (JUDGE), was born in Chicago on June 13, 1950, attended Chicago Public Schools and graduated from Lake View High School in 1968. She attended North Park College in Chicago, and graduated in 1972. Lynne taught in the Chicago Public Schools from 1972 to 1980 at Clemente High School. During her career as a teacher she sponsored various extra-curricular activities and received the Teacher of the Year Award in 1975.

While still teaching at Clemente, Lynne attended law school at night at DePaul University College of Law. In January, 1981 she received her Juris Doctor degree and began her career in the Cook County State's Attorney's Office in May, 1981.

Judge Kawamoto has had an extensive range of experiences within the State's Attorney's Office. She has tried cases before bench and jury, worked in the Felony Review Unit as consultant to the Chicago Police Department, presented cases at Preliminary Hearing Court and to the Cook County Grand Jury. She has extensive Felony and jury and bench trial experiences including complicated Double Juries, Repeat offender Cases and Capital Litigation Cases. Lynne was also assigned to the Special Prosecution Unit for Gang Crimes Prosecutions to handle difficult gang-related trials and Hate Crimes Prosecutions. From this Special Prosecution Unit Ms. Kawamoto was promoted to the positions of Supervisor of the Juvenile Division of the State's Attorney's Office where she supervised 50 attorneys and a legal support staff. She also coordinated law enforcement efforts between her office and the Chicago Police Department and over 100 suburban Police Departments. She also supervised efforts towards the "Best Interest of the Child", in child abuse and neglect cases with other health, social and law enforcement agencies throughout Cook County. In her supervisory position Lynne was the Chief Administrator for the seven Delinquency and the seven Abuse and Neglect Calendars that comprise the Cook County Juvenile Court system, the largest in the country.

Besides her teaching career in the Chicago Public Schools Ms. Kawamoto has become certified as a teacher for the National Institute for Trial Advocacy and has taught in-house courses at the Cook County State's Attorney's Office and the DuPage County State's Attorney's Office. She also presented on-going training to the 50 attorneys under her supervision. Lynne has also kept up-to date in her profession by attending courses at Northwestern University College of Law and the National College of District Attorneys in Houston, Texas.

Lynne Kawamoto is a member of the Japanese American Service Committee, the Japanese American Citizen's League, the Governor's Illinois Asian-American Advisory Council. She is also a founding member of the Asian-American Bar Association of the Greater Chicago Area and is currently serving on the Board of Directors and as Co-Chair of the Membership Committee and as a member of the Legislative and Judicial Committee. Lynne is also a member of the National Association of Asian-American Professionals, the Women's Bar Association, the Chicago Bar Association, the Illinois State Bar Association and the American Bar Association.

Lynne is active in community affairs including the 1990 Asian Lunar New Year, the opening of Kan-WIN, the Korean American Women in Need; A Crisis Line for Women Who Need Help, the JASC Keiro Nursing Home Ground-Breaking Ceremony, the JASC Law Day Program, the JASC Fuji Festival, and as a patron and supporter of the Angel Island Theater Company.

Lynne Kawamoto was the first candidate recommended by the Asian-American Bar Association in August, 1989 to be the first Asian-American Judge in Illinois. Lynne was rated

"Qualified" by the Chicago Bar Association for the Office of Associate Judge in Cook County. She has received much community support from a variety of community organizations including the Chinese American Service League, The Chinese American Civic Council of Chicago, the Illinois Ethnic Consultation, the Filipino American Political Association and, The Commission on Asian-American Affairs for the City of Chicago. She has received over 50 letters of support and endorsement from individuals from the Asian American Community.

Lynne Kawamoto is married to Thomas E. Epach Jr. and has one step-daughter. She is now an Associate Cook County Judge.

ESTHER OSWIANZA KEGAN, it is difficult for me to acknowledge that I celebrated my 78th birthday this June 29, 1991.

Northwestern University has been an important part of my life - with an award of Phi Beta Kappa and Bachelor of Arts degree in 1933 and an award of Order of the Coif and Juris Doctor degree in 1936. I was licensed to practice law in Illinois in 1936 and was admitted to the US Supreme Court bar in 1943 and have thereafter continually practiced law as a registered patent attorney before the US Patent and Trademark Office and also as a specialist in the field of trademarks, copyrights, and food and drug law.

In 1939 I was married to Albert I Kegan. I moved his admission as a lawyer before the Patent and Trademark Office in 1941; we practiced together as Kegan & Kegan until 1963 when he died of cancer. My son Daniel joined the Kegan & Kegan firm in 1984. Daniel is a trademark computer and copyright specialist and we are both active in the law firm at present.

From time to time I authored law review articles on our specialities. Back in 1961-62 I was Law Lecturer on Patents and Trademarks at Northwestern Law School. During 1965-67 I was a member of the Illinois Food, Drug, Cosmetic and Pesticide Law Study Commission and during 1968-73 a member of the Comprehensive Health Planning Advisory Council Arbitration has been, and still is, an active area for me.

I have been a member of the Women's Bar Association of Illinois continuously since 1936. During the past 50 years I have been a member of the Chicago Illinois, and American Bar Associations, the Patent Law Association of Chicago, the International Association for the Protection of Industrial Property and World Peace through Law.

I am happy that clients still come to me even in the present to have me counsel them in my fields of intellectual property-patents, trademarks, copyrights and trade secrets. I am also happy that I have three wonderful children and five grandchildren, all while continuing to practice law. I have announced that I do not intend to retire and am still at my office every day.

HELEN KELLEHER (JUDGE), retired associate Judge of Cook County Circuit Court, was on the bench for 32 years and was the first woman to become an assistant judge in the county's Probate Division. She was in the probate division from 1955 to 1978. She received her law degree from the DePaul University Law School in 1938, and a doctorate from John Marshall Law School.

She was an attorney for the Chicago Motor Club and then was an assistant Cook State's attorney in the venile Division. She helped organize the Democratic ...omen's Club of Oak Park and served as its president.

In an unsuccessful race for Congress in 1954, she ...gued in a debate, "Only 11 women sit in Congress ...compared with 424 men. Is this equal ...presentation? Shouldn't women's point of view on ...r, on matters relating to the home and family and ...ance, be known? Women have always been known ...r their progressive attitude on the issues of the day. ...ey should be heard in Congress. We need more ...men-competent women- in Congress."

Judge Kelleher was a member of the Women's ...r Association, the Federation of Illinois Women's ...mocratic Clubs, the Catholic Lawyers Guild of ...icago and the Big Sisters organization. She was ...st president of the Illinois Federation of Business ...d Professional Women, the Kappa Beta Pi legal ...rority, the West Suburban Bar Association and the ...tional Association of Women Lawyers.

In 1975, she was among 36 associate judges ...nored by the Chicago Bar Association for their ...orts to improve judge-lawyer relations.

She has one daughter, Helen Marie Orr, and ...o grandchildren.

Judge Helen Kelleher is deceased.

DOLORES TORRES KENNEY, intellectual ...operty attorney specializing in patents, trademarks, ...pyrights and related matters, partner in Olson & ...erl Ltd., 20 N. Wacker Drive, Suite 3000, Chicago, ...ceived her JD from Chicago Kent College of Law- ...inois Institute of Technology in 1984 and was ...mitted to the bar and registered to practice in the ...ited States Patent and Trademark Office the same ...ar. This event culminated a mid-life change in her ...orking career from chemist to consultant to ...unselor. It also meant entering the male-dominated ...ld of patent law, but "Dee", as she is know to her ...ends, has never been intimidated from entering ...her similarly dominated arenas.

Prior to entering law, Dee, a native Chicagoan, ...ceived her BS degree in chemistry in 1956 from the ...llege of St. Francis in Joliet. She began her career ...a chemist in an era when women were being told ...be technical secretaries, get married and have ...bies. Indeed, industrial laboratories were generally ...t designed to accommodate women and, in fact, ...e was the only female chemist on the staff in her ...st job. Shortly thereafter she went to work for the ...e then Toni Company (later Personal Care Division ...the Gillette Company), an enlightened company ...ere women were not considered oddities in either ...e lab or the legal department, where WBAI member ...eodora Gordon was already on board. Dee spent ...e next 18 years researching and developing personal ...re products for women, competing side by side ...th male scientists, and providing technical support ...he legal patent and consumer service departments, ...til Gillette moved from Chicago.

In 1974, Dee and her husband, Jerome, formed ...n-Quest, Ltd. at technical information and ...nsultancy support service, of which she is still a ...incipal. Her varied activities included writing ...chnical articles and monthly columns as a ...tributing editor to trade journals and being active in ...e professional technical societies. She became the first ...man President of the Chicago Chemists' Club (a ...oup which once held a special meeting to decide if they ...uld allow a woman to be a member) and the first

woman Business Manager of Publications of the Chicago Section of the American Chemical Society. In 1977, she decided to get a Certificate of Business Administration from Keller Graduate School of Management. Then, in 1981, through the encouragement of her husband, she entered law school.

In her present career, she finds that many women entrepreneurs do not understand the importance of intellectual property and tries to advise them whenever possible. Toward this end, she has contributed editorial columns for publications aimed for women in business. In 1989, she was one of the recipients of the "Women's Voices" awards given for her editorial contribution to the 1988 Metro Chicago Women in Business Yellow Pages.

Someone recently asked Dee who her role model was in achieving her goals. She believes every woman is her own role model, who will achieve whatever she is motivated to do. Dee has always been self-motivated. While she does not consider herself a role model for others, the Mexican-American Business and Professional Women of Chicago apparently thought otherwise. In 1985, she received a contemporary woman of the year award from that organization. Dee later learned that among the factors which swayed one of the judge's vote was Dee's entry into male-oriented fields.

In addition to keeping up with her new legal discipline, Dee maintains memberships in technical societies, as well as various legal bar associations. She is also a member of the National Association of Science Writers. For relaxation, she enjoys oil painting, some of which have won ribbons, and sings with the Niles College Concert Choir. She and her husband have also traveled extensively.

JUDITH MOTTL KERR, childhood was spent in Riverside, Illinois and attended college at the University of Wisconsin, Madison, Wisconsin from 1960-1964 where received her B.S. She then taught school in Hinsdale, Illinois for two years. Ms. Kerr attended Northwestern University, Chicago, Illinois from 1966-1969 where earned J.D.

I was the judicial chairperson for all University of Wisconsin women students during my senior year in college. I supervised the transformation by individual living unit plans from "hours" to "no hours" and key privileges. This experience triggered my interest in the law.

I found the practice of law to be different from the study of law in that additional skills are required, and that there is an additional value in obtaining greater judgement through experience.

1970-1973 - attorney at Tidewater Legal Aid Society, Norfolk, Virginia; 1973-1974 - resided in and took Bar exam in Pennsylvania; 1974 to date - sole practitioner in LaGrange, Illinois.

I am a general practitioner practicing primarily in areas of real estate, estate planing, family law, and small business.

I enjoy the great activity of legal matters in which I become involved as a general practitioner to positively affect people's lives. Married Alexander D. Kerr Jr. in 1969. Two children Matthew, and Joshua. Due to children, an office was established in a portion of the home and, with outside help when the children were young, was able to successfully and satisfyingly combine a law practice and family life.

SHARON L. KING

CAROL A. KIPPERMAN (ASSOCIATE JUDGE), was born on January 30, 1942. She has one daughter, Anna Lynne Kipperman. She attended the University of Pennsylvania, where received B.A. with honors and distinction in Political Science, 1962. University of Pennsylvania Law School, J.D., 1965.

Judge Kipperman has in-depth experience in many areas of law, including civil, criminal, and administrative experience. Her many activities include Women's Law Fund, Board of Trustee, Chicago Symphony Orchestra, Junior Governing Board, Chicago Heart Association, Management Services Committee, Children's Rights Project, Advisory Board, University of Pennsylvania Law School Annual Giving, Chicago Regional Committee.

Bar admissions include: United States Supreme Court, 1969; Supreme Court of Illinois, 1972; Supreme Court of Ohio, 1970; District of Columbia Court of Appeals, 1966; United States Courts of Appeals; Seventh Circuit, 1973; Sixth Circuit, 1970; District of Columbia, 1967; United States District Courts: Northern District of Illinois, 1972; Northern District of Ohio, 1970; District of Columbia, 1966; Northern District of Illinois Trial Bar, 1982.

JEWEL N. KLEIN, like many of my law school classmates, I did not start our really wanting to be a lawyer. I went to law school because I didn't really know what I wanted to do with my life but I knew that the law, as an avenue of public service.

There were nine females in my class of 133 at the University of Chicago Law School. Whatever sex discrimination existed did not register with me. From the old school, I assumed that men just naturally treated women as stupid and that we always had to prove ourselves. In those days, I did not question those ancient perceptions. While the sixties heightened my sensitivity to race discrimination, I was not really aware of the sexism in our society.

In the summer of 1965, I worked for the Law Students' Civil Rights Research Council which sent me to clerk at a subsistence wage for the law firm of Tucker & Marsh in Richmond, Virginia. That firm was counsel for the local branch of the NAACP and had handled all of the major school and public accommodation desegregation cases in Virginia. There, I met my husband and we were married the following year. It never occurred to me to keep my maiden name. In those days, women took their husband's name so that they could show the world that they were smart enough to do what women were supposed to do — get married!

Married for only eight weeks, Steve and I took the Illinois Bar exam together (and passed) and then went into the Peace Corps where our government taught me to speak Spanish. From 1966 to 1968 we lived in Peru and learned about that culture while, at the same time, we watched our country from afar. It was a time of great turmoil in our country and we gained new insights as we saw our country through the eyes of a supposedly underdeveloped country.

When I returned from Peru, five months pregnant, I began to realize how difficult it was for a woman lawyer to get a job. I opened up a practice with a female classmate.

Later, and for almost 12 years, I worked for the Illinois Racing Board which, in those days, governed an all male industry. During that time, I became active in the WBAI. I quickly found that other women lawyers had interests like my own. WBAI provided camaraderie and networking that were a great source of moral support. WBAI taught me to see the sexism that had been around me for years.

My year as 75th WBAI President has been a highlight of my life. My goal was to speak for our members with dignity and vision on the critical issues of our time. The task was a joy because of the untold hours of support and encouragement from our members. The hard work of my WBAI predecessors paved the way.

RALLA KLEPAK, attended Carter Harrison High School, Nicholas Senn High School, Northwestern University where a B.A. and M.S. were obtained and John Marshall Law School for J. D. degree.

Prior to Law profession employed by the Board of Education, City of Chicago as a teacher specializing in language arts, reading difficulties and English as a second language. Also was employed by the Department of Vocational Rehabilitation, State of Illinois as a special consultant in literacy problems.

Currently a attorney licensed in Illinois; U.S. Supreme Court; Real Estate Broker, licensed in the state of Illinois and Commonwealth of Puerto Rico; Insurance Broker, licensed in the state of Illinois; Educator, in Real Estate Law and Transactions; Lecturer in the area of prison reform, women's issues, civil rights, ERA and family law; Certified Financial Planner.

Engaged in private practice, specializing in trial practice in the areas of matrimonial and family law matters, real estate law and chancery matters, estate planning and small business planning.

First woman civilian attorney to try a major criminal matter before full court martial proceedings at Great Lakes Naval Training Station, Court of Military Appeals. Wrote several legal articles and outlines for use by other attorneys. Also involved in numerous controversial cases which are of signifcance such as, Nelson vs. Nuccio, Johnkol vs. License Appeal Commission of Chicago.

Professional associations include: American Trial Lawyers Association; Advocates Society, Chicago Bar Association, Illinois Bar Association, World Peace Through Law, Women's Bar Association of Illinois, American Coalition for the Third Century (WC3), Director of Prison Project, Institute of Women Today; Northside Real Estate Board of Realtors, Association of Defense Lawyers, member of the Association of Trial Lawyers of America and International Association for Financial Planners.

ALICE KOLNICK, attended DePaul University and Chicago Teachers College from 1935-1942 acquiring a B.A., M.A., Ph.D, and Ed M. degrees. From 1942-45 attended DePaul University at night for the J. D. degree.

Areas of law practiced are Real Estate, Probate, Estate planning. Was aware since high school that I wanted to be a lawyer. Immediately upon graduating from law school, I hung up my shingle.

MARILYN ROZMAREK KOMOSA, appointed a Magistrate in 1964, the title of the office was changed to that of Associate Judge in 1971 and in

1976 she was elected a Judge of the Circuit Court of Cook County, having led a field of 39 candidates in the Democratic primary and coming in second in the general election that followed for 15 newly created judicial positions. In 1982 and in 1986 she was retained for additional six year terms.

At the time of her appointment as Magistrate, she was the youngest woman ever to have been so appointed in Cook County and now is believed to have the longest tenure of any woman on the trial bench in Cook County and probably the state. She is currently assigned to the miscellaneous Tax & Remedies Sections of the Law Division.

Judge Marilyn Rozmarek Komosa is a Phi Beta Kappa graduate of Northwestern University and received her J. D. "cum laude" from the Loyola School of Law. She began her legal career in 1956 with the firm of Pope & Ballard and from 1957 until her appointment as a Magistrate served as an Assistant Public Defender, primarily in Women's Court.

She is a past president of the Women's Bar Association, was the first woman president of the Advocate Society and the first Illinois Director of the National Association of Women Judges. The recipient of a number of awards, academic and otherwise, she is a linguist, world traveler and has spent several of her more recent vacations taking courses at universities around the world.

The third of her four children, who is also named Marilyn and who is probably the first child born to a woman judge in this state, was recently sworn in as an attorney.

Since 1985 Judge Marilyn Rozmarek Komosa has served as chairperson of the Law Day Reception for New Citizens which is jointly sponsored by the WBAI, the CBA, the ISBA and the Chicago Chapter of the Federal Bar in cooperation with the Citizenship Council of Metropolitan Chicago.

CAROLYN H. KRAUSE, attended the University of Wisconsin for B.A. degree in 1960, and IIT-Chicago Kent College of Law for J. D. degree, graduating with honors in 1966.

Currently is in private practice with the law firm of Krause & Krause in the Village of Mount prospect. She has held positions as both the Mayor and the local Liquor Control Commissioner in Mount Prospect.

Professional affiliations include the Chicago Bar Association, the Illinois State Bar Association, Northwest Suburban Bar Association and the Women's Bar Association of Illinois.

LILLIAN K. KUBICEK, WBAI suffered a sad loss on January 12th. 1990 with the sudden death

of life member Lillian K. Kubicek from a heart atta Her many longtime friends are grieving for her a. remembering her cheerful and friendly personali

Lillian had been an active member of the Boa of Directors of the WBAI Foundations for many yea and had also taken an active part in WBAI activit as a former treasurer and committee member. S was a 1935 graduate of the University of Illin College of Law, and from law school went directly the law firm of Kirkland & Ellis, where she specializ in corporate law and became one of the firms fi woman partners. She left the Kirkland firm in 19 for Seeburg Corp., in Chicago, and then in New Yo where she became Vice President, Director, Secreta and General Counsel of the company and its U.S. a foreign subsidiaries. After retirement she return to the Chicago area, where she became active in t WBAI Foundation's auction committee each year to the time of her death. She was also active in otl charitable organizations, including the Slov American Charitable Association and the W Suburban Humane Society.

She is survived by her sister Anne, with whc she lived at 1058 Dartmouth Drive, Wheaton, Illin 60187. Her newspaper obituary designated the WB Foundation as a recipient of memorials in lieu flowers, and the Foundation hopes to be able award a Lillian K. Kubicek memorial scholarship 1990.

EVALYN WALSH LAIRD, lives in Gra Beach, Michigan. She has five children, grandchildren, 24 great grandchildren and stays touch with all of them. A few years ago years ago s had a broken hip, two broken legs and 100 stitches her head from an auto accident. Now, two days ea week she takes the South Shore Railroad from l home to her law office in Chicago on Michig Avenue. Evalyn has been practicing law for 65 yea In February, 1992, Evalyn celebrated her 90th birthd and was the subject of a "Chicago Profile" in t *Chicago Sun-Times.*

Evalyn arrives at the office promptly at 9:15 a. on Tuesdays and Fridays. There she manages Edwa J. Walsh Reporting Services, a court reporting serv founded by her father who was also a lawyer. "We listed in Sullivan's." A drawing of her father taki notes during a trial hangs on the wall. Evalyn a handles her law practice, primarily probate wo She probates wills for people she has known many years, "some from the 30's and 40's."

In 1907, Evalyn, her mother, sister, grandmot and grandfather lived in a one room "soddy" Oklahoma for nine months. By homesteading, grandfather, a Civil War veteran, was able to obtain the 160 acres of land he fenced in. The "soddy" was dug out of the ground, one wall was earth, the roof was sod, a stove stood in the middle. "There were no trees and 2 or 3 times a week we had to gather buffalo chips to burn." Homesteading was well worth living with rattlesnakes. Now Evalyn and her sister own the land which profitably produces gas.

Evalyn was the only woman graduate in the 1926 class of DePaul Law School. The previous year she had married Charles Hamilton Laird, an engineer. He always encouraged and supported her law work. While their five children were small, she practiced in the afternoon out of an office in her father's court reporting service. "They would take messages for me in the morning,"

With the children growing, Evalyn took a job as an estate planer with Prudential Insurance Company. Then upon her father's death came the management of the court reporting service and finally more time to devote to practicing law. She lost only one case in front of a judge who thought women had no right to practice law. Another judge, after ruling in her favor, invited her into chambers to suggest elocution lessons so her voice would carry better. She graciously proposes he was "only trying to be helpful." She did not take elocution lessons.

Evalyn, did, however, make time to ice skate every day. She is a 73 year member of the Chicago Figure Skating Club, and until her accident, had skated twice weekly with the Skokie Valley Figure Skating Club.

She has been a Women's Bar member for more than 50 years, active with Speakers Bureau, May Day citizenship celebrations and Mayor Daley's Committee on Women Lawyers. She has also been involved with Boy Scouts, Girl Scouts, and the Glenola Club, a Catholic Women's group.

When Evalyn is not attending meetings of the Environmental Law of Real Property Committees at the Chicago Bar Association she is eating lunch at the CBA with other members of the Roundtable, a group of 40 for whom Evalyn the CBA reserves a lunch table. Except that this is a special table. It was purchased by the Roundtable members back when Evalyn's father was a member. They rolled it down LaSalle Street when the CBA moved to its LaSalle Street quarters.

Evalyn is Chairman of the Environmental Committee of Grand Beach, Michigan. She has lived there, at least part of each year, since 1912 in a house built by her parents.

She was admitted to the Michigan Bar in 1982 and is, of course, a member of the Michigan WBA.

She proudly proclaims that three of her granddaughters are lawyers.

ROSEMARY DUSCHENE LaPORTA,

spent her childhood in Chicago and the surrounding area. She attended Wilson Junior College from 1945-1947 and DePaul University College of Liberal Arts from 1947-1950. She received a Bachelor of Arts degree from DePaul. She received her Juris Doctor degree from DePaul University College of Law in 1957.

For ten years while working as a secretary in the office of the College of Law at DePaul, she worked with and for the Dean and law faculty and was

encourage by several of them to consider a law career. She was greatly impressed by the focus, concentration and love of law exhibited by the law students. She started taking classes and loved the give and take of legal debate. Retired Supreme Court Justice Daniel P. Ward was then one of her professors. She considered him to be her role model for his brilliance and his integrity in the law.

She enjoyed her law school years. She found them challenging, difficult, expensive and exhausting because she worked full-time and attended evening law classes year round. 18 hour days were difficult and she found her fellow students to be older than the day students, with families to support, and little time for the camaraderie enjoyed by the full-time students.

Upon graduation from law school in August 1957 and getting her license in November of that year, she went to work for attorney Robert C. Eardley as a combination secretary, law clerk and associate. His general practice included every area of the law. She became a partner in this firm and stayed there until she became an associate judge of the circuit court of Cook County in 1975. In 1982 she was appointed by the Supreme Court as a circuit judge and elected to that office in 1984. In 1989 the Supreme Court assigned her to the Illinois Appellate Court, First District, where she is presently serving.

She has been impressed with the large numbers of fine women attorneys who have joined the private practice field since 1957 when she began. She has always found the profession stimulating, all-engrossing, challenging and immensely satisfying. She looks forward to each mentally challenging day.

She has been a member of WBAI since 1957, serving on many committees and holding office during those years. She served as the 1966-67 president of WBAI and as the first woman president of the Illinois Judges Association. The IJA is an organization representing all state court judges in Illinois.

She has been married to Frank LaPorta since 1957. They are both workaholics and have no children.

DIXIE L. LASWELL, received her Bachelor of

Arts degree from the University of Colorado in 1970. She graduated Summa Cum Laude (first in class) from the John Marshall Law School with her Juris Doctor in 1975. She is a very active member of the Chicago Bar Association and the Illinois State Bar Association.

She started work in 1975 at the firm of Rooks, Pitts & Poust where she became a partner. In 1985 she became the principal and secretary at the firm of Gessler, Flynn, Laswell, Fleischmann, Hughes and Socol, Ltd.. In February of 1989 she became a partner at Coffield Ungaretti & Harris where she is currently employed.

Working at Coffield Ungaretti & Harris she concentrates practice in Environmental Law including client counseling in interpretation and application of state and federal environmental statutes and regulations; client representation in a broad range of environmental litigation; participation on behalf of clients in state and federal rulemaking proceedings; client counseling regarding permitting procedures; performance of on-site environmental assessments; and counseling regarding environmental issues which arise in real estate transactions and merger, acquisitions and divestitures.

She has written several articles for publication, mostly on the subject of environmental issues. She has also spoken on numerous occasions about issues of the environment and the implications of the law on those issues. She is frequently requested to speak at regular meetings of various professional groups on environmental topics.

IRENE LEFKOW, a retired lawyer, Mrs.

Lefkow was a resident of Glen Ellyn for two years. She was born in Kansas City on October 18, 1884.

Mrs. Lefkow had helped defend former Lt. Carl O. Wanderer in a celebrated 1920 murder trial.

When she died in 1966 she left one son, seven grandchildren, and one great grandchild.

BETH A. LEHMAN, attended Carleton College where she received a Bachelor of Arts Degree in 1966. She attended the University of Chicago for her Master of Arts Degree in Comparative Literature, which she received in 1967. She received her Juris Doctor from the John Marshall Law School in 1975.

She used her education to teach in the City Colleges of Chicago, but wanted an alternative career, so she went to law school at night. Teaching and lawyering overlapped for a few years, then she gave up teaching.

After she graduated she has worked in small firms of three, and as a sole practitioner. Now she shares space with her husband, Horace Fox, but they have separate practices. Her practice deals with domestic relations, bankruptcy, real estate and general practice. She also works as a conciliator for the City of Chicago Department of Housing mediating complaints of housing discrimination.

She considers her accomplishments to be the melding of professional and family life. This was made easier by the freedom of working for herself. Also providing varied legal services to individuals at moderate cost.

She is married with two children. Both children spent a great deal of time with their parents in the office during their early years. When the children got too old for the office, Beth worked part time. She has resumed full time practice now that the children are in school.

She co-chaired the 1990 Joint-Professional Dinner for WBAI.

IAN H. LEVIN, (JUDGE), spent his childhood in Chicago. He attended the University of Illinois from 1957 to 1959, and graduated for DePaul University in 1961 with a degree in Commerce. After graduation he worked as a C.P.A. working with the Internal Revenue Service. There he became interested in Tax Law. He was law clerk to Justice Daniel P. Ward, Supreme Court of Illinois, who was and is his professional role model. He attended DePaul University Law School as a night school student graduating as Valedictorian in 1966 with his Juris Doctor, cum laude, Law Review staff member.

He said that his professors were excellent and he had very motivated excellent classmates. As an assistant Public Defender he was Chief of Appeals Division and tried murder, rape, armed robbery and other felony cases. He was appointed as a full circuit court judge by the Illinois Supreme Court in Sptember 1989 after 23 years as an attorney. He hears civil jury and bench trials. Ultimately he would like to be a judge at the appellate level.

He has been married for 26 years and has two children. It was a difficult balance with great tension, tying to both excel professionally and in his home life.

He has done work for WBAI by promoting and encouraging the professional equality for the advancement and recognition of women attorney

GEORGIA LEE LIPKE, When I graduated from college shortly after World War II I didn't exactly expect to take the world by storm but neither did I expect rejection at every turn. I considered myself reasonably bright, reasonably intelligent, and certainly educated (after all, I had the paper to prove it) but I was just as certainly unprepared for what faced me. The only thing anyone asked me was could I type.

Since I could type and had taught myself shorthand, I became a secretary and resigned myself to becoming a good one. That is, I was resigned until the day, coming through customs after a trip, an agent asked me in a bored voice, "school teacher or secretary?"

I have the greatest respect for school teachers but had decided early in life it was not for me. I had even become satisfied with being a good secretary. Now I suddenly wondered if I had not sold myself short.

So I enrolled in Chicago-Kent College of Law of night classes, four nights a week for four years. I graduated in June 1959 as one of two women in my class and was admitted to practice in November of that year. Once again I was faced with rejection.

I wish now I had saved some of the letters received from law firms in answer to my requests for an interview. There was one which stated the firm had no "facilities" for women attorneys. Another said they didn't hire women because their attorneys had to travel a great deal. One offered to hire me "as a secretary."

Finally I was fortunate enough to get an appointment as an Assistant State's Attorney in Cook County. When I left that office a year later, it was to go into a small law firm.

There are many stories that could be told by those of us who practiced law in the days when women lawyers were either looked upon with awe or as freaks. We were sometimes ostracized and sometimes patronized. Court clerks ignored us and judges called us "honey" from the bench. They often asked if we were lawyers while our male opponents were never asked the same question. To be fair, there were also times when we were treated with respect and admiration.

Being a member of the General Assembly of the I.S.B.A. and working on committees of the C.B.A. was gratifying and stimulating but joining the Women's Bar Association of Illinois was one of the wisest moves I ever made.

The association taught me to appreciate the sacrifices and contributions of the brilliant and dedicated women who paved the way for all of us. The night I was installed as its president in 1971 will always be one of my proudest and happiest memories. Thank you W.B.A.I.

NANCY G. LISCHER , was born in Davenport, IA.. She attended Valparaiso University from 1970-1974 with a break from 1972-1973 where she studied at Schiller College in Madrid, Spain. After she graduated she spent 2 years travelling in South America and Europe, then 2 years working in a women's health center. She went to law school in 1977 and graduated in 1981. Her tort professor said women law students were no longer unusual. Like men, they now could be mediocre, not exceptional.

She says the women's movement of the 1960's raised her expectations of herself and directly influenced her choice to go to law school. She refused to work in the medical center or be a secretary so she took the LSAT's and went to law school. Forty percent of her classmates at DePaul were women.

When she graduated she was surprised that there were as few women in the practice considering the amount of women as fellow students. After graduation she was an assistant attorney general from 1981-1984. The she joined Hinshaw, Culbertson, Moelman, Hoban and Fuller and became a partner in 1989. At the firm she works in the appellate department handling all types of appeals.

She is single and this has helped out in the practice because of no family obligations. In WBAI she was 1984-85 co-editor of the newsletter with Jewel Klein, and co-chairman of the Installation Dinner when Jewel was president.

REBECCA WILLNER LISS, prominent attorney and wife of Max Liss had a joint law practice.

Mrs. Liss was 1928-29 president of the Women's Bar Association, and as chairman of the legislative committee of the organization worked for all legislation of a remedial nature and that affecting women. The endorsement of the eight hour law for women by the Women's Bar was brought about through her efforts.

She did much work in Springfield and especially in the senate in connection with the women's jury bills. Mrs. Liss was chosen to speak before women's clubs, conventions and other groups in various parts of the state in an educational campaign on the need of women jurors under the auspices of the Women's Bar Association.

Mrs. Liss is deceased.

ANN LOUSIN, Professor, The John Marshall Law School. Professor Lousin was born in Chicago in 1943 and attended the Chicago public Schools. She attended Grinnell College (Iowa), where she primarily studied history, political science and German, and received a B.A. in 1964. From 1964 to 1965 she spent nine months studying political science and German at the University of Heidelberg (Germany) and travelling throughout Europe. In 1965, she matriculated at the University of Chicago Law School, from which she received her J. D. in 1968.

Her first big professional break came in 1970, when she spent six months as a research assistant at the Sixth Illinois Constitutional Convention. She served as legal researcher for The Committee on Revenue and Finance, which drafted the Revenue and Finance articles of the 1970 Illinois Constitution, and aided other committees. She wrote the original draft of the Official explanations of each section distributed to the voters. This job led to becoming staff assistant to the Speaker of the Illinois House of Representative, W. Robert Blair, from 1971 to 1975. She staffed the Committee on Constitution Implementation and the Revenue Committee, drafted many bills in those fields and aided the Speaker on legal and constitutional issues. From 1973-75, she was also Parliamentarian of the House, the first woman to hold that position in Illinois and probably in any state legislature.

In 1975 she joined the faculty of the John Marshall Law School in Chicago, where she primarily taught Sales Transactions and Secured Transactions. In 1980 she became a full professor, probably one of the first 125 women in legal education to obtain that rank at an accredited law school. She has served on many bar association committees on Commercial law, specialty, the Illinois constitution, and is a recognized authority, lecturer and author in the Uniform Commercial Code, the Illinois constitution and legislation. Recently, she has begun to expand her interests in international trade and comparative commercial law.

Besides her academic duties, she has held several governmental and civic posts, including a term as Chairman of the Illinois State Civil Service Commission from 1977 to 1983 and memberships on the boards of the Illinois State Historical Society, The Women's Bar Association of Illinois and The Blind Service Association of Chicago. Single, she enjoys opera, theater, travelling, keeping up with friends

and writing on legal subjects for non-lawyers in newspapers. She says it's ironic that one of the reasons she went into law as "to avoid being a teacher...and now look what I'm doing!"

JACQUELINE STANLEY LUSTIC (JACKIE), lives in the Lakeview neighborhood of Chicago with her husband Christopher Hallett. Jackie was born and raised in Manhattan. She went to Hunter College elementary and high school and City College of New York. She describes herself as a committed city dweller.

After graduating college in 1970 Jackie lived in Mexico teaching English, was an editorial assistant for House Beautiful Magazine and worked for NYC Public Broadcasting Station. Jackie always wanted to be a lawyer, both her parents having been lawyers. However, when she expressed that goal in college teachers and guidance counselors acted oblivious to such ambitions in a woman. Encouragement from a friend who had completed law school resparked Jackie's interest. She took the LSAT's in Mexico scored high and decided to apply. Jackie viewed law school as a tradeschool...a means to an end. When she attended DePaul, in Chicago, the student body was integrated by age, gender, and race. Jackie didn't realize this was not the norm in the legal world until 1979. When presenting a motion in federal court she observed that, aside from herself, the only other woman in the courtroom out of about 25 people, was the court reporter.

After working for a private firm for a couple of years, Jackie had an opportunity to work in the Illinois govenor's office. Finding this a way to have her law license benefit the most people she has made this her career for the past ten years. She is legal counsel for the Illinois Department of Human Rights which investigates complaints of discrimination in housing, employment and public accommodations on basis of race, sex, national origin or disability. She also monitors affirmative action efforts of state agencies and public contractors. Her job causes her to fly back and forth between Chicago and Springfield especially during legislative sessions.

One of Jackie's most exhausting experiences was being president of the WBAI. She observes that for every step forward women lawyers take one half step backward. She cites as an example the failure of law firms to deal with life styles of dual career couples with children. Jackie is on the Chicago Bar Association's Board of Managers.

Jackie is an avid scuba diver. Why? Because there are no fax machines or telephones underwater and her office has to work really hard to reach her in the ocean's depths. (Even on a sail boat they got to her by phone.) Husband Chris shares this hobby with her.

ANN GOGGIN LUTTERBECK, grew up in Elgin, Illinois. She attended DePaul Univiersty where she received her J. D. in 1949 and University of Illinois (L.L.M., 1957).

A strong desire to have a career which would give her independence and her extensive reading about accomplished women gave her the desire to become a lawyer. In an era when few women attended law school she thought the entire experience was of high quality.

Her speciality was in the area of Employment Discrimination law. She is retired. Presently volunteers for the Executive Service Corps. Her legal education has given her the ability to be analytical and objective both professionally and personally.

She has enjoyed the freedom and independence being a lawyer has helped her achieve, but dislikes the wall of intimidation it seems to set up when first meeting people.

She has raised three children to productive adulthood, mostly as a single parent, after being widowed. She feels this has influenced her two daughters to pursue serious careers and her son to encourage his wife to pursue a career.

Ann feels that women have made great progress business and the professions since she first became lawyer. However, she thinks that women will not ve achieved real equality until mediocre women ve the same opportunities as mediocre men.

ANDREA LYON, spent her childhood in ve different states: Massachusetts, New Hampshire, nsas, Pennsylvania, and Illinois. She attended tgers University in New Brunswick, NJ. Went to e Antioch School of Law in Washington D.C. from 73-1976. She became interested in law because she as a civil rights activist in high school.

She loved law school. Of course, Antioch with ' diverse program and radical politics was hardly e normal law school experience. She found that in coming a lawyer that it is taking longer to change e world than she thought it would be.

She was a public defender for 14 years and was ief of a Homicide Task force. She is now the director the Capital Resource Cent, assisting lawyers presenting death row inmates.

She likes being an attorney, but finds it ustrating to do what she does in the hysterical publican political climate. She has saved 16 people om the death penalty at trial. In WBAI she chaired e trial lawyers committee for three years and was the board for two years.

She is a single parent with one daughter, mantha. Samantha is the reason she is doing less al work.

LOUISE ERB MADDEN, my sister, Ruth nna Erb, and I were both born and reared in Chicago. 'e were graduated from John Marshall Law School June 1925. I was admitted to the Illinois Bar in ctober 1925; my sister was admitted in February 27.

By that time we had our own court reporting sinesses well launched.

In January 1927 I was married to Marlow J. adden; we had been admitted to the Bar on the me day in 1925. Incidentally, his mother, Pauline S. adden, had been admitted to the Illinois Bar in 15, and for some years before her death in 1929 had en a member of WBAI.

My sister, who had married Varian B. Adams, Illinois lawyer, was a member of WBAI from 1927 til her death in 1965. Thereafter I continued to erate the court reporting business alone. Such law actice as I undertook was for relatives or neighbors-ually real estate transactions or probate matters. y husband continued to practice law in Chicago for er 45 years.

I always maintained my interest in WBAI. I served on various committees, was Treasurer, was Second Vice-President, and worked enthusiastically on the Women on Juries project, both in Chicago and by lobbying in Springfield.

My husband and I have one child, Barbara, 59, who chose journalism as her career. She received her degree from the University of Illinois in 1952. She married Donald W. Peterson in 1955. She had progressed to the position of Assistant Editor on the Journal of Medical Education when she retired in 1958 on the birth of her first child.

We have two grandchildren. Our granddaughter Amy Peterson Kiley, 32, received her degree, Bachelor of Liberal Arts, from Drake University, Des Moines, Iowa in 1979. After working several years in law offices, and marrying Robert J. Kiley, she decided to study law and, with the complete approval of her husband, is now in her third years of law at the University of Wisconsin.

Our grandson, Andrew D. Peterson, 29, after working several years in the communications field, received is Bachelor of Science degree from Southern Illinois University in 1987. He is now with a video firm in Morton Grove, Illinois.

We had always loved travel, and by 1955 had visited all of the 50 states. From then through 1981 we visited approximately 100 foreign countries on the five continents, with many wonderful experiences and only one disaster - having our plane ditch in flames in the South China Sea at 4:00 a.m., in July 1960. We lost one of our party, a good friend, who was drowned. We were rescued by the U. S. Coast Guard stationed near Manila, and finished our trip around the world in six more weeks.

The year 1971 brought complete retirement for both of us. We moved to Fort Lauderdale in 1982. I have been a WBAI member since 1925. Since I am nearly blind; my husband has written this for me. (Editor's note: Mrs. Madden died in March 1992.)

EARLE A. MALKIN, was admitted to practice in the Illinois Supreme Court in 1956; he is also a member of the US District Court, Norther District of Georgia, Northern District of Illinois; 7th Circuit; US Supreme Court; Court of Military Appeals; and the US Court of Claims.

His professional activities include civil litigation, with emphasis on chancery and domestic relation matters, both at trial and appellate levels. He was appointed as member of Domestic Relations Management Advisory Committee and as an attorney for minor children in contested custody, visitation and abuse matters. He is also the arbitration chairperson for the Circuit Court of Cook County Mandatory Arbitration Program.

His legislation experience includes being the principal drafter of the Spousal Health Insurance Rights Act of Illinois (1st state to enact this type of legislation) and the Illinois Qualified Domestic Relations Order Act. He was the drafter of amendments to many pending legislative proposals and enactments on behalf of the CBA and the ISBA. His bar association memberships include the Illinois State Bar Associaiton, the Chicago Bar Association, the American Academy of Matrimonial Lawyers, the North Suburban Bar Association, and the Women's Bar Associaiton of Illinois where he is on the Matrimonial Law Committee.

BLANCHE M. MANNING, as a 23 year old legal secretary in a thriving law firm, I developed an insatiable desire to become more acquainted with the law. That desire persisted even though I had a substantial period remaining before receiving my undergraduate degree. While working as a secretary, I vigorously pursued (part-time) my undergraduate degree at DePaul University and later went on to matriculate full-time at Chicago Teachers College.

When I finally entered law school two years later, I discovered that I would be the token woman and Black in my class. However, I was not to be

deterred by this. I attended the John Marshall Law School during the afternoon, and later I attended day classes while teaching full-time in the Chicago Public School system.

Upon graduation from law school, I considered several options and various geographical locations. After all was said and done, however, I decided to remain in Chicago, my birthplace, where I attended Corpus Christi Catholic Elementary School, Christian Fenger High School, Chicago Musical College, DePaul University, Chicago Teachers College, as well as The John Marshall Law School. So I took the bar exam and became licensed to practice in Illinois.

My first job as a lawyer was the most exciting challenge I had encountered up to that time. As an assistant State's Attorney for the Cook County State's Attorney's Office, I prosecuted major felony cases at 26th and California (the Criminal Courts building). Remaining in that position for five years, I learned how to be a trial lawyer. While serving as an assistant State's Attorney, I attended Roosevelt University and received a Master of Arts Degree.

One day I received a telephone call from the director of a fledgling government litigation office of the Equal Employment Opportunity commission (EEOC), inviting me to apply for a position as a trial lawyer-team leader for their new Chicago Litigation Center. I applied and I was hired. For the next four and a half years I spent my time prosecuting major corporations for alleged practices of employment discrimination. We fought such practices in the Federal district courts throughout a ten state Midwest region. When I left that position I had attained the rank of supervisory trial attorney with duties of supervising a number of trial lawyers and support staff.

While still working at EEOC, I received a telephone call from a former colleague with whom I had worked in the State's Attorney's Office, who was now a lawyer for United Airlines (UAL). He advised me that UAL was seeking a lawyer and invited me to apply. Once again, I applied and I was hired as a general attorney in the labor law section. I represented management in arbitration proceedings and also defended UAL in discrimination cases. By this time, I aspired to become a member of the judiciary and felt that my changes would improve if I went back to the litigation end of the law. So I applied and was hired by the U. S. Attorney's office as an assistant U. S. Attorney in the Civil Division. I handled my civil caseload, assisted in criminal prosecutions and handled appeals.

One year later my dream was fulfilled. I was appointed as an associate judge for the Circuit Court of Cook County. Five years later I was honored by an appointment to serve as the Supervising Judge of the Municipal Department in the First District. Two years later I was elected to the Circuit Court, and shortly thereafter (1987), the Illinois Supreme Court assigned me to sit as an appellate judge in the Illinois Appellate Court. I then ran successfully for election to that seat in 1988.

During most of my legal career I have continued to teach—while as an assistant U. S. Attorney I was an adjunct professor at the Attorney General's Advocacy Institute, Department of Justice, in Washington, D.C.; and as an adjunct professor at the NCBL College of Law; while an assistant State's Attorney as a professional lecturer at Malcolm X College; and while a judge as a faculty member of the New Judges Seminar and the annual judges meeting, both sponsored by the Illinois Judicial Conference; and the Professional Development seminar for new associate judges and other continuing legal and judicial education seminars.

I am a member of various legal and civic organizations, including the Cook County and Women's Bar Associations, a member and former Chairperson of the Illinois Judicial Council, and a former second vice-president and board member of the Cook County Bar Association.

My husband, William, and I have reared five children (orphaned nephews and a niece).

IRENE V. MCCORMICK, a member of the Women's Bar Association of Illinois since 1921 and president of the association in 1929-30, was born in Chicago. She passed away in April of 1965 at the age of 76.

Ms. McCormick received her academic education in the Chicago Public Schools, her Ph.B. degree in 1913 from the University of Chicago, and her LL.B. degree in 1921 from the Chicago Kent College of Law. She was admitted to practice in Illinois in 1931.

After graduation she entered the law office of her brother, Howard H. McCormick, where she remained until 1924, at which time she joined the Legal Aid Bureau of the United Charities of Chicago. She gave many years of loyal service to that organization, rising to the rank of Chief Trial Attorney. During this period she not only assisted the thousands of clients who could not afford private counsel to solve their legal problems and protect their rights, but she gained the highest respect for her knowledge of the law and her courtroom skill from the hundreds of law students who obtained their court experience under her guidance, many of whom are now highly successful practicing attorneys and judges of our courts, and all of whom remember her with gratitude, affection and admiration.

She resigned from the Legal Aid Bureau in 1945 to engage in the private practice of law, in which she continued almost to the date of her death.

In addition to her membership in the Women's Bar Association of Illinois, she was a member of the Chicago Bar Association, Illinois State Bar Association, American Bar Association, and the National Association of Women Lawyers. She was conferred the honor and title of Senior Counsellor by the Illinois State Bar Association.

Ms. McCormick was also a member of Kappa Beta Pi legal sorority, Chicago College Club, the Alumnae of the University of Chicago, Chicago Business and Professional Women's Club, Illinois League of Women Voters, and the Lakeside Chapter of the Order of Eastern Star. In all of these organizations, Bar Associations and professional and civic clubs, she participated actively, serving as Chairman of many important committees, and giving most generously of her time, talents and financial resources.

She was a staunch Republican and in earlier years served as Chairman of the Women Lawyers of Illinois in the Ruth Hanna McCormick campaign and as a member of the Women's National Republican Club of Chicago.

MARGARET H. (PEGGY) MCCORMICK, a recent member of the Womens Bar Association of Illinois, is a principal in the five-lawyer immigration law firm of Minsky, McCormick & Hallagan, P.C. in Chicago. She is nationally recognized as an expert in the field immigration of law. Named in Woodard/White's 191-92 Best Lawyer's in America, she represents top level executives for multinational companies. She has particular expertise in immigration issues relating to high tech professionals. Over the years she has provided counsel to numerous Chicago lawyers and law firms on matters involving immigration law.

In 1990, Ms. McCormick was appointed by Mayor Daley to serve on the Advisory Council, Immigrant and Refugee Affairs for Chicago's Commission on Human Relations. She currently chairs a subcommittee on Legal and Legislative Affairs for the Council and, in this capacity, she is initiating a community program to provide informational legal forums in various ethnic communities.

Ms. McCormick has been an adjunct professor of immigration law at Loyola Law School since 1986. Spanish speaking, she began her career as staff attorney for Travelers & Immigrants Aid in 1978 where she handled asylum matters. In 1980 she started a private immigration practice with her brother and, in 1986 their firm was merged with another immigration law firm. Her practice is primarily employment based immigration, although she continues to serve on the lawyers expert panel for the Midwest Immigrants Rights Center, a pro-bono legal services program which provides free legal services to applicants for political asylum.

Ms. McCormick has served as Chair of the Chicago Bar Association (CBA) Section on Immigration law, Chair of the Chicago Chapter of the American Immigration Lawyer's Association (AILA) and is currently an elected member of AILA's national Board of Governors. As an AILA Governor, she is Chair of two national Task Forces on Business non-immigrants and Employment Based Immigration. She also Chairs AILA's local Pro Bono committee.

Last fall Congress passed major legislation profoundly affecting employment based immigration. Ms. McCormick was Program Chair for the 1991, five day AILA conference on the new law. Held in Chicago June 5-11, top government officials and over 1200 lawyers were in attendance.

Ms. McCormick has spoken regularly at immigration seminars and conferences sponsored by the Illinois Institute of Continuing Education (IICLE), by the CBA and by both national and local AILA. She spoke at the Practicing Law institute's (PLI) Chicago immigration law program in December of 1991. She has contributed to the IICLE Handbook on Immigration Law and to several AILA publications.

Raised in Chicago, the second of 12 children, she is a graduate of Mudelein College (1973) and DePaul Law School (1977). She is married to Steve McCormick, a partner at Kirkland & Ellis and they have three children, Kevin, age nine, Marjorie, age six and Daniel, age one.

CATHERINE GOUGER WAUGH MC CULLOCH, she was born on a farm near Ransomville, New York. When she was five the family moved to a farm near New Milford, Illinois, where she attended a village school. She was deeply influenced by her father, who, though untrained in the law often handled his neighbors' legal claims. Three years after her graduation from nearby Rockford Female Seminary, she enrolled in the Union College of Law in Chicago, forerunner of the Northwestern University Law School. Upon completing the law course the following year she was admitted to the Illinois bar in 1886. Her efforts to overcome the firm prejudice against women lawyers in Chicago were discouraging, however, and she returned to Rockford to begin her practice there. She took further work at Rockford Seminary, and having written a thesis on "Woman's Wages," was awarded both a B. A. and an M. A. degree.

She became increasingly involved in the women's suffrage movement. She had become

legislative superintendent of the Illinois Equ[...] Suffrage Association. With the adoption of the fede[...] suffrage amendment, she joined the new League[...] Women Voters, serving as chairman of its Commit[...] on Uniform Laws Concerning Women. She belong[...] to a number of prohibition groups, including[...] Woman's Christian Temperance Union, of which s[...] was legal adviser for many years. Her major energ[...] however, were always reserved for her own city a[...] state. (See: Notable American Women) She and [...] husband lived in Evanston and from 1917 to 1925 s[...] served as Master in Chancery. She was 1916-19[...] WBAI president.

HELEN F. MCGILLICUDDY, the fi[...] woman to serve as an Appelate Court Justice[...] Illinois. She passed away in March of 1990.

Ms. McGillicuddy sat on the bench for 24 ye[...] and retired in 1986 due to health problems t[...] limited her mobility.

She made the record books in December 19[...] when she was elected as a judge in the 1st Distr[...] Appellate Court. She sat as a circuit court judge fr[...] 1962 to 1976. Three of those years were spent a[...] judge in the juvenile Court Division. Though she w[...] not married and had no children of her own, [...] concern for children before her was so deep that s[...] often offered troubled youths her home telepho[...] number in case they wanted someone to call.

Justice McGillicuddy was born in Chicago a[...] educated in the Chicago public schools. She attend[...] Northwestern University, graduating with a pub[...] accounting degree. She scored the second high[...] score in the state on the CPA exam and began worki[...] for an accounting firm, she opted for law school a[...] began studying at DePaul University.

When she was graduated in 1949, she was one[...] only six women in the class.

Most female lawyers were in probate or r[...] estate law, but McGillicuddy chose trial work. S[...] said she found the experience quite pleasant. [...] addition to her legal work, she spent ten ye[...] lecturing on accounting at Northwestern Univers[...] School of Business.

She participated actively in the Women's [...] Association of Illinois and was the 1960-61 preside[...] She was an active member of the 25 year old Wome[...] Bar Foundation and served as its first president. S[...] spent eight years on the board of directors of the G[...] Scouts of America in Chicago and is a former memb[...] of the board of managers of Mary Bartelme Home [...] Girls.

BERTHA L. MCGREGOR

CAROL MCHUGH, she attended and received a J. D. from DePaul University College of Law and a B. A. from the University of Illinois. She is a member of the Chicago Bar Association and worked as a staff writer for The Independent-Register and the Chicago Daily Law Bulletin. She was a Law Clerk to the Justice Daniel P. Ward of the Illinois Supreme Court. She is currently an associate in the law firm of Arnstein & Lehr concentrating in employment law, representing management.

MARY ANN GROHWIN MCMORROW, (JUSTICE), was born and raised and attended schools on the northwest side of Chicago. I have a brother who is two years older, and a sister who is two years younger. We were extremely close-knit and affectionate family. My parents felt the effects of the depression and worked hard to insure that all of us receive good educations. As a result, each of us graduated from Loyola University.

I graduated form Loyola Law School in 1953. prior to going to law school, I attended Rosary College. My primary reason for going to law school was to implement a suggestion made by my mother. My mother piqued my interest in becoming a lawyer when she suggested that I utilize my debating skills, one of my fortés to become a lawyer.

During my first two years of law school the classes had only two women students. In my third year and last year of law school I was the only woman, and the only woman graduate. Irrespective of the small female enrollment, I was an associate editor of our Law Review for two years, authored two articles which were published in the Illinois Bar Journal, and elected class President for two years. The male students were extremely welcoming to me and I experienced no distinction because I was a woman. Upon graduation, I worked for Loyola Law School, doing research on racial integration in the schools in conjunction with a Ford Foundation grant to the school. After that project was completed, I became an associate in a small law firm, Riordan & Linklater. I handled all sorts of civil matters. After doing that for approximately two years, I was appointed an assistant state's attorney and assigned to the criminal division of the State's Attorney's Office. Being thrust into the criminal law field was a real shock. Never did I expect to be practicing criminal law. However, my time in the State's Attorney's Office was invaluable because of the tremendous and varied experience I acquired. I was the first woman to prosecute major criminal cases in Cook County, and received extensive publicity in connection with some of the more notorious cases I prosecuted. I learned trial procedure, how to try cases, argue to juries, and be a forceful advocate. The trial experience I acquired at that time remained useful when I preside over complex trials in the Circuit Court and also in making decisions in the Appellate Court.

Emmett McMorrow swept me off my feet and we married in 1962. We were blessed with the birth of our daughter and only child in 1963. As of this writing, she is a graduate student studying clinical psychology. I lost my greatest supporter and the love of my life when my husband died of cancer three years ago.

After the birth of my daughter, I practiced law as a general practitioner.

In 1976, at the urging of friends, I ran for and was elected to the Circuit Court of Cook County. I was assigned to the Domestic Relations Division for approximately four years, after which I was assigned to the Law Jury Division until the Supreme Court appointed me in 1985 to the Appellate Court of Illinois. In 1986 I was elected to the Appellate Court of Illinois. In 1989, fortified by 15 years of judicial experience, the urgings of my friends and family, and "highly qualified" Bar Association evaluations regarding my qualifications to sit on the Illinois Supreme Court, I ran, as an independent, to fill one of the vacancies being created on the Illinois Supreme Court in 1990. No woman has ever sat on the Illinois Supreme Court. Four candidates vied for election in the primary. Although I came in second, the overwhelming consensus was that the effort was worthwhile. The major political parties and the electorate became aware that qualified women should be considered for this office, and that Illinois, a major industrial state, should join the other 35 states which have a woman on their supreme courts.

I think that my career and my philosophies regarding law were profoundly influenced by one of my law school teachers and by my law school classmates. We did everything intensely: we studied, worked, played, and lived intensely. My judicial career is the result of a foresighted mother, and a very supportive husband. He worked very hard for my election and was very proud of women in law. I liked being a student, a practicing attorney, and a judge. Each phase brought new challenges and opportunities.

While my career is essentially the result of a lot of hard work and support of family and good friends, I hope that in some way I have paved roads for women attorneys. Now, women practice in all fields of law and can be great litigators. It was not always so. When I became an attorney, very few women tried cases in many of the courts. Over the years, I have noticed an increase in women attorneys in the courtroom setting. I am happy to see this recent development, but am even happier about the excellent way in which they perform.

The WBAI has always been an invaluable resource for me. Many of my dearest and oldest friends are women I met in conjunction with my membership in the WBAI. The WBAI has always been helpful and I trust will continue to do so in the future. The possibilities for women in law are exciting and limitless. If I had to do it all over again, I would do it exactly the same way.

PADDY MCNAMARA

MARGUERITE MCNEILL, a Chicago lawyer for almost 40 year, was an associate in Pam & Hurd, which later became Schiff Hardin & Waite.

Ms. McNeill was a resident of Tuscon when she passed away in 1989.

She became a lawyer and practiced law when few women did. She earned her recognition the hard way, going to law school at night and then becoming an associate at a law firm when it just not was the common practice.

McNeill was a classmate of former President Ronald Reagan at Eureka College. She attended Chicago-Kent College of Law and was admitted to the bar in 1936. She also earned a master's degree in business administration at the University of Chicago.

Ms. McNeill, a director in the 1940's of the Women's Bar Association of Illinois was a delegate in November, 1947, to the Conference of the Inter-American Bar Association. While there, she learned of women lawyers in France and Britan whose careers were interrupted and, in some cases, ruined as a result of World War II. She returned to Chicago and collected money and clothing for those women.

She retired to Tucson in the early 1970's.

JILL K. McNULTY, was born and raised in Peoria, IL. and graduated from Peoria High School in 1953. Her father was an attorney who practiced in Illinois for over 30 years. She attended Vassar College in Poughkeepsie, NY. from 1953 to 1955 then attended Northwestern University where she received a Bachelor of Arts degree in June 1957.

She attended the University of Washington School of Law from 1957 to 1958, placing second in her class, then attended Northwestern University School of Law, receiving a J.D. degree in June 1960.

She had several influencing factors in becoming a lawyer. Her father was a lawyer so she grew up with law around her. She had a history teacher who encouraged her and made her strive for excellence. And her aunt was a M.D. specializing in psychiatry. She made her realize that women could achieve anything if they worked hard enough for it.

She has mixed feelings about law school. She says that the women in her classes were discriminated against and were called upon to read so-called embarassing court cases. There seemed to be a resentment toward them for taking up the seats of men who were there to support their families.

After law school she found that she would not be hired for the respected jobs because she was a woman. Those were the days before the Civil Rights Act of 1964. She had a rough time until she secured employment with the firm of Ross, Hardies & O'Keefe. She was a "pioneer" - the first female attorney ever hired.

From 1964 to 1972 she raised her two sons and worked for the Council for Diagnosis and Evaluation of Criminal Defendants and for the Illinois Law Enforcement Commission. In 1972 she became a Professor of Law at IIT - Chicago Kent College of Law, resigning on March 1, 1981. She taught Criminal Law, Criminal Procedure, Juvenile Law, Poverty Law Seminar, Secured Transactions, and Custody Aspects of Family Law.

From 1979 to the present she has worked as a judge in the Circuit Court of Cook County. She is presently a Justice for the Illinois Appellate Court, First District, in the Divorce Division. She is looking forward to being a generalist as an appellate court judge.

The most dramatic change over the years has been the great influx of women into the profession. She began to notice this in the mid-70's when she was a professor. She thinks it is a most welcome event and will change the profession for the better.

She has always felt a great support from the WBAI in her career endeavors and especially in her quest for judicial office. The organization has been steadfast in its support when things were going well, and more importantly when things were not. She would like to work in helping to reduce gender bias in the court and also assist women and other minority attorneys who aspire to judicial office.

SOIA MENTSCHIKOFF,

was a former active member and great contributor to WBAI, Ms. Mentschikoff passed away in 1984.

She was an internationally known expert in commercial law and is well-remembered as the co-author, with her husband, Karl Llewellyn, of the Uniform Commercial Code.

Soia Mentschikoff earned her J. D. in 1937 from Columbia University Law School.

She was the first woman to teach at Harvard Law School. In 1951 she came to the University of Chicago to join its law faculty. In 1974 she became the first woman dean at the University of Miami School of Law and remained there until her retirement in 1982.

Under both the Johnson and Nixon administrations, she was mentioned as a nominee for the U. S. Supreme Court.

University of Chicago Dean Casper stated, 'by any standard, Ms. Mentschikoff was one of the great law teachers of her generation who inspired students and colleagues alike.

BARBARA MATUSIK MILLER,

graduated from DePaul University Law School in 1963 and was one of three women law graduates that year. After graduation and passing the Bar, jobs for women attorneys were difficult to find. Barbara went to work in a small financial institution in her home town of Lyons. She served the customers of the institution through good and bad times while the financial institution grew to the third largest thrift institution in the State of Illinois with the 13th largest mortgage banking operation in the nation and a real estate development subsidary and a financing subsidary to administer collateralized mortgage obligations. She served the institution for 24 years achieving the position of Chief Executive Officer and President. In the late 1980's the institution was purchased by the Pritzker family and Barbara left to work with another financial services company.

Presently Barbara is working with LaSalle St. Securities doing underwritings for stock and bond issues. She also represents individual, commercial and institutional clients in making investments.

In 1986 DePaul University honored Barbara by naming her as Outstanding Law Graduate.

Barbara has worked to promote the interests of women by serving as president of the Illinois Appointments Coalition which seeks to have women appointed to corporate Boards. She is serving as President of the LaGrange Business and Professional Women's Organization. During her tenure at the financial institution, 40% of the officers were women.

Barbara's three children are each interesting people making a contribution to society in different ways and supporting equality for women.

Throughout Barbara's career she was an active member of the Women's Bar Association of Illinois and found support and cooperation from other Bar members.

BENJAMIN K. MILLER,

Chief Justice Miller, a native of Springfield, received a Bachelor of Arts degree from Southern Illinois University in Carbondale in 1958. He then went to Vanderbilt University in Nashville, TN, where he received a Doctor of Jurisprudence degree in 1961. Following graduation from Vanderbilt, Justice Miller returned to Springfield where he was actively engaged in the private practice of law from 1961 to 1976. In 1976 he was appointed a Judge of the Circuit Court for the Seventh Judicial Circuit by the State Supreme Court. He was elected to that position in 1978.

Justice Miller served as presiding judge in the Criminal Felony Division of the circuit court in Sangamon County from 1976 to 1980. In 1981, he was elected chief judge of the Seventh Circuit and served in that capacity until 1982 when he was elected to the Fourth District Appellate Court. In 1984, he was elected to the Supreme Court of Illinois. He was elected chief justice of the court in 1991.

In addition to his judicial duties, Justice Miller is currently a member of the board of directors of the American Judicature Society. Justice Miller served as the chairman of the Illinois Courts Commission from 1988 to 1991. He has also served as a member of the Illinois Law Enforcement Commission, as a member of the Board of Govenors and as Treasurer of the Illinois State Bar Association, and as a chairman and a member of many committees of that Association. He is a member of the American and Illinois State Bar Associations, the Illinois Bar Foundation, Sangamon County Bar Association, Women's Bar Association. In 1991, Justice Miller was the recipient of an Honorary Doctor of Law Degree from The John Marshall Law School in Chicago and also received the Lawyers' Assistance Program Carl Rolewick Memorial Award.

Justice Miller has also been active in academic and community affairs. He is currently on the board of directors of the Abraham Lincoln Association and is a member of the advisory board of The Lincoln Legal papers. He served as president of the Greater Springfield Chamber of Commerce, as president of the Central Illinois Mental Health Association, and as an officer and member of the board of directors of other civic and charitable organizations.

Justice Miller is also an adjunct professor at Southern Illinois University School of Medicine where he assisted in the development of the medical-legal curriculum.

While serving on active duty as an enlisted man in the U. S. Army Reserve, Justice Miller graduated from the U. S. Army Intelligence School at Fort Holabird, Maryland. Following his discharge from the Army Reserve, he served as Lieutenant J. G. in the U. S. Navy Reserve.

MARTHA A. MILLS,

in 1990, Martha joined Schaefer, Rosenwein & Fleming, a six lawyer firm dedicated to top quality litigation. The firm's litigation practice includes both complex and not so complex business and commercial litigation, international law, intellectual property, insurance law, bankruptcy litigation, environmental litigation, professional liability, premises liability, some areas of employment law, constitutional law and appellate work. In addition, the firm handles some federal criminal litigation.

Martha was inducted into the American College of Trial Lawyers in 1989. She was the second woman from Illinois to receive this honor.

Martha graduated cum laude from the University of Minnesota Law School in 1965. She was one of three women in her law school class. Upon graduation she became the first female associate with White & Case, a prominent New York Wall Street firm.

Martha joined the Lawyer's Committee for Civil Rights Under Law in Jackson, Mississippi, in 1967 for reasons of social commitment. Coincidentally she obtained a wealth of trial experience that it would have been difficult to acquire elsewhere. In the course of this, she worked on two cases which resulted in landmark Supreme Court opinions. In addition, she won, for the Estate of a black person who had been murdered, $1,021,500 verdict in a civil case against the whites who were believe to have murdered him. This was the first such verdict since Reconstruction.

In 1969, Martha was appointed City Attorney of Fayette, Mississippi, by Charles Evers, its first black Mayor. She remained in that position long enough to straighten out a budget left in disarray by the outgoing white administration and to train new city officials.

In late 1969 she became Chief Counsel of the Lawyer's Committee office in Cairo, Illinois. She remembers a terribly depressing looking area with an appalling inventory of problems. Cairo's shortsided administration would rather give up swimming pools, little League and Golden Gloves than share them with blacks.

In 1970 Martha moved back to Chicago. She became an associate at Schiff Hardin & Waite. Five years later, she decided to start her own firm. In 1986 she became a partner in Foss Schuman Drake & Barnard, where she practiced with great satisfaction until that firm merged its practice into a larger firm.

Martha is a frequent participant in NITA programs as a teaching team member, and in continuing legal education projects. She is active in various bar associations, having been on Governing Council of the Litigation Section of the American Bar Association and on the Board of Governor's of the Chicago Council of Lawyers. She has served on the Federal Defender Panel since 1970, and is a frequent legal volunteer for various organizations.

Martha is also very active at St. Andrew's Greek Orthodox Church in Chicago, having been picnic chairman, sung in the choir and been adult advisor to high school youth for some years. She is happily married to A. Patrick Papas who is also active at and on the Board at St. Andrew's.

ANNA L. MINAHAN,

born in Aurora, Illinois on July 16, 1882. Deceased September 26, 1962.

Ms. Minahan attended the Aurora Elementary School, the Englewood High School in Chicago, the University of Chicago, and the John Marshall Law School. She earned her Bachelor's of Law Degree from

e John Marshall Law School by night school
tendance, and who, although her law studies were
terrupted due to her transfer while in Government
rvice from Chicago to Washington, D. C., did
rservere in her studies and on her transfer back to
nicago some years later reentered her law course
udy thereby earning her degree in 1946.

She was admitted to the Illinois Bar and to
ractice before the United States District Court in
nuary 1948, was then age 66 and an inspiration to
l who have endeavored to attain a cherished goal.

She worked in various capacities of 34 years
rm February 1918 to July 1952 in the United States
ederal Government Service and who, at the time of
er retirement, was an Assistant United States
ttorney, having been appointed June 1951, by Otto
erner Jr., who was then United States Attorney, of
e Northern District of Illinois.

She was honored, beloved, and respected member
Kappa Beta Pi International Legal Sorority and who
rved in various offices including Dean of Zeta Chapter,
e school chapter of John Marshall Law School and who,
the time of her death, was a member of the Chicago
lumanae Chapter, Epsilon Alumnae.

In the 14 years she was a member of the Women's
ar Association of Illinois served on various committees
nong them the Legislative, Judges Dinner, Current
aw, and, because she was an accomplished pianist, on
e Entertainment Committee.

She had two brothers, Mark and Edwin, a niece
nd two grandnephews.

CORINNE SEITHER MORRISSEY, Born
efiance, OH on December 5, 1937. She attended
rathmore College where she earned B. A. in 1959;
niversity of Chicago in 1963-64 where she earned 30
ours of U. S. History; Loyola University of Chicago,
here she earned J. D. degree in 1985.

She was admitted to the Illinois Bar in 1985 and
came an associate of Baker & McKenzie in 1987-
89. Currently the Director of Advising at the John
larshall Law School.

She has done pro bono work for Chicago
olunteer Legal services through clinic at Visitation
hurch on Garfield Boulevard in Chicago. Taught
hool from 1959-63 while first husband attended
niversity of Chicago Law School. She worked as
dministrative Assistant in Litigation Department
Baker & McKenzie 1969-1987 and attended law
hool evenings.

Married partner, Francis D. Morrissey,
dministrator of Litigation Department of Baker &
IcKenzie, January 1989, and left firm thereafter due
general policy as to nepotism.

PATRICIA E. MULLIN, president of
'omen's Bar Association 1970-1971, was born in
ubuque, Iowa.

Graduated from the Visitation Academy and
larke College. My B. A. degree included a major in
iology, a minor in Chemistry and Education. I
terned a year at Lila Post Hospital, Battle Creek,
lichigan and took the national exam to obtain an MT
SCP) Medical Technologist—American Society of
linical Pathology. While I was in charge of the
ood Bank at St. Anne's Hospital, Chicago, Illinois,
ttended DePaul University Law School and I have
ris Doctorate from that school. I am a member of

the Iowa Bar, the Illinois Bar, and was admitted to the
Supreme Court of the United States.

I am a Vice President, the Corporate Secretary,
and Senior Counsel for Bankers Life and Casualty
Company, and Illinois Insurance Corporation. Since
working for an insurance company, I obtained the
CLU Degree (Chartered Life Underwriter), the FLMI
(Fellowship in Life Insurance with specialty in Pension
Planning), and ChFC (Chartered Financial
Consultant) Degree.

I am on the Board of the Equal Employment
Advisory Council, Washington, D. C. I was its
chairman in 1986. From 1985 until 1990 I was a
Director for the National Foundation for the study of
Equal Employment Policy, Washington, D. C.

I am a Commissioner of the Illinois Supreme
Court - Character and Fitness Committee, of which I
was chairman for 1990-1991. I am a Director of the
Women's Bar Association of Illinois Foundation. I
was Chairman of the Committee to select outstanding
Supervisory Employe of 1971 for the Chicago Federal
Executive Board.

During the year that I was President of the
Women's Bar Association three of our members were
elected as delegates to the Constitutional Convention,
and they kept us advised of their activities. They
spoke before the group and helped us to decide on
the adoption of the revised Constitution and especially
the four sections that were left to the general public.

The most gala event was our reception for the
Consular Corps. It was a lovely and interesting affair.
I was pleased to preside at the program for the reception
for new citizens. All in all it was a delightful year!

VICTORIA MUNIZZO, has spent her life
in and around Chicago. She attended Northern Illinois
University from 1981 to 1986 and the John Marshall
Law School from 1986 to 1989. She became interested
in law while working as a court clerk. She thought
that judges had the easiest job around. She found out
she was wrong.

Going straight from college into law school, she
feels that law school forced out the true independent
and aggressive woman that she is today. One of the
first things she learned in law school was that there
are many people that still believe women don't belong
in the legal field. She is now proving them wrong. She
also found out that theory and practice are sometimes
two very different things.

As a relatively new lawyer, she dreads
watching more experienced lawyers practice as
though they were fresh out of law school with little
or no experience but with great vanity. She is
working in the domestic relations field, which is all
she ever wanted to do. She works for the firm of
Nottage and Ward.

She and her husband are newlyweds living in
Chicago. Her husband is also an attorney so family
and work blend nicely.

HELEN WALTER MUNSERT, was brought
up in a legal atmosphere and maintained that tradition
in her adult life. A practicing lawyer, she was the first
woman to serve as attorney and hearing examiner for
the Illinois Commerce Commission.

She married Kenneth Munsert in 1929. She and
her husband both attended Kent Law School. She
was first in a graduating class of more than 100.

Ms. Munsert volunteered for many associations.
One of her accomplishments being that she was the
first woman to serve as director of the Chicago
Regional Chapter of the Association of Interstate
Commerce Commission Practitioners.

She has served as legislative chairman of the
Alliance of Business and Professional Women of
Chicago, and as a member of the local and national
bar associations, has served innumerable terms as
secretary of various committees.

One of her special interests was the concern for
the promotion of qualified women in public service.
In addition to city life, she and her husband bought a
13 acre sheep and steer farm.

SANDRA R. MURPHY, admitted to Illinois
Bar in 1976 and the United States Federal District
Court for the Northern District of Illinois in 1976.
Received J. D. from Loyola University in June 1976
and B.A. from Northwestern University in 1971.
Capital Partner in Trial Department of McDermott,
Will & Emery head of domestic relations department.

Chairman of the Matrimonial Law Committee of
the Chicago Bar Association (1985-1986); chairman of
the Family Law Council of the Illinois State Bar
Association Family Law Section (1987-1988); chairman
of Legislation Subcommittee of Matrimonial Law
Committee (1981-1982); member of the Family Counsel
(1987-1989), and secretary (1990) of the American
Academy of Matrimonial Lawyers; and vice president
of Board of Managers for the Illinois Chapter of the
American Academy of Matrimonial Lawyers.

Guest lecturer on negotiation of and settlement
of matrimonial law cases at Loyola University and
guest matrimonial law professor at Loyola University.
Guest lecturer regarding negotiation of matrimonial
law cases John Marshall Law School. Given frequent
lectures on family law topics including: "Tax Reform
Act of 1984 and Its Implications for the Family Law
Practitioner"; Drafting Marital Settlement
Agreements Under the Tax Reform Act of 1986";
"Highlights of 1982 Court Decisions and Legislation";
"Development of Mediation Guidelines"; "The
Retirement Equity Act of 1984 and Its Implications
for the Family Law Practioner"; Client Relations and
Management"; "Joint Custody and Alternatives to
Trial Today: Its Strengths and Weaknesses"; "The
Art of Negotiating a Domestic Relations Case";
Drafting Antenuptial and Marital Settlement
Agreements; and "Problems in Awarding
Maintenance and Child Support".

Ms. Murphy has written several articles and
publications. She has been published in Illinois Family
Law Newsletter, Family Law and the Family
Advocate - a journal by the ABA Family Law Section.

SHEILA M. MURPHY, (JUDGE), born in
Colorado Springs in 1937. I was the only daughter born
to Martin and Gertrude Murphy. I have four brothers.

My father's dad died when he was six weeks old so
he was raised in an orphanage, perhaps this is where he
got an enlightened view of a girl's right to be fully herself.
He proved this when I was about ten years old.

My brother Marty was sick so I went to Pauline
Chapel to serve Mass in his stead. When the priest
wouldn't permit me to serve, my father defended my
right to serve. Later my mother encouraged me to
become an attorney. After I married I asked mom
when would be the best time to attend law school.
My son, Patrick, was one month old. She looked me
in the eye and said, "There is never a perfect time for
any mother to do anything for herself. Just do it!"

I graduated from DePaul University law school
in 1970. There was acute prejudice against women by
some of the faculty, Kathryn Bigley and Mary Conrad
and I all encouraged each other. (I needed a lot of
encouragement since our daughter, Brigid, was born
during Law School). The greatest asset to my legal
career has been my husband, Patrick Racey who
made it all possible, and is my confidant and adviser.

When I joined the Cook County public
Defender's Office in 1971, women were not assigned
to the Criminal Court. Since one woman had

previously been assigned there and it didn't work out well, the administration wouldn't allow any women to try felony cases.

When the 1964 Civil Rights Act was made applicable to county government, I threatened to sue if the discrimination didn't stop. I was then transferred to the Criminal Court and given the worst assignments for some time.

One judge forbade me to wear slacks in the courtroom, so I wore only slacks in his courtroom. The same judge is now a great advocate for women and his daughter is a freshman in law school. Most of the men who tried to keep me from trying felonies have also become enlightened and I forgive them for their former myopia.

The worst thing about my early years as an Assistant Public Defender was that there were no role models. (Prior to my time Mary Ann Grohwin McMorrow was a great trail blazer for the women in the States Attorney's Office.) The years were lonely and for a time, I became embittered. I find that resentment and bitterness is like an evil acid, it burns the container it is in. However I learned that prayer blows resentment away. I thank the Women's Bar Association members for their encouragement in those years. What WBAI does for each other, we do for ourselves as we as women, continue to climb the peaks that our founding sisters sighted for us long ago.

REGINA G. FIRANT NARUSIS, was born in Kaunas, Lithuania on October 12, 1936, and became a naturalized citizen of the United States in 1955. She attended the University of Illinois-Urbana from 1953 to 1959 gaining both her undergraduate degree and her law degree.

She became a lawyer because of her love for the American Justice System and the American way of life. She was one of very few women in law school so she had to prove herself.

She started her career as an Assistant State's Attorney for McHenry County and became Chief Juvenile division. She now has a private practice of her own. She specializes mostly in Family Law at this time, but has been engaged in the general practice of law as well. She says that the image of lawyer has changed in the 30 years of her practice. Lawyers have lost respect for themselves.

She is married with three children and two grandchildren. This has placed on her a constant balancing of her many rolls and demands. She has had few experiences with WBAI because of distance but has been very involved in community affairs. She is actively involved in the Lithuanian Freedom Cause.

NANCY NICOL

NANCY NEEDLES

DAWN CLARK NETSCH, was born in Cincinnati, OH on September 16, 1926. She attended public elementary and high schools in Cincinnati. She attended Northwestern University in 1948 earning a B.A. with distinction. She graduated in 1952 from Northwestern's School of Law, receiving her Juris Doctor degree magna cum laude (first in class). She was elected to the Order of the COIF.

Following graduation, Netsch worked from 1952 to 1954 at the Washington firm of Covington and Burling. She then served as a law clerk to Federal Judge Julius J. Hoffman, U.S. Distric Court for the Northern District of Illinois, from 1954 to 1956. From 1957 to 1961 she was employed at the Chicago law firm of Snyder, Chadwell, Keck, Kayser & Ruggles, where she specialized in antitrust law. From 1965 to the present she has been a member of the faculty at Northwestern University School of Law. She teaches state and local government law and antitrust, real estate and race relations law.

As a delegate to the Illinois Constitutional Convention in 1970, she served as vice-chair of the Revenue and Finance Committee and played a major role in writing the Illinois State Constitution. Two years after serving as a delegate to Contitutional convention, she was elected to the Illinois Senate and has been reelected five times. She is the first woman to be elected to a State Constitutional Office in Illinois. She is currently the Comptroller for the State of Illinois. Dawn has been frequently honored for her accomplishments in government.

Dawn is married to the internationally known architect, Walter A. Netsch. They live in Chicago in a house he designed.

GRACE NEWTON (JERRY), spent her childhood in Washington D.C.. She graduated for the University of Michigan in 1963 and graduated from Kent Law School in 1982. She found her law school years to be stimulating.

Since obtaining her law degree, she has worked as an Assistant Attorney General, specializing in litigation of employment discrimination.

She is in her 2nd marriage with two wonderful children. It has been tough combining her career and her family.

ODAS NICHOLSON, Judge, Circuit Court of Cook County. When I was growing up on a farm in Pickens, Mississippi, I never dreamed that I would become a lawyer in Chicago, or a judge. As the youngest of seven children, I was the odd one, I read

everything I could find, and I aspired to be a teache a profession of most of the women in my family.

Two fortuitous things happened in my l however. When I was 13, my father consented to r coming to live with a brother and sister, following r mother's death. While a student at Wilson Jr. Colle (now Kennedy-King College) I represented the colle in an Oratorical Contest sponsored by the Old Hera American Newspaper annually, on a city wide bas and including all of the college. I participated in t contest on "Thomas Jefferson - A Great Americar

It was my good fortune to meet the late Dr. T. Smith of the University of Chicago, who was one the judges. It was he who suggested that I become lawyer.

When I attended DePaul University College Law there was only one other woman in my class ar only four women in the entire Law School. Tod women comprise from 40-45% of the student boc One could count the minorities on one hand then compared to today when there is a 10% minor enrollment. I am told that I am the first black wom to graduate from DePaul.

It was a blessing in disguise that I had to wc during college and law school since I had the privile of working as a secretary for a very outstandi lawyer, Mr. Earl B. Dickerson. Upon receiving r Juris Doctor Degree from DePaul and being admitt to the Illinois Bar in 1948, I became Trial Attorney Supreme Life Insurance Company of America whe Mr. Dickerson served as General Counsel.

Aside from the many rewarding experiences derives from the general practice of law, three ever stand out in my legal career: (1) Being elected a Delegate to the Sixth Illinois Constitutior Convention, and being elected Secretary of t Convention by the delegates, and helping to write t 1970 Constitution, especially the Equal Righ provision. (2) Serving as head of the Office of Gene Counsel for the U. S. Equal Employment Opportun Commission for the Chicago an Kansas City Regio which comprised ten states in the midwest. (3) N selection as a Fellow by the National Endowment Humanities "Law and Justice in American Societ Seminar at Harvard University.

Among my many professional affiliations deem my membership in WBAI since 1962 and honor of having served as its President (1973- most rewarding. As a founding member of the Joir Negro Appeal and past president I was able to ma a contribution to agencies serving under privileg youth. I was privileged to serve as president of Illinois Judicial Counsel as well as a Board Member the NAACP and the Chicago Youth Centers.

I presently serve as a member of the Visiti Advisory Committee of the DePaul University Colle of Law and am a member of the President's Club

A great source of strength has been membership in the Metropolitan Community Chu where I have served as Trustee since 1956.

Due in large measure to my membership in legal profession and as a member of the judiciar have been the recipient of many honors and awar including the following: Alpha Gamma Pi Medalli Cook County Bar Association Public Service Awa Operation Push Achievement Award for la Sojourner Truth Award of the National Associati of Negro Business and Professional Women's Clu

DePaul University Distinguished Alumni Award, Edith S. Sampson Memorial Award, Illinois Judicial Council, Outstanding Achievement in the Legal Community Award, Women's Law Caucus DePaul University, Operation Push Award for Exemplary Service in a Leadership Role in Law, Kenneth E. Wilson Award, Cook County Bar Association Distinguished Service Award, Cook County Bar Association, Listed in Who's Who of American Women 9th Edition, Listed in Who's Who among Black Americans.

JENNIFER T. NIJMAN, was born and raised in Toronto, Canada. She became a U.S. Citizen in 1988. She attended the University of Illinois, Champaign-Urbana from 1980 to 1984 and attended the University of Illinois Law School from 1984 to 1987.

She became interested in the practice of law as a child. Her mother was a legal secretary and Jennifer enjoyed watching and learning from her mother's boss.

She works as a litigator in the areas of commercial litigation and environmental. She loves her job because she always has something different to do and she learns from each situation.

She was married on September 8, 1990 and she and her husband reside in Chicago.

CHERYL I. NIRO, I spent the bulk of my childhood in Park Forest, Illinois, the south-suburbs of Chicago. Attended the University of Illinois, Champaign-Urbana from 1968-1972, undergraduate, B. S. Fine and Applied Arts, highest honors. Did graduate work from 1973-75, straight "A" grade point average, Graduate School of Education. Attended Law School at Northern Illinois University, College of Law from 1976-1980.

I think I first decided that I would like to be a lawyer when I was about ten years old, while sitting in the office of Mr. Robert Navid, my parent's attorney in Park Forest. His wife was an elementary school teacher, and I admired both of them. A high school teacher, Jim Smith, at Rich Central H. S. was instrumental, because he let me know that he thought I was very smart and capable of accomplishing great things—which made him unique and memorable.

Thinking back on law school some feelings surface: Lack of positive female role models—I have dedicated a lot of time to law related education programs because I feel that I would have been helped greatly if I had more images of professional women while growing up. My law school may have been unique in its lack of women on the faculty—but, unfortunately, I think it was not. Law school was definantly a love/hate experience. I would do it again in a second, but I remember the joy of suffering together with my fellow classmates. My view of becoming a lawyer is constantly changing. Everyday, I seem to gain some new insight as to what it is all about. The things that remain the same are my ideals. I went to law school with idealized notions of justice, and professional service and integrity—and I refuse to lose sight of these values.

After graduation from law school I gave birth to my first child, Christopher, and worked part-time at Pope, Ballard, Shepard and Fowle, in Chicago. My daughter, Melissa, was born two years later. I wasn't

very good at "juggling" so, I left the firm. Later, I was appointed by the Illinois Supreme Court to head the statewide programs to commemorate the Bicentennial of the United States Constitution. This was a wonderful experience. I continued to work, both on my own, and with my husband's intellectual property firm. I have devoted much time to bar association projects, and have been instrumental in the founding of the Illinois Supreme Court Legal Historical Society. At this time, I concentrate on appellate practice, and am heading several important projects, including the ISBA Task Force on Children.

As a law student, I was the Dean's teaching assistant for the Legal Research and Writing program, and taught the course for two semesters. Perhaps it was that experience that explains my focus on appellate work. I suppose I dream of sitting on the bench in an appellate court someday.

Truth and justice are my two highest held values. I am also a tireless worker for the underdog, and helpless. I have a need to help people, which is satisfied by my career in the law. What I don't like about this career is that occasionally, the system doesn't work to create either truth or justice.

My major accomplishment is achieving balance. I never thought that at this point in my life I would value such a thing—but it seems that it is what I am currently most proud of. I can list many professional accomplishments, although, not as many as I would like. But, I can honestly say that I have a wonderful personal life as well. "Having it all" isn't as easy as it looks, and getting to a point of "balance" and fulfillment is tricky! I am married to William L. Niro since July 1, 1979. We have two children, Christopher and Melissa. We both had to make balancing a big part of our lives—trying to meet the needs of our children and families, professions, and selves. My perspective changes, I guess. Experience helps, and wisdom, hopefully, results.

As a new member of WBAI, I look forward to my involvement in this organization with a renewed commitment and realization that we owe those women who preceded us, those who will follow us, and ourselves, our best efforts to be organized and supportive of women in our profession.

My younger years were spent in the arts—primarily music. I have toured Europe with a concert orchestra through the People-to-People Program of the State Department, and studied music quite seriously. Contrary to what many engineers and others might think-I have found that my past serves me well in the practice of law. In all professions, including law, the truly great practitioners are those who can see new possibilities and creative solutions to problems. My life in the creative arts has served me well, and, hopefully, enhances my ability to serve the profession well.

KATHERINE NOHELTY, Chicago's first woman Municipal Court Judge in November, 1956, Miss Nohelty feels that being elected wasn't just her victory. "I think it's the culmination of the work of all women who have been active in politics since women were given the vote."

A referee in Traffic court since 1953 and an attorney since 1937 she once thought social service was her field. "But I went to work for a firm of lawyers, first as a receptionist, then as a secretary,

and finally as a court reporter," she said. "I found the work so fascinating I decided to become an attorney." It wasn't easy. She took both her pre-law and law work at Loyola University, graduating in 1937 after ten years of night school work. Miss Nohelty believes that a woman judge makes a special contribution in that she believes a woman is concerned with humanitarion values in every case. "I believe in considering a case where she may find a defendant guilty, she is aware of rehabilitation as well as punishment.

When elected in 1956, she said: "I hope my election is an encouragement to other women to participate actively in their political parties. And as more women lawyers become more active in politics, there will be more women judges."

Judge Nohelty's debut in politics began in the 1930s when she joined the Federation of Illinois Woman's Democratic clubs. She became active in the 50th ward Democratic organization. For 4 1/2 years she was captain in the ward's 1st precinct.

Judge Nohelty served as WBAI president in 1945-46. She celebrated her 90th birthday on December 3, 1991, the day, in 1956 she was sworn in as first woman elected Municipal Court Judge in Chicago.

ROSAIRE NOTTAGE, she is in partnership with Eunice Ward, and both are as close as sisters. Their partnership is like a well-oiled marriage. They finish each other's sentences, laugh at each other's jokes, and act as cheerleader or critic depending on othe other's need. To the outsider, they seem like girls who grew to womanhood together, lifelong friends. To the insider, they are attorneys, whose reputation for toughness and speed has built a dynamic new divorce practice in town - Nottage & Ward.

They met over lunch and some favorable impressions were formed. During several lunches they discovered a shared phiosphy about the deeper responsibility of being a divorce attorney. Responsibility like honesty towards the client about their legal position; the difference between what they want and what they'll get (there's usually a big gap): and whatit's likely to cost them.

Eunice received a phone call from Rosaire in July which said "Come on, let's do it." They got themselves a business advisor, a line of credit, an accountant, and a three-year business plan. in December 1987, the firm of Nottage & Ward was born, and has since thrived beyond all their carefully planned expectations. In the past two years, this marriage of colleagues has evolved into a marriage of minds. The women now practice what they call 'team-lawyering.'

It's clear that the contrasts between these two women have only served to complement each other, and they have become, "tremendous friends." They intend to be in business together for a long time, taking on, maybe, one or two more associates.

J. S. NOTTINGHAM, spent her childhood in Chicago and attended DePaul University for both her undergraduate and her law degrees. She became interested in law when she was involved in a law suit when she was seven years old.

During law school she never stopped to analyze what was going on around her. After law school she went into a private practice and eventually a partnership specializing in domestic relations, probate, and personal injury. She states that lawyers today must continue their legal education to remain current.

She is married to Otto C. Kohivek, M.D.. They are both active in their practices, and have many outside interests such as flying, herpetology research, photography and writing.

RITA NOVAK, graduated from law school in 1978. She currently works at the American Bar Association on a project which assists appellate courts in implementing methods to reduce case backlog and delay. She has also worked at the Illinois Attorney General's office doing civil appeals,

She has taught at Indiana University - Indianapolis for three years and was a law clerk to a federal district court judge. She received her L.L.M. in 1981.

Generally, She would like to see WBAI assist in placing women in leadership positions, particularly in public office but also within their firms and businesses.

TERESA NUCCIO, attended Donnelley College in Kansas City, KS. then attended Northeastern Illinois University where she received a B.A. Psychology in August 1977. She attended the Loyola University of Chicago School of Law from 1977 to 1981, receiving her Juris Doctor in June 1981. She also received her Master of Social Work from Loyola in June 1981.

She began her legal work in the town of Cicero as the Assistant Town Attorney. She then became the law clerk for the Honorable Olga Jurco, United States Magistrate, United State District Court, Northern District of Illinois. From August 1985 to October 1990 she was a part-time associate to the law offices of Penny Nathan Kahan. She has been a part-time sole practioner since 1990.

She has worked as a Network TV Specialist and a Social Worker before entering the field of law. She is very active in her community and has been published in several publications.

She is a member of the Chicago Bar Association, the Illinois State Bar Association, the National Employment Lawyers Association, and the Women's Bar Association of Illinois.

DENISE O'MALLEY, she spent her childhood on the South side of Chicago. She attended and received a M. A. from the University of Chicago. She received a J. D. from John Marshall Law School. She became interested in law through her aunt who was a lawyer. After graduation, she became a State's Attorney. She doesn't just like being a lawyer, she loves it!

MARGARET G. O'MALLEY, I am a lifelong resident of Chicago and have received my formal education here. I graduated from Mercy High School and received my pre-legal training at Saint Xavier's College for women. I graduated from DePaul College of Law with a Doctor of Jurisprudence.

My legal experience includes six years in private practice, two years as an Assistant State's Attorney, three years in the legal department of what is now the

Cook County Department of Public Aid, ten years as Referee of the Juvenile Court. I've been Magistrate, Associate Judge, and now full Judge of the Circuit Court of Cook County. I was selected in 1971 by the Supreme Court of Illinois to fill a judicial vacancy.

I was slated by the Democratic Party to run as a judicial candidate in 1974 on a county wide basis. I led the judicial slate with the highest number of votes cast.

I have sat in the Juvenile Court, various police courts, and such special assignments as Women's Court and Paternity Court. I sat for 18 months in Small Claims. I had four different assignments to Traffic Court. I spent over a year at Monroe Street Court which handled the "Drunk Call." For several years I head a trial call in the Divorce Section. While assigned to the County Division, I head adoptions - contested and non-contested. Mental health cases were also part of the assignments. I heard contested election cases and matters of taxation. These were my main assignments but I filled in on vacations in various other court areas.

I resigned my position as Circuit Court Judge of Cook County effective as of November 1, 1979. I was recalled to the Bench as of January 1, 1988. I was assigned to Marriage Court and have continued to serve there.

I am past president of the Women's Bar Association of Illinois. I am presently active on the Board of Managers and a member of various committees. I served on the Mental Health, Juvenile, Adoption and Matrimonial Committees of the Chicago Bar Association.

I have continued my "formal" legal education by attending four sessions of from two to four weeks each at the State College of the Judiciary in Reno, Nevada. I complete two separate 13-week courses sponsored by the American Academy of Matrimonial Law. I have attended more than 15 seminars organized by the Continuing Committee of Legal Education.

I have been active in civic and legal circles. I am a member of the following professional organizations: Chicago Bar Association, Women's Bar Association, Catholic Lawyers Guild, National Association of Women Lawyers and the National Association of Women Judges. I am a member of the Women's Board of Saint Joseph's Hospital and of the Women's Board of DePaul University. I am active in my church and have been a Eucharistic minister for four years.

MARY G. OPPENHEIM, spent her childhood on the North Side of Chicago. She graduated from the University of Illinois in 1930 and attended DePaul University from 1931 to 1934.

Her mother was a business woman and Mary assumed responsibilities of the family financial matters early in high school. She felt very positive about law school that it gave her a good solid basis.

She suffered discrimination as a female and found it extremely difficult to establish a practice. She was employed by the U.S. Department of Justice as the 1st woman Immigration Examiner and during WWII in Contract Division. She has had a General Practice of Law since 1945.

She has found that the practice of law has lost civility and loyalty, but it still is a great career. She is proud that she is helpful in solving problems for people of all ages, sex, and colors, and being in public service. The practice of law has become much more competitive, accelerated, and stressful.

She is married with no children. She says that she have been to busy with her husband and office to fully utilize WBAI and regrets her failure to do so.

MARIA PAPPAS, received her B. A. in Sociology for the West Liberty State College in West Virginia. She received her M.A. in Guidance and Counseling from the West Virginia State University. After receiving her teaching certification in 1972 she taught at West Virginia State University and Loyola University as a teaching assistant. She has had her

present private practice since July 1972, dealing with individual and group therapy, child adolescent family, and marital counseling.

She became a community professor at DePaul in 1974, and worked for the Society of Individual Psychology in Austria. After receiving her Ph.D. in counseling and Psychology, she has worked in the field of psychology at the Adlerian Psychology Center, Holland; the Society of Individual Psychology, Essex, England; the Governors State University, Park Forest South, IL; the Greek Society of Psychology, Athen, Greece; the International Adlerian Summer School, Zurich; and the Dreikurs Institute, Tel-Aviv. She became a certified graphoanalyst in 1979.

She received her Juris Doctor from the Illinois Institute of Technology in January 1982. She established a private practice in 1982 and was appointed to the Ministry of Justice in Athens, Greece in 1983.

She is a consultant of Family Education Association of Chicago, Daniel Williams Hill Elementary School, Jewish Vocational Service, Northbrook School District, Ohio Valley Homemakers Association, National Teachers College, St. Thomas Apostle Elementary School, Chicago Council on Medicine and Religion, Morraine Valley College, Morman Society of Salt Lake City, Utah, Depot, Latin School, Joliet School District, and Safari - Day-One Drug Abuse Center.

She has been published in numerous publications. Her professional memberships include Individual Psychologist, Most Notable Americans, the American Society of Adlerian Psychology, Who's Who in American Women, the ASAP Task Force on Minorities, Day-One Safari, and the American Bar Association.

In 1990, from "outta nowhere", as far as the regulars could tell, Pappas was elected, on her first try for public office, to the Cook County Board.

MARY AVGERIN PAPPAS, Currently Chief Administrative Judge. Federal Sector Hearings Chicago District Office, U. S. Equal Employment Opportunity Commission, since January, 1979 conducting administrative hearings on complaints of discrimination against Federal agencies by Federal employees or applicants for Federal employment. I has been a most rewarding experience helping eradicate discrimination.

I graduated from Loyola University School of Law in 1950 and was admitted to the Illinois Bar that same year. In contrast to the high percentage of female law students today, I was the only female in a class of 83 back then. Until entering federal service, was in the general practice of law for many years.

Shortly after graduation from law school, in 50, I became a WBAI member and worked on any of its activities. I recall that one of the most atifying experiences was to chair the Paternity Act ommittee. That committee drafted and lobbied into w, the 1957 Illinois Paternity Act which provided ildren born out of wedlock more adequate financial pport than its predecessor did. Threatened by a st minute veto by Governor William G. Stratton ıless provision was made for a blood test, I rsonally drafted the Illinois Blood Test act which came law together with the Illinois Paternity Act.

Another committee of long standing of which I d the privilege to be a member and ultimately one its chairmen was the Family Court Committee. For ay years, the members of this committee lunteered their services representing indigents in at court, without any renumeration whatsoever. In 68, I had the privilege of accepting on behalf of BAI, the Certificate of Merit and Appreciation ɔm the National Council of Juvenile Court Judges, · the many years of service by that WBAI committee.

During my term as WBAI President, and in nor of the first elected woman jurist in Illinois, the ɪdge Mary M. Bartleme Scholarship Fund, was ɪablished, to provide scholarships for worthy law ɪdents. The first scholarship was awarded in July 66. This was later renamed as the WBAI Foundation nd.

Over the many years, aside from my professional tivity, I have been active in public service. In the rly 60's, I was elected to the Elementary School ʌard of Lake Bluff, and became its first female ɪesident.

In 1969, I was elected a Delegate-Member to the 70 Illinois Constitutional Convention by the ɪctorate of the then 51st Senatorial District. I had ɪ privilege to serve with Judge Odas M. Nicholson, ɪo was another delegate. The result of the efforts of ɪt Convention, was the present Illinois state ɪnstitution was presented to the voters in a form ɪsed upon Member Resolution #1 which I submitted. ɪat resolution mandated separate submission to the ɪctorate, of controversial subjects and thereby ɪured successful passage of the Constitution.

My husband and I were married in 1951, and ɪre blessed with our wonderful son, Michael who w resides in the charming coastal community of ɪuth Bristol, Maine, with his lovely wife, Gail. though our work keeps us in Chicago most of the ɪe, we do visit Maine several times during the year be with our children and to stay in our lovely year-ɪnd ocean-side home in York Beach, Maine.

My very best wishes to the members of the ɔmen's Bar Association and its continued success.

MARY SINCLAIR PEARCE, was born ɪry Hazel Sinclair in 1952 and spent my childhood Lake Bluff, Illinois. In 1974 I graduated from Beloit ɪllege, Beloit, Wisconsin, earning a B.A. degree, th majors in English Literature and Philosophy.

After college, I wanted to get some work ɪerience before deciding on a career. I was among ɪ first class in Roosevelt University's Lawyer's ɪsistant Program, and, beginning in 1974, I worked a paralegal in a large Chicago law firm. In 1976 I ɪered DePaul University College of Law, and was e to support myself during law school by working part-time at the law firm. During law school I met my husband, George Pearce, and we graduated, married, and were admitted to the bar in 1979.

Later in 1979 I began my present job as an attorney with the Office of the General Counsel for the United States Department of Agriculture. Along with the other attorneys in our office, I provide legal advice to the agencies of the Department located within our region. Although I worked full-time during the first five years of my employment, after the birth of our second child I changed to part-time, working four days a week. My children receive excellent care from their grandparents while I am at work, and I feel much more satisfied with my life because I am able to spend that extra day with them. I enjoy being able to contribute time to volunteer at school and church activities, and my life seems busy and full.

MARY L. PERISIN, spent her childhood in Chicago. She received a secretarial degree from DePaul University and her law degree from the John Marshall Law School, graduating in 1942.

From 1942 to 1948 she worked at the Social Security Administration. Since 1948 she has been in her present private practice dealing with real estate, probate, and trusts.

She is a life member of the American Bar Association, the Women's Bar Association of Illinois, and the Illinois State Bar Association. She is also a member of the Judicature Society.

She is a widow and has two children who are both attorneys, and two grandchildren, Daniel A. and Michele A. Aljinovic. She lives in Chicago.

FANNIE PERRON, taught French at the Lachine High School, Montreal, after graduating from McGill University, Montreal, before coming to Chicago and enrolling at the University of Chicago law school, from which she received the degree of Doctor of Law, 1930. She was graduated cum laude in the department of modern languages at McGill University. She was the only woman in her class at the University of Chicago, and successfully passed the November bar examinations.

Fannie Perron was a very active member of the WBAI before her retirement several years ago from the Corporation Counsel's office, where she was assigned to the Traffic Court.

She speaks fluent French, Russian, Hebrew and Yiddish. In addition to her interest in the law and languages she has carried on a life-long love affair with literature, music and the writing of poetry.

MILDRED PETERS

ANN CHRISTINE PETERSEN, is the general counsel of the Air Force. She acts as the final legal authority on all matters arising within or referred to the Air Force, except those involving military justice. Her father is a sole practioner in Iowa and served as her role model and teacher in the art of lawyering. As general counsel, she also serves as a member of the Intelligence Oversight Panel, advises the Debarment and Suspension Review Board, and performs liaison duties with the Department of Justice.

Ms. Petersen was born 25 December 1950, in Muscatine, Iowa, and graduated from Muscatine High School in 1969. She received a bachelor of arts degree, with highest distinction, from the University of Iowa in 1973. She was elected to Phi Beta Kappa and graduated with honors in political science. She received her juris doctorate, cum laude, from the University of Michigan in 1976.

Ms. Petersen was admitted to practice law in Illinois in 1976. She is admitted to practice before the 7th U.S. Circuit Court of Appeals and the U.S. District Court of the Northern District of Illinois, where she is a member of the trial bar.

After graduating from law school in 1976, Ms. Peterson joined the Chicago law firm of Wildman, Harrold, Allen & Dixon, where she practiced principally in civil litigation. She became a partner of the firm in January 1983. She assumed her current position in December 1989.

Ms. Petersen belongs to the American Bar Association and its antitrust, litigation and law practice management sections. She is a member of the Trade Associations Committee of the antitrust section, Illinois State Bar Association, Chicago Bar Association, Women's Bar Association of Illinois and the Legal Club of Chicago.

She has taught employment discrimination law as an adjunct professor at DePaul University College of Law in Chicago.

Ms. Petersen is married to Bruce H. Weitzman, a Chicago attorney.

MARIA P. PETERSON, was admitted to the Bar in May 1989. She has been practicing law at the U.S. Department of Labor-Office of the Solicitor.

She would like to see more programs where women politicians are focused. Seeing more women in power allows someone such as herself to pick and choose whom they would like to follow. A few years ago there was not a large selection of what a women could be in politics or law.

As a new lawyer, she doesn't have too many memorable experiences yet. However, the women attorneys she has met on the WBAI Board are kind and trustworthy. She hope to meet more women attorneys like them.

PAMELA PFRANG, became a lawyer in May 1984. She was an associate in a small firm for six months, she left law for six months, then came back as a P.P. in DuPage County. She has been at Cook County P.D. since April 1986, most recently months in appeals.

She would like to see WBAI put on more substantive topic programs and more political involvement on behalf of poor and imprisoned women.

JOANNE P. PITULLA, an ethics research attorney on the staff of the Center for Professional responsibility of the ABA in Chicago. I was born and raised in Chicago. I received my undergraduate degree from the University of Illinois in Champaign-Urbana, in 1957. Attended law school at Chicago-Kent in 1981 when I was divorced. I had a longing to be an attorney since my sophomore year in high school, probably inspired by Portia in The Merchant of Venice by Shakespeare. I enjoyed the verbal sparring and camaraderie of law school since Chicago-Kent had a great student mixture of different ages and life experiences and careers.

I taught English in high school and junior colleges for approximately ten years. I have never regretted becoming a lawyer, but I also believe my life experiences and English training and background have given me a depth, maturity, and resilience that I would not have if I became an attorney as a callow youth.

I worked as a reference librarian in the Chicago-Kent Law Library and then went into sole practice for five years working primarily in divorce and appeals. Now I do research in professional responsibility issues. I savor the knowledge of how the system of justice works and the access it gives me to advocate the principles I espouse. What I dislike is the cowardice I find fairly common among attorneys, including women, which causes them to go along with corruption rather than make waves.

In the broadest sense, I believe my accomplishments are in living my life with intensity and integrity, especially in raising three now-adult children who are such individuals in their own right. As to my brief legal career, I believe I have brought a new perspective and awareness of abuses in the area of attorneys fees through appellate cases I have won. I also have been active in working for reform in marital property law and divorce law.

I am single, with two sons and a daughter; no grandchildren yet, unfortunately. My children are very supportive and encouraged me through law school and my—quite literally—trials and tribulations since then. They also believe that it is important to stand up for principle, even when it costs—as it usually does.

I have yet to be really involved in the WBAI, although I have been a member since law school. I have not yet seen the support in the WBAI for the reforms in the profession which I fervently believe are needed. Rather, I have experienced the WBAI as a pleasant organization where people can network, but which exists mainly to further careers rather than to further what I believe should be the concerns of professionals in the public interest.

MARIJANE PLACEK, decided at the age of six years to make the law an integral part of her life and has spent the majority of the subsequent years working toward that goal, and at her young age, has become a trial attorney of widely-acknowledged high calibre.

As an aggressive and outstanding high school student, Marijane was captain of her school's debating team for four years and in 1966 was president of the Student Body. Believing that a successful person acknowledges no limitations on his or her abilities, she became a member of the National Honor Society, as well as being finalist in the Illinois State Science Fair for two consecutive years.

Working her way through Rosary College in River Forest, and while maintaining a 4.5 grade average, she was editor and founder of the freshman newspaper, Vice-President of the Junior Class, and President of the Student Government Association; she was selected for the College's summer program to study at Oxford University in England and was mentioned in the National Student Registry. She was on the Dean's list and graduated with honors.

At DePaul College of Law, she was on the national Moot Court team and International Moot Court team, respectively for two years. Founder and President of the Women's Caucus, she co-edited Women in Law, a two-volume textbook used at DePaul. She was recipient of a Yale summer scholarship to attend its course "Women in the Law." She was also Vice-President of the International Law Society, and is listed in the Colleges of Law Who's Who.

Sworn into the Illinois State Bar and shortly thereafter into the Federal Bar; she was law clerk to the general counsel for the McDonald's Corporation. Soon there after she started work for the Appellate Division of the Office of the Public Defender. Promotions came quickly and she served as Senior Trial Lawyer in both the Juvenile Division and in the Fourth Municipal District of Cook County. In this later assignment, she filed a neglect petition against the Department of Children and Family Services following the death of three year old Tina McCord, a child placed by the agency in the care of a foster home and in which the child was killed by her foster brother. After an eight hour contested hearing, the petition was granted. It is believed that his is the first time that any state agency has been found in neglect.

Also, while in the Fourth District, Ms. Placek successfully defended Mr. Roberto Salanis. Charged with Murder in the beating death of a 21 year old, Marijane convinced the Courts that the true cause of death was not the actions of Mr. Salanis but rather due to the gross negligence of the hospital treating the victim. A first for any suburban Criminal District.

As a senior trial attorney at the Criminal Court Building, Marijane has involved herself with such vigor in defending her clients that she will often find herself appointed by the Court to cases at request of defendants who know her by reputation alone. As of March, 1990 she had handled over 50 capital cases (cases where the prosecution is asking for the death penalty).

Ms. Placek has conducted seminars for the league of Women Voters and for senior citizen's groups. She presently belongs to eight different legal organizations, including the American Bar Association, American Judiciary Association, Advocated, and the American Trial Lawyer's Association. Among her many honors are the Treasures of the Women's Bar Association and a membership on the WBA's Board of Directors. She was nominated by both the Bohemian Bar Associations prestigious Weigle Award.

She served as the first woman President to the Coalition of Suburban Bar Associations, and is currently on the board of the West Suburban Bar Association and the Treasurer and Vice President of the Bohemian Lawyer's Association. Always mindful of her roots; she recently initiated and signed a Declaration of Freedom for Czechoslovakia and is currently negotiating with certain Lawyer's Guilds in Prague for a lawyer exchange and to aid the newly formed democracy in the formation of a New Constitution.

Recently she has accepted the American Bar Association's Public Service Award for her sponsorship, through the Coalition of Suburban Bar Association, of an awareness program dealing with drunk driving.

She has taught seminars for local police and the training academy of the Cook County Sheriff's Department.

HELEN VINEY PORTER, during my senior year at the University of Louisville School of Law, I

clerked for a Circuit Court Judge. He told me that federal court judge would even interview me fo clerkship and even though his recommendati would get me an interview at local law firms, hiring door would be slammed in my face becaus was female.

I interviewed with the Internal Revenue Serv and was offered work in the Chicago Region Counsel's Office. When I arrived to start work, I w told that I would be assigned to the Tax Court Divisi I got this choice position because the head of Collection Division refused to have a woman worki in his department, Alcohol and Firearms Divisi required three to five years experience, and Regional Counsel thought a woman was too delic to work in the Criminal Fraud Division.

At my first appearance before the United Sta Tax Court, the Clerk of the court inquired as to wh I was representing. He was astounded to find ou was the Commissioner of Internal Revenue. Outsi of Washington, D.C., there were no other women this position.

My boss, the Regional Counsel, encouraged to become active in bar association work. I joined Chicago Bar Association and became Chairman the Young Lawyers Committee, forerunner of Young Lawyers Section. After much participati and long hours of work, I was elected President of Women's Bar Association of Illinois, 1972-7 President of the National Association of Wom Lawyers, 1973-74; and President of the Chica Chapter of the Federal Bar Association, 1974-75. I w also an Assembly Delegate, Illinois State Association and active in the American B Association. I am currently a member of the Board Editors of the American Bar Journal.

I met my husband, Lewis Morgan Porter, Jr. at Regional Counsel's office. Our daughter Alicia was b in 1979. I continued to practice full time, be active in association work and be a wife and mother.

I left the IRS to become Associate Region Counsel, Equal Employment Opportuni Commission. There I supervised two trial teams. 1975, I became Associate Professor of law at Le University College of Law (now Northern Illin University College of Law). I taught federal taxati of individuals, corporations and partnerships; est and gift tax. Lewis was the first law school to hav full time day care center.

I left Lewis and entered private practice Northbrook specializing in tax law. In 1987 I joined by my husband and the firm Porter and Por was established.

At the time I entered law school and whe began practicing, women comprised only th percent of lawyers. It is good to see the percentage women increase so dramatically. The opportunit are there for women in the law as never before. still have the problems of child care and fam conflicts. But it is good to know that these proble can and are being resolved.

JANE HARTLEY PRATT, was born Southern Indiana and spent her childhood there a in Indianapolis. She attended Franklin College wh she graduated cum laude in 1952. She attend Indiana University School of Law at Blooming where she received her Juris Doctor in 1955.

As a college senior she was President of her Greek social fraternity. A horse-drawn float in the homecoming parade caused damage to vehicles along the route and it was her responsibility to deal with the problem. She was impressed with the assistance given by a local lawyer. In July, after graduation, she talked with him again and also to a woman lawyer in Indianapolis. Both encouraged her to enter law school. She applied, was admitted and started classes a month and a half later.

She says the subject matter in law school was almost totally theory oriented with absolutely no help as to the realities of law practice. She was the only female student enrolled in the law school there when she entered but, with one noteable exception, teachers were not biased. It was a totally male oriented atmosphere but they treated her as any other fellow student.

Her view of herself being a lawyer has not particularly changed. However, she sees long range detriment in the increasing emphasis of law as a business rather than a profession because that totally changes the emphasis as to a lawyer's responsibility. Her first job was as a legislative assistant to a congressman on Capitol Hill in Washington. Therafter her lawyer husband and she moved to Monmouth and became associated with and eventually partners in their present firm, Beal, Pratt, & Pratt. The firm is a small basically agricultural community. They do general practice with each partner keeping the others advised about current problems and changes.

She notices the most obvious change being the substantial increase in number and percentage of women in the field of law. There has been a corresponding increase in governmental regulations as affecting many areas of practice.

Because 95% or more of the WBAI activities are in Chicago, she has had little direct participation. She does meet with women lawyers in her judicial district but that has been difficult to maintain on a regular basis.

She remembers entering the law building on the first day of law school. Three male students standing at the top of the stairs snickered loudly, "She's in the wrong building." She smiled and responded, "No, she is not."

On her first trip to the Appellate Court in Ottawa, Illinois, for oral argument, there were no public restroom facilities for women in that building. One of the ladies in the Appellate Clerk's office graciously made available the facilities in one of the judge's chambers.

It has been her privilege to see and be a part of the evolution in acceptance of women as lawyers. She believes we should all be grateful to the true pioneers who in the 1800s began forcing open the door through which we can now proudly walk.

As one of the pioneer women lawyers in this geographic area, she has demonstrated that a women can successfully combine a career in law with raising a family and with community involvement.

She is married to Channing L. Pratt Sr.. They have three grown children. Their daughter is married and has two sons. Their two sons are bachelors. One is an attorney practicing in Indianapolis, specializing in health care law. She combined her family and work through the help of her partners and the support and recognition they gave to her family responsibilities.

MARY (MAMIE) KENNEDY PRESCOTT,

she was born September 3, 1878 in Galva, Illinois, the youngest of six children, raised by her widowed mother. After finishing high school, she took a business course at Brown's Business College, Galesburg, Illinois, came alone at 16 to Chicago, got a room on the near north side for $4.00 per week room and board, looked for a job as a stenographer. One of the offices she applied at was an attorney by the name of Proudfoot. He gave her the names and addresses of other lawyers to whom she went but was unsuccessful. Then Mr. Proudfoot told her he had a 16 year old daughter

whom he would not want roving the offices looking for a job. So, he hired her. She enrolled evenings at Chicago-kent College of Law and in June, 1899 was graduated, the only woman in her class. She said Henry Horner, also a member of that class buttoned on her gloves for her. She was the seventh woman in Illinois admitted to the bar.

She practiced for many years as a member of Mr. Proudfoot's office - criminal law. She told her daughter, Edith Prescott, of her first case - the lawyer was out of town, but she had done the work on the case which came up for a hearing. The judge asked if the lawyer for the prosecution was present - Ms. Prescott stood up - all 100 pounds of her - said she was present and ready. She said the man was sent to jail.

Edith Prescott, says that yer mother practiced for several years until her marriage in 1908. Edith Prescott arrived in 1910, the only child of her mother's marriage. This ended her active practice, but she did some probate work.

She did on June 18, 1956.

SANDRA K. PRINCIPE, has over 15 years
of experience primarily focussed on real estate related matters in corporate environment. She possesses additional expertise she gained from the role of General Counsel, coordinating all in-house legal matters. She has supervised ongoing interaction with outside counsel while actively involved with internal corporate issues from developing policies to negotiating complex contracts. She earned both her B.S. and J.D. from the University of Wisconsin.

She has worked for Seay Companies from 1976 to 1982 as General Counsel; Burnham Companies from 1982 to 1987 as General Counsel, Vice President and Secretary; and Continental Bank from 1987 to 1991 as Associate General Counsel. She is presently at Dalan/Jupiter, Inc. where she works as General Counsel.

AURELIA (AURIE) PUCINSKI, was
elected to Clerk of the Circuit Court of Cook County, in November of 1988, by beating former Mayor Jane Byrne in the April primary and former Alderman Edward Vrdolyak in the general election. Aurie has pledged to restore the public's confidence in the integrity of the judicial system by making the Cook County system fair, efficient and effective.

Aurie's clerk victory capped a ten year public career.

In 1980, she was elected a Carter-Mondale Delegate to the Democratic National Convention with more votes than any other delegate candidate in the nation. Aurie also began a four year position with the U.S. Small Business Administration as Regional Counsel. During that time, she assisted in the administration of a $5-billion economic development program and more than $500-million in federal loans. At the SBA Aurie was responsible for the supervision of 22 attorneys and the delivery of legal services to a staff of 430.

In 1984, Aurie established her own law firm, and was elected Commissioner to the Metropolitan Sanitary District (now known as the Water Reclamation District) with 1.2 million votes in Cook County, leading the slate of candidates for that office.

As a commissioner of the Water Reclamation District, Aurie worked to deliver new sensitivity and

responsiveness to the residents of Cook County. She led the way for the District to work cooperatively with suburban communities and local industries to resolve problems and achieve long term solutions.

Aurie prepared for her political career by working and receiving degrees in History from Catholic University in Washington, D.C. and a J. D. degree in Law from DePaul College of Law in Chicago.

Aurie is married to Jim Keithley, General Manager of WEDC Radio in Chicago. The couple lives on the Northwest side of Chicago with their three children: Rebecca, 12, Annie, 10 and Jimmy, 9.

M. DOLORES QUIROZ, passed the Illinois
Bar in 1977. From 1978 to the present she has worked as an Assistant Corporation Counsel for the City of Chicago Law Department. She has worked in the Housing Court, Traffic Court, Chancery, Municipal Branches, and Demolition Court.

She would like to see the WBAI present a nationwide policy for all the women in the U.S.A..

Her best experiences have been bringing her children to court so they can see their "mom" in action! She also liked winning some rather tough cases against some very rude male attorneys.

She is proud to be a role model to younger Hispanic women.

LESLIE RECHT, Leslie developed an early
interest in public policy issues at the University of Chicago, where she majored in political science and urban studies, graduating with a B. A. in 1970. Leslie joined the legal department of Peoples Energy Corporation upon graduation with high honors from IIT Chicago-Kent College of Law in 1974. At that time, Peoples Energy was the holding company for Peoples Gas, a local distribution company regulated by the Illinois Commerce Commission, and natural Gas Pipeline Company of America, an interstate gas pipeline company regulated by the Federal Energy Regulatory Commission. During the 1970's, the gas industry was heavily regulated, and Leslie represented these companies in regulatory proceedings concerning their rates, certificates to expand their facilities or service, in customer complaint cases, in appeals of those proceedings, and in contract negotiations. She was one of the few women then practicing energy law, and she obtained broad experience using her trial and negotiating skills, her knowledge of accounting, environmental and tax issues, as well as political and public policy issues working with engineers and technicians in the natural gas industry.

In 1981 Leslie entered private practice, becoming a partner in Springer, Castedet & Kurlander, a firm specializing in public utility and energy law, representing a major gas and electric distribution company in Iowa, Illinois, Minnesota and at FERC. Leslie's firm merged with Defrees & Fiske in 1985, and her practice has changed as the utility industry has changed from heavy regulation to a competitive environment. These changes have required energy lawyers to work in new areas such as anti-trust. Leslie enjoys practicing in an exciting area of the law, dealing with public policy energy issues which affect everyone.

Leslie and her husband, Mike Fultz, have restored a Victorian home and garden on Chicago's

Near West Side in the West Jackson Boulevard Historic District and support historic preservation. She is active in her neighborhood association in area development issues, and as a board member of Friends of Downtown and an officer of the Grant Park Advisory Council she works to shape public policy discussion and decisions. Leslie was a Board member of WBAI from 1985-87, was a member of the WBAI Lawyer Referral Service Commission from 1986-88, and has been an active member of the WBAI Foundation.

CATHERINE C. REITER, born New York, NY, May 8, 1950; admitted to bar, 1981, Illinois. U. S. District Court, Northern District of Illinois. Member of the trial bar of the U. S. District Court, Northern District of Illinois.

Education: University of Michigan (B.S. in Nursing, cum laude, 1972); DePaul University (J.D., 1981).

Honoraries: Sigma Theta Tau, Mortar Board. Member: Chicago, Illinois State and American Bar Associations, Women's Bar Association, Illinois Association of Defense Trial Counsel, Illinois Association of Hospital Attorneys. Concentrating in medical, nursing and hospital malpractice and products liability as a trial lawyer and director of Pretzel & Stouffer, Chtd.

MONICA D. REYNOLDS, born November 5, 1920 in Gibson City, Illinois. Married June 19, 1948 to Jay J. Reynolds, Jr., Children: one daughter-deceased, five sons.

Graduated DePaul University College of Law 1947 (J.D.). Admitted to State and Federal Court in 1947.

Judge Reynolds has been in private practice, travelled with husband, worked with the Corporation Counsel's Office, has been a Judge in the Mechanics Lien Division and Domestic Relations Division and is currently a Chancellor.

She has been a frequent lecturer, mostly in the field of Domestic Relations. Lectured at Loyola Academy, Regina High School, Deerfield High School, Phoenix Club Meetings, Mothers Without Custody Meetings, and First National Bank Employee Assistance Program; also a guest lecturer on Oprah Winfrey Show, twice on the Norman Marx Show, Carol Marin Show and the Lee Phillips Show.

She was one of five judges appointed to serve on the Judicial Selections Committee for the Circuit Court to evaluate judicial candidates for the years 1985 through the present; selected to serve as an assignment judge and "team captain" in the Domestic

Relations Division; "uniformly rated among the highest in legal knowledge, judicial conduct and temperament" of the judges in the Domestic Relations Division by an opinion survey conducted by the Chicago Tribune in October, 1982 of the lawyers who appear in that division; selected to chair the Domestic Relations Section seminar at the Illinois Judicial Conference for the third time; one of five judges chosen to serve on the Committee to Evaluate and Select Candidates to fill the vacancy on the Board of Elections; selected as a guest lecturer by Loyola University School of Law, Rome Center, Italy, and not only lectured there, but also presented papers to the Italian Parliament on the subjects of comparative divorce law and malpractice in the United states; named in Chicago Magazine as one of the City's "Hidden Treasures" being referred to as a "Voice of Wisdom and Sanity", one of five judges on the Committee of Finance of the Circuit Court; lectured frequently on topics ranging from motion practice to mediation.

Reynolds has been a WBAI member since 1946. She has served on many committees, and chaired the Judges' reception for several years.

KATHRYN BARASA RINELLA, born in Wilmette, Illinois. My parents moved to Chicago when I was very young. I attended DePaul University and at the age of 18, I entered the DePaul College of Law. I was admitted to practice in the State of Illinois in 1928. Shortly after I was admitted, I became an attorney in the City Attorney's Office of Chicago. Only personal injury cases against the City were tried in this office. After three years in the City Attorney's Office, I joined my father, Bernard P. Barasa's law firm. In 1934 I was married to Samuel A. Rinella also an attorney. We had two sons, Bernard and Richard, who are married and living in the Chicago area. Both are practicing attorneys in Chicago. I have three grandchildren. I was president of the Women's Bar Association of Illinois in 1937-38. During my term of office we worked diligently for the passage of legislation giving women the right to serve on juries and the requiring of a license to drive a car. It was a most interesting and rewarding year for me. In 1941 the Rinella family moved to the suburb of Northbrook, Illinois. In 1942 I became a charter member of a Northbrook Service Club which is very active to this day engaging in civic projects. In 1947 I was one of the founders of the Northbrook Chapter of the League of Women Voters of Illinois. In 1971 my husband and I moved to Chicago where I am now a resident. In 1975 I was made a trustee of DePaul University. For six years I served as an active trustee and then was made an honorary trustee which I am today. In 1982 my husband passed away after we had enjoyed 48 years of a happy married life. I proudly look at the legacy that our two sons are continuing in the law firm of Rinella and Rinella, Ltd.

The contrast between the status of women in the law today and in my day is almost unbelievable with 40% of the students in the law schools being women and women attorneys in every field of the law. I am sure the women lawyers of my day who are still alive must be saying, "Well Done".

Ms. Rinella passed away in August of 1991 after submitting her biography, four days after her 85th birthday.

JOAN M. RIORDAN, I decided to be a lawyer at the ripe old age of ten. It was a decidedly unusual choice of profession for the times, and considering the fact that my family did not even know a lawyer in those days.

For the younger daughter of immigrant parents, it was an ambition unusual enough for my teachers and classmates at St. Thomas the Apostle Grammar School on the south side of Chicago, to remember years later.

Throughout the rest of grammar school and high school, the idea persisted. It was fostered by my parents supportive attitude. From the time my sister and I had started first grade, we had know that we were to be the first college graduates in the family. We also knew that although our parents would help as much as they could, we would have to work our way through school or get scholarships to pay the tuition. We did both!

By the time I graduated from DePaul Law School my sister, who had a Masters Degree in History, was working on a Master's Degree in Library Science. I was a good thing that my parents liked going to graduations!

When I graduated from DePaul Law School in the mid 1960s, law was still regarded as a man's profession. The school placement service did no help women find legal jobs. We were still being told by law firms: "Sorry, we don't hire women lawyers". Most firms would not even grant us an interview.

After several months of hearing the same thing when I called for an interview, I finally told the head of one law firm on the telephone that I wasn't a woman but a female impersonator. I certainly would not suggest saying anything like that today, but back in the mid 1960s, it was brash enough thing to say to get me the interview and the job.

It wasn't a good job, but at least it was a job finally as a lawyer! I didn't stay long in my first job but then neither did any of my male counterparts. Although no one accused them of leaving simply because they were "men". Within a few years, once more with the encouragement of my parents, I opened my own law office and remained a sole practioner until 1981, when my husband and I formed the partnership of Riordan & Robbins.

During those first years as a lawyer, I formed lasting friendships with other young attorneys who were members of the WBA. We were "networking" before we knew what "networking" meant. We met for lunch one day a week at a big round table at the CBA (the only one regularly reserved by females) surrounded by our male counterparts, and shared our legal experiences and knowledge. We encouraged each other and supported each other, and we sure laughed a lot at those lunch meetings! It was in the time honored tradition of the WBA and one that hope never ends!

DEBORAH SULLIVAN ROBERTS, born in Oak Park, Illinois in 1953 to Anne M. Sullivan and John R. Sullivan, the youngest of eight children (Actually nine, however one died in infancy). Both o my parents were attorneys, however my father deceased. I attended DePaul University from 1971 1974 and then transferred to Southern Illinoi University where I received my B. S. degree in 1975 i Speech Communications. I attended Portland Stat University form 1976-1978 and there received my M S. in Speech Communications, I went to work fo communications companies including MCI until 198 when I entered DePaul University Law School an graduated in 1990. I was admitted in May of 1990 a the age of 37.

My parents naturally played a big role in m desire to become an attorney. My father practice general law. My mother specializes in probate an real estate. She is my real mentor. I admired how sh could comfortably juggle her career and home life and with eight children. I never felt slighted as a chil even though she was working. I admire her for all he great organizational skills, her ability to enter a man ld and not feel bitter about the competition but rather face it as a positive challenge. For me the areas probate and real estate are ideal. I enjoy these areas cause I truly feel I am helping people. With the right to die" issue so important today we can make tremendous impact on our society. I am especially interested in helping the elderly and in the future would like to do more in this area. I feel their rights are especially in jeopardy and they are not educated to take full advantage of the law. I also enjoy residential real estate work as it often benefits people when they are making a big step in their lives. It is often an exciting period and generally accomplished easily and without conflict. We have handled a few adoptions as well which are most rewarding. It's a win-win situation. The areas of probate and real estate are especially well fitted to my role as a wife and mother of three. Julia is three and one half years, Steward is two and one half years, and Anne (named after my mother) is three months. Julia and Stewart were born while I was in law school. Both within weeks of my last final. I was pregnant with Anne while studying for the bar. I feel this made both labors (of birth and school) easier as I had little time to worry about one or the other. My husband was tremendously supportive as well!

Since graduation I have joined my mother in our partnership of Sullivan and Sullivan. From the start I wanted to follow in her foot steps. I feel so fortunate to have such a tremendous role model. I work only three days per week so that I can be with my children. She still works five to six days and she is 80 years old. She has as much or more energy than I do. We both take advantage of afternoon naps or breaks to get over the afternoon slumps. We are one of the few mother-daughter partnerships I know of. I hope and expect to see more and more of this in the future. I am currently a member of the WBAI association and find it very helpful. The Probate committee is especially enjoyable and interesting. We keep up with current issues and share information and ideas which is invaluable.

RONNIE I. ROBBINS, partner, Robbins & Robbins, Ltd., in 1953 I was one of two females in a freshman law school class of 77. These numbers were standard for the time. People often asked me if my father was an attorney. Typically early women law students were daughters of attorneys or came from educated families, where their aspirations were nurtured and the way was smoothed for future employment.

My dad was not an attorney, he was a taxi-cab driver. My orientation was akin to many of the males at DePaul University. I resided at home with my parents during my undergraduate and law school days, commuting to school by way of the elevated train, straphanging with an armful of law books pressed to my chest. (It was unfashionable for women to carry briefcases in the '50's) To finance my education I worked full time each summer and part-time 20 hours weekly, during the school year. Student loans were then unknown.

My working contemporaries and I exemplified the American dream. We were upwardly mobile and the law was our vehicle. All one needed was the ability and the will!

Without connections and absent "clout" of any

kind upon graduation, resume in hand, I attacked LaSalle Street seeking employment. I went from building to building "cold calling" on lawyers and law firms. Surprisingly enough I obtained a number of interviews. I suspect that, in many instances, the hiring attorney merely wanted to see this female oddity that had presented herself to his receptionist requesting legal employment.

In my numerous interviews the question I was most often asked was, "do you type?" I did type. However, any job offers I received from those questioners, I summarily rejected. I knew what I would be doing for them and it would not be practicing law. In the '50's, in the average law office, a good secretary earned more than an entry level attorney. Thereupon, to hire an attorney who could also double as a secretary, that was a real find.

My persistence was rewarded. I obtained an excellent job with an insurance company law firm doing personal injury defense. I was with them for three years and obtained an invaluable education in the field of torts. I carried a case load of 300 files from the inception of litigation to closure, by either settlement or verdict. In the late '50's, I think I was the only woman in Chicago handling volume personal injury defense.

During this period I married a young, gutsy attorney similiar to myself. He was self-employed. I joined him, switching to the plaintiff's side of personal injury. We formed our own firm and have practiced law together for 30 years. We're now serving our second generation of clients.

Family oriented in the law, my younger brother worked his way through law school as our law clerk. Our son joined us in the practice, upon his law school graduation in 1986. Our daughter, an industrial psychologist, is often consulted for ideas.

In those precious free hours, I arbitrate uninsured motorist claims for the American Arbitration Association. This June I will complete the University of Chicago's four year evening course of study in the Great Books.

My advice to all young women coping with the dual responsibilities of career and family, - with planning, persistence and discipline you can have it all!

MARY STRETCH ROOT, following her admittance to the Bar in 1933 was employed in the legal department of Century Metalcraft Corporation. Subsequently she was employed during the depression by the Chicago Title and Trust Company in its Release Department. After serving as a volunteer in the Probate Court, to gain experience, she was recommended to the American Surety Company to close their two hundred open estates. When the estates were closed she entered private practice, mainly in the field of drafting wills, probating estates and handling real estate transactions. In addition she represented the National Catholic Society of Foresters, a fraternal insurance company, for twenty two years, a large Chicago Dairy and the Resurrection Hospital while serving on its Lay Advisory Board. She was President of the Resurrection Hospital Auxiliary and served as it Counselor from 1954 to date.

In 1937 she married John E. Root and had four children, one of whom is an attorney, specializing in mining and environmental Law in Colorado. She

volunteers her services every Friday evening in the Resurrection Hospital Auxiliary Retail Shop. Since December of 1987, she practices law on a limited basis.

ALLEN F. ROSIN

ESTHER ROTHSTEIN, back in 1946, I was urged to go to law school by two members of the Women's Bar Association of Illinois, namely, Phyllis M. Kelley, the first woman to be appointed an Assistant Probate Judge and Etha Beartrice Fox who had an outstanding career in government service. Both were graduates of Chicago-Kent College of Law which had a night law school. I am forever grateful to them, and to McCarthy and Levin, the law firm where I was then working as a secretary, and where I am presently a partner, for setting me on the legal path. I graduated in 1949 and my love affair with the legal profession has never dimmed.

I have had a satisfying and gratifying career. It has been more than a good living—it has been a good life. I, early on, became impressed with the benefits of legal training besides that of earning a livelihood. It also was a means for serving the community, of contributing towards making government more responsive and in meeting unmet legal needs of the less fortunate and indigent.

I was privileged to serve as president of the Women's Bar in 1961-1962, which proved to be a wonderfully fertile field for lifelong friendships, a great learning experience for leadership and a stepping stone to many achievements.

I was also gratified to be the first woman in 103 years to serve as president of the largest urban bar in the United States, The Chicago Bar Association, and a few years later, to serve as president of its Foundation. There were other firsts I hope helped smooth the path for others. I was the first woman to serve as a director of the Illinois Bell Telephone Company, the first woman trustee of Illinois Institute of Technology and presently a Life Trustee, the first to chair a committee of the American Bar Association, the Gavel Awards Committee, and the first woman lawyer to be elected to the Chicago Hall of Fame.

I am pleased to have been instrumental in encouraging many young men and women to enter the legal profession. In looking back over 40 years, I feel that there are many unmet challenges. While women have made some dramatic strides, there are many, many closed avenues. For the profession as a whole, the challenges are equally as great. The attendant pressures of new techniques, the erosion of professionalism and the shrinking world give real need for solutions to problems in reaching the goal of equal justice for all.

Certainly the law has been the bulwark of our democracy, and if we are to be a strong beacon for the future, our profession needs strengthening. I am proud to be a part of the Women's Bar Association of Illinois which is playing a major role in facing important issues and working toward their solution, and through its Foundation Scholarship Program for deserving and needy young women law students, in making it possible for them to become lawyers and leaders for a better society.

ILANA DIAMOND ROVNER, I am often asked whether it was always my ambition to be a federal judge. Not only was it never my ambition, it was not even something I dared dream about. In 1960, when I entered law school, only two women in the history of this country had ever been federal judges. They were viewed as super humans of some sort. How could I even dare to imagine that I might someday join them. Further, mine was an era in which very few women attended law school. I was one of three women in my freshman class at Georgetown Law School, and, after Thanksgiving break, one of only two women.

I am incredibly fortunate to have the opportunity to serve in the federal judiciary, and I am very aware of how grateful I should be. I was born in Riga, Latvia in August of 1938. My parents and I were able to escape the madness of World War II. When other children were told bedtime stories, I was taught how the rule of law had failed — how men had misused constitutions and laws, and how whole bodies of government had been undermined by madness. Small wonder that by age seven I was writing school essays on being a lawyer — wanting to use the law for good ends — "to do good", in the words of a seven year old. The neighbors called me Portia. It never occured to me that there were few women lawyers — nor did it ever occur to me that I could not try to be a lawyer or that I could not try to be a useful person and make society better somehow.

I view myself as someone who has had enormous good fortune and been the beneficiary of very good timing. After I graduated from law school, I retired to have a family and did not return to work until 1972, when our son started school. My timing could not have been better. After doing research for Richard J. Phelan, presently of Phelan, Pope & John, I was hired by Judge James B. Parsons of the federal bench, who was making a concerted effort to hire a female law clerk — his first. I was with the judge of a year and a half, and in 1973 I joined the U. S. Attorney's Office as an Assistant U. S. Attorney under Governor James R. Thompson. In early 1974, I became the first woman in the history of the office to be a supervisor. After four years in that office, I joined Governor Thompson as his deputy and legal counsel. In November 1984 I was sworn in as United States District Judge for the Northern District of Illinois.

The Woman's Bar Association of Illinois has been a great part of my professional life. I recall luncheon meetings that took place some 21 years ago at a solitary table at the far end of the Chicago Bar Association's dining room. What a joy it is to see the remarkable changes that have occured for women in the law since those years.

Above all, I realized how fortunate I have been to have parents who would not give up, a land such as this one to flee to, the educational and professional opportunities that have come my way; and above all, supportive and caring family and friends.

LINDA-LILLIAN B. ROZHON, an active trial lawyer and native of Berwyn, Illinois, Ms. Rozhon worked as a lawyer since 1955. She served in the Army during World War II, where she was a First Lieutenant in the Military Intelligence Division of the War Department attached to the Adjutant General's Office. She finished her tour of duty in Germany where she assisted in the evacuation of hundreds of Czechs to freedom from the Nazis and the Russian occupation.

After the war, Ms. Rozhon attended DePaul University, where she graduated Magna Cum Laude with her degree in philosophy and then her doctorate in law.

During her years as a practicing attorney in Berwyn and Oak Park, Ms. Rozhon was very active in community and veteran affairs. In addition to WBAI and other bar associations, Ms. Rozhon was also active and held office in the Veteran of Foreign Wars Berwyn Post 2378, and the Fourth district Department of the VFW. She was a member of the Disabled American Veterans Westown Chapter #22.

Ms. Rozhon passed away in 1986 after a short illness. She was survived by one sister Geraldine Rozhon Kolarik and nieces Barbara Sedivec and GeraLind Kolarik and grand niece Mary A. Sedivec.

AUDREY HOLZER RUBIN, is Senior Counsel at Covia Partnership, one of the world's largest developers and distributors of computer systems and software for the travel industry.

Prior to joining Covia, she was a partner at the Chicago law firm of Gottleib and Schwartz, specializing in commercial litigation. She was an associate with Burditt Bowles and Radzius (formerly Burditt and Clakins) from 1978-1982.

Ms. Rubin graduated cum laude from Yale University in 1975 and received her law degree from Northwestern University Law School in 1978.

She was the chairperson of the "Illinois Task Force on Gender Bias in the Courts", which, after two years of extensive research, published its several hundred page report in July, 1990. Ms. Rubin has served as a member of the Chicago Bar Association Board of Managers and as a director of the Illinois State Bar Association Young Lawyers Division. She has served on numerous committees of the Chicago, Illinois and Women's Bar Associations. The Chicago Sun Times and Today's Chicago Woman selected her as one of "One Hundred Women Shaping Chicago's Future".

Ms. Rubin is a a frequent lecturer and author on the topic of Gender Bias in the Law and Courts. She also has been a featured performer in the Chicago Bar Association's annual Christmas Spirits production since joining the show in 1978. She is married to lawyer and Christmas Spirits director E. Leonard Rubin, with whom Ms. Rubin has two children: Margot, born January 1985 and Bette, born December 1988.

EVELYN STARR RUPERT, in 1930 I was the one woman in the day class of DePaul Law

School. I gave the fact no real thought a I wanted be a lawyer like my hero Clarence Darrow - peri

But, when I walked on the stage of the Op House where our graduation was held I was gree by thunderous applause. I realized the public accep and fully approved a woman as a lawyer. Followi this experience I did not further question my stat

I had the wonderful opportunity of associati in the very early years of the Woman's Bar Associati with lawyers like Irene McCormick, Helen Cir and Pearl Hart. We must not forget these real pionee

My first legal experience was the Legal Aid the United Charities. Following this for six year was in private practice as a member of a four lawy firm. This prepared me for my real legal goal-the C of Chicago then Cook County Department of Welfa where we legally, socially and financially servic the indigent. Judge Komosa, then a Magistra presided over our "Welfare Court" where Patern Cases were heard. My thanks to her.

Our Division worked closely with the Juven Court involving dependent children, the Cour Court on independent adoptions, the enforcement divorce orders of alimony and child support, a liens on personal injury cases, insurance matters,

A number of attorney's working with me ha become judges, politicians and prominent attorne

After a 31 year period I retired with a "thank to the people who indicated approval at r graduation and sent me on my way to become Direc of Court Services of Cook County Department Welfare.

There are many paths to travel in the practice law.

MIRIAM SANTOS, she has combined gr personal motivation with a deep community conce to become a rising star in Chicago city governme At age 33 she became the first female and first Hispa to serve as City Treasurer of Chicago. She w appointed to the position in April of 1989 by Ma Richard M. Daley, and was later elected to the offi receiving 71% of the vote, in April 1991.

In the two years since taking office she h embarked on an ambitious campaign to modern her office and to maximize its productivity for c taxpayers.

As the city's banker, the Office of the C Treasurer manages an annual cash flow of $40 billi Santos' accomplishments in the Treasurer's Off include the privatization of a former costly employ check cashing service at City Hall; the full automati of the office resulting in more efficient investm practices; and a 55.2 % cut in city banking fees. T

Changes implemented under Santos have resulted in an additional $7 million in investable city revenue.

Miriam Santos has also aggressively worked with minority and other community-based financial institutions, and has provided equity in the distribution of contracts, as well as office hiring. Recently, she announced the creation of a linked deposit program which would provide loans to minority and women-owned businesses.

Prior to her appointment as Treasurer, Santos was at Illinois Bell's manager of customer and community relations. She directed a division of 60 employees and served as the company's link to area schools, community programs and human service agencies. Ms. Santos was also a senior attorney for the company.

Santos' public service career began in 1983 as a deputy director of the Child Support Enforcement Division in the Cook County State's Attorney's Ofice. She also directed the Aspira Center for Educational Equity in Washington, D.C. — a national organization promoting educational opportunities for HIspanics — and later served with Chicago United, working to bring business resources to bear on problems confronting the city's Hispanic community. Santos was the statewide Hispanic coordinator for Adlai Stevenson's gubernatorial campaign in 1982.

Miriam Santos was born in Gary, Indiana to a steelworker father and a homemaker mother. Her Puerto Rican-born parents always stressed the importance of education to their five children, and in 1973 Miriam became the first member of her family to attend college.

She obtained a bachelor's degree from DePaul University in 1977, and in 1980 a law degree. In June 1990 she received her master's of management degree (M.B.A.) from Northwestern University's Kellogg School of Business. Santos has been the recipient of three fellowships and is a member of numerous civic boards and foundations including the Finance Council of the Archdiocese of Chicago, the Executive Committee of the Board of Directors of the Illinois Democratic Leadership Council, the Advisory Board of the Make-A-Wish Foundation, the Junior League Advisory Board, and the University of Illinois College of Medicine Corporate Advisory Board.

MARCIA SABESIN, spent her childhood in New York City. She attended Russell Sage College, in Troy, N.Y. for a Business degree in Computer Programming. She attended Memphis State University School of Law for her law degree from 1976 to 1979.

She decided to be a lawyer because her father was a lawyer. She grew up in an atmosphere of law practice—always was interested in legal and business-related situations.

She enjoyed her studies of law. She found her general experiences with the law school unpleasant, because the faculty and administration were narrow minded regarding women.

She worked for one law firm in Memphis for six years, concentrating in business law, tax and estate planning. She moved to Chicago when her husband accepted a position there. She now practices as a sole practitioner specializing in business law, tax and estate planning. She enjoys working with people and helping them solve their problems.

She enjoyed serving as chair of Probate and Estate Planning Committee for WBAI and attending committee meetings over the past three years and networking with female attorneys. She says moving to Chicago has been difficult for her career, and this is a problem for female professionals, who have to move because their husbands make a career change.

She has successfully accomplished combining an important professional career without too much sacrifice of what she considers her responsibilities to her husband, her children, and her home.

She is married with three children. She went to law school after the children were born. She has found that by working hard and being efficient she could successfully combine her work with family reponsibilities and not sacrifice either.

SUSAN CAROL SALITA, she is admitted to the Illinois Supreme Court, Federal District Court for the Northern District of Illinois and the United States Court of Appeals, Seventh Circuit.

She is currently Assistant State's Attorney in the Cook County State's Attorney's Office. She has worked for the Civil Actions Bureau, Criminal Prosecutions Bureau, and the City Colleges of Chicago, Office of the Attorney.

She received a J.D. from DePaul University in 1985, an M.A. in Higher Education Administration from The Ohio State University, and a B.A. in History from the University of Colorado.

EDITH S. SAMPSON, she was trim and dynamic and knew that the eyes of the world were on her as she stepped onto the stage of the United Nations as one of the alternate U. S. Delegates to the Fifth General Assembly. It was still something akin to fantasy, that she had been chosen as the first Negro to represent the United States in the world organization.

Sitting at the great conference table of nations, she was a bright symbol of the progress the United States had made in race relations - an eloquent example of the kind of opportunity that can come in a free society to anyone who serves wholeheartedly. She was a prominent Chicago attorney, and was in Boston to deliver a lecture when the momentous phone call from the State Department trilled in her room. "I am calling for the President of the United States," said a voice to her. "Just who is ribbing me?" she laughed, then grew silent as the voice continued, "The President wonders if you would accept his invitation to become a member of the American delegation to the United Nations General Assembly." She accepted the position.

JOANNE H. SAUNDERS, she was one of three women admitted to the United States District Court for the District of Columbia in 1959. She was the only woman graduate from DePaul Law School that year. Since then she has been in active practice.

She was employed by the Federal Government until she entered private practice specializing in Family Law and Labor Law with emphasis in Immigration matters. She has been an active bar association member and chaired various committees of the Illinois State Bar Association and the Chicago Bar Association. She presently is a Director of the Illinois Bar Foundation.

She was a Commissioner of the Department of Energy and Environmental Protection of the City of Chicago.

LONNA SAUNDERS, she has been a member of WBAI since 1985. She was graduated from Northwestern University School of Law and received her bachelor's degree from Vassar College with Departmental Honors in Political Science. She currently serves as chair of the Law and Media Committee of the American Bar Association, Young Lawyers Division.

She is also a staff attorney for the Better Government Association; litigation associate at Arvey,

Hodes, Costello & Burman; and volunteer attorney for Lawyers for the Creative Arts and Chicago Volunteer Legal Service. She has worked as a television news anchor at WCIV-TV in Chicago and a radio call-in talk host for WIND and WMAQ, Chicago.

SIMA Z. SAVIN, she was born in Chicago, Illinois and graduated with honors from Chicago-Kent College of Law. She was the only woman member of the June, 1938 graduating class. She attended night classes while employed full-time as a legal secretary; admitted to the Illinois Bar in December of 1938. Married Bernard Savin, a lawyer, and devoted the years 1946-1956 to rearing four children.

She was employed by the State of Illinois in the Division of Unemployment Compensation—Claims Deputy and Deputy Reviewer; Federal Government, Office of Price Administration—Attorney, Regional Rent Office, Commerce Clearing House, Inc.

ANDREA M. SCHLEIFER, graduated from Indiana University with her A.B. in 1970. She attended Loyola University and received her Juris Doctor in 1979. She has worked for Mullane & Schiller, 1980-81; Kaszak & Schleifer, 1986-87; and presently at Andrea M. Schleifer & Associates, from 1981-86 and 1987 to the present.

She is a general practitioner with an emphasis in family law, discrimination, employment and general civil litigation. She has handled over 2000 contested hearings and trials in dissolution, paternity, custody, post decree, appeals, discrimination, juvenile and misdemeanor. She has been appointed by the court as attorney for children in approximately 35 domestic relations and paternity cases.

She belongs to the following professional organizations: the Illinois State Bar Association, the Chicago Bar Association, the American Bar Association, the Decalogue Society, and the Women's Bar Association of Illinois. Served on the Planning and Steering Committes of the Illinois Task Force on Gender Bias in the Courts, the American Arbitration Association, Neighborhood Justice of Chicago, was the 1987-88 president of the Illinois Women's Agenda, was the founder of the Illinois Task Force on Child Support, was the legal advisor for the Illinois Council Against Parental Child Abduction, the Child Abused Women Coalition, and is on the steering committee of the Cook County Democratic Women.

RUTH ANN SCHMITT, was born on January 19, 1949 in Rochester, NY. She received her

Certificate d'Assiditute from the Universite de Grenoble, France, in 1970; her B.A. from Valparaiso University, Valparaise, IN., in 1971; and her Juris Doctor from Depaul University College of Law in 1974.

She is affiliate with the American Bar Association, the Chicago Bar Association, the Illinois State Bar Association, the Women's Bar Association of Illinois, the Chicago Council of Lawyers, the National Association of IOLTA Programs, and the Donors Forum of Chicago.

She has been employed by the American Bar Association as National Pro Bono Coordinator, the Chicago Volunteer Legal Services Foundation as Assistant Director, and presently with the Lawyers Trust Fund of Illinois as Executive Director.

She feels her accomplishments are having a child, building the organizational structure of the Lawyers Trust Fund, securing funding for the Illinois Legal Needs Study, and producing a video on Pro Bono Attorneys. She has notices that she has gotten more tolerant thru her years as a lawyer.

Ruth's honors include the 1984 Maurice Weigle Award, 1985 South Chicago Legal Clinic Outstanding Service Award and 1990 Public Interest Law Institute Distinguished Public Service award.

MARILYN JEAN SCHRAMM, she was born and raised in Elmwood Park, a northwest middle class suburb of Chicago. While working full-time as a data processing clerk, she began to realize the need for and benefit of a college education. With the help of scholarships and loans and working 25-30 hours per week as a keypunch operator, she managed to get through DePaul University in four years, graduating with a B.A. in Political Science.

She attended Northwestern University Law School. The competitiveness of the first year of law school caught her by surprise and she began to question her choice of profession. She decided to join the Joint Degree Program (JD/PhD) at Northwestern adding at least another year of schooling studying Law and Politics at the Graduate School in Evanston.

She took her Law Degree and a Master of Arts in 1981 (choosing not to finish the PhD Program) and actually began to practice law. When the objective of becoming a lawyer was first set, it was not with the thought in mind of aspiring to work in a large law firm.

Nevertheless, the first four years of this career were spent as an Associate at Sidley & Austin never quite satisfied and never quite sure what would satisfy. The last five years have been spent as corporate counsel at The Quaker Oats Company. The following questions remain unanswered today but hopefully will have answers in the future: "Was it all worth it?" and "Where do we go from here?"

ANASTASIA LUKA SCHUPP, grew up on the southwest side of Chicago. She attended Loyola University from 1962 to 1966 and graduated with her Juris Doctor from Loyola in 1977.

She found law school to be exhilarating, but the practice of law became more clerical than she anticipated. She has been in general practice since 1982. She would like to do some issue oriented volunteer work in varied fields such as elder care and mental health law.

She dislikes the lack of preparation of other attorneys. She feels accomplished in gaining her professional status. She has noticed the change from law as a profession to law as a business because it is becoming more commercialized.

In WBAI she chaired a committee and wrote for the newsletter. She comments that the amount of responsibility an attorney undertakes is not commensurate with solo practitioner fees.

She is married with one son Bill.

JOANNE SEVICK SHEA, grew up in Chicago's west suburban area. She attended Marquette University from 1955-1957, transferred to DePaul and received her B.A. in 1958. She received her J.D. from DePaul University in 1961.

She was one of two females in her law school class in the late 50's and early 60's. Attitudes ranged from a feeling of total protection from other students or professors — or one of why are you here? The subject matter of her classes was not as elective as it is today.

Her father and uncles were lawyers and this influenced her to go into law. When she entered the work force the public was not ready to accept female attorneys in many areas.

She has been employed as an attorney at the Northern Trust Company. She presently has her own practice acting in capacities with the government. She is a member of the Prisoner Review Board appointed by the governor. She is one of two attorneys sitting on the board which enable, her to weigh evidence more readily in violation, good conduct and clemency than her fellow members.

She considers her accomplishments to be trying to do it all, wife, mother, and lawyer, in the 60's and early 70's when that wasn't a very popular position. She has noticed more acceptance of the woman attorney. She has served on the board of WBAI and various committees through the years.

She is married to an attorney. They have one daughter who is a J.D./M.B.A.. She feels comfortable with her life — had she been born 15 years later she would have put more emphasis on her career and less on her family.

NANCY DREW SHEEHAN, she was elected Commissioner of the Metropolitan Water Reclamation District and became the first woman vice president of the nine member Board of Commissioners.

Prior to her election, she worked as a prosecutor for the Cook County State's Attorney's Office in the Environmental Law and Child Support Divisions. She was a high school teacher for the Chicago Board of Education for seventeen years.

She graduated from Mother McAuley Liberal Arts High School in Chicago and received a Bachelor of Arts Degree from St. Mary's College of Notre Dame, a Master of Science Degree in Education at Northeastern Illinois University and a Juris Doctor from The John Marshall Law School. She also studied at the London School of Economics.

She is Chairperson of the Committees on Judiciary and Purchasing for the District. She developed an educational program in which qualified staff members go to schools within the District, teaching the history of the District and the role it plays in the protection of our waters. She also initiated

the production of an educational coloring book for the lower grades.

She was the first woman to be elected President of the Illinois Association of Wastewater Agencies.

KAREN G. SHIELDS, grew up in southwest Florida in a very small unicorporated community called New Zion. She graduated high school in Arcadia, FL. She atteded the University of Illinois, Chicago Circle, from September 1974 through August 1977. She then attended the DePaul University School of Law from September 1977 through June 1980.

She wanted to be a public defender, defending those who had no one to defend them. She did not understand what law school was about until the end of the first year. Then she began to enjoy it and could not wait to get hands on training. Since graduating, she has loved the practice of law — something she anticipated, but did not know for sure until she experienced it. She loves being a lawyer, but hates asking for money.

She spent the first two years in private practice doing whatever came her way and doing many cases for one of the CVLS clinics. In May 1982, she became an assistant public defender. She worked in Juvenile Court in Abuse and Neglect and in Delinquency for three and one half years, then Felony Trial and Homicide Task Force for five and one half years. Recently, she went into private solo practice with a special emphasis on criminal defense.

In her estimation, her most major accomplishment is to have graduated from high school, college and law school while coming from an environment which did not especially value the high school graduation.

For over ten years she has worked in support of abortion rights. She has been on the board of Illinois NARAL for all these years, serving as its chair for three. She also served on the National NARAL board for five years, serving as its chair for three. It is important that women support the right to control their own bodies and destinies. It is a struggle which will not, unfortunately, go away in her lifetime and one which she will never desert.

CAROLE SIEGEL, she was a native of the Back of the Yards neighborhood of Chicago and a graduate of St. Basil's grammar school and Lindblom High School. The Yards are, of course, the stockyards for which Chicago was world-famous. After high school she began her professional career as a secretary for Hertz, the rent-a-car company.

She went to college part time until the children could make their own lunches, and eventually was able to go full time at Rosary College where she majored in English and Philosophy. At Loyola Law School WBAI member, now Dean Nina Appel, was Carole's torte professor. Carole recalls her as a "wonderful teacher." She clerked for a small firm then worked on "space for services" from them, and finally established her own practice specializing in domestic relations. Husband Gerald is head of Gerald Siegel and Associates which designed WBAI's 70th & 75th Anniversary Calendars and assorted flyers. Carole was WBAI's 1991-92 president.

GERALDINE C. SIMMONS, Native Chicagoan. Graduate of Chicago public schools osevelt University, John Marshall Law School (John arshall Law Review). Divorced; mother of one ughter. Practice of Law: Partner in Salone, nmons, Murray & Associates, concentrating in al estate, probate, and general civil practice. Former structor, Lawyer's Assistance Program, Roosevelt niversity. Former judicial law clerk, Illinois ppellate Court. Former Staff Appointments; ommission on Judicial Compensation; Commission Judicial Redistricting; Ad Hoc Committee on dicial Evaluations; Commitee on Law Related ucation. CCBA: Board of Directors. Member: icago Bar Association, American Bar Association, omen's Bar Association, Former Board Member, ack Women Lawyer's Association Memeber, nerican Bar Association Treasurer, Women wyers Division, National Bar Association Board ember, Women's Law Group. John Marshall Law hool Alumni Association, 2nd Vice President. Civic tivities: Alpha Gamma Pi Sorority, nic., Bylaws ommittee Parkway Community House, Board ember. African-American Economical evelopment Task Force, member. CCBA ommunity Law Project, panel attorney. lawyers for e Creative Arts, panel attorney. Judge and Brief rader for Moot Court Competitions at John Marshall w School and DePaul University Law School. urch Attorney, member of Lincoln Guild, Lincoln emorical Congregational United Church of Christ. .B.E.L.D.E.F., Inc., panel attorney. ISBA/CCBA ople's Law School, instructor. Past president, Cook unty Bar Association.

JEANNE HURLEY SIMON, she was elected the Illinois House of Representatives in 1956 to present the district including Evanston, Wilmette, innetka and Glencoe. She won reelection two ars later. It was there she met Paul Simon, a presentative from Troy in Southern Illinois, now a .S. Senator from Illinois. They married on April 21, 60, becoming the first husband-wife team in the story of the Illinois General Assembly.

She is a graduate of Barat College in Lake Forest d Northwestern University Law School. An torney, she began her career as an assistant Cook unty State's Attorney. She did not seek reelection the House after moving with her husband to Troy. e has been active helping her husband in his mpaigns for the legislature, lieutenant governor, ngress, Senate and President.

She was appointed a member of the Advisory uncil to the White House conference on Libraries. e also served as a legislative analyst for the National dvisory Council on Women's Educational ograms. She is admitted to the bar in Illinois and e District of Columbia and is a former president of e Women's Bar Association of Illinois. Other ganizations she belongs to include the League of omen Voters, the American Library Association, e American Association of University Women, the omen's National Democratic Club, and ngressional Wives for Soviet Jews. She has written book about her campaign experiences during her sband's yearlong bid for the presidency in 1987-88 lled, *Codename: Scarlet.*

JOHN B. SIMON, was born on August 8, 42. He attended the University of Wisconsin and graduated with a BS Degree in 1964. He then attend DePaul University and graduated with his Juris Doctor degree in 1967. He was a member of the Law Review and received two Bancroft-Whitney American Jurisprudence Awards while at DePaul.

He was admitted to the Illinois Bar in 1967 and the bars of the United States District Court for the Northern District of Illinois and the United States Court of Appeals for the Seventh Circuit in 1968.

He was an Assistant United States Attorney, 1967-1974; Special Counsel to the Director of the Illinois Department of Public Aid, 1974-1975; Principal consultant to the Commission on the Review of the National Policy Toward Gambling, 1975-1976; Special Counsel to the Administrator of the Drug Enforcement Administration. From 1977-1980 he was Counsel for both Illinois Governor's Revenue Study Commission of Legalized Gambling and special Counsel 1979-80 for the Illinois Racing Board. From 1983-1985 he was the Director of the Chicago World's Fair-1992 Authority.

He was the commissioner of the Illinois Racing Board and a trustee of Depaul University in 1990. He has been a partner in two firms, Friedman & Koven from 1975-1985 and Jenner & Block from 1986-present.

He is a member of numerous organizations and committees. He lives in Chicago with his family.

THELMA BROOK SIMON, in 1940 she graduated from the University of Chicago Law School, and was admitted to the Illinois Bar, became a member of the WBAI, and landed her first job as a lawyer with the firm of Angerstein & Angerstein. There she learned to write scholarly briefs and argue law in the various courts. Although she left the firm after two years, her name was kept on the door as a "welcome mat."

She was asked by Justice Bristow before whom she had once argued a case in the Circuit Court, to serve as Law Clerk, since he was then on the Appellate Court. The job with its flexible hours, was ideal. She continued to work for Justice Bristow after he became a Justice on the Supreme Court of Illinois, until his death. She worked briefly afterwards as "clerk at large" for all the other Justices of that Court. During this period she was admitted to the U.S. Supreme Court Bar.

Another legal vista opened when Senior Federal District Judge Walter J. LaBuy asked her to serve as Law Clerk and assist in organizing, researching, and drafting a manual, subsequently published as "Jury Instructions in Federal Criminal Cases." She was WBAI's 1956 president, a Wilmette Board Trustee from 1961-1969 and counts as highlights hosting 1968

WBAI picnic, helping to elect B. Fain Tucker to the bench and working to elect Justice McMorrow to the Illinois Supreme Court.

SANDRA J. SLAGA, she graduated from St. Louis University School of Law and moved to the Chicago area later. She has been searching for her niche in the law. Perhaps not so strangely, her husband and children have helped her significantly in her search.

One of their many gifts to her has been a confirmation that her inner voice does indeed know what's best for her and that she can trust her instincts. Those instincts have always included a commitment to one day use her talents and skills to help women, children and the individual. For years she allowed society and others to convince her that she could not be valuable unless she practiced high-powered, high-paying, full-time law. Now she knows that her value is determined not by the impressiveness of her title nor the size of her paycheck, but by the content of her character and the dedication and sincerity of her practice - whatever law she may choose. The workplace is crying out for revolutionary changes in attitude toward part time work, parental leave and child care. She intends to work with WBAI and other colleagues on this.

PATRICIA S. SMART, graduated from the University of Illinois in 1975 with and English major and a chemistry/mathematics minor. She graduated magnum cum laude in 1978 from the University of Illinois. There she received the Rickert Award for Academic Excellence.

She is a partner in the firm of Pattishall, McAuliffe, Newbury, Hilliard & Geraldson. There she is engaged in federal civil litigation in the areas of trademark, unfair competition, advertising, copyright, and computer law; trademark licensing, advertising approval, and related counseling. She also practices before the United States Patent and Trademark Office prosecuting trademark applications, oppositions, and cancellations.

She is a member of these organizations: the American Bar Association, the American Intellectual Property Law Association, the Chicago Bar Association, the Computer Law Association, the Copyright Society, the Illinois State Bar Association, the Legal Aid Clinic for Disabled, and the Legal Club. She has given speeches and been published for several of the organizations she belongs to as well as being the co-author of "Recent Developments in Trademark Law".

GAIL T. SMITH, she grew up in the Chicago area. She attended Barat College in Lake Forest, Illinois and the Institut Catholique de Paris. She graduated magna cum laude from Barat. After teaching high school in Chicago for several years, she enrolled in New York University School of Law. During law school, she began working with child custody issues for women prisoners and served as chair of programming for the 16th National Conference on Women and the Law.

Upon graduating from law school, she was awarded a grant by the Berkley Law Foundation to found Chicago Legal Aid to Incarcerated Mothers (CLAIM). CLAIM provides legal services and educational programs on family law to help the families of women prisoners remain intact whenever possible. She is author of the handbook for Incarcerated Parents in Illinois, which has become a model for programs nationwide.

She received Barat College's Margaret Burke Award in recognition of her dedication to the community through her work with CLAIM. She has served on the Citizens Advisory Committee to Jessie "Ma" Houston Community Correctional Center. She has been a member of the Board of Directors of the National Women and the Law Association since 1987. She founded the Women in Prison Project at New York University School of Law. She is an active member of WBAI's Matrimonial committee and served as 1989-91 co-chair of the committee.

THEDA C. SNYDER, received her B.A. cum laude from the State University of New York at Buffalo in 1969. She then attended the Loyola University School of Law for her J.D., graduating 12th of 164 students in 1977; she was Law Review.

From 1982 - 1985 she was a consultant to Illinois Institute for Continuing Legal Education, creating, organizing and presenting seminars on subjects covering the breadth of legal practice. From 1987 - 1989 she was a consultant to Jenner & Block on in-house associate development program, creating curricula and recruiting faculty for a semi-monthly litigation series.

From 1986 to the present she has been a consultant to Continuing Legal Education Satellite Network, creating, organizing, and presenting seminars on a variety of subjects. These subjects include product liability litigation, estate planning, family law, land use, document control in complex cases, Immigration Reform and Control Act, international trade, insurance law, environmental law, transportation law, social security claims, and tax law. She is currently working on programs on professional liability litigation and succession planning for the closely held business.

She is a member of the following bar associations: the Illinois State Bar, the American Bar, the Chicago Bar, and the Women's Bar of Illinois. She is also a member of the Commercial Law League of America.

She is a Chicago resident married for 23 years to Myron Snyder, a manufacturer's representative. They have one son who is a student at the University of Illinois School of Engineering.

LOIS SOLOMON, she lives in Wilmette with her husband. She attended the University of Chicago Law School. She loved law school. She found it intellectually stimulating. She enjoyed her fellow classmates, especially Arthur, whom she met and married in law school. Although invited to be on Law Review, Lois declined.

After law school, she was unable to find work in her chosen field of labor law. She did legal research for U of C Professor Allison Dunham on an open space project. Then she clerked for U.S. District Court Judge Julius Hoffman. Then she worked for Legal Aid Society, leaving that when she became pregnant. She returned to the law, joining her husband's law firm (Solomon & Behrant). She concentrates in appeals and probate. She and her husband are both members of the Executive

Committee of the New Trier Democratic Organization. Lois has been involved in pro-choice and anti-war activities. She loves reading mysteries, gardening and eating candy.

JEROLD S. SOLOVY, he was born in Chicago, Illinois. He received a B.A. (with high honors and distinction in Political Science) from the University of Michigan. He was admitted to the bar in 1955. He received his Legal education from Harvard Law School where he graduated cum laude with a LL.B degree. He was also a member of several honor societies such as, Phi Beta Kappa; Phi Kappa Phi; Pi Sigma Alpha; and Phi Eta Sigma. He is a partner at Jenner and Block and chairman of the Special Commission on the Administration of Justice in Cook County.

SUSAN PIERSON SONDERBY, she was appointed as a Judge of the United States Bankruptcy Court on October 1, 1986. She was the first woman appointed in the Seventh Circuit Court of Appeals (Illinois, Indiana, and Wisconsin) to the bankruptcy bench.

A native of Joliet, she graduated from Joliet East High School, Joliet Junior College, the University of Illinois and The John Marshall Law School. Prior to her present position, she was the United States Trustee for the Northern District of Illinois. She was appointed by former United States Attorney General William French Smith. She was Assistant Attorney General and Chief of the Consumer Protection Division for the Office of the Illinois Attorney General. Formerly, she was a partner in the Joliet law firm of O'Brien, Garrison, Berard, Kusta and DeWitt.

She is a member of the Chicago Law Club, National Conference of Bankruptcy Judges, American Bankruptcy Institute, The Legal Club of Chicago, the Union League Club and The John Marshall Law School Alumni Association Board of Directors. She is a member of the Commercial Law League of America and serves on the Executive Council of the Bankruptcy and Insolvency Section.

Her accomplishments include being the commencement speaker at Joliet Junior College, the keynote speaker at the Business and Professional Women's District Conference and the keynote speaker at the University of Illinois Women's Day Conference. She was featured in "Illinois Issues" and received the International Organization of Women Executives Leadership Award. She was also chosen the Business and Professional Women's Young Career Woman.

DOROTHY W. SPINKA, spent her childhood in the Englewood neighborhood of Chicago. She attended Central YMCA and Northwestern University for 1932-1942. She then attended the Kent College of Law from 1942-1946.

She became interested in law in high school from a civics teacher. Her law school years were during WWII so there were only eight students in her class.

After graduation she worked in the legal department of Zurich Insurance Company. She married in 1944, limited her time at practice because of her three children, and returned to practice in 1970. Her practice includes probate, real estate, trust, small business, and family law.

She dislikes the hours required for lawyers keep current. She is not especially active in WB because her practice is on the far south side of Chica Over the years, she observes, law has become m litigous.

FRANCES EDGERTON SPOONER, w born on February 12, 1876 in Cincinnati, OH, Lincoln's birthday. She was educated at the hi school in Woodhull, IL, and graduated from Central High School at Minneoplis. She prepared the Illinois State Bar Examination during six years reading law, and 24 weeks study at the Illinois Colle of Law in Chicago. She was admitted to practice December 15, 1911.

In 1912 she presented a three-hour argument the Judiciary Committee of the Illinois Sta Legislature and persuaded that august body t women had the right to seek and hold judicial offi She was a pioneer suffragist and for many year national speaker for the Republican party.

She was a life member of the WBAI and of National Association of Women Lawyers. She wa member of the Rebekah Lodge, 90, I.O.O.F., and h been a State Officer. When she died she had completely retired and seemed always to be handli a few cases. From her own statements, it appe music represented a vital force in her life. Her favor composer was Mozart. Until her eyesight failed; was a master marksman, donig range practice w the Chicago Police.

Although her failing health curtailed h activities, she remained interested in the law and women lawyers. At the time of her death she w engaged in research for a series of articles on famo women attorneys with emphasis on members of Women's Bar Association of Illinois.

She died on March 6, 1962. She outlived close relatives and all those contemporaries w knew her best. Even the younger women, such Elsa Beck and Edna Perraton, who were most famil with her life and career, are gone.

LETITIA SPUNAR-SHEATS, she spent of her childhood on the Northwest side of Chica She went to high school at Schurz High School a thereafter went to college at Lake Forest College, three years, and the University of Illinois Champaig Urbana her last year.

She attended John Marshall Law School and substitute teaching to put herself through law sch She became a member of the bar in 1972. Her school years were fun for her because she enjoy going to school and being a student. She did realize that being a lawyer was such an intense and that you really have to be "up" all the time w you are dealing with people on a constant basis trying cases. Being a lawyer does allow a lot of ro for individual expression which she thinks is v encouraging.

After she got out of law school she worked in Corporation Council's Office, Department of Build and Housing, for a couple of years and then went in partnership with a gentleman who had been a practitioner for thirty five years. Since he died, she been a sole practitioner. She has noticed women attorr are becoming less competitive with each other and realizing they have to help each other out.

SUSAN STAFFORD, spent her childhood in Oregon, Georgia, Indiana, Michigan, and New Jersey. She attended Barnard College, NYC from 1960 to 1961 and the University of Wisconsin, Parkside Campus from 1973 to 1976.

She became interested in law from a woman lawyer who talked to her history class on career options. she loved law school. The caliber of teachers and students was high and she enjoyed the reading of cases. She disliked some of the pressure.

Her view of becoming a lawyer changed after law work. She found the work took 26 hours a day and 8 days a week. She missed her freedom for travel and hobbies. She worked for the U.S. Dept. of Commerce during the 1980 census, then for a small loop law firm. She left when she moved 40 miles west because it was too much commuting for little satisfaction.

She now works as a volunteer for various community groups. She serves on the boards of Not-for-Profit organizations. When she was a lawyer she felt good about helping people, sometime in just little ways, but it really made a difference in their lives. The bad part was the feeling the you didn't do enough and would like to do more, but there was not time.

She thinks of herself as a role model, giving good advice. She was instrumental in opening Eastview Women's Resource Center in Geneva, IL. in 1987. She notices lots of "Lady Lawyers" now. Other women are leaving the law because they find it is not enough (or too much) to personally satisfy them.

She has been married for 29 years. They have two sons, 23 and 27. They became self-sufficient and more independent because she was not at home all the time. They are proud of her and she is proud of them.

SARAH STEGEMOELLER, she is a relatively new member of the Women's Bar Association of Illinois, and she was reluctant to add her biography to those of members of long-standing, such as her partner, Eleanor Guthrie, whom she views as true pioneers of the profession. She did not join WBAI for more than ten years after becoming a member of the Illinois Bar and, on reflection, she thinks that it was probably her loss for not having done so earlier. You see, her 1978 law school class at Washington University in St. Louis was composed 48% of women. Women students predominated in positions of significance at the school.

She was a member of the moot court team that won the Eighth Circuit competition, and represented it at the national competition. She came to Chicago (on the enlightened attitude of her first employer) neither knowing of, nor expecting significant gender based obstacles to her pursuit of a legal career. She was not sure how membership in a "women's" bar association would be relevant to her when she was interested in becoming, and being perceived as, a good lawyer, period...not a good woman lawyer, or worse, a good lawyer...for a woman.

JOAN E. STEINMAN, she received her bachelor's degree in philosophy from the University of Rochester, and her law degree from Harvard Law School, where she served on the Harvard Civil Rights - Civil Liberties Law Review. She was admitted to the Illinois Bar in 1973 and practiced with the Chicago

law firm of Schiff Hardin & Waite, specializing in civil litigation. She joined the faculty of IIT Chicago-Kent in 1977, and was named interim dean of the law school in 1990.

She has authored articles on the status of class members in federal class actions, the associational privacy privilege in civil litigation, suits for money damages to vindicate first Amendment rights, pseudonymous litigation, law of the case doctrine and other procedural issues. She also teaches courses in civil procedure and complex litigation.

GEOFFREY R. STONE, Dean of the University of Chicago Law School, he received his undergraduate B.A. degree from the Wharton School of Finance and Commerce of the University of Pennsylvania. He then attended the University of Chicago Law School, where he served as editor-in-chief of the Law Review, was awarded his J.D. degree cum laude, and was elected to membership in the Order of the Coif.

Following graduation, he served as law clerk to Judge J. Skelly Wright of the U.S. Court of Appeals for the District of Columbia Circuit, He spent the next year as law clerk to Justice William J. Brennan, Jr. of the Supreme Court of the United States. He was admitted to the New York Bar in 1972 and has been a member of the faculty since 1973. He served on the Board of Governors of the Chicago Council of Lawyers, the Board of Directors of the American Civil Liberties Union, Illinois Division. He is currently a Fellow of the American Academy of Arts and Sciences, an ex-officio member of the American Law Institute, a member of the Executive Committee of the Association of American Law Schools, a member of the Board of Advisers of the National Association of Public Interest Law - The Public Service Challenge, a member of the Advisory Board of the Legal Aid Society, and a member of the Advisory Board of the Chicago Volunteer Legal Services Foundation.

ZITA J. STONE, she was born in Greenfield, Nebraska. She received her degree of LL.B. from Loyola University College of Law . In 1928 and was licensed to practice law by the Supreme Court of Illinois.

At the time of her death in 1967, she held the position of Associate Counsel of Bankers Life and Casuality Company of Chicago, Illinois. Prior to joining Bankers, she was an attorney for the Illinois Insurance Department; previous to that, she was in private practice and also fulfilled public service appointments. She was the first woman public defender to be appointed by the City of Chicago.

She was a member of the Illinois Bar Association, the American Bar Association, the Law Institute and Alpha Theta Chaper of Kappa Beta Pi Legal Sorority: she served on several committees of the Women's Bar Association and supported the activities of the Association.

ANNE SULLIVAN, Probate has been her speciality since she was admitted to the bar in 1934. At that time the Probate Court was desperately in need of house cleaning. Old estates had to be closed. On the recommendation of her friend Phyllis Kelly, the first woman assistant probate judge, she was hired by Judge O'Connell to help the court. Then Judge O'Connell recommended her to the National Surety Co., which had just gone through a reorganization due to the Great Depression. Two years later the law firm of DeFreese, Fiske, O'Brien and Thompson lost its probate attorney. "We don't usually hire women," they explained. But with her experience they did.

She and her husband founded Law Clerk, Inc. as a family business. Trained clerks were employed during the day, but "at 4 o'clock we put the kids to work picking up work from the lawyers, of which there were eight". Since the death of her husband, she has been in probate practice on her own.

ELINOR PORTER SWINGER, A farmgirl in the forties, she was pushed and pulled to law against the more traditional tides of those times. Her tiny high school (graduating 25 per year) deserved A+ for confidence building in crucial years. Ohio State University (at 25,000) was the perfect counterweight, a campus awash with competitive challenges of the real world. A shrewed professor propelled her to law school early...noting that she could begin her first year in the final undergraduate year, a useful saving of time and money. If in doubt, he said she could take a new (not required) LSAT test "alleged" to measure law aptitude. She did and it did and she entered law school aglow. Upon graduation, the job scene was a jarring contrast.

Armed with a good class rank and some tax skill, she trooped to the top firms in the state where she was: 1) warmly received; 2) warmly rejected as an attorney; and 3) offered jobs as secretary or librarian (both then better paid than new attorneys). Luckily, discrimination—at least at entry level—was far less in government. She spent golden years in a first legal career in the Chief Counsel's Office of the IRS in Washington, D.C.

After years of writing (four of her published books dealt with the law) and lecturing "about" law, she returned to practice when her youngest left for college. She joined a loop law firm that has many governmental clients, including schools and colleges. This has dovetailed nicely with long service on governing boards; allows her to participate heavily in bar activities and is an altogether satisfying third legal career.

BRENDA A. SZEJA, was born in Dorset, England and came to Chicago at age 13. Dorset is the home of Thomas Hardy, the Powys brothers, and John Fowles. She attended Circle, SIU, and the University of Chicago from 1965-1970. She graduated with her Juris Doctor from Lewis University in 1975.

She was a fundraising associate, and met one of her many older "mentors" in her formative professional years. He is still practicing, and he is the one who urged her to attend law school.

Her view of becoming a lawyer became much less an academic pursuit and much more a demand on one's time, dedication, and competitive spirit. She learned about the peculiar comraderia between men lawyers and judges, and about the difficulties of being a female sole practitioner. She says "Thank God, I still have my looks!"

After graduation she worked with the great Julius Lucius Echeles until 1989, and she is now on her own, though she works in tandem with a number of other lawyers. She has no particular preference in her law area, but she enjoys trial work. The dedication, hard work and long hours she put in working for Julius are skills which helps her do the best for each client.

She found honors in being the best, staying afloat financially, and confronting ethical problems that she had not anticipated. She enjoys knowing the answers to people's legal problems. She regularly attends WBAI luncheons, reads the newsletter, and supports WBAI candidates.

She is very happy in her life as a wife, sister, daughter, aunt, and she has many friends.

SUSAN B. TATNALL, she is a partner of Drendel, Schanlaber, Horwitz, Tatnall, & McCracken, in Kane County, Illinois. She is one of the many women who after being a traditional wife, mother and homemaker, entered the profession of law "later in life" than normal. In the late 1960s and early 1970s she became increasingly active in the Women's Movement and increasingly aware of the inequities present in our society. Because of this interest, she was drawn to the legal profession as a way of empowering herself and hopefully other women.

She applied to the University of Kentucky, College of Law and was accepted and began her 3 year law school career at the ripe age of 37. Upon graduating, she moved to the Chicago area, took the Illinois Bar Exam and began a solo practice in Geneva, Illinois.

She became a partner in an Aurora and Geneva base law firm, and is currently the first woman President of the Kane County Bar Association.

BERNIECE P. TAYLOR, she received her J.D. in 1931 from the University of Chicago Law School, in the general practice of law. She worked her way through Indiana University at Bloomington, Indiana by teaching eight months of the year rural and secondary schools and then making up the work the rest of the year at the University. She earned her B.A. six years out of high school during which she had taught five years. She then earned her way through law school by doing secretarial work for the Law professors as well as night teaching at Bird Memorial Community Center in South Chicago.

Since few law firms would even interview women, she edited a book on automobile law and a review of many volumes of Supreme Court law of Indiana for Callaghan Publishing. She was a law clerk to Judge Alschuler of the Seventh Court of Appeals—an invaluable experience in researching and writing briefs.

1916-20 WBAI President Katherin McCulloch and her husband Frank did Berniece a favor by hiring Berniece's husband to work in their law firm. Later, when he graduated law school during the depression, he became a partner. An artist, Berniece has even sold some of her paintings. She is also a gardener in the yard of her house that she and her husband built in 1953.

HELEN THATCHER, she was a highly respected and very much loved individual who was many years ahead of her time. She served for 40 years as an administrator at the John Marshall Law School, where in 1948 she received her degree. She served as registrar, becoming the assistant dean in 1973. She was promoted thereafter to associate dean in 1975, the first woman to hold that post at John Marshall.

When she first became an administrator at John Marshall, there were no women on the faculty. Because of her strength and determination, doors were opened for women. She was one of the founders of the National Association on Law Placement, an organization that created an orderly process of placement between law schools and private firms, and she was the first editor of its newsletter. She was also the first woman to serve on the board of directors of the Executive Club of Chicago as well as on the board of the University Club of Chicago. She

mattered to the law school, to the people who knew her, and obviously, to the Chicago and Illinois Legal Community.

LUCIA THEODOSIA THOMAS, Dreams do come true!!! When she was fice years old she decided she wanted to become a lawyer so she could help her 80 year old "Uncle Charlie". Uncle Benjamin Crockett took her to visit a court that did it!!! She was born in Cheyenne, Wyoming and grew up in San Antonio, Texas. She attended Xavier University in New Orleans, Louisiana, and graduated with a B.A. degree. She attended the University of Michigan Law School and graduated in 1940 from the Robert H. Terrell Law School in Washington, D.C. with a LL.B. degree.

She was admitted to the District of Columbia Bar, the U.S. Court of Appeals, and the United States Supreme Court. She received a Master of Laws Degree, a Master of Patent Law Degree, and a Juris Doctor Degree from the John Marshall Law School in Chicago, Illinois. She was admitted to the Illinois Bar in 1942.

She joined the Women's Bar Association of Illinois and is now a Life Member. She served on the Board with Coula Butler, and as Secretary. She is a member of all the National, State, and local Women's Bar Associations and Foundations, the National, local and State Judicial Associations and Foundations, and a Life Fellow of the Chicago Bar Foundation and a sustaining Member of the American Judicature Society.

She was in private practice, an Assistant State's Attorney, Assistant Corporation Counsel, Appellate Law Clerk, and was the first woman lawyer appointed to a Full Circuit Court Judgeship.

She has received numerous Legal, Civic, Social, Religious, and Judicial Awards and donates to many scholarships, especially the Women's Bar Foundation.

MARY C. THOMPSON, she attended the University of Illinois, Champaign, as an undergraduate. She attended Northern Illinois Law School and passed the Illinois Bar in 1981.

Since she started the practice of law, she has truly found her niche in life. Her real reason for wanting to be a lawyer is because it justified her personality.

DONNA ANASTAZIA TOULMIN, she is currently a Legal Officer in Domestic Relations Division, of the Circuit Court of Cook County. She has been in private practice in Rochester, Vermont and Chicago, Illinois. She specialized in the areas of domestic law, notably representation of children affected by custody disputes; estates planning; legal representation of working artists.

She has taught at De Paul University, teaching undergraduate courses on Law and Society. She was admitted to practice before the Supreme Courts of Illinois, New York, and Vermont. She is a member of the American Bar Association, Chicago Bar Association, and the Illinois State Bar.

She received her J. D. from De Paul University College of Law, a M. A. from the University of Chicago, and a B.A. from the University of California.

JOAN SCHILLER TRAVIS, she is an attorney in general practice in Park Ridge. She is an Assistant Corporation Counsel of Skokie, and is a licensed real estate broker. She is the former President of the North Suburban Bar Association. She was Chairman of the Skokie Consumer Affairs Commission and Collector of Niles Township.

She is listed in "Who's Who of American Women", "Who's Who in the Midwest", and Who's Who in American Law". She hosts, produces and directs a Public Access Cable television program which appears in Chicago and Skokie. She was graduated form the John Marshall Law School and holds a Bachelor of Philosophy degree from Northwestern University. Prior to practicing law, she was a freelance writer with credits in a broad range of national and local magazines and newspapers.

VASILIKI B. TSAGANOS, she is an associate of Baker & McKenzie, Chicago, Illinois. She received her J.D. degree from the Northwestern University School of Law in 1990 and served as an Note and Comment Editor of the Journal of International Law & Business. She received a B.A., from The American University, in Washington, D.C. and also studied at the Institute of European Studies in Brussels, Belgium.

She is also a member of the Chicago, Illinois, Women's and American Bar Associations.

B. FAIN TUCKER, she was born in Greencastle, Indiana, reared amid a closely knit family, and imbued with a philosophy valuing knowledge, democracy, service and the dignity of the individual. Her scholastic excellence and literary skills at De Pauw University earned her admission to Phi Beta Kappa, and Theta Sigma Phi, honorary journalism society, and later, she was awarded a citation from De Pauw University "in recognition of outstanding achievements and services which reflect honor on the University."

She actively practiced law with the esteemed firm of Pope and Ballard, and at the same time served as Lecturer on Family Law at the University of Chicago

Law School. She was elected and served as President of the Women's Bar Association of Illinois in 1941. Her devotion to law held the highest priority in her life, consequently, as the most qualified of all woman lawyers in the area she was selected to rum for Judge of the Circuit Court of Cook County, and was elected after a vigorously contested election, becoming the second woman in the history of the County to be a Judge.

She was a member of the Women's Bar Association and given the most challenging assignment—to serve as Judge of the Criminal Court—the first woman in the State of Illinois to preside in that Court. She also was assigned to the Common Law Division and the Chancery Division and heard cases in all fields of law. She died on September 26, 1970.

CORNELIA HONCHAR TUITE, she was born in Chicago, Illinois and attended DePaul College of Law where she received a J. D. summa cum laude, La Sorbonne, University of Paris (France), University of Grenoble (France), and received a N. H. and a B. A. from New England College. Her current professional activities at the American Bar Association include, Assistant Counsel for Standing Committee on Ethics and Professional Responsibility, Principal Editor, Second Edition, Annotated Model Rules of Professional Conduct, American Bar Association, Columnist, ABA Journal, Ethics, monthly column devoted to ethics problems, Contributor, ABA/BNA Lawyers' Manual on Professional Conduct.

Her current professional activities in addition to her work at the American Bar Association include, Reporter, Seventh Federal Judicial Circuit Committee on Civility in Federal Litigation Practice (on-going study of civility problems, Committee Chair, Hon. Marvin E. Aspen), Member, Editorial Board, CBA Record, Member Board of Directors, Community & Economic Development Association of Cook County, Inc., Cook County Circuit Court, Juvenile Division, Lawyer Referral Panel.

VALERIE MOEHLE UMHOLTZ, she spent her childhood in Pekin, Illinois. She attended and received a B. S. in Finance from the University of Illinois and also attended Southern Methodist University and Illinois Central College. She received a J. D. summa cum laude from Northern Illinois University College of Law.

She became interested in law while working in her father's law office during high school. After graduation from law school she clerked for Justice Ben Miller and then joined the law firm of Moehle, Swearingen & Associates. She is currently in general civil practice which is the type of work she always wanted to do. She would enjoy doing more appellate work.

She is a member of the Tazewell County Bar Association, and the Illinois State Bar Association.

EDITH VAUGHAN, she spent her childhood in Oklahoma and Oak Park, Illinois. She attended Rockford College, and went to night Law School at Chicago-Kent College of Law, graduating in 1946. She became interested in law through curiosity while working in the personnel department of Sears, Roebuck and Company. After graduation from law school, she continued to work for Sears, Roebuck and Company. She is now retired. Over the years, she

observes, more women are studying law and making use of their law degrees.

LESLIE L. VEON, she was born in Kent, Ohio. She was admitted to the Illinois Bar in 1978. She received a A.B. degree cum laude from Miami University, and her J.D. degree, Phi Beta Kappa, from the University of Cincinnati. She is Co-Author of "Hidden Assets", A.B.A. Family Advocate; "Illinois Child Custody Law: An Overview," Illinois Bar Journal, Vol. 76, No. 1; "Antenuptial Agreements and Malpractice: Is the Risk Worth the Reward?" American Journal of Family Law, Vol. 2, No. 2; "Family Law in Illinois," The Cambridge Institute. Chapter Author: "How to Handle Goodwill Valuation of Professional Practices," Handling Business Interest In divorce Proceedings, Illinois Institute of Continuing Legal Education; "Antenuptial Agreements: To Draft Or Not to Draft," Seminar On Matrimonial Law, American Academy of Matrimonial Lawyers; "Attorneys' Fees in Divorce Actions: Judicial Intervention and the contingent Fee Bar," presentation to Illinois Chapter, American Academy of Matrimonial Lawyers; "Valuations of closely Held Corporations," Illinois Divorce Practice, Professional Education Systems, Inc.

Seminar Lecturer: Professional Practice Goodwill, and Antenuptial Agreements, Illinois Institute of Continuing Legal Education; Goodwill Valuation, Professional Education Systems, Inc.; Illinois Family Law, The Cambridge Institute. She is also a member of the Chicago and Illinois State Bar Associations; Appellate Lawyers Association.

MARJORIE JUDITH VINCENT, she is from Oak Park, Illinois. She was a 3rd year Post Graduate at Duke University Law School, and the recipient of a $25,000.00 scholarship. She was an Undergraduate at DePaul University and graduated with a B.A. in music.

Her ambition is to obtain a Juris Doctorate Degree and practice Corporate Law. She has had 14 years of classical piano training and has performed in national and international piano competitions since the age of 12. She is fluent in French and Creole. She is a member of the Alpha Kappa Alpha, Inc.

During her year-long reign as Miss America 1991, she spoke out on the issue of domestic violence, with a specific concentration in the area of battered women. She visited women's shelters and community centers and addressed national, state, and local associations as well as colleges and universities throughout the country, in an effort to increase public awareness of this growing problem.

DIANE N. WALSH, she spent her childhood in Chicago, Illinois. She attended college at Loyola University of Chicago. She attended law school at Northern University College of Law. She became interested in law while in high school and worked in several law-related fields.

Since graduation, she has been working as an Assistant State's Attorney. She has worked with criminal appeals, and prosecuted cases in juvenile court, both in abuse and neglect of children and in the delinquency courts. She is currently assigned to the Felony Review Unit and will progress through the office until reaching her ultimate goal as a Felony Trial Assistant.

LEANNE WALSH

EUNICE WARD *Biography on page 120*

WILLIE M. WHITING, she is a Judge of the Circuit Court of Cook County, Illinois. Although this title is no longer an oddity for women, when she made her debut, it was not necessarily the usual for any woman lawyer of her race. She was born in Chicago, and a product of the public school system. Early teaching by those lovable professional educators, made her know that dreams could come true if one was adequately prepared. The introduction to college commenced at Fisk University of Tennessee, but only for a short period.

A stint in the military (which provided the base for a return to college), the pre-law courses at Roosevelt University and finally, she was graduating from the John Marshall Law School. The law degree and state licensing, allowed her to join her uncle's law practice. It also provided the groundwork for later becoming the executive secretary for the Chicago branch of the N.A.A.C.P.

This led into her becoming an Assistant Corporation Counsel, Assistant State's Attorney and Assistant U.S. Attorney. Before becoming a

prosecuting attorney she, for a one year period, became a Resource Consultant for the Illinois Department of Public Aid. These various occupations prior to her appointment as a Magistrate, an Associate Judge and subsequently becoming an elected Judge, aided her immeasurably in her present occupation on the bench.

JANE S. WHITMAN, she attended William Smith College and received a B. A. in English. She received a J. D. from Michigan Law School in 1952. She works for the Law Firm of McDermott, Will, & Emery and was a member of the WBAI in earlier years and always found it very rewarding.

ANN CLAIRE WILLIAMS, she attended and received a Juris Doctor from the University of Notre Dame Law School, a M. A. in Guidance and Counseling from the University of Michigan, and a Bachelor of Science in Education from Wayne State University. She has been a Faculty member in Trial Advocacy Courses at Harvard Law School, University of Chicago Law School and Loyola University School of Law, a Adjunct Professor and Lecturer in trial advocacy courses at Northwestern University Law School and John Marshall Law School, and is presently a Faculty Member for regional, national, in-house and advanced advocacy programs for the National Institute for Trial Advocacy.

She has been a Law Clerk to the Honorable Judge Robert A. Sprecher, an Assistant United States Attorney, Chief of the Organized Crime Drug Enforcement Task Force for the North Central Region, and is currently a Judge in the United States District Court. She is a member of the Illinois State Bar Association, Cook County Bar Association, Women's Bar Association of Illinois, National Association of Women Judges, Federal Judges Association, Federal Bar Association, and Black Women Lawyers Association.

KATHRYN E. WILLIAMS, she enjoyed a full and positive career in nursing and health care administration prior to her entry into the legal profession. She practiced first as a Registered professional nurse and was active in advancing the cause of women in health care, advocating advanced education for the health care practitioner and equal employment opportunity for women in health care. She was an active speaker and writer for this cause and she continues to hold active licensure as an R.N. in several states. She advanced as a nursing administrator and then moved into general health care administration. She was an early health care risk manager and a consultant to the Illinois Hospital Association.

Having served as one of the first presidents of the Illinois Society of Nursing Administrators, she now counts as a favored client the successor professional association, the Illinois Organization of Nurse Executives. She teaches Legal Aspects of Nursing Administration and stays active as counsel to several professional nursing associations.

At the encouragement of her four children, she entered law school after her children had finished school. She was drawn to the area of family law and is delighted that she has the opportunity to use all the

skills acquired in her "prior life" in this emotional difficult area of the law.

While she continues to practice in the area corporate law, concentrating in small (and frequen women owned) business enterprise; an increasing large part of her practice is devoted to family law. S volunteers for pro bono with the Chicago volunte legal services Foundation and sits on their Board Directors. She is an active member of several B Associations, has been co-chair and chair of t Matrimonial Law Committee of the WBAI.

JILL WINE-BANKS, was the deputy attorn general of Illinois, and was named executive direct of the American Bar Association. She was educat at the University of Illinois at Urbana, where s received an undergraduate degree in communicatio She received her J.D. degree from Columb University School of Law.

She served as assistant prosecutor in t Watergate investigation and as a trial attorney in Justice Department's Criminal Division of t Organized Crime Racketeering Section. She was attorney with the Washington, D.C. law firm of Frie Frank, Harris, Shriver & Kampelman. She served general counsel to the Army and was a partner in Chicago law firm of Jenner & Block.

INA S. WINSTON, she was 1987-88 preside of the Women's Bar Association of Illinois.

She initiated the WBAI Woman's Issues Awa one of which was presented to State Senator Dav Clark Netsch and one to State Senator Adeline G Karis.

M. LEE WITTE, was raised by parents w were resolute that she and her sister would get college education denied them by the depressi Lee attended and graduated the University Wisconsin where she was inducted into Mortar Boa nominated for a Fullbright and received a B.A. c laude in English. She met and married Richard Mi a leading campus anti-war activist with a wick sense of humor and a real, rare respect for wom Her concept of lawyers was limited to crusadi attorneys on TV, but her husband didn't blink wl she told him she wanted to go to law school Chicago.

She was shocked that despite fine LSAT sco the then-Dean of DePaul University College of L had no use for female students. She was interview only after her husband faked an appointment himself. "What right have you to take a ma position here?", this Constitutional law scholar-D screamed. Sympathetic secretaries suggested her odds would increase if they could remove her first name (Mary) from all paperwork.

She paid for law school writing carpet ads for Montgomery Ward, computing taxes for Continental Bank, pushing drinks at John Barleycorn, and interviewing clients at Legal Aid Bureau. Totally ignorant of Chicago ways—she never really knew an attorney until she wa one—she just assumed that the Public Defender would be thrilled to sign the #2 graduate in her class. Wrong. She found her best chance for immediate trial work in the U.S. Army Judge Advocate General's Corps. She joined as a Captain in the spring of 1975, the 16th woman ever accepted. Three months later, her name was placed on a plaque in Charlottesville, Virginia as the first female class valedictorian. She tried a wide variety of civil and criminal matters before military juries and eventually became Chief of Criminal Defense and Legal Assistance at HQ, Fort Sheridan. Evenings, she completed a double masters in Public Administration and Management from Webster College, summa cum laude.

Her passion for defending the defenseless took her to Chicago Volunteer Legal Services Foundation, the nation's oldest and largest pro bono legal services agency. Beginning as a staff attorney handling divorces, she became Executive Director in 1985.

ILENE F. WOLF, admitted Illinois Bar (1975); U.S. Supreme Court (1984). partner in the firm of Wolfe & Wolf, of Arlington Heights; graduate of John Marshall Law School (J.D. 1975), graduate of Northwestern University (B.S. 1966). ISBA Assembly (1989-92); Assembly Meeting and Agenda Committee (1991-92); ISBA Family Law Sect. Council (Association Member, 1991-92); Participant in the ISBA Long Range Planning Meeting (1982); Past President of the Northwestern Suburban Bar Association (1987-88); also served in offices of Executive Vice-President, 2nd Vice-President, 1st Vice-President, Secretary and Treasurer and a member of the Board Of Governors. Served on the following committees of hte NWSBA: By-Law Committee (Chair two times) and member of the committee for 12 years; Quality of Life Committee (as co-chairman helped to develop the Lawyers for Lawyers Committee, a peer support group fro Dissolution prove-ups in the suburban district courts; Public Relations Committee; Co-chariman of the Continuing Legal Eduacation Committee; speaker on matrimonial Law "Nuts and Bolts" over several years for the NWSBA. Member of the Women's Bar Association of Illinois. Member of the Women's American ORT (Past Vice-President of the West Suburban Region).

Mother of two children; Natalie (20) and Daniel (16).

ELLEN A. YEARWOOD, originally she had no intention to be a lawyer; she just wanted not to be a teacher! (They work too hard for too little pay), she was born and grew up in Georgia. She studied mathematics at Emory University in Atlanta, got a job offer from a steel manufacturer in Illinois, and immediately left the red clay of Georgia for the beautiful black earth of the Midwestern plains. During her fourth year as a computer programmer/analyst, a friend said, "Let's go to law school," and thinking it would be fun and interesting, she said, "Sure".

She moved to Des Plaines and went to DePaul at night while working full time. It was hard. During the first year she realized that to succeed while working full time would require giving up all social, political, and personal life, and she did. What a pleasure it was to pass the bar and take up politics, personal life, and entertainment again!

After trying for months to get interviews with Chicago intellectual property firms and getting only one (and no offer), she started her own practice, volunteering with Pro Bono Advocates to learn domestic relations courts and taking referrals from the Des Plaines domestic violence advocacy agency to start. Her practice has grown very general— domestic relations, basic estate planning, residential real estate, employment discrimination and unlawful termination, an occasional criminal misdemeanor of personal injury. She is kept fascinated by helping women's campaigns for public office, networking on women's issues and other (unpaid) volunteer activities.

BARBARA L. YONG, she is an associate (hoping, to make partner) in the litigation division of the law firm of Siegan, Barbakoff & Gomberg. She grew up on the southwest side of Chicago. She was valedictorian of her high school class at Hubbard High School. She graduated Phi Beta Kappa from the University of Illinois in Urbana-Champaign. She attended law school at Loyola University School of Law from which she received and award for leadership and service. She was editor and writer for the Woman's Law Reporter, President of Phi Alpha Delta and Vice-President of the Decalogue Society.

Special Assistant Attorney General in the Welfare Litigation Division of the Illinois Attorney General's Office was her first legal position after law school. While there, she handled hundreds of administrative review cases, tried class action suits in federal court and briefed and argued cases before the Illinois Appellate and Supreme Courts.

She first tasted private practice in Wheaton, Illinois with Guerard & Drenk, Ltd., then the largest

firm in DuPage County. Following the firm's break-up, she became a partner of Drenk, Yong, & Smith, Ltd. She left that firm to join Siegan, Barbakoff & Gomberg.

She currently chairs the joint Committee on Women's Rights of the Chicago Bar and Women's Bar Associations. She co-founded the Chicago Bar Association Runaway and Homeless Youth Project. She also belongs to the American and DuPage County Bar Associations, and is an arbitrator for the New York Stock Exchange and Cook County's new mandatory arbitration program. She devotes as much time as she can to her husband and their two adorable, bright and happy daughters. She wants her children to grow up knowing how much they are loved, how important it is to find a loving and supportive man like their dad to marry and, most importantly, with hard work, determination and a little bit of luck their dreams will come true.

VEVA I. YOUNG, in Memphis, TN, my hometown, after finishing college, I worked for six years before returning to school to pursue a career in law and graduated from Howard University in Washington, in 1947 with a LLB degree. My love for the law was heightened by the courses in government I had taken in undergraduate school, and I was familiar with many U.S. Supreme Court decisions. After studying ethics and religion, I felt there was a kinship between the law of God and the law of man.

In January 1948 we were admitted to the bar in Springfield, Illinois. On the train trip to Springfield, my seat mate (who was also admitted at that term) was a Jew who was employed at a large corporation in Chicago. During our conversation, he told me that I should immediately join the Chicago Bar Association because as a member one could "get away with murder." At that time, I was sure he was being facetious.

After arrived in Springfield, we were instructed to pick our kits. I was given a kit which did not have a ticket for the reception after the swearing-in-ceremony. In fact, I did not know about the reception until some of the black applicants were discussing the matter. Since I was the only black woman admitted, I decided it was sexism or inadvertance. I returned to the clerk, explained the situation, was given a ticket and an apology. Inadvertance won the day.

I was rudely awakened again. I made an application for membership to the Chicago Bar Association which was ignored. I thought that it was strange that the Supreme Court of Illinois would designate a body to pass on the candidates for the bar which discriminate against some lawyers for membership. My first thought was to write the Justices to inform them of the racial or sexism displayed by a body which it had "annoited" to pass on applicants for admission to the bar of Illinois.. After discussing the matter with other black lawyers, I was advised to forget the whole matter.

This was a horrendous beginning, but looking back, the practice of law was inspirational, rewarding and an ongoing learning experience.

My first day in Court was on a divorce motion. After the ruling, the Court stated: "prepare your order." Time wasted in writing the order. Afterward, I would go to court with two orders typed (pro and con which required very few changes to conform to the court's ruling) in trying to be prepared. I spent 2 years practicing in Memphis, and I never met the racism in the court which I experienced in Chicago.

When you are fresh out of school, you think you know the the substantive law, but one soon learns that it was not used in the police court, nor small claim courts, where the clerks ran the "show." At Eleventh and State when "cash register Bob" was "King", a list of traffic cases would be posted in the corridor. Fifty lawyers would be there to give the clerk $1.00 to call his or her case first. It should not have taken a Rhodes Scholar to figure out that the money was wasted as one lawyer would be #1 and one would be #50 to be called. In most of the other divisions the going rate was $2.00 to get a case called in order and you may stay until the end of the call, or day if you did not conform.

In the earlier days you would try to discern whether a judge's remarks were racist or sexist. At a pre-trial before a circuit jduge (who had been a States Attorney of Cook County),we were asked the color of the litigants. My reply in my best lawyerlike voice was "I did not think that would be an issue." The judge recovered quickly and stated, "Of course not, I just asked." The laughable part was that my opponent was also black, but you would not know it from the color of his skin.

Several of my foreclosure cases were assigned to the same chancellor, and the rumor was that he was under the grip of the "Mafia." He had a favorite master-in-chancery, who followed me one day from te courtroom to the corridor, greeted me and stated: "I notice that you have quite a few foreclosure cases. I would appreciate it if you would ask for me to be the master, I would see that we both make money." Shocked, I mumbled, "Is that so." I have never figured out how we would "make money", as the chancellors used a fee schedule to award fees.

Joining the WBAI was most rewarding. In discussing my experience with women lawyers, many had faced the same problems, so I felt that sexism was rampart rather than racism. The corporation counsels and assistant states attorneys are still asking women lawyers: "Are you a lawyer?" A question, after 40 years, that I have not heard ask of a male attorney. Worse is the habit of some judges in the Municipal division who look on the appearance form and call women attorneys by their first name. This happened to me in 1985. I told the judge that I thought my client may not feel that I was a member of the bar when I was addressed by my first name in court.

For the past 15 or 20 years, the chancellors, probate and tax court judges have been most helpful in helping lawyers resolve problems. They are professional, learned, and display judicial temperament, and it is a pleasure to practice.

When you take from the community, you try to give back something to the community by becoming involved in community activities. In working with children at a settlement house, doing pro bono work for welfare recipients at a neighborhood agency and working with a local hospital board, was a result of practicing law. Many doors were opened, and I got a glimpse of the board room at a black corporation, and an offer of work at a white corporation. After 40 years, I still find the work satisfying and challenging.

In the earlier days, maybe the lawyers were as much at fault as the judges, when we did not complain of the money-hungry clerks, dishonest and corrupt judges who were selling justice and not mercy. But we can be hopeful, for I can assure you that the practicing of law is not the same as it was 40 years ago.

PEARL A. ZAGER, she spent her childhood in West Bend, Wisconsin. She attended college at Florida Atlantic University and law school at the University of Wisconsin. Her parents owned a restaurant which was opened 7 days a week, 22 hours a day. She didn't like being that committed to work, so her father told her to become a doctor or a lawyer. Since graduation from law school she has been in private practice. She was with a small firm of 6-8 lawyers for 9 years, then merged twice to end up at Vedder, Price which has 140+ attorneys.

She works in the areas of business counseling, commercial real estate & loan transactions.

KATHRYN E. ZENOFF, she was born in Chicago, Illinois and spent her childhood growing up in the Chicago area. She graduated from New Trier High Scool in the top five percent of her class. She then attended college at Stanford University in Palo Alto, California. During her junior year of college she was a guest student with the Smith College Junior Year Abroad Program. She spent the year in Paris, France and Geneva, Switzerland, taking courses at the University of Geneva and the Institute for International and European Studies in Geneva. She returned to Stanford and received her B.A. with honors.

Following graduation from college, she entered Columbia Law School in the fall of 1968. While at Columbia she was the first female law student to become part of the International Fellows Program at Columbia University. During law school, she worked for District Attorney Frank Hogan as well as for the Mayor's Commission for the United Nations. After graduation from law school, she worked with the New York City law firm of Aranow, Brodsky Bohlinger, Benetar and Einhorn. She practiced with that law firm for four and a half years and then moved back to Chicago, where she joined her father in his law practice. She also spent approximately one year in the Cook County State's Attorney's Office prosecuting child abuse and neglect cases.

She moved to Rockford, Illinois and began working for the State's Attorney's Office in Winnebago County as Chief of the Juvenile Division. She has spent nine years in this office, as Chief of the Juvenile Division and Chief of the Misdemeanor Unit and as a senior felony prosecutor, prosecuting adult felony cases. She is currently Facilitator of the Winnebago County Children's Advocacy Project and is Supervisor of the Child Protection Division of the State's Attorney's Office.

Married to a physician, mother of two children, she finds it a challenge to balance her family life and a full time career as a lawyer. She finds both, though, make her life fulfilling and rewarding.

EDITOR'S NOTE: ORIGINAL BIOGRAPHIES ARE LOCATED AT THE CHICAGO HISTORICAL SOCIETY.

EUNICE WARD, she was born in Chicago but spent her early years in what she considered to be a small town, Kenosha, Wisconsin. She attended Kent Law School and after college she took the usual tour of Europe for a year and then went to Chicago without money or friends to find fame and fortune. She worked for government agencies including but not limited to the Department of Children & Family Services. She quickly realized no one of authority would listen to her opinions or ideas. When she presented her Title 6 civil rights & affirmative action program for children, she observed those in charge really wanted her to go away. After being passed over for a position, she quit, filed a discrimination suit and went to law school, to obtain what she really needed to be effective: a license to speak. In law school she was a partner in a fashion design business which she really loved. It was artistic and creative and she got to play dress up every day. In the fashion business, where your hemline was at was considered important.

After becoming an attorney, she opened her own practice and 1980. Since 1988 she has been partners with Rosaire Nottage, also a WBAI member. They were "fixed up" after the annual WBAI judicial reception by another member of WBAI> She is currently working on the WBAI joint professional dinner and she and Carole Siegel are trying to re-establish the WBAI speaker's bureau.

Photo on page 118.

MATILDA FENBERG
Admitted to Ohio Bar, July 11, 1922; Illinois Bar, October 11, 1923.
Yale University School of Law, L.L.B
Practice—General.
Member: Women's Bar Association of Illinois, Chicago Bar Association, Illinois State Bar Association, Hancock County Bar Association, Ohio.

BERTHA D. BAUR
Admitted to Illinois Bar, June, 1908. Chicago-Kent College of Law, L.L.B.
Practice—General.
Member: Women's Bar Association of Illinois.

NELLIE CARLIN
Admitted to Illinois Bar in 1896.
Chicago College of Law, L.L.B.
Practice—Probate and Chancery.
Assistant State's Attorney.
(Appointed August, 1917.)
Member: Women's Bar Association of Illinois, Chicago Bar Association, American Bar Association.

ELIZABETH H. BUCHHALTER
Admitted to Illinois Bar April, 1914.
Chicago Kent College of Law, L.L.B.
Webster College of Law.
Practice—General.
Attorney for West Park Board, appointed July, 1924.
Member: Women's Bar Association of Illinois, Illinois State Bar Association.

Fannie N. Perron
(currently employed as an
Asst. Corp. Counsel

Kathryn M. Barasa
(Rinella)

Rose A. Matelson
(Adelman)

Photos above re rinted from the WBAI 20th Anniversary Journal & Directory issued in 1934-35.

WBAI's First President
1914-1915
Nettie Rothblum Loew

NETTIE ROTHBLUM (MRS. EDWARD C. LOEW)

Nettie Rothblum was born in Baltimore, Maryland, coming to Chicago with her parents when a young girl. She received her prelegal education in Boston, Massachusetts.

Miss Rothblum was the only woman member of her class at Chicago-Kent College, where she was a general favorite because of her outstanding brilliance and scholarship.

She maintained a law office continuously since her admissioninois bar in 1909, practicing under the modest name of N. Rothblum. She is a clever lawyer and has met with much success.

On June 18,1919, she was married to Mr. Edward C. Loew, a Chicago business man. Their home is on the north side.

Mrs. Loew is one of the founders of the Women's Bar Association of Illinois, of which she was the first president. She is also a member of the Chicago Law Institute. In 1915-1916 she served as a member of the Board of Directors of Kappa Beta Pi, and in the latter year was elected Associate Grand Dean. She is a member of the Order of the eastern star.

Nettie is tall, with black hair and sparkling black eyes. She is a forceful speaker and still retains a charming eastern accent. She asserts that she is a docile wife and says that her cheif hobby is experimenting with new recipes, although she has not permitted the historian to include any of them in this sketch.

(Biography from *The History of Kappa Beta Pi*, June, 1937 by Alice C. Edgerton, Grand Historian.

Photographs from *The Golden Anniversary History of Kappa Beta Pi, 1908-1958*.)

WBAI's Second President

NELLIE CARLIN
Admitted to Illinois Bar in 1896.
Chicago College of Law, I.L.B.
Practice—Probate and Chancery
Assistant State's Attorney (Appointed August 17, 1917)
Member: Women's Bar Association, Chicago Bar Association, American Bar Association

WBAI's Third President

CATHARINE WAUGH McCULLOCH
Admitted to Illinois Bar November, 1886.
Union College of Law, L.I.B.
Master in Chancery, Superior Court of Cook County 1917-1925 (Appointed.)
Practice—General
Member: Women's Bar Association of Illinois, Chicago Bar Association, Illinois State Bar Association, American Bar Association

In June 1914, when WBAI was formed, the New York City based *Women Lawyer's Journal*, ran a headline as follows:

Abolish Capital Punishment

It noted, "Illinois, Tennessee, Indiana and Oregon have practically discontinued capital punishment, Louisiana and Minnesota almost so."

In its November, 1914 issue it ran (among other items) two of particular interest to Illinois women lawyers.

ILLINOIS WOMEN WIN NEW RIGHT.

Woman suffrage gained another victory at Chicago Monday when Judge Owens, in the county court, ruled that the newly-enfranchised voters were entitled to vote for county commissioners. Their right to do so has been vigorously opposed. The campaign for this additional right was led vigorously by Mrs. Catherine Waugh McCulloch.

WOMEN SEEK MEMBERSHIP.

The retiring council of the American Bar Association declined to act on the matter of admitting to membership in the association three women whose names were proposed, leaving the decision with the new council, which was elected to-night. The council consists of one member from each state and territory.

The women proposed for membership are the Misses Eva L. Bean, Maine; Marion L. Tyler, Massachusetts, and Margaret C. Wish, Illinois; also Mrs. Jean H. Norris, whose name was presented by Mr. Charles K. Boston, Vice-President of American Bar Association, of New York City.

The Golden Anniversary History of Kappa Beta Pi, 1908-1958, contains some information about early Illinois women lawyers. At page 12 it recount that in addition to various appointments or starting offices of their own they:

established a number of "firsts" for women. Sue Brown was the first woman in Illinois to hold the position of Assistant United States District Attorney. Phyllis Kelley was the first woman to be appointed assistant to the Probate Judge of Cook County, Illinois. Three of them, Mary Sellers, Phyllis Kelley and Katharine Clark, formed a firm of lawyers in Chicago, this being the first firm of women lawyers in Illinois. Cupid broke this up when Mary Sellers married, but years later, after her husband's death, she and one of the members of the original firm, Phyllis Kelley, again practiced law together. Claire Gleason was the first woman lawyer in Illinois to specialize in the examination of abstracts. Two of the Founders served as Justices of the Peace for several years, Katharine Clark in Oak Park, Illinois, and Alice Craig Edgerton in Mukwonago, Wisconsin, where she went to live with her father after her mother's death in 1923. Even the one who didn't finish law school established a "first" for women by being the first woman to serve on the Board of Education in Madison, New Jersey, the town to which she and her husband moved in 1921.

Not content with founding a legal sorority, several of the Founders went on to found the Women's Bar Association of Illinois. The 1937 History mentions Nettie Rothblum and Alice Craig Edgerton as being among the founders of that organization, and refers to Charlotte Doolittle as one of the charter members. Nettie Rothblum was the first president of the organization. In addition to their activities in the Sorority, where they rendered yeoman service on all levels, the Founders were members and active participants in bar associations and organizations of many kinds, some having to do with their cultural interests, some with their avocations, some with public affairs.

The following was their view of the future:

The future looks precarious. It probably always has looked that way to thoughtful people. Whatever that future, we need to be concerned about our place in it. Is a legal sorority going to be useful in the next fifty years of the world's history, and if so, what functions can it perform? In speaking of the situation in 1908 when the Sorority was organized, Alice Craig Edgerton pointed out that there were no associations to bind women lawyers together, to inspire them or to encourage other women to enter the profession. An organization that would be a bond between women law students before and after graduation seemed to be needed. It is still needed. Women still need the bonds of fellowship, they still need inspiration, they still need encouragement to study law and to practice law. To a greater or lesser extent, a legal sorority can satisfy these needs; it all depends upon its leadership. Some years it will be good; other years it will be less so. But as long as the organization is there, lethargic though it may be at times, an instrumentality for action is available.

Above all, the Sorority serves as a means of communication in a day when communication of ideas is of paramount importance. It is a means of communication between women lawyers in our own country, in Canada, in some of the European countries and between individual members throughout the world. Through personal contacts, through local meetings and international conventions, and especially through our QUARTERLY, we can all communicate with each other. We can learn of other women's ideas, aspirations and achievements, share in them and be inspired by them; we can learn of their needs and lend a helping hand; we can communicate to the world, opinions representing the concerted thinking of women lawyers on the many problems which confront not only women but all mankind. Clearly, then, the Sorority is an organization with a great potential for service in this precarious future. Let us face that future together and give it the best we have.

CPSIA information can be obtained at www.ICGtesting.com
Printed in the USA
BVOW04s1004180416

444616BV00009B/36/P